BLACK PLOTS
&
BLACK CHARACTERS

BLACK PLOTS

&

BLACK

CHARACTERS

A HANDBOOK FOR AFRO-AMERICAN LITERATURE

by ROBERT L. SOUTHGATE

GAYLORD PROFESSIONAL PUBLICATIONS

SYRACUSE, NEW YORK
1979

© Robert L Southgate 1979

First published 1979

by GAYLORD PROFESSIONAL PUBLICATIONS

Syracuse, New York 13221

Printed in the United States of America

Library of Congress Cataloging in Publication Data

Southgate, Robert L., 1921-
Black plots & black characters.

Bibliography: p.
Includes index.
1. American literature—Afro-American authors—
Handbooks, manuals, etc. 2. Afro-Americans—
Handbooks, manuals, etc. 3. American literature—
Afro-American authors—Bibliography.
4. Afro-Americans—Bibliography. 5. Afro-Americans—
Bibliography I. Title.
PS153.N5S65   810′.9′896073   78-14394
ISBN 0-915794-14-4

Permissions

To the Black Writers of the United States

CONTENTS

PART I

Plot Summaries

Black Plots & Black Characters

10

FOREWORD

Black Plots and Black Characters is a significant and long-needed contribution to the development and study of Afro-American literature. This volume comes out at a time when there appears to be a lull in the publication of works by Afro-American authors, especially poetry and fiction. One is reminded of that devastating decade after the Harlem Renaissance when the number of works by Afro-Americans plummeted. Certainly during the Great Depression literary output by other American authors also dipped. However, black American authors as a group would not enjoy such attention from the American public for another twenty-five years. During the sixties, the American public once again encountered the eloquence of black activists. These voices were joined by the voices of the seers, of the creative writers, of the "prophets for a new day." Yet a decade hence we witness the onset of the familiar slowdown: The popularity of black creative literature is on the wane.

Yet far from the glitter and noise of the marketplace, the necessary work continues. If the writers and the committed reading public must live with such cycles, there must also be steady work to sustain us between the peaks. There are the continued attempts to establish black literature courses at the upper academic levels. There are the critical articles and the development of fresh insights as vital, complex, and engaging as the works themselves. Bibliographies fit well within this context, for they can demonstrate the quantity and make note of the quality of the existing literature.

This work by Robert Southgate is unique among bibliographies of Afro-American literature in a number of significant ways. The arrangement broadens from concise summaries of specific novels,

11

plays, and long poems to a chronological index for Afro-American literature. Within this framework are included a short dictionary for Afro-American literature, biographical sketches of the writers and an extensive bibliography of their works, and a more general bibliography for Afro-American history and literature. The plot summaries, a feature long overdue for the study of the literature, deal with the principal contributions and include many less popular, though no less provocative, pieces.

This handbook will prove invaluable for students, teachers, librarians, researchers, and all interested readers in the general area of Afro-American literature and culture. It is a thorough and discriminating volume that will complement and encourage continuing efforts to sustain one of the most vital literatures on the planet.

JOHN MCCLUSKEY, JR.

Associate Professor of
Afro-American Studies
Indiana University

PREFACE

For anyone interested in studying the literature of the blacks of the United States, it is almost impossible to find adequate reference books. A handbook for Afro-American literature containing summaries of novels, plays, speeches, folktales, and poems is virtually nonexistent; and the general works on United States literature give little or no information about the black authors of this country. Only in the third edition of *A Handbook for Literature* by William Flint Thrall, Addison Hibbard, and C. Hugh Holman is there any mention of black American writers, and then only a long paragraph is included. Thus there is an urgent need for a reference book that will fill this gap to some extent. It is hoped that this volume will serve this purpose.

Works by blacks about blacks are included here, but the writings of whites about blacks are not represented to a great extent because this aspect of Afro-American literature has been written about in other books that are readily available. Several of these have been listed in the general bibliography.

The choice of entries included in this volume and the comments upon them are entirely personal and will possibly be unacceptable to many. However, it is hoped that twenty years of teaching the history and culture of the blacks of the United States to many students who prodded me with thousands of questions while the book was in the process of being written will suffice to render the choices valid. Although this book is not a biographical dictionary, some biographical sketches have been given as well as information pertaining to Afro-American history. An effort has been made to

13

include the works of authors who are not as well known, as well as those whose writings are relatively famous.

Although the general bibliography is highly selective and lists only those materials that are easily obtained, it is hoped that the entries will be useful to all who wish to study in detail the history and literature of the blacks of the United States.

Cleveland, Ohio   ROBERT L. SOUTHGATE
1978

Robert L. Southgate is a junior high school librarian in the Cleveland Public Schools, a position he has held since getting his Master's degree in Library Science at Western Reserve University. Before that he was a classroom teacher, and he has continued to be a teacher and lecturer on the History and Culture of Black Americans, and a consultant in Afro-American studies. He is at present lecturing at Baldwin-Wallace College and assisting part-time on the evenings and week ends at the East Cleveland Branch of the Cleveland Public Library System, in addition to his school library-media work and his writing. He is greatly in demand as well for workshops, seminars and staff development sessions for teachers, and for psychiatric and other staff members at the Cleveland State Hospital and other institutions.

Southgate has taken an active leadership role for many years in such organizations as NAACP and CORE. He knows at first hand how much it will mean to young people, as well as to their elders, to learn about a black contribution to literature whose history spans two centuries, a cultural heritage rarely even hinted at in textbooks on American literature.

ACKNOWLEDGMENTS

When writing a book of any kind, one cannot claim to have produced it alone. It is very often the sum of the ideas that result from interchange between friends, students, scholars, and many others. To list the books and essays of the many persons, both black and white, whose writings have been useful in producing this book would constitute a separate volume. Therefore, I wish to thank all those pioneering and present-day writers and scholars whose works opened the way for the study of Afro-American literature.

The work of John Hope Franklin, Sterling Brown, Benjamin Quarles, Vernon Loggins, Alain Locke, Hugh Gloster, Robert Bone, Noel Schraufnagel, Darwin Turner, Jean Wagner, William Gibson, Stephen Henderson, John McCluskey, Houston A. Baker, Jr., and Eugene Redmond has been especially useful.

Without the generous aid of the staffs of the Moorland Research Center at Howard University, the Schomburg Collection of the New York Public Library, the Cleveland Public Library, and the Freiberger Library of Case Western Reserve University, this book could not have been produced. Many friends have helped me while I was writing this volume, but I especially want to thank my good friend Professor John McCluskey of Case Western Reserve and Indiana universities, who wrote the foreword for this book and made many helpful suggestions.

A special vote of thanks must also go to my friends Mrs. Carol R. Jones and Mr. Lee Lassic, who listened to me talk almost daily about my writing problems and offered encouragement and numerous useful suggestions to help me solve them. I wish to thank my editors, Ms. Virginia Mathews and Mrs. Jewell Harris, for their

15

constant support when problems arose and the deadline grew closer. A very special thank-you must go to fifteen-year-old Miss Mary E. Roberts, who very skillfully typed the entire manuscript. Most of all I wish to thank Joan Southgate, my wife, and my children for their patience and understanding during the time this book was being written. Any defects that may be found in this book are entirely my responsibility.

R.L.S.

PART I

Plot Summaries

An Address to the Negroes of the State of New York

Kind of work: Speech
Writer: Jupiter Hammon
Time: 1782
Setting: New York
First published: 1786

Comment

Jupiter Hammon, the first black poet to write in the United States, was a man trapped by his religious views and the fervor of them. The influence of Methodism pervades almost all of his poetry as well as his prose. He saw religion as the only way in which the blacks, both slave and free, could solve their problems.

Hammon refers only once to liberty in his speech and then in a wistful and remote manner. He was so affected by his religious outlook that he could see the problems of slavery only in religious terms, and this limited the kind of poetry and prose he produced.

Summary

The author states that he is speaking to the blacks of New York State for their own good. He is pained at the wickedness, ignorance, and stupidity of most of them. He wishes to give them the advice of an old man of seventy.

The blacks are urged to obey thier masters whether or not it is right for their owners to make slaves of them. This must be done because the apostle Paul commands all servants to be obedient. This is taken as a command from God, therefore the slaves ought to do it happily. If the master is cruel and unjust, the slaves must cry out to God for redress. Slaves should be honest, trustworthy, and faithful to the masters. It is wicked for a slave not to care for the master's goods; it is also wicked to steal from a master, for God will punish all who do this. It is pointed out that slaves must not use profanity since this is forbidden by God's command through Jesus Christ.

AN ADDRESS TO THE SLAVES OF THE UNITED STATES OF AMERICA

Kind of work: Speech
Writer: Henry Highland Garnet
Time: 1843
Setting: Buffalo, New York
First published: 1843

Comment

As early as 1830, free blacks were meeting in convention to decide how to solve the problem of slavery and other related problems. In 1840, a convention of free blacks met in Buffalo, New York, to discuss the plight of the blacks and to develop a course of action. Two prominent free blacks were trying for leadership of the convention: Henry Highland Garnet and Frederick Douglass.

In his speech, *An Address to the Slaves of the United States of America* Mr. Garnet urged the enslaved blacks to stage open rebellion to gain their freedom. The violent tone of his speech aroused opposition to his position and cost him the chance to become the leader of the free blacks. Frederick Douglass was more persuasive in his efforts to sway the convention in his favor and as a result he eventually became the leader of the blacks.

Summary

The speaker indicates that free blacks sometimes met in conventions and wept over the plight of their fellow blacks who were enslaved. Slavery has caused a gulf to exist between free blacks and enslaved blacks. Garnet states that blacks were brought to the United States two hundred and twenty-seven years ago. They did not come seeking homes or freedom of religion; the blacks came as extremely reluctant immigrants to these shores. Nearly three million blacks are enslaved and prevented from learning to read or write. Families are broken up and slave women are forced to endure all types of indignity.

It is sinful for the enslaved blacks to submit to slavery; the slaves should die rather than remain slaves. The enslaved blacks are urged to follow the path of William Tell, Robert Bruce, Nat Turner, and Denmark Vesey, rebels all. All black slaves must rebel together and throw off the clanking chains of slavery. They should remember that there are four million blacks and their motto must be "resistance, resistance, resistance."

ALIEN LAND

Kind of work: Novel
Writer: Willard Savoy
Time: 1938-1948
Setting: Vermont; Alabama; Harlem, N.Y.; Washington, D.C.
First published: 1949

Important Characters

Kern Roberts—a young black man
Charles Roberts—*Kern's father*
Laura Roberts—*Kern's mother*
Paula Roberts—*Kern's aunt*

Alien Land

Nettie Hoskins—*Charles's cook and housekeeper*
Jeff Mason—*a black man who is tried for murder*
Jake Caulfield—*Paula's husband*
Bill Noble—*a white sheriff*
Mariane—*a beautiful white girl whom Kern marries*

Comment

Alien Land is a protest novel concerned with the problem of passing and the hero is the tragic mulatto stereotype. In some novels of this kind, Nella Larsen's *Passing* and Jesse Faucet's *Plum Bum*, for example, those who pass either die tragically (Nella Larsen's heroine leaps out a window) or return repentant to live among the blacks (as Jesse Fauset's heroine does). Using a modified stream of consciousness technique as well as flashback, the author presents Kern Roberts as a hero similar to James Weldon Johnson's nameless protagonist in his novel, *The Autobiography of An Ex-Colored Man*. Both Kern Roberts and Johnson's hero remain in the white world.

Johnson's protagonist seems urban and sophisticated; Kern Roberts is almost always in a state of intense rage. The author's viewpoint is presented in various speeches in the novel that are not at all related to the narrative. The lynching of Jake Caulfield and the slaying of Paula are indicative of the kind of treatment blacks received in the South during the period the author covers. The problem of color barriers among the blacks themselves is evident in the treatment Kern receives when he goes to an all-black school; it is further shown by the intense conflict between Kern and Nettie Hoskins.

Summary

The novel begins with a prologue in which Kern Roberts, the protagonist, decides that he will pass for white permanently. Kern's father, Charles Roberts, a Washington, D.C., lawyer who passes for white, decides to reveal that he is a black man in order to work in behalf of the blacks and help them secure their rights. To do this, he begins to work with the Freedom League, an NAACP type of organization. Kern's mother who is white is devastated because it means that the Roberts family will have to live as blacks. Later Kern's mother is assaulted and Kern identifies Jeff Mason, a black man, as the attacker.

When Mason is indicted, Kern's father and the Freedom League defend him. This causes a strained relationship to develop between

Kern and his father. Laura Roberts returns home to Vermont [becomes ill and dies.] Because of his father's revelation that he is black, Kern must go to a school for blacks. Here he encounters hostility because of his near-white complexion. At the same time, he faces difficulties with his father and dark-skinned housekeeper, Nettie Hoskins, who hates Kern because he is half white. Kern's father thinks that his son is a coward because he is sensitive to art and literature. Kern answers a newspaper ad for a delivery boy, reveals that he is black, and does not get the job.

Kern writes a story that helps him win a scholarship to an exclusive writing school in New York, but his identity is revealed and he loses it. During his summer vacation Kern meets his Aunt Paula Caulfield, who wants him to come South to school. He decides to go. In the South he encounters severe racial prejudice directed against the blacks. Blacks are killed wantonly. Eventually, Jake Caulfield, Paula's husband, a strong black man who resists the racial prejudice, is killed by Bill Noble, the white sheriff who wants Paula for his mistress.

Paula resists Noble. She stabs him and he in turns kills her. Kern flees the South for New York, where he passes for white and obtains a job as a radio script writer. He meets a beautiful white girl, Mariane, and falls in love with her. He tells her he is black and she breaks off their relationship. However, she returns and marries Kern who, although he has decided to remain white, is reconciled with his father as the novel ends.

ALL THE REST HAVE DIED

Kind of work: Novel
Writer: Bill Gunn
Time: 1960s
Setting: Philadelphia; New York
First published: 1964

All the Rest Have Died

Important Characters

Barney Gifford—*a young black actor*
Marty—*a young black poet*
Bernard—*a friend of Barney's*
Maggie—*Barney's girl*

Comment

In *All The Rest Have Died* the author's concern is with responsibility and its acceptance by the individual. Each person must be aware that he must lead his own life in an absurd world. Barney, for example, cannot allow himself to cling to his cousin Taylor's memory; he must live for himself and be responsible for his own actions. The author employs a stream of consciousness method to show the environment as seen through the eyes of Barney Gifford. Race is seen as merely another facet of the already unreal condition of society. Although racism is woven through the book, its significance is diminished. The novel is not about blacks and whites as such; it is about a group of nice people trying to sort out their lives.

Summary

As the novel begins, Barney Gifford has come home to Philadelphia to visit his parents. Using a flashback technique, the author reveals Barney's past. Barney's cousin Taylor, to whom he was very close, had been killed in a holdup. Taylor had planned to become an actor. After Taylor's death Barney decides that he will try to be the actor that his cousin wanted to be. In New York he meets a group of people with whom he develops close relationships.

He has success as an actor and meets Maggie, a beautiful white model. They fall in love and decide to live together. Their affair is stormy and at times it threatens to break up. When Barney's friend Bernard, a rich young white man, commits suicide right in front of him, Barney is shocked into facing the reality of the rather pointless life he has been leading. He asks Maggie to marry him and goes home to Philadelphia to visit his parents as the novel ends.

AND THEN WE HEARD THE THUNDER

Kind of work: Novel
Writer: John O. Killens
Time: World War II
Setting: The southern United States; Australia
First published: 1963

Important Characters

Sergeant Solly Saunders—*a black soldier*
Millie Saunders—*Solly Saunders's wife*
Fannie Mae Branton—*a beautiful black woman who loves Solly Saunders*
Joe Taylor, "Bucket-head" Baker, Lanky Lincoln—*Solly Saunders's buddies*
Celia—*An Australian nurse who falls in love with Solly Saunders*

Comment

The point that the author is trying to make in *And Then We Heard the Thunder* is that unless the racism directed against the blacks is dealt with, there will be clashes between blacks and whites in the United States itself. The various descriptions of the racial affronts that the black soldiers encounter indicate the extent of the racism that permeated the U.S. armed forces during World War II. This problem has not yet been solved; note the recent racial fighting on board the U.S. carrier *Kitty Hawk* and the various negative encounters between black and white armed services personnel in Vietnam, Germany, and elsewhere.

Summary

The novel opens in a barracks where the black U.S. soldiers live. Solly, a college-educated corporal, is laughing and joking with several of his buddies. News arrives that the unit is being moved to Georgia near a town called Ebbensville. When the black soldiers are settled in their barracks, trouble begins. They face racial prejudice, harassment, and assaults from the white M.P.s, the local police, and the citizens of Ebbensville whenever they go into town.

And Then We Heard the Thunder

The commanding officer of the black unit does not like blacks and treats his men as inferiors, giving them little or no respect. Solly Saunders tries to overlook the indignities that he and the other black soldiers face because he promised his wife Millie that he would try to do it. Although Solly loves his wife, who is about to have their first child; he meets and begins an affair with Fannie Mae Branton, a beautiful black girl. As he comes to know her, he realizes that he cannot seduce her as he planned and finally tells her that he is married. One evening when he is in Ebbensville, Saunders and his buddies are beaten by the police. While they are in the hospital recovering, Solly writes a letter condemning the racism directed against black soldiers in the U.S. forces and sends it to a well-known black newspaper. As a result of this action, the NAACP demands an investigation.

When Captain Polke finds out who wrote the letter, Solly and his friends are shipped to the Pacific Theater. They take part in several battles and in one of them Solly, Lieutenant Samuels, and several of Solly's buddies are badly wounded. They are taken to Australia and hospitalized. Solly nearly dies but recovers. As he is convalescing, he learns that his wife died giving birth to their son. Celia, an Australian nurse assigned to Solly's group, tries to soften the impact; but in the process she falls in love with Solly. At first Solly cannot respond because she is white, but the barrier is overcome. Everything goes well until a unit of southern troops from the United States is moved to the town of Bainbridge. They bring with them their racial prejudice and soon tension between the blacks and whites increases. Finally a violent gun battle, in which the black and white U.S. soldiers fight each other, breaks out in the center of Bainbridge. Solly joins the blacks and when the battle ends he finds that several of his buddies have been killed. As the novel closes, Solly is sitting in the street crying.

THE AUTOBIOGRAPHY OF AN EX-COLORED MAN

Kind of work: Novel
Writer: James Weldon Johnson
Time: 1900s
Setting: New York; Florida; Europe
First published: 1912

Important Characters

The nameless protagonist
The hero's mother
The hero's wife
"Red Head"—*a white school companion*
"Shiny"—*a black school companion*

Comment

The Autobiography of an Ex-Colored Man is one of the many novels of passing that black authors of the United States have written. In this novel James Weldon Johnson has presented many aspects of the life of the blacks of his time: black Pullman porters, Cuban factory workers, Connecticut schoolchildren, educated and well-off blacks of Washington, and the members of New York's black cabaret society as well as New York's black elite and aristocrats. Southern black preachers and religious singers such as the Reverend John Brown and "Singing" Johnson are present and also European musicians, white middle-class New Yorkers, and last, if not least, a black man being burned at the stake in the South. The Autobiography of an Ex-Colored Man is different from the novels of many black writers of this period in that the South is not the main setting. The author's discussion of the problems of the race prejudice that blacks faced is straightforward for its time and in many ways is still valid today, especially the idea that blacks should not allow themselves to be demeaned and should use all their resources in the struggle to eliminate the problems that hinder their progress. One unusual feature of the novel is that all or nearly all of the characters, including the hero, are nameless.

27

The Autobiography of an Ex-Colored Man

Summary

As the story begins, the hero is taken by his mother, the mistress of a rich southern planter, from a small town in rural Georgia to a large city in Connecticut. In this city he gains his early education and enters high school. He forms a strong friendship with "Red Head," a rather dull white schoolmate, and "Shiny," a brilliant black. Very early it is discovered that he has a talent for music. One day at school he accidentally discovers he is black. He had always thought he was white. He goes home to his mother and asks her if he is a "nigger."

His mother does not tell him everything about her relationship with his father. One day he meets his father for the first time but does not know how to react to him. Shortly after the hero graduates from high school, his mother dies and he makes plans to go to Atlanta University for his college education, using the money raised from a benefit his music teacher held for him.

Upon reaching Atlanta, he prepares to enter school but his money is stolen and he is unable to carry out his plans. He leaves Atlanta for Jacksonville, Florida, and finds work in a cigar factory. He does well and soon has enough money to take him to New York. When he arrives in New York, the hero goes to a cabaret and wins a large sum of money in a crap game. As a result, he becomes involved with the Harlem cabaret society and gets a job playing the piano at a cabaret called the Club. While he is at the Club, he meets an attractive woman, "the widow," who takes a liking to him. One night at the Club the hero meets an enigmatic millionaire and begins to work for him.

Later the attractive widow flirts with him just to make her boyfriend jealous. One night the boyfriend becomes enraged, pulls a pistol, and kills his girlfriend; the hero finds that he must leave. He becomes the traveling companion of the eccentric millionaire for whom he had worked. They visit the principal cities of Europe. While abroad he decides that he will return to the United States to study and transcribe the folk music of the southern blacks. His millionaire employer tells him he is foolish to think of himself as a black man but wishes him well in his project and gives him extra money to help him begin. Sickened by the sight of a black man being lynched, the protagonist abandons his project and returns to New York.

Once he has returned to the city, he passes for white and becomes prosperous in the real estate business. He meets a beautiful white woman and falls in love with her. He wants to tell her his story and reveal that he is a black man, but he does not know how she will react. Finally he does tell her everything. She leaves him for awhile, then returns and marries him. The hero's beautiful wife bears him two children but dies suddenly after the birth of the second child. Although he has a strange longing for his mother's people, the blacks, he remains among the whites and lives as one of them.

BAD MAN

Kind of work: Play
Writer: Randolph Edmonds
Time: 1920s
Setting: Rural Alabama
First published: 1934

Important Characters

Tom Joiner—*a sawmill worker in his thirties*
Ted James—*a sawmill worker*
Hubbard Bailey—*a sawmill worker*
Percy Hardy—*a sawmill worker*
Burt Ross—*the white manager of the sawmill*
Maybell Joiner—*Tom Joiner's sister*
Thea Dugger—*a giant sawmill worker and bad man*

Comment

Like George Broadus in Willis Richardson's play, *Idle Head,* Thea Dugger is a rebel but on a much larger and more heroic scale. Although he is a stereotype of the bad brute nigger, he is fearless and refuses to play the role that whites have designated for him. When the mob arrives, Thea hands out the six pistols that he owns and prepares to fight.

Bad Man

Although he has killed several men, fought, gambled, and in general led a rather disreputable life, he still gives his life for his fellow blacks. During the period with which the play is concerned, any black man who acted as Thea Dugger did would have been considered too demented or too stupid to know better and would have been lynched or burned at the stake. In Jean Toomer's short story, *Blood Burning Moon,* a Thea Dugger type, Tom Burwell, is burned after killing a white man in a fight over a black woman.

Summary

As the play begins, Tom Joiner, Ted James, and Tom's sister, Maybell, are waiting in the rough bunkhouse where the black sawmill workers live. They are waiting for Tom and Maybell's father, to come and take Maybell home. Tom does not want her to stay in the camp overnight and tells her that if their father does not come, they will walk home. The men who work in the sawmills are of all types, including murderers, gamblers, and convicts newly escaped from jail. Ted, who is secretly in love with Maybell, suggests that the men sleep on pallets in the main part of the shanty and give Maybell their room so that she will not have to walk home.

Tom goes to the commissary, leaving Maybell alone with Ted. Ted tries to tell Maybell how much he cares for her but Tom returns and becomes furious, telling Ted that he does not want his sister to become involved with a sawmill worker. Before he can say any more, several of the workers enter the shanty. The men are surprised to see Maybell, but before they can say anything Thea Dugger comes in to the shanty. He is a giant and everyone is afraid of him except Ted, to whom Dugger has taken a liking.

The men have come to gamble and play cards and soon a game is started. While the game is in progress, Percy Hardy, one of the workers, comes in and tells the group that old Sam, a white recluse who lived in the woods by himself, has been killed. The game goes on. Jack Burchard, one of the cardplayers, accuses Thea Dugger of cheating, reaches for his gun, and threatens to shoot him. Thea calmly faces Burchard, takes away his pistol, and prepares to kill him with it. Maybell, seeing that Thea really means to shoot Jack, pleads with him not to do it. Thea has spent his life fighting, drinking, and gambling. He has already killed six men and Jack will be just one more. Maybell tells Thea that he must have some good in him in spite of the dissolute life he has led. Thea decides not to kill Jack and to forget the entire incident.

Burt Ross, the white camp foreman, rushes into the shanty and tells the workers to scatter because a mob has formed and plans to lynch a black man, any black man, from their camp for the murder of old Sam. Everyone except Thea Dugger prepares to flee, but Percy tells the group that their escape route has been cut off and the mob is coming. When the mob arrives, Thea passes out his six guns and prepares to fight; but the mob leader threatens to burn down the shanty with everyone in it. Ross intervenes; he asks the mob leader to spare his workers because he needs them to run the mill. The leader tells Ross to send out the murderer of old Sam and the others will be spared. Even though the workers are innocent, they know that someone will have to go out to the mob in order to save the lives of the others. Ted decides to go out, but Thea Dugger stops him and goes out to the mob himself. As the play ends Thea is being burned at the stake amidst the cheers of the mob.

BALLAD OF BIRMINGHAM

Kind of work: Ballad
Writer: Dudley Randall
Time: 1963
Setting: Birmingham, Alabama

Important Characters

A black mother
A young black girl

Comment

The poem is written in standard ballad form with an *a b a b* metric pattern. The poet is without a doubt making reference to a bomb explosion that occurred at the Sixteenth Street Baptist Church on September 15, 1963. In the blast four little black girls attending Sunday school were killed. In 1977 an ex Ku Klux clansman was convicted of this crime.

Summary

In this ballad a black mother refuses her daughter permission to participate in a civil rights march and sends her to church to sing in the choir instead. The mother hears an explosion and rushes to the church to find her daughter, but finds only her shoe. Her daughter is dead, killed in the explosion.

BALO

Kind of work: Play
Writer: Jean Toomer
Time: 1924
Setting: Rural Georgia
First published: 1941

Important Characters

Will Lee—*a black farmer*
Susan Lee—*Will's wife*
Tom Lee—*Will's oldest son*
Balo—*a younger son*
Jennings—*a white neighbor*
Cousin Mamie—*a relative of Will's*
Uncle Ned—*an old black man*
Sam—*Ned's companion*

Comment

Balo is a play about the religious ecstasy and conversion of a young black farm boy. The simple life of rural blacks and whites is shown and nothing much seems to happen to anyone except Balo.

Will's relatives and neighbors visit, talk, play cards, and watch Balo undergo a religious conversion. That is all, or so it would seem.

One important thing to remember about this play is that it seems to have been written to be read rather than to be acted out on a stage. The author's stage directions are elaborate, detailed, and poetic; and it is through these directions that one feels the complete impact of Balo's emotional experience.

Summary

As the play opens, it is Sunday. Will Lee, a fairly well off farmer, is whittling kindling so his wife, Susan, can begin breakfast. Soon Will goes to the kitchen and breakfast begins. Will prays and blesses the food. While he is doing this, his two sons, Tom and Balo, come in the front door, hear their father praying, and stand with their heads bowed until he finishes. Will calls his sons to ask them if they have had their breakfast. When they indicate that they have, Will tells them to lie before the fireplace and get some sleep since they have been up all night boiling cane syrup. Before he goes back to the kitchen, Will tells his sons to be sure and read their Bible for a few minutes before they go to sleep. Tom begins reading and soon falls asleep, but Balo continues reading and becomes strangely excited. His religious ecstasy mounts as he reads. He has reached an intense emotional state when he hears the younger children come into the room. Balo pretends that he is asleep and soon actually does fall asleep.

While Tom and Balo are sleeping, Will and Susan come into the room to sit and talk quietly. Will is thinking seriously about becoming a preacher. From outside the house someone calls. Will recognizes the voice of Jennings, his white neighbor, also a farmer. Jennings comes in and Will's desire to become a preacher is discussed. Susan is opposed to the idea. Will and Jennings talk about crops and the market. Finally Jennings wishes the family good morning and leaves.

Tom and Balo are still sleeping. In the evening Will's cousin Bob arrives with his wife and six children for a friendly visit. Everyone gathers around the fireplace. They begin to talk and the children laugh and play. There is a knock at the door and Uncle Ned, an old respected member of the community, comes in. He is immediately invited to supper. Susan and Mamie prepare the meal while the men talk. As supper is being served, Balo comes in but cannot find a chair near the fire so he goes to the organ and begins to play a spiritual. Soon everyone is singing. While the singing continues, Balo exhibits the same intense excitement that he had shown earlier in the day. His feelings are so strong that he rises from his chair.

Banjo

There is a knock on the door and two new couples join the group. Almost immediately a card game is begun and everyone is enjoying himself. Uncle Ned and Will are talking about sin in the world and suddenly Will begins what is tantamount to a sermon. Everyone around the fire begins to sing and hum and soon the room has the atmosphere of a church. Balo is immediately affected by this singing, leaps to his feet, crying out that he has found Jesus, and falls to his knees in supplication. As the play closes, Uncle Ned is blessing Balo for his conversion.

BANJO

Kind of work: Novel
Writer: Claude McKay
Time: 1929
Setting: Marseilles, France
First published: 1929

Important Characters

Ray—a young black man
Banjo—a black jazz musician

Comment

In *Banjo* the author, speaking through Ray, is waging an intense war against white civilization and its mores. He sees this society as sterile, moribund, and unworthy of emulation. Not only is white society dying but the blacks of the middle class are hypocritical, color conscious, and practice color prejudice among themselves. The author maintains that the quality of the culture of primitive Africans is superior to that of the U.S. and the West Indian blacks. In general, *Banjo* is a platform from which the author makes his attacks on Western culture.

Summary

As the novel opens, Banjo is on board a ship entering the port of Marseilles. The story follows Banjo and the jazz band that he organizes as they move from one cafe to another, playing jazz music mostly, because they like it. Ray meets Banjo in one of the these cafes. They become friends and roam Marseilles together. They become well known throughout the Ditch, a section of Marseilles where hustlers, prostitutes, pimps, and workers mix to form the lower class of the city. Ray and Banjo continue wandering for a while, but Banjo decides to leave the city. He signs on a ship under a false name, collects some wages, and persuades Ray to go wandering with him as the novel ends.

BEETLECREEK

Kind of work: Novel
Writer: William Demby
Time: 1950
Setting: Beetle Creek, Virginia
First published: 1950

Important Characters

Johnny Johnson—*a young black boy*
David Diggs—*Johnny's uncle*
Mary Diggs—*David's wife*
Bill Trapp—*an old white recluse who lives near the black ghetto of Beetlecreek.*

Comment

The novel *Beetlecreek* is a study in despair and hopelessness. The characters in it are sleepwalkers in a dead town. No one is able to help himself or anyone else. Only Johnny Johnson, Bill Trapp, and

Johnny's uncle, David, have a chance to emerge from the stagnant pool of life in Beetlecreek; and even they fail when they make the effort. When Trapp tries to reach out from his self-imposed exile, he is rejected. Johnny Johnson, toward whom Trapp reached, becomes the instrument of Trapp's death when, at the insistence of his gang the "Nightriders", he sets fire to the old man's house. Johnny's Uncle David fails when he discovers that Edith, his old flame, is simply an urban version of his wife, Mary, whom he no longer loves. In the end David and his nephew, Johnny, remain engulfed in the stagnant and dead environment of the town. *Beetle Creek* has been called an existentialist novel.

Summary

The novel opens with Johnny Johnson and three of his friends trying to steal fruit from the tree on Bill Trapp's property. Bill Trapp sees them; the three boys on the ground run away but Johnny is caught in the tree. Trapp waits for him to come down, then invites him to sit on the porch and have a glass of cider with him. While they are talking, Johnny's Uncle David rushes through Bill Trapp's gate and demands to know what Trapp is doing to his nephew. When he discovers that Johnny is not hurt, he calms down and Trapp invites him in for a drink of wine that he has made.

Johnny's uncle and Bill Trapp talk and drink and finally David leaves but promises to return. Although Trapp is really a recluse, David becomes his drinking partner. When an old flame of David's comes to town to attend a funeral, he has an affair with her. Johnny becomes friendly with Bill Trapp but the gang of young blacks, the Nightriders, want him to break off his relationship with Trapp before they will accept him as a member.

Eventually Trapp invites several black and white children to his home for a picnic, but everyone becomes suspicious of him and accuse him of being a child molester. Then both blacks and whites turn against him. Bill Trapp withdraws into his shell again. David's love affair with his old girlfriend fades out and Johnny, in order to become a member of the Nightriders, sets fire to Bill Trapp's house.

BEHOLD A CRY

Kind of work: Novel
Writer: Alden Bland
Time: 1918
Setting: Chicago
First published: 1947

Important Characters

Ed Tyler—a young black man
Phom Tyler—*Ed's wife*
Mamie Jenkins—*Ed's mistress*
Son Tyler—*Ed's oldest son*
Dan Tyler—*Ed's youngest son*
Joe Davis—*Ed's younger friend*
Cleo Davis—*Joe's wife*
Sam Brown—*Ed's coworker at the packing plant*
Clara Brown—*Sam's wife*

Comment

In *Behold A Cry* the author is concerned with the migration of blacks from the rural South to the cities of the North, the problem of the blacks working as scabs, and the pressures that result from such conditions. With housing in short supply, the blacks had to live wherever they could. Under these conditions Ed Tyler moves from rural Georgia to Chicago, where he works as a scab laborer. When his family arrives, Ed is forced to find another place to live. The apartment he finds is small and uncomfortable; Ed becomes estranged from his wife and family and eventually abandons them to run away with another woman.

Summary

Walking down State Street in Chicago in 1918, looking at the crowd and admiring the various attractive women, Ed Tyler hears his name called. The caller is Joe Davis, a young man from his hometown in Georgia. Joe tells Ed that he has a message from his wife, Phom, and his two sons, whom he has left in the South with the promise that he will send for them soon. Ed and Joe go to a bar to have a drink and Joe does nothing but talk about his new wife, Cleo. After leaving the bar, Ed goes home to Mamie Jenkins, his beautiful mistress.

Ed has been exempted from the draft because he has a wife and children; he neglected to mention that his family is in the South. When Ed discusses this problem with Mamie and suggests that he should bring his wife and children to live with them, Mamie agrees. Ed sends for them.

Ed goes to the station to meet his family and suddenly is ashamed of their "just from the country look." He takes them home to his and Mamie's apartment. At first Phom's suspicions of Ed and Mamie's relationship are minimal, but gradually she senses that it is not casual as it seems to be. Ed's deception begins to crumble. His relationship with his sons begins to change and they think he does not like them. One day Ed takes his sons to the lake. While they are there, a race riot breaks out but Ed manages to get them home safely. Ed and his fellow worker, Sam Brown, discuss the problems of organizing a union at the plant where they work. Sam is for the union, but Ed is uncertain; when the union decides to strike, he becomes a scab worker. In the first day on the job Ed does not encounter difficulty in spite of the angry union workers. However, on his way home he gets on a streetcar, discovers that he is the only black on the car, and realizes that he is in a difficult position.

Near his house the motorman opens the streetcar door and urges Ed to try to outrun the white mob that has formed. The mob catches Ed and he is beaten badly; the police rescue him and take him home. When Ed is brought home badly hurt, Mamie breaks down completely and Phom finally realizes what the relationship between Ed and Mamie has really been. After Ed recovers from his injuries, Phom insists that they move to a new house. Ed breaks off his relationship with Mamie and for a while everything seems to go well for the Tyler family.

One Sunday Ed goes to visit young Joe Davis who is ill, and meets Joe's wife, Cleo. Ed suggests to Phom that Cleo and Joe move into the extra upstairs rooms in their home. Phom reluctantly agrees, and Joe and Cleo move in. Joe and Ed spend much time together while Joe is recovering. Ed becomes attracted to Cleo and she to him. Soon Ed finds that he is in love with Cleo and wants to live with her. He continues to work as a scab and the other black workers join him. For a time Ed and Cleo avoid each other but finally they both decide to leave their respective mates and live together.

BIRD AT MY WINDOW

Kind of work: Novel
Writer: Rosa Guy
Time: 1960
Setting: Harlem, New York
First published: 1966

Important Characters

Wade Williams—*a young black man*
Faith Williams—*Wade's sister*
Mumma—*Wade's mother*
Uncle Dan—*Wade's uncle*
Gay Sommers—*a beautiful black girl with whom Wade falls in love*
Dr. Forest—*A psychiatrist who treats Wade*
Professor Jones—*A white professor who helps Wade and Uncle Dan escape from a mob*

Comment

In *Bird at my Window* the author is basically concerned with the psychological results of race prejudice and discrimination and the negative effects upon the victims. The only time Wade feels free is when he is in the army, and even there he cannot escape the racism that blacks encounter. It is the officers calling Wade a "nigger" that results in the fight in which a captain is killed and racial slurs are hurled at him during the school integration case in which he is involved. On another level Wade's tangled love-hate relationship with his mother is a factor in his destruction; at one point he is pleased when he notes that Mumma fears him. The ghetto environment with its almost constant violence and death is the factor that breaks Wade's mind and destroys him.

Summary

Bird at my Window begins with Wade Williams waking in a ward of a mental hospital. He has been put there because he attacked his sister and beat her badly. By flashback techniques it is revealed that Wade was very close to his sister, Faith, and had once saved her from being raped when they were children. As a young boy in junior high school in New York City, Wade was discovered to be brilliant and an attempt was made to have him enter a special school in the Bronx. The effort only results in trouble and an arrest for Wade.

In spite of this, Wade finishes school and finds a job. One day he meets an intelligent beautiful black girl who works with him. He falls in love with her and she becomes pregnant with his child. When she tells Wade about her condition, he becomes angry and tells her to abort her pregnancy. Later she marries a medical student who also loves her and Wade realizes he made a mistake in rejecting her. In remorse he quits his job and goes into the army. Stationed outside Paris, he meets a French girl and eventually becomes her lover.

One evening he takes the girl out to a cafe, where he is insulted by the negative racial remarks of a white southern officer. Wade waits for the officer to come after him, and in the fight that follows he beats the man to death. He and his girl dig a grave and bury the dead man, then Wade goes back to his outfit. When Wade returns home to Harlem, he is immediately caught up in its more sordid aspects. He lives at a furious pace and at times has blackouts in which he become enraged. In one of these periods he savagely beats up his sister and finds himself in a mental hospital.

Eventually Wade returns to normal and goes home, where his insensitive mother; who has always disliked him, begins to taunt him. One day Wade, in a fit of rage, tries to stab his mother, but Faith jumps between them and he stabs her instead. The final scene shows Wade staring at Faith's body.

BLACK NO MORE

Kind of work: Novel
Writer: George S. Schuyler
Time: 1933
Setting: Harlem, New York
First published: 1931

Important Characters

Dr. Junius Crookman—*a black doctor*
Max Disher (Matthew Fisher)—*a young black man*
Bunny Brown—*a close friend of Max*
Hank Johnson—*a backer of Dr. Crookman*
Chuck Foster—*a backer of Dr. Crookman*
Henry Givens—*a white minister*
Helen Givens—*Henry's daughter*
Sandol—*a formerly black Sengolese*
Santop Licorice—*leader of the Back to Africa Society*
Shakespear A. Beard—*a leader of the National Social Equality League*
Sissereta Blandish—*Harlem's leading hairdresser*

Comment

In this novel the author assaults everyone and everything. His satire is savage and no individual or institution is immune from his attack. He ridicules the crassness, stupidity, materialsim, and what he considers the general opportunism of Americans, blacks as well as whites. How neatly and cynically Max swindles poor whites out of a fortune by playing upon their racial prejudices. Blacks, too, are taken to task; the satiric portrait of Shakespeare Agamemnon Beard is clearly a sketch of Dr. W. E. B. DuBois. Santop Licorice and the Back to Africa Society are without a doubt references to Marcus Garvey and the Universal Negro Improvement Association.

The N.A.A.C.P. appears in the guise of the National Social Equality League; the Urban League is lampooned as the National League. The leaders of these organizations are depicted in ill-tempered, crusty prose as individuals deeply involved in debauchery, thievery, adultery, and graft. All are almost without redeeming features of any kind. In the author's view the blacks are just as bad as the whites and the only difference between them is color.

Summary

The novel opens on New Years Eve, 1933. Max Disher, a handsome young black man, is standing in front of a Harlem night club. Max is disconcerted because his fair-skinned girlfriend has left him and he has no woman companion to use the tickets that he has bought for the New Year's party at the club. Max's friend Bunny Brown arrives and they decide to use the two tickets themselves. Shortly after Max and Bunny enter the club, a group of whites come in. Among them is a ravishingly beautiful girl who immediately captures Max's attention. He insists on asking her to dance in spite of the fact that she is white and from Atlanta, Georgia. He is rebuffed and goes home to bed, where he dreams of the young white girl who refused to dance with him.

The next morning his friend Bunny calls to tell him about an article in the *New York Times* that says that a black doctor in Harlem had developed a method to change blacks to whites almost instantly. Max goes to see Dr. Crookman, the inventor of the Black No More process, and becomes the first black to take the treatment. Newly changed from black to white, Max sets out for Atlanta to find the girl of his dreams. He changes his name to Matthew Fisher and, pretending to be a member of a New York Anthropological Society, interviews Reverend Henry Givens, leader of the Knights of Nordica, a Ku Klux Klan-like organization. He becomes a member of the group and eventually becomes Grand Exalted Giraw of the Knights of Nordica. Max and Reverend Givens devise an elaborate plan to use the threat of the Black No More process to white purity as a way of swindling hundreds of thousands of dollars out of the whites of the South. While working with Givens, Max meets his daughter and discovers that she is the white girl whom he had met in Harlem. Immediately he proceeds to court and marry her.

Dr. Crookman's process is an immense success and blacks appear at Black No More sanitoriums in droves to undergo it and turn white. Black organizations and businesses lose support quickly; black politicians lose power; and Mme. Sissereta Blandish, queen of the beauty and hairdressing trade in Harlem, goes broke because the blacks abandon her. In the South, economic and social structures are violently changed when the blacks no longer use Jim Crow facilities. An extra burden is placed on the white taxpayers when equal salaries have to be paid to the erstwhile blacks. The national political parties are affected by the Black No More process as well. The Republicans take on the Democrats on their home ground, the solid South. The Republicans run Gump and Gussie for president and vice-president, respectively, against the Democrats Reverend Givens and Arthur Snobcraft and win. After the election is over the southern Democrats employ Dr. Sam Buggerie to examine the geneological backgrounds of the southern whites for purity; he discovers that at least fifty-million whites, including Givens and Snobcraft, are part black.

The entire country is thrown into a state of panic and shock. Max's wife gives birth to a darker than usual son and Max tells her that he, too, has blacks in his family tree. Mobs rage and Max's position becomes untenable. He arranges an escape for Givens and his family and for his own family as well. Hiring a plane, he departs for Mexico, taking with him the entire treasury of the Knights of Nordica. Buggerie and Snobcraft are trapped in rural Mississippi and try to disguise themselves by putting black shoe polish on their faces. As a result, they are lynched by a white mob that mistakes them for real blacks. All the black leaders, including Santop Licorice, the leader of the Back to Africa Society, have become white via the Black No More process. Dr. Crookman announces a discovery that he has made. The real whites are darker than the ersatz ones. As a result of this revelation, Americans whites begin to take sun baths and stain their skins to appear darker. Bunny Brown meets and marries the last genuine black woman in the United States; she refused out of race pride to undergo the Black No More process.

BLACK THUNDER

Kind of work: Novel
Writer: Arna Bontemps
Time: 1800
Setting: Virginia
First published: 1936

Important Characters

Gabriel Prosser—*a twenty-six-year-old slave*
Solomon Prosser—*Gabriel's older brother*
Martin Prosser—*Gabriel's second brother*

Black Thunder

Juba—*Gabriel's woman*
Mingo—*a free black man*
Thomas Prosser—*a salve owner*
Ben and Pharaoh—*slaves*

Comment

Using the scant materials that were available when *Black Thunder* was written, the author has produced a historical novel showing that the longing to be free was in the thoughts of many slaves in the early United States. It is only in very recent times that books and articles closely examining the several black slave revolts have been written. In *Black Thunder* the characters are seen as heroic and idealistic, especially the central character, Gabriel.

Summary

A statement about the trial of the participants in the Prosser Uprising, which occurred in Virginia in 1800, opens the book. In flashbacks it is revealed that the revolt was caused by the brutal treatment of the slaves by their owners. Gabriel, a twenty-six-year-old slave of Thomas Prosser, a slave owner who treats his slaves harshly, plans a revolt when Prosser beats an old slave, Bundy, so badly that he dies. It is decided that all whites will be killed except Quakers, Frenchmen, and Methodists.

Gabriel plans to attack the city of Richmond in late August 1800. However, because of a violent rainstorm and because of two slaves who tell their owners of the plans for the rebellion, it becomes necessary to cancel the revolt. Gabriel's followers are dispersed and he goes into hiding. Eventually he is captured and with the other leaders of the uprising hanged. Juba, Gabriel's woman, is sold at public auction.

BLOOD ON THE FORGE

Kind of work: Novel
Writer: William Attaway
Time: 1930s
Setting: Kentucky; Pennsylvania
First published: 1941

Important Characters

Big Mat Moss—*a black tenant farmer*
Melody Moss—*Big Mat's brother*
Chinatown Moss—*Big Mat's brother*
Mr. Johnson—*a white landowner*
Hattie Moss—*Big Mat's wife*
Anna—*Big Mat's girlfriend*

Comment

Blood on the Forge is a proletarian novel. The author is concerned with the economic exploitation of the blacks. Big Mat and his brothers are forced to leave their tenant farm, which is one form of economic exploitation, and work in the steel mills of Pennsylvania, where they are not only away from the land but must face a situation that is worse than the one they left. The blacks must compete with white workers and usually are given the worst and most dangerous jobs in the mills. The author protests against this environment, which not only destroys the workers but dehumanizes them as well. Mat is able to gain his self-respect through violence. He becomes a minion of the mill owners and is killed in a clash with the union members. The author is attacking the capitalist system, which allows its workers to be crushed economically and psychologically.

Summary

Big Mat Moss, his wife, Hattie, and his brothers, Chinatown and Melody, are living as sharecroppers on a run-down farm in Kentucky. When Big Mat's mother died behind a plow, she was caught in the traces and the mule dragged her home through the fields, mutilating her body in the process. Big Mat killed the mule in a rage. As a result of this, the Moss family has no credit on the books of Mr. Johnson, the landowner, and no food in their cabin. Mat goes to Mr. Johnson to kill hogs for him in the hope that he will be given some of the meat and to try and persuade Johnson to give him another mule. Johnson agrees to give Mat another mule and gives him a bag of chitterlings to take home, but nothing else. The next day Big Mat returns to the Johnson house to finish cutting up the hogs and to get the mule promised to him. Mrs. Johnson knows nothing of her husband's agreement and sends Mat to the riding boss or overseer.

On his way to find the riding boss, Big Mat stops to admire the mules and decide which one he will take. When Mat swats a bee on the back of one of the mules, the overseer, who has just ridden up, chastizes him. Mat reminds him that they used to play together as children. The riding boss strikes him across the face with a quirt. Mat does not respond to this offense. However, when the riding boss says that any mule is worth more than any black woman, Mat beats the overseer so badly that he thinks he has killed him. He leaves the Johnson place at a run. While Mat is at the Johnson house, a labor recruiter comes to the Moss shack and offers Chinatown and Melody money to come to Pennsylvania and work in the steel mills.

When Big Mat comes home and tells what he has done, the three brothers know that they must leave Kentucky. Leaving Hattie behind to run the farm, the brothers take off.

The Moss brothers are carried to their destination in a boxcar filled with other black men going to work in the mills. When the new men arrive in Pennsylvania, they find that the situation is an unpleasant one. They must live in bunkhouses and are victims of racial prejudice directed at them by the Slavs, Italians, and other groups working in the mills. It is finally pointed out to the Moss brothers that they were hired as strike breakers and therefore paid much less in wages. The work is grueling and dangerous with death or injury a possibility every minute. There is nothing for them to do in their spare time except gamble, watch dog fights, drink bad whisky, and visit the local prostitutes.

Big Mat misses the farm and is frustrated until he learns the job. Because of his great size and strength, his coworkers come to admire him, especially when he saves a well-liked foreman's life. Mat becomes known as Black Irish. He plans to send for his wife, Hattie; but before he can do so he meets Anna, a beautiful prostitute who falls in love with him and decides to become his mistress. For a while they are happy, but Mat broods over the fact that other men admire her and often he beats her.

One day on the job, Melody's hand is injured severely and he can no longer play the guitar. Mat comes to see him in the hospital. While he is there, one of the blast furnaces explodes, killing fourteen men and injuring many more, among them Chinatown, who is blinded. Mat's relationship with Anna deteriorates and she finally taunts him, calling him "peon" and "nigger". He responds by giving her a vicious beating and leaves.

In the labor conflict between the mills and the workers the blacks have been used to break the union. Big Mat becomes a deputy for the mill owners. In this capacity he feels that he is like the riding boss he had known in Kentucky and begins to enjoy the violence of his job. Big Mat is killed in a labor fight, Chinatown is blind, and Melody will not play his guitar for a long time because of his injury. The novel ends with the two surviving brothers boarding a train that will take them away from the steel mills to Pittsburgh and an uncertain future.

BOY AT THE WINDOW

Kind of work: Novel
Writer: Owen Dodson
Time: 1938
Setting: New York; Washington D.C.
First published: 1951

Important Characters

Coin Foreman—*a nine-year-old black boy*
Naomi Foreman—*Coin's mother*
Mr. Foreman—*Coin's father*
Agnes Foreman—*Coin's sister*
Woddy—*Coin's brother*

Boy at the Window

Berniece Foreman—*Coin's younger sister*
Uncle Troy Starr—*Coin's blind uncle*
Ferris—*a boy that Troy meets at the station*
Mrs. Walker—*Uncle Troy's lover and landlady*

Comment

This short novel is primarily concerned with a young boy's growing up and the shattering of his relatively secure and sheltered world. Whenever Coin encounters difficulties he cannot solve or has questions he cannot answer, he goes to his mother, Naomi, who answers his questions, helps him solve his problems, and provides love and affection for him in spite of her own handicap. One day he is called a "nigger" by another boy. When he asks his mother what the word means, she has him look it up in the dictionary. He discovers that the definition given means a bad person and decides that it does not apply to him.

When Coin's mother dies, his sheltered world begins to crumble. He has no one to whom he can turn for affection and understanding, as he could to Naomi. Agnes, his sister, takes over the task of caring for the Foreman children and as a result her fiance leaves her. Coin's father, a reserved and religious man, is unable to provide the warmth his son needs. Coin is sent away to Washington. While on the train that carries him from New York to Washington, Coin encounters a group of blacks. They are a jovial, noisy group and some of the passengers complain. Someone calls them "niggers." Coin overhears this and surmises that the term is one that is applied to blacks even if they are not bad. Racial prejudice as such is not dealt with to any great extent by the author. The main concern is with Coin's search for a replacement for Naomi.

In his meeting with Ferris, who provides him with a feeling of warmth and friendliness, Coin thinks he has found a companion and replacement for his mother. This illusion is soon broken when Ferris leaves. The author uses a form of the stream of consciousness technique to show Coin's thoughts. It is in this way that the author's views of life in the black ghetto and the disadvantages of living there are shown. The novel is basically concerned with Coin's personal efforts to find fulfillment. As a novel of a boy's growing up in the black ghettoes of two cities, it is similar to Al Young's novel, *Snakes*.

Summary

Nine-year-old Coin Foreman lives in Brooklyn with his family in a gently decaying integrated neighborhood peopled by blacks, Irish, Italians, and Jews. He goes to school and plays with his friends. On Sunday he attends church with his parents. Coin's mother, Naomi, is suffering from the aftereffects of a stroke and is partially crippled. He is very close to her. Eventually Naomi dies and Coin must go to live in Washington, D.C., with his blind uncle, Troy Starr, who sells pencils and chewing gum on the streets.

One day while attending a movie, Coin meets Ferris, a boy a little older than he. They spend the day together, but Coin discovers that Ferris is merely waiting for his train to take him home to Kentucky to his aunt. Coin goes to the station to see him off, then returns to a local cafe to meet his uncle and guide him home. While at the cafe, he meets several of his uncle's friends, who order ginger ale for him. The bartender mixes highballs, thinking they are for the adults. Coin drinks three "ginger ales" and passes out. His uncle's friends take Coin home. When he awakens the next morning, he sees his uncle and Mrs. Walker, the landlady, making love. He hears Mrs. Walker urge Uncle Troy to send him back to New York. He returns to his room and makes plans to run away the next day.

BROWN GIRL, BROWNSTONES

Kind of work: Novel
Writer: Paule Marshall
Time: 1940s-1960s
Setting: Brooklyn, New York
First published: 1959

Important Characters

Selina Boyce—*a young black girl*
Deighton Boyce—*Selina's father*

Brown Girl, Brownstones

Silla Boyce—*Selina's mother*
Ina—*Selina's sister*
Miss Thompson—*a nearby hairdresser*
Miss Suggie—a friend of Selina's

Comment

This novel is similar to Gwenolyn Brooks's novel, *Maud Martha*, in that it is episodic, showing the life of Selina Boyce between the ages of ten and nineteen. In the various episodes Selina grows and matures in an environment that prepares her for the obstacles she will encounter. Like Maud Martha Brown in the novel *Maud Martha*, Selina learns that life is not as easy as it seems. With each scene her relationship with her family changes so that eventually she is able to adjust to her mother's betrayal of her father.

This beautifully written novel, with its warm, poetic, yet precise imagery, is unusual in that it is about a West Indian family that retains a special cultural heritage that sometimes separates them from U.S. blacks.

Summary

As *Brown Girl, Brownstones* opens, Selina Boyce, ten years old, is sitting on the second-floor landing of the old brownstone house where her family lives. She leaves the landing to go downstairs and annoy her older sister, Ina. When Ina becomes angry, Selina goes to meet her father, who is just coming in the house. In a later scene Selina becomes friends with Miss Suggie, a boarder at the house. She becomes a special friend of Miss Thompson, a hairdresser, who listens patiently to Selina's problems and provides the warmth Selina's mother, Silla, lacks. Selina's father, Deighton, who dreams of returning to Barbados and settling on a piece of land he owns, does not get along with his wife. Silla considers him a ne'er-do-well and a daydreamer. She wants to buy the brownstone that they live in, but Deighton won't sell his land so that she can make a down payment.

Silla schemes and eventually forges Deighton's signature on the necessary papers to sell the land. But only Deighton can get the money; and when he does, instead of bringing it home to Silla, he spends it all on presents for everyone. Silla is enraged. Selina, who loves her father, is shattered by her mother's actions.

Later her father is injured in a factory accident and must stop work. After he is well, Deighton becomes a follower of Father

Devine and the Peace Movement. Eventually he leaves the house and moves to Harlem to become a member of the movement. Selina goes to visit every week. Silla becomes angry and one day swears out a warrent for Deighton's arrest as an illegal alien. He is taken away by the police and deported.

Later that evening, when they have gone to bed, Selina suddenly strikes her mother and calls her Hitler. After this episode Selina's relationship with her mother is never the same. She goes to school and soon is a young woman ready to make her own way. While she is at college in New York, she meets Clive, a young black artist and war veteran who cannot seem to find himself. She falls in love with him but realizes after a while that she has become his crutch. When she receives a monetary award, she turns it down and tells her mother that she can no longer live with her. In the final scene she takes one last walk through the neighbrohood.

CAPTAIN BLACKMAN

Kind of work: Novel
Writer: John A. Williams
Time: 1970
Setting: Vietnam
First published: 1972

Important Characters

Abaraham Blackman—*a black soldier*
Whittman—*a white soldier*
Doctorow—*a soldier*
Mimosa Rogers—*a beautiful black woman*
Woodcock—*a soldier*

Captain Blackman

Comment

Captain Blackman is a historical novel in that it traces the history of the blacks as military personnel in the United States armed forces from the American Revolution to the Vietnam War. In each period in which Blackman appears the author shows the injustice the blacks suffered at the hands of the whites. Farmers during the revolutionary episode want to take away the weapons of the blacks. Later segments of the novel show that the blacks were almost constantly on the receiving end not only of the racial prejudice directed against them but of bullets as well. The author suggests that throughout United States history the black soldier has been used as cannon fodder. Thorough research has been done to support the author's contentions.

Summary

The novel begins with Captain Abraham Blackman leading a search and destroy mission in the Vietnam War. In the fighting that occurs, he is badly wounded and falls unconscious in the mud. As the novel continues, Blackman awakens periodically from a coma and in his hallucinations he sees himself as a soldier in all the wars the United States has fought. He is first a soldier in the Colonial army at the Battle of Bunker Hill, then a sailor at the Battle of New Orleans. Later he is in the Union Army during the Civil War. He is a Buffalo Soldier during the American Indian wars. He is present at San Juan Hill in the Spanish-American War and in World Wars I and II as a soldier. Captain Blackman has his leg amputated as a result of the wound he received in Viet Nam and is given a medal for bravery as the novel closes.

CATHERINE CARMIER

Kind of work: Novel
Writer: Ernest Gaines
Time: 1960s
Setting: A Louisiana plantation
First published: 1954

Important Characters

Catherine Carmier—*a beautiful black Cajun woman*
Raoul Carmier—*Catherine's father*
Lillian Carmier—*Catherine's sister*
Della Johnson Carmier—*Raoul's wife*
Jackson Bradley—*a young black man who falls in love with Catherine*
Aunt Charlotte—*Jackson's aunt*
Madame Bayonne—*Jackson's old teacher*

Comment

In *Catherine Carmier* the author is concerned with the psychological aspects of racism and its effects upon its victims, the blacks. Although Raoul Carmier is, for all intents and purposes, a white Cajun in appearance, the fact that he has some black branches in his family tree delivers a devastating psychological blow to him and he clings to his beautiful daughter, Catherine, for support. Raoul does not permit Catherine to have any black suitors for fear of adding more black blood to his already tainted bloodline. When Jackson begins to call on Catherine, Raoul sees him as a threat.

On another level the author is concerned with manhood and its loss. Raoul feels a loss of manhood when he is rejected by the Cajuns. Jackson Bradley also feels uncertain about his manhood. He has come home to find himself but things have changed and he is no longer at ease. When Jackson fights Raoul, both men are trying to prove their manhood. In the end Catherine bears the brunt of the psychological blows resulting from the fight between Jackson and her father. When she goes into the house to attend to her father's injuries, it seems that Jackson has lost her.

Catherine Carmier

Summary

Jackson Bradley, a young black man, returns home to Louisiana after ten years in San Francisco, where he had completed a college education. He has come home to visit his Aunt Charlotte and other relatives. Aunt Charlotte, who has cared for Jackson from childhood, wants him to remain in the region and teach the blacks now that he has finished college. Jackson, however, does not intend to remain because he knows he cannot endure the racism and oppression that the blacks suffer at the hands of the Cajuns, the dominant group in the area. For some time this group has been forcing the blacks from their farms and taking them over. The Cajuns consider themselves white in spite of the admixture of black and Indian blood in their backgrounds. The blacks are imposed upon and segregated. When Jackson refuses to use the local segregated facilities, the Cajuns become suspicious of him and think he is a civil rights activist. In a conversation with Madame Bayonne, who taught him as a boy and understands his restlessness, the Carmier family is discussed. Jackson decides to renew his acquaintance with the beautiful Catherine Carmier, whom he had known when he was a boy. Madame Bayonne immediately senses that he will encounter difficulty with Raoul Carmier, Catherine's father, who, because of the presence of blacks in his geneological background, is considered black by the Cajuns. They will not accept him on the same terms as white Cajuns. Thus he is caught in the strange position of not belonging to either group. He will not accept the blacks as his people and is unacceptable to the Cajuns in spite of the fact that the Carmiers are all light-skinned enough to pass for white and Catherine's sister, Lillian, does just that.

At first Jackson wants only to resume his friendship with Catherine; but after several meetings with her, he finds himself deeply in love and asks her to leave her father and come away with him. Raoul knows nothing of this relationship; but he is told of it by the Cajuns, who welcome a chance to turn Carmier against Jackson. When Raoul discovers Catherine in the act of leaving, a bitter fight between Raoul and Jackson occurs in which Raoul is badly beaten. Catherine tells Jackson that she must attend her to her father's various bruises and lacerations. She asks Jackson to wait for her and goes into the house with a promise to return.

CLOTEL

Kind of work: Novel
Writer: William Wells Brown
Time: Nineteenth century
Setting: The South
First published: 1853

Important Characters

Currer Bell—*a beautiful mulatto slave woman*
Clotel—*Currer's sixteen-year old daughter*
Althesa—*Currer's fourteen year-old daughter*
Horatio Green—*a wealthy white citizen of Richmond*
Mary—*Clotel's daughter*
Dick Walker—*a slave trader*

Comment

In *Clotel*, the first novel by a black American author, William Wells Brown reveals the many and generally horrible aspects of slavery as practiced in the United States. The particular horrors described are slave auctions, coffles of slaves, slave pens, miscegenation, Christian hypocrisy, and murder. The action literally whirls the reader from one incident to another. The numerous, somewhat melodramatic accounts provide enough material for several novels.

Currer's having been the mistress of Thomas Jefferson in her youth is a reference to the relationship that is said to have existed between Jefferson and his beautiful slave, Sally Hemmings. It is obvious that the author drew upon his own experience as a slave in the descriptions of the activities of the slave traders and of slave auctions. The author uses the complex plot of the novel as a hook on which to hang the views of the Abolitionist Movement, in which he participated. *Clotel*, in spite of its defects, serves as a protest against slavery and was quite effective at the time it was written.

Comedy American Style

Summary

The story begins at a slave auction in Richmond, Virginia, in which three beautiful mulatto women, Currer Bell and her two daughters, Clotel and Althesa, are for sale. Currer, said to have been the mistress of Thomas Jefferson in her youth, and her daughter Althesa are sold to Dick Walker, a slave trader. Clotel is bought by Horatio Green, a prominent citizen of Richmond, who makes her his mistress and has a daughter, Mary, by her. Currer and Althesa are carried south to New Orleans by Dick Walker. After a while Horatio Green decides to marry. He takes his daughter Mary to be a servant for his new wife and Clotel is sold to a slave trader.

In New Orleans both Currer and Althesa are sold; Currer is sold to a Methodist minister and Althesa to a young doctor, who eventually marries her. While Clotel is being carried south in a coffle of slaves, she manages to escape with the help of a black man, a slave named William. After their escape Clotel returns to Virginia to find her daughter. After reaching Richmond Clotel tries to rescue Mary. She is put in a slave pen near the nation's capitol; but she again escapes the slave traders and tries to cross a bridge over the Potomac River with slave catchers at her heels. When she discovers that she cannot escape from her pursuers, she leaps leaps into the Potomac River and drowns within sight of the White House.

COMEDY AMERICAN STYLE

Kind of work: Novel
Writer: Jessie Fauset
Time: 1930
Setting: Philadelphia
First published: 1933

Important Characters

Olivia Blanchard Cary—*a very light-colored black woman*
Christopher Cary—*Olivia's husband*

56

Teresa, Christopher, and Oliver—*the Cary children*
Henry Bates—*a young black man whom Teresa loves*
Phoebe Grant—*a beautiful young black woman whom Christopher loves*

Comment

The author is concerned in Comedy American Style with a woman's obsessive desire to be white. Olivia literally destroys her family in her desperate urge toward whiteness. She breaks up Teresa's romance with a black man from MIT and forces her to marry a white Frenchman. Even when whites insult her, Olivia admires them. She dislikes blacks almost as much as she loves whites. She has no relationship with any blacks, prominent or not. In the end it is her mania to be white that causes her to be alone in Paris and forced to live in shabby and wretched circumstances.

The author shows that passing is to be condemned and blacks should be proud of their color and heritage. It is black Phoebe Grant who finally is able to force Olivia to leave for Paris.

Summary

Olivia Blanchard is a little girl going to a white school when the novel opens. She is not thought to be black, but one day a teacher mistakes her for an Italian. The effect of this affront upon her is so devastating that she becomes determined to marry a man who is as light-skinned as she is.

When she grows up, she marries Dr. Cary, a very light-skinned black man, in the belief that her children would be near white and pass over the color line into the world of white Americans. Two of her three children come close to her desires since they are for all intents and purpose white. However, her son Oliver is brown and is immediately rejected by Olivia.

As Oliver grows up, his mother continues to reject him and constantly ridicules him. Olivia's daughter, Teresa, meets Henry Bates, a young, well-educated black man, and falls in love with him. Olivia finds out about the relationship and breaks up the romance, forcing Teresa to marry a parsimonious, dull Frenchman. Oliver, suffering from Olivia's rejection, commits suicide. Olivia's second son, Christopher, meets a beautiful black woman and marries her. After Teresa's unhappy marriage, Dr. Cary deteriorates and eventually goes into bankruptcy.

Phoebe Grant maneuvers Olivia into a position where she

leaves Philadephia for Paris, where she expects to live with Teresa. However, she is rejected by Teresa's husband. Olivia is stranded in Paris and is forced to live on the small sum of fifty dollars a month that her husband sends her.

COMING HOME

Kind of work: Novel
Writer: George Davis
Time: 1970
Setting: U.S.A.; Thailand
First published: 1971

Important Characters

Lt. Ben Williams—*a black American fighter pilot*
Rose Williams—*Ben's wife*
Lt. James Childress—*a black American fighter pilot*
Lt. Stacy—*a white fighter pilot*
Damg—*a Thai woman with whom Ben falls in love*
Roxanne—*a girl loved by Lt. Stacy*

Comment

Coming Home is a novel about the racism that exists in the United States armed forces and is directed not only against the blacks, but also against the Thais. White fighter pilots among themselves refer to the black pilots as niggers and darkies. Using a unique and modified stream of consciousness style, the author reveals the thoughts of each character. Rose, Ben Williams's wife, has an affair with Lt. Childress, who sought her out in Washington, D.C., where she works. She does not really love Ben at all. In the author's view racism that extended itself all the way from the United States to Vietnam demolishes personal relationships not only between blacks and whites but also between the blacks themselves.

Summary

As the novel begins, Lt. Ben Williams, a black stationed in Thailand, awakens in the tent he shares with two other American fighter pilots, one black and one white. Lt. Childress, the other black pilot, is going home to the United States and he does not want Ben to have his girl, Damg, who is attracted to Ben.

Ben makes his flights but comes to like the war less and less. He thinks about his wife in the states, who does not write to him. After Childress leaves, Ben meets Damg and they become lovers. He is relatively happy with her, but he is growing to dislike the war more and more.

Finally he refuses, on one mission, to drop his bombs and states that he will not fly any more. When Lt. Stacy, the white fighter pilot, is questioned, it is discovered that Lt. Childress has killed a policeman in Baltimore and Ben Williams is being investigated because he knows Childress. He is to be court martialed for refusing to fly. One evening in a bar in Bangkok, Ben meets a black soldier who is deserting the army because he had been ordered to shoot a child. After thinking everything over, Ben leaves Damg a note and some money and deserts.

THE CONJURE MAN DIES

Kind of work: Novel
Writer: Rudolph Fisher
Time: 1930s
Setting: Harlem, New York
First published: 1932

Important Characters

Dr. John Archer—*a black doctor*
Perry Dart—*a detective on the New York City police force*
Bubber Brown—*a cheap Harlem private detective*

The Conjure Man Dies

Jinx Jenkins—*Bubber's partner*
Samuel Crouch—*an undertaker*

Comment

This is the first detective novel written by a black American author. There is no mention of the issue of race or race problems in the entire novel; what is presented is a murder mystery along the lines of S. S. Van Dine's Philo Vance stories. The author's medical background is fully brought into play, and comic relief is provided by the characters Bubber Brown and Jinx Jenkins, carryovers from Fisher's previous novel, the *Walls of Jericho*. In addition to writing a first-rate mystery story about the murder of a Harvard-trained African conjure man, the author provides views of the various aspects of the life of the Harlem of his time.

Summary

The novel begins at midnight in a building occupied by Samuel Crouch and N. Frimbo, psychist. There is a commotion. As Bubber Brown, a fake private detective, runs out of the building seeking a doctor, he finds Dr. John Archer and takes him back to the building to show him the corpse of N. Frimbo, a Harvard-trained conjure man. Dr. Archer examines the body and calls the police. Perry Dart, a black detective of the New York City Police Department, is assigned to the case. Dart and Dr. Archer, using Philo Vance type methods, follow all the clues and eventually provide a solution to the mystery, with the doubtful help of Bubber Brown and his friend Jinx Jenkins. As the novel ends, Bubber and Jinx are walking down Lennox Avenue, listening to someone sing "I'll be Glad When You're Dead, You Rascal You."

CORREGIDORA

Kind of work: Novel
Writer: Gayl Jones
Time: 1947
Setting: Kentucky
First published: 1974

Important Characters

Ursa Corregidora—*a blues singer*
Mutt Thomas—*Ursa's first husband*
Tadpole McCormic—*Ursa's second husband*

Comment

Corregidora is concerned with black female sexuality. In Ursa's case her problems are compounded by her past, as revealed in flashbacks. The cause for her present crisis is her savage and brutal progenitor, after whom she is named; he haunts her like an evil phantom. A Portuguese slave owner who fathered his own slaves, Corregidora raped the females when they were old enough and later set them to work as prostitutes. From childhood, Ursa Corregidora has this seemingly evil spell cast over her as had all the Corregidora women before her. The violence and degradation inherent in the slave-master relationship in regard to black female slaves during the period of American slavery still has a direct effect on black female and male sexual relations. However, the reader does wonder how Ursa, who has spent a large part of her life in night clubs, remains so passive and resigns herself to abuse.

Summary

As the novel begins, Ursa is recovering from a hysterectomy, the result of her being knocked down a flight of stairs by her husband, Mutt Thomas. When she recovers, she goes to sing in a cafe owned by Tadpole McCormic. He is strongly attracted to Ursa, eventually they become lovers, and she finally marries him. She soon realizes that she cannot return his love and give him sexual satisfaction. Ursa takes a job at another cafe across town so that she can decide what to do.

C'ruiter

On night Ursa comes home to find Tadpole in bed with his new singer, a fifteen-year-old girl. She leaves him and returns to her first husband, Mutt.

C'RUITER

Kind of work: Play
Writer: John Matheus
Time: 1918
Setting: Rural Georgia
First published: 1926

Important Characters

Granny—*a black woman*
Sonny—*Granny's twenty-three-year-old grandson*
Sissy—*Sonny's twenty-year-old wife*
A white man—*an agent recruiting workers for a munitions factory in Detroit*

Comment

In *C'ruiter* the author is concerned with the Great Migration of blacks out of the South to the North during World War I (1915-1918). At this time hundreds of thousands of blacks left the South in search of better jobs and living conditions in the northern cities. Southern plantation owners saw their labor force disappearing and tried to stop the flow. Recruiting agents were arrested and newspapers such as the *Chicago Defender*, which urged the blacks to leave, were confiscated. Railroad ticket agents refused to sell the blacks tickets and in some instances blacks were arrested to prevent them from leaving.

Several writers have written about this period. In George W. Lee's novel *River George*, some of the blacks leave the farms they sharecrop to go to the cities and work. Alden Bland, in *Behold a Cry*, has as the hero Ed Tyler, who has left the South to work in Chicago. Big Matt and his brothers leave their farm in Kentucky to work in the steel mills of Pennsylvania in William Attaways novel, *Blood on the Forge.*

Summary

As the play opens, Granny is in the main room of a sharecropper's cabin preparing breakfast for her grandson and his wife. Sonny and Sissy come in from the fields, where they have been working since sunup. While they are eating breakfast, Sonny tells Granny to come with them. Sonny has been recruited to go North and work in a Detroit munitions factory. While they are talking, a well-dressed white man comes in and tells everyone to be ready to leave that night. Sissy prepares to pack while Sonny tries to persuade Granny to go North with them. He is afraid that when he is gone the white plantation owner will put Granny off the land. Finally Granny agrees to go.

In the second scene Sonny and Sissy are waiting for the recruiter to take them to the train. When the agent comes, he tells everyone to hurry; but Granny reminds him not to forget Benny, the family dog. The agent says that he cannot take the dog along and Granny refuses to go, but she urges Sonny and Sissy to go on. She returns to the cabin and releases the dog from the crate. As she sits alone in the cabin, the play closes.

CURLING

Kind of work: Novel
Writer: Robert Boles
Time: 1960s
Setting: Boston, Massachusetts
First published: 1967

Curling

Important Characters

Chelsea Burlingame—*the black adopted son of a rich white couple*
Anne Megathlin—*a woman whom Chelsea once loved*
Roger—*Chelsea's close friend*
Cade-Hoover-Ward—*a young white southerner with whom Chelsea works*

Comment

In this unusual novel the author's basic concern is with the protagonist's lack of racial identity, which places him in the position of belonging nowhere. His color makes him feel he does not belong with the whites in whose circle he moves. He buys a building in the black ghetto of Boston to have a reason to visit the section, but he feels ill at ease there as well. These feelings affect his relationship with Anne, a beautiful white girl he once loved. Most of the action takes place in Chelsea's mind. The memories of incidents in his past curl into one another until his world seems chaotic.

There is very little about racial protest in *Curling*. It deals with the identity problem of a highly intelligent black man living in an environment that he did not make but must live in. Chelsea leaves his white friends for a time but soon realizes that he has become dependent upon them. When he kills a pickpocket, it is his white father's lawyer who extricates him from the affair.

Summary

As the novel opens, Chelsea is working in his office at a Boston engineering firm. Since it is a gray, dreary, winter Friday, Chelsea decides to leave work early and later go to dinner with his friends, Roger and Anne Megathlin. Chelsea has had a brief love affair with Anne and wants to see her again. It is decided at dinner that everyone will spend the weekend at Chelsea's house on Cape Cod.

The group, Chelsea, Roger, Anne, and Cade Hoover-Ward, attend a party and the next morning leave for the cape. As part of the weekend excursion everyone goes to a zoo and then on a drinking spree. Chelsea winds up in a New Bedford bar, where his wallet is stolen. He follows the pickpocket out of the bar and kills him in a fight. Chelsea is jailed but eventually he is cleared and released.

DADDY WAS A NUMBER RUNNER

Kind of work: Novel
Writer: Louise Meriwether
Time: 1930s
Setting: Harlem, New York
First published: 1970

Important Characters

Francie Coffin—*a twelve-year-old black girl who lives in Harlem*
Adam Coffin—*Francie's father, a number runner*
Sterling Coffin—*Francie's fourteen-year-old brother*
China Doll—*a local prostitute*
Henrietta Coffin—*Francie's mother*
Miss Peters—*a social worker*
Miss Mackey—*a lady who plays numbers and runs a floating crap game*
Sukie—*Francie's girlfriend*

Comment

Daddy Was a Number Runner is an episodic novel in which various incidents reveal the relentless pressures on the inhabitants of the black ghettos, especially the urban ones. There is an air of almost complete hopelessness at one point. Francie pleadingly asks her mother if they will ever be able to leave the street where they live in such poverty and squalor, among bed bugs and rats.

When Adam Coffin gives in under the pressures of black ghetto living, the Coffin family begins to collapse. James becomes a pimp and a hustler; Sterling quits school; and Francie's mother becomes a wage slave to make ends meet. The author is concerned with the harsh and violent environment that destroys so many young blacks trying to survive in spite of it. Francie is one of those who may be trapped and demolished.

Summary

Twelve-year-old Francie Coffin helps her father, Adam Coffin, a number runner, pick up bets from his customers. Many things happen to Francie in the Harlem ghetto where she lives. Almost every day she has to fight Sukie, with whom she eventually becomes friends. Francie's oldest brother, James Junior, drops out of school and joins a street gang.

Economic problems increase as Francie's father finds his number racket dwindling because of police pressure. Eventually the Coffin family goes on welfare and finds itself harassed constantly by Miss Peters, a social worker. She forces them off the welfare rolls.

Throughout all these various difficulties Francie roams her depressed neighborhood, observing everything. Once she is almost raped by a man in a movie theater. When her father leaves the family, Francie is upset and tries to find him. When a white man is mugged and killed, James Junior and several street gang members are arrested. James is proven innocent but leaves home to become a pimp.

Under the pressures of the depression and racial discrimination, the blacks riot. Francie sees this, too. As final blows her brother, Sterling, a brilliant student, drops out of school and China Doll, a local prostitute whom Francie liked, kills her pimp and is jailed. In the final scene Francie and her brother Sterling are sitting on the front stoop in the evening and she is wondering if she will ever be able to leave the mean street she lives on.

A DIFFERENT DRUMMER

Kind of work: Novel
Writer: William Melvin Delley
Time: 1957
Setting: Sutton, a southern town
First published: 1962

Important Characters

Tucker Caliban—*a black southern farmer*

Bennet T Bradshaw—*a black minister*
David Wilson—*a white southern aristocrat*
Dewey Wilson—*David's son*
Dymphna Wilson—*David's wife*

Comment

A Different Drummer is a protest novel that reflects the desperation the blacks felt for decades and gave vent to during the violent decade of the 1960s, in which they broke out of the pattern of race relations that had been in existence in the United States for centuries.

Tucker Caliban is a special kind of rebel and sets the tone for the mass departure of the blacks from Sutton. Tucker does not appear directly in the novel; but he is seen through the eyes of others, including the whites, who do not understand his revolt. When the blacks begin to leave, the whites respond with violence.

Bradshaw is blamed for the exodus of the blacks and lynched. The nonviolent aspect of the quiet rebellion of the blacks of Sutton was a forecast of things to come in the 1960s, when Martin Luther King led the blacks in what was tantamount to a nonviolent revolt against the status quo. The title of the novel is taken from a passage found in chapter 18 of Henry David Thoreau's *Literary Journal*.

Summary

A group of white men are sitting on the porch of the local grocery company watching the blacks of Sutton leave and head North. In a flashback scene the story of Tucker Caliban's ancester who refused to become a slave is told. Tucker Caliban, a black farmer, one day sprinkled salt on his fields, burned his house, shot all of his livestock, and with his wife and child left the little southern town of Sutton. Soon all the blacks in the entire state begin a mass exodus to the North.

At first the whites laugh about the exodus; but when they realize that all of the blacks are really leaving, they become anxious, angry, and confused. The whites try to find reasons for the blacks leaving but cannot. About the time the blacks begin to leave, Bennet Bradshaw, a black minister and cult leader, comes to Sutton. He was the college classmate of the town's leading white citizen. Soon the townspeople become suspicious and accuse him of organizing the mass exodus of all the blacks. Bradshaw is lynched as the novel closes.

THE DUTCHMAN

Kind of work: Play
Writer: Imamu Amiri Baraka (LeRoi Jones)
Time: 1960s
Setting: New York
First published: 1964

Important Characters

Clay—*a twenty-year-old black man*
Lula—*a thirty-year-old white woman*
An unnamed young black man
Subway riders

Comment

The Dutchman is a savage, biting play that is in reality a commentary on the racial conflict between blacks and whites in the United States. Lula is symbolic of the machinations of white America in its relations with the blacks. The play suggests that whites tend to tease the blacks, then humiliate them. When the blacks are resentful and enraged at such treatment, they are put down hard. And the process is repetitive.

Summary

As the play opens, Clay, a studious young black man with books under his arm, is seated alone on a subway coach. The train stops. Lula enters and comes down the aisle toward Clay. She stops beside his seat, and speaks to him, then sits down beside him. As Lula begins a conversation with him, he is surprised at how much she seems to know about him. Clay begins to think she is a friend of some of the people he knows.

Lula teases and entices Clay until he finally asks her to come to a party with him. She continues to tease him and suggest that they go to her apartment, where he will make love to her. Suddenly she insults him. Clay is taken aback for a moment as Lula begins to taunt him and ridicule his background. She accuses him of being simply a white black man. After he recovers from the initial shock of Lula's comment, Clay is enraged. He slaps her and angrily begins to berate her and all whites. Finally he exhausts his anger, reaches for his books, and prepares to leave the train. While he is doing this Lula takes out a small knife and kills him.

The riders throw his body out of the coach and leave at the next stop. Lula straightens her clothing and takes her seat. A young black man about twenty comes into the coach. He is carrying a couple of books under his arm. An old black conductor shuffles through the coach as Lula gives the young black a long, enticing look and the play ends.

FAITH AND THE GOOD THING

Kind of work: Novel
Writer: Charles Johnson
Time: Present
Setting: Georgia; Chicago
First Published: 1974

Important Characters

Faith Cross—*a young southern black woman*
Todd Cross—*Faith's father*
Lavidia Cross—*Faith's mother*
Dr. Lynch—*a local physician*
Reverend Brown—*the minister of Faith's church*
Isaac Maxwell—*Faith's lover*
The Swamp Woman—*a conjure woman*

Comment

The novel *Faith and the Good Thing* is a mixture of folklore, voodoo, and good storytelling. The story is comic in many respects but, as in all comedy, there is sadness and tragedy as well. While the novel is not about race conflict as such, the author touches on several negative aspects of black ghetto life as well as the part that voodoo and folklore play in the culture of the blacks.

Summary

The novel begins with the death of Faith's mother, Lavidia Cross. Before dying she tells Faith to find a "good thing" and hold on to it. Faith goes to her minister, Reverend Brown, and asks him what a good thing is. He tells her that it is her mother's relation to God. Not satisfied with this explanation, Faith goes to the Swamp Woman for an answer. Her answer is couched in philosophical jargon and Faith still does not know what the good thing is.

Faith's search takes her to Chicago. Almost as soon as she arrives, she is mistaken for a prostitute by Arnold Tapp, who leaves her twenty dollars. Faith finds this money helpful.

Later she meets Isaac Maxwell, who falls in love with her. Thinking he is the good thing, Faith says yes when he proposes to her. She becomes a typical housewife, but Isaac tires of her and leaves. The apartment where Faith lives catches fire and she is badly burned. She decides to return to Georgia. As the novel ends, Faith becomes a conjure woman.

THE FLAGELLANTS

Kind of work: Novel
Writer: Carlene Polite
Time: 1960s
Setting: New York
First published: 1966

Important Characters

Jimson—*a young black poet*

Ideal—*Jimson's girlfriend*
Rehba—*a white female librarian*

Comment

In this unusual novel the protagonists Jimson and Ideal are constantly flaying one another verbally. They make speeches to one another in bars, in bed, on the street, and just about anywhere else. The subject of these harangues is usually the experience of the blacks in the United States. When Jimson takes a job in an art library and a white woman librarian falls in love with him, Ideal becomes angry and goads him into an argument. Jimson's response is a lecture on the theory of the black matriarch who emasculates and dominates the black male both sexually and emotionally. Jimson resents the fact that Ideal takes the dominant role in their relationship. Ideal defends the idea of the dominant black female role on economic grounds since black women are often able to secure employment easier than the black men.

While Ideal appears to want Jimson to assume the proper role, neither she nor Jimson is able to break out of the pattern the whites have put them in. Implicit in all these speeches that Jimson and Ideal hurl at each other is the belief that blacks must maintain race pride and respect and must make an unusually strong effort to adjust to the white world that overshadows and oppresses them. Although it was written in 1966, the problems with which the novel is concerned remain today.

Summary

The Flagellants opens with a brief introductory chapter in which Ideal appears as a child dancing on the top of a large brass bed in her grandmother's house in the South. The main action of the novel occurs in Greenwich Village. Ideal and Jimson, a young black poet, live together and spend their time lacerating one another verbally. Jimson moves from job to job and Ideal works in a drug store. While working in an art library, Jimson meets a white woman librarian who falls in love with him; but he rejects her and quits the job.

One evening Ideal tries to prevent Jimson from committing suicide. She severely cuts her hand in the process. Jimson changes his mind, leaves Ideal waiting for an ambulance, and goes out for the evening. Jimson finally takes a job at Beaureaucratique, a United

Nations type agency. He meets Johnny Lowell, who urges him to live for today and love as many women as he can. Jimson has an affair with a beautiful black woman. Ideal begins to watch him closely and, as the novel ends, she decides she must leave Jimson for her own good.

FOR UNBORN CHILDREN

Kind of work: Play
Writer: Myrtle Smith Livingston
Time: 1926
Setting: The South
First published: 1926

Important Characters

Leroy Carlson—*a young black lawyer*
Marion Carlson—*Leroy's sister*
Selma Frazier—*a young white woman*

Comment

This short play has as its theme the subject of miscegenation and the concomitant problems of such a relationship, especially during the period with which the author is concerned. Usually the situation involved a southern white man and a black woman. Here the reverse is true; it is a black man who loves a white woman. This problem has still not really been solved and Marion's outburst concerning black women has echoes that are heard today. The author's view of this kind of relationship may possibly be expressed in her amazing and bizarre ending of the play. The idea seems to be that any black man who becomes involved with a white woman ought to meet his doom and be lynched by a mob. This is bizarre indeed.

Summary

The play opens in the living room of the Carlson home in the South. Grandmother Carlson and Marion are discussing the fact that Leroy Carlson is in love with a young white girl, Selma Frazier, whom he wants to marry. Grandma is prepared if necessary to tell Leroy something about his past that will cause him to give up Selma, but she does not tell Marion what it is. When Leroy comes home, Grandma Carlson and Marion try to persuade him to give up Selma. Marion becomes angry and denounces Leroy because he wants to marry a white woman instead of a black woman. Leroy does not want to give Selma up and is in a quandary as to what his course of action should be. Grandma Carlson tells Leroy that his own mother was white and that she rejected him because of his color. While Leroy is trying to decide what to do, Selma comes into the room, almost hysterical. She urges Leroy to run away because there is a mob coming to lynch him. He finds that it is too late to run.

Grandma Carlson and Marion return and are much afraid for Leroy because the mob leader threatens to burn down the house if Leroy does not come out. Leroy hugs his Grandmother and Marion and tells them he will make a sacrifice for unborn children. He walks out the front door to be lynched by the waiting mob.

THE FOURTEENTH CADILLAC

Kind of work: Novel for young people
Writer: Jesse Jackson
Time: 1925
Setting: Columbus, Ohio
First published: 1972

Important Characters

Stonewall Jackson—*a seventeen-year-old black youth*
Ben Jackson—*Stonewall's father*

The Fourteenth Cadillac

Maybell Jackson—*Stonewall's mother*
Steeple—*a friend of Stonewall's*
Moses Jackson—*Stonewall's older brother*
Talitha—*Stonewall's girlfriend*
Ed Coffin—*a local black undertaker*
Uncle Ernie—*Stonewall's uncle*

Comment

In this short novel for young people the author tells the story of the efforts of a black youth to grow to manhood in a midwestern city during the 1920s. Stonewall Jackson's problems seem relatively mild compared to those of M.C. in Al Young's *Snakes*, John Grimes in James Baldwin's *Go Tell It on the Mountain*, or Joe Brooks in Sharon Bell Mathis's *Teacup Full of Roses*, in which the protagonists are also black youth in the process of growing up in a negative environment. Stonewall Jackson's surroundings are negative in a mild way. Although he meets racial discrimination when he tries to find a job, he does not encounter the intense pressure of the urban black ghetto that M.C. and John Grimes both face. He certainly does not encounter the kinds of obstacles that Joe Brooks in *Teacup Full of Roses* has to deal with in his young life.

There is a warmth in *The Fourteenth Cadillac* that Stonewall displays toward his brother and his friend Steeple that is similar to what Joe Brooks feels for his younger brother David in *Teacup Full of Roses*. In Stonewall's father, Ben Jackson, one finds a steady, level-headed black man who loves his son and finds the means to tell him so.

Summary

The story begins with seventeen-year-old Stonewall Jackson attending his aunt's funeral. Although he is still in high school he is failing, but only his brother Moses knows this. After the funeral is over, Stonewall goes to his aunt's house to join everyone. On the way he sees Steeple, a friend from school, and asks him to come along with him to have some food with everyone else. When everyone leaves Ernie's house, Stonewall and his family go home.

After they reach home, Stonewall's mother scolds him for asking Steeple, whom she does not like because he is three years older than Stonewall and roams about the country working as a groom in stables. Stonewall stands quietly but his father says that

74

after Stonewall graduates from high school in the summer they will paint the houses and fences. At this point Stonewall tells his parents that he will not graduate.

His father tells Stonewall that he will have to go to work since he is not graduating and while he is job hunting he will have to paint the house. Stonewall tries to find a job in several places, including a hotel, and a garage, but no one will hire him. One Sunday Steeple tells Stonewall that he can earn some money in the Battle Royal but does not tell him what that means. When the boys reach the spot where the event is to take place Stonewall discovers that he is to fight blindfolded in a ring with thirteen other youths. Stonewall is knocked out and has to be taken home.

Steeple helps Stonewall get a job as an exercise boy on a large horse farm. The job lasts only until the horse show that is being held on the farm is over. Soon Stonewall is out of work. He takes a job with Ed Coffin, the undertaker, but finds that he does not like working with corpses. After leaving Coffin, Stonewall decides that he will leave home to take a job at Bolt Farm.

GORILLA MY LOVE

Kind of work: Fifteen short stories
Writer: Toni Cade Bambara
Time: 1940s
Setting: Harlem, New York
First published: 1972

Important Characters

Hazel—*a young black girl about ten years old*
Jefferson Winston Vale—*Hazel's uncle*
Big Brood and Baby Jason—*Hazel's younger brothers*
Grandaddy Vale—*Hazel's grandfather*

Gorilla My Love

Comment

In the title story, *Gorilla My Love,* the author is concerned about grown-ups keeping their promises. To ten-year-old Hazel, keeping one's word is very important. She demanded her money back from the movie manager when he did not show the film *Gorilla My Love* as he had promised. When Hazel's uncle does not keep his promise as she thinks he should, it is tragic and it hurts. What the author has done in all the stories in this collection is to capture the innate beauty in black language. The reader is allowed to see life in the black world through the eyes of Hazel and all the other beautiful young blacks who people these stories.

Summary

The collection *Gorilla My Love* opens with Hazel, a young black girl, riding in her grandfather's truck. She and her younger brothers are visiting Grandaddy Vale for the summer. Mr. Vale is taking a load of pecans to the market and Hazel is sitting in the passenger's seat. Her grandfather lets her give him directions. Hazel's uncle, Jefferson Winston Vale, whom she calls "Hunca Bubba" because she couldnt't say uncle when when she was a little girl, is in the back of the truck with her brothers. In a flashback Hazel remembers the time, Easter a year ago, when she and her brothers went to see a movie. On the marquee the movie *Gorilla My Love* was advertised. However, when the children got inside, they found that a religious picture was being shown instead. Hazel joined the other kids in the movie yelling and stomping until the movie usher made them stop. Then Hazel took her brothers to the manager's office to demand their money back because the manager did not keep his word and show *Gorilla My Love.*

In the truck Hazel turns to her uncle, who is looking at a picture of a younger woman whom he is going to marry and asks him if he is going to marry her. When he says yes Hazel reminds him that he is not keeping his word because he promised Hazel he would marry her. Hazel's uncle explains that he was only kidding and besides, he is her uncle. She is hurt, but her grandfather tells her that Hunca Bubba was the one who told her that. The uncle she knows now is a man named Jefferson Winston Vale. This does not help the hurt, however, and as the story ends Hazel is crying so hard that she can not see the road map in her hands.

Go Tell It on the Mountain

Kind of work: Novel
Writer: James Baldwin
Time: 1935
Setting: Harlem, New York
First published: 1953

Important Characters

Gabriel Grimes—*a religious zealot*
John Grimes—*the oldest of four children and Gabriel's stepson*
Elizabeth Grimes—*John's gentle mother*
Roy—*John's brother, the favorite of his father*
Sarah—*John's sister*
Aunt Florence—*Gabriel's sister*
Father James—*the pastor of the Temple of the Fire Baptized*
Brother Elisha—*Father James's nephew*
Praying Mother Washington—*a pillar of the church*
Sister McCandlers and Sister Price—*Two saints who come to church every night*

Comment

This is the story of the attempt of a sensitive, intelligent, young black boy, John Grimes, to maintain his equilibrium in a hostile and almost savage environment mitigated only by the gentleness of his mother. Although there are references to racial prejudice and its effects in the novel, the primary concern is how John copes with his surroundings and adapts to them so that he can go his own way. On another level John's intense religion is a shield that protects him from the hostility both of the outer world and of the inner world of his home. John's religious conversion shows the maturity he has reached.

Summary

As the novel opens, it is John Grimes's fourteenth birthday and as he wakes he feels apprehensive. He wonders whether anyone will remember his birthday. As he does his house chores, he thinks bitterly about his stepfather, whom he fears and has grown to dislike intensely. His mother gives him the small amount of money she had saved.

John is overwhelmed by his mother's action and leaves the apartment before his father comes home from work. He spends the cold wintry afternoon in Central Park imagining how he will become a great leader. As he nears the apartment on his return home, he senses that something is wrong. He sees his sister Sarah rush from the house. When he enters the apartment, he finds his Aunt Florence, his mother, and his father, Gabriel. His brother Roy has been stabbed by a group of white boys when he went into their neighborhood. Gabriel takes his bitterness out on his family. When his wife becomes nervous, he slaps her across the face. In spite of his wound, Roy is enraged by this and curses his father, threatening to kill him if he strikes her again. Gabriel becomes furious, takes off his belt, and begins to beat Roy severely. Roy is saved only by the intercession of his Aunt Florence. That evening everyone goes to the temple as usual and in the bouts of praying and singing the early lives of several of the characters are revealed. Using the flashback technique, the author tells the life stories of Gabriel and Elizabeth.

In his youth Gabriel had been wild and uncontrollable, but he is converted and becomes a preacher. He marries and seems to settle down but becomes involved in a love affair with another woman, who bears him a child. He sends her away to Chicago, using the money his wife, Deborah, had saved. He gradually loses his status as a preacher. After the death of his first wife Gabriel decides to go north to New York. He meets Elizabeth, John's mother, and they marry.

Elizabeth's story is also told in flashback. When she was eight years old, Elizabeth's mother died and it was necessary for her to go to live with an aunt away from her father, who ran a bawdy house. Elizabeth's aunt disliked him because of his activities, but to Elizabeth her father was simply someone she loved intensely. Elizabeth grew to hate her aunt because of this dislike the aunt had for her father. Elizabeth meets Richard, a young man who takes her from her aunt's house to New York, where they plan to marry.

For a while Richard and Elizabeth are happy, then Richard is accused of a crime of which he is innocent and is taken to jail where he is badly beaten. Richard is broken as a result of the brutal treatment. One day when Elizabeth is out of the apartment, he commits suicide. Elizabeth had not told Richard she was pregnant and they had not married. She meets Gabriel and he proposes to her.

John's Aunt Florence's background, too, is revealed in flashback. She had been married to an easygoing, somewhat impractical, and happy-go-lucky man whose life-style was unlike her own. She was practical, religious, and a striver while her husband Frank was just a few notches above being a rounder. After ten years with Florence, Frank deserted her and was killed in battle in World War I. Near the end of the evening at the temple John undergoes an intense religious conversion.

HARLEM SUMMER

Kind of work: Novel for young people
Writer: Mary Elizabeth Vroman
Time: 1960s
Setting: Harlem, New York
First published: 1967

Important Characters

John Brown—*a sixteen year-old black youth*
Marcus Garvey Mason—*"Mark Two" a black youth*
Deena Johnson—*Mark's girl*
Sam Block—*a white grocery store owner*
Old Paul Mason—*Mark's grandfather*
Duke and Pippy—*two black youths*
Candy Matthews—*John's aunt*
Ernie Matthews—*Candy's husband*

Harlem Summer

Comment

In *Harlem Summer* the author is writing about the rapid maturation of a black youth from Alabama during a summer he spends in Harlem. John Brown learns fast that life in a black urban ghetto the size of Harlem is quite different from the life he knew at home. Each incident in which is is involved helps him mature more quickly. It is interesting to note that the author has presented a side of Harlem that everyone seems to forget is there. These young people are representative of the hardworking, respectable citizens of Harlem who are generally overlooked. The usual picture of Harlem is of an immense ghetto filled with drug addicts, pushers, whores, and pimps. The issue of race is touched upon but not to any great extent. Sam Block, the white grocery store owner, is portrayed in a sympathetic manner.

Summary

Sixteen-year-old John Brown, who is visiting his aunt and uncle in Harlem, New York, for the summer, asks Sam Block, a local grocery store owner, for a job. John gets the job and meets seventeen-year-old Marcus Garvey Mason, who also works at the store. The two boys become friends. Mark introduces John to Deena Johnson, his girl, and also to Paul Mason, his grandfather, with whom he lives. The three young people spend time together when they are not working. One evening, while waiting for Mark at the Apollo Theater, John and Deena are accosted by Duke and Dippy, two tough young men of the neighborhood. Just as John is about to fight them to protect Deena, Mark arrives and Dippy and Duke withdraw.

One evening after leaving a movie theater, John stops to listen to a street corner orator. While he is listening, he notices a man about to pick a lady's purse. John attempts to stop him and the pickpocket pulls a knife. John fights him and wins. When the fight ends, John is arrested and taken to jail. He calls Mark and Old Paul and they in turn call his aunt and uncle. While John is still at the police station, the woman whose purse was about to be picked comes in an explains what happened. Old Paul and Mark arrive and the detective who arrested John immediately recognizes Old Paul as an friend of his. John is released and returns home with his aunt and uncle.

One day John is alone in Sam Block's store when Duke and Dippy come in. Dippy is carrying a pistol. He points it at John and forces him to be quiet. Dippy says that he has come to settle a score with Mark, who had beat him in a fight earlier. When Mark comes in,

Dippy hits him over the head with the butt of the pistol and dazes him. At this point John jumps Duke, and Mark, recovering from the blow, jumps Dippy. In the ensuing fight Dippy and Duke are badly beaten. After the fight ends, Mark takes Dippy's gun away from him and throws both boys out of the store. Mark takes the pistol to Old Paul, who disposes of it. John does not understand why Mark let Duke and Dippy go without calling the police. Mark explains that Duke and Dippy are in trouble enough without going to reform school. The novel ends as the summer does with everyone, including Sam Block, at the train station to see John off to Montgomery.

A HERO AIN'T NOTHIN BUT A SANDWICH

Kind of work: Novel
Writer: Alice Childress
Setting: New York, the present
First published: 1973

Important Characters

Benjie Johnson—*a thirteen-year-old black boy*
Rose Johnson—*Benjie's mother*
Jimmy Lee Powell—*Benjie's friend*
Butler Craig—*Benjie's "stepfather"*
Bernard Cohen—*a white teacher of Benjie's*
Nigeria Greene—*a black teacher of Benjie's*

Comment

This short novel was written for young people, but it can be read with pleasure by adults as well. The author has written about a difficult subject with marked skill. She has been able to incorporate the language of the street into the novel in such a way as to provide a smooth, flowing narrative. The story has an unusual structure. A stream of consciousness technique is employed and each character's thoughts and ideas are presented. There is almost no direct description in the entire novel. The subject of race emerges only in the relationship between Nigeria Greene and Bernard Cohen.

Summary

Thirteen-year-old Benjie Johnson is a black youth who is about to become hooked on heroin. In class Benjie nods and cannot pay attention because of his heroin addiction. His teachers, Bernard Cohen and Nigeria Greene, are aware that Benjie is a junkie; but Mr. Cohen will not turn Benjie in to the authorities. Benjie's friend, Jimmy Lee Powell, tries to talk to Benjie and get him to stop using heroin, without much success. Benjie's mother cannot communicate with her son and feels helpless. Finally Nigeria Greene and Mr. Cohen turn Benjie in and he has to take withdrawal treatments.

Butler Craig, Benjie's "stepfather" and his mother's boyfriend, finds out that Benjie is an addict, gives up his own apartment, and rents a room in the same building as Benjie and his mother so that he can help them. Although Benjie comes home from the center, he is not completely cured and steals Butler's clothes in order to get a fix. Butler becomes angry and leaves. Benjie's mother goes to a reader, a kind of conjure man, who says that he can cure Benjie. He gives her a blue substance that she is to bathe Benjie with to enable him to withdraw from the drug.

After thinking about Benjie and his mother, Butler returns but catches Benjie stealing a toaster from a nearby apartment and chases him. Benjie tries to leap across an air shaft and does not quite make it. Butler catches him, saves his life, and the two return to Benjie's mother's apartment. Shortly after Bulter and Benjie come back, Mrs. Johnson takes Benjie to the funeral of a friend of his who died of an overdose of heroin. She makes Benjie go to the coffin and look at his dead friend. This angers Butler, who tells her she must give up the voodoo advice from the conjure man and get Benjie back to the treatment center. Since Butler saved his life, Benjie considers him to be his real father. When Butler asks him to return to the center, he agrees to do so. The novel ends with Butler waiting outside the center to take Benjie home.

His Own Where

Kind of work: Novel
Writer: June Jordon
Time: 1970
Setting: Brooklyn, New York
First published: 1971

Important Characters

Buddy Rivers—a sixteen-year-old black youth
Angela Figueroa—Buddy's girlfriend
Mr. Hickey—a school principal

Comment

In this short but unusual novel the author has successfully employed black urban idiomatic expression in describing the actions of protagonists and their surroundings. She has combined standard English words and phrases with black English terms to develop a special kind of stream of consciousness that makes the reader aware of the internal experiences of the characters as well as of their words. On the whole the author has provided a positive image of a black youth that is worthy of emulation.

Summary

Sixteen-year-old Buddy Rivers and his girl, Angela Figueroa, are on their way to a cemetery where they plan to hide. Gradually the story of Buddy and Angela unfolds. Buddy meets and falls in love with Angela, but her parents object to her seeing him. Buddy's father is in the hospital as the result of having been struck by an automobile and Buddy must look after the brownstone house where they live. He spends much time at the hospital with his father. It is there that he meets Angela when she comes to see her mother, a nurse there.

One evening Angela has an argument with her mother and leaves angrily. Buddy walks out with her. They become close friends and eventually fall in love. Angela's parents try to keep her from seeing him. One evening her father beats her so severely that

83

she leaves home and Buddy takes her to the hospital. The hospital officials think that Buddy has beaten her and they question him. However, they soon find out her father is the guilty one.

The authorities send Angela to a shelter for wayward and abused children. Buddy writes to her. When she is temporarily released and returns to the city, she moves out of her mother's home to Buddy's house. They stay there for a while, but Buddy is afraid that the juvenile authorities will take Angela away. To avoid this, Angela and Buddy run away from the house to live in an abandoned shed in a no-longer-used cemetery near the city reservoir. As the novel closes they prepare to set up housekeeping.

THE HOUSE BEHIND THE CEDARS

Kind of work: Novel
Writer: Charles Chesnutt
Setting: The South
Time: 1890
First published: 1900

Important Characters

Rena Walden—a beautiful young mulatto woman
John Warwick—Rena's brother
Miss Molly—Rena's mother
George Tryon—a young white man
Jeff Wain—a childhood friend of Rena's

Comment

The author in *The House Behind the Cedars* is using the "tragic mulatto" theme to show the harshness of the repression of the blacks at the turn of the century. The author focuses his attention on the racial attitudes of both groups. When Jeff Wain, a childhood friend, tries to help Rena as she wanders around fevered and in delirium, she tells him not to touch her. George Tyron will not marry Rena, but he certainly does not reject her as a mistress. John, Rena's brother, passes for white. An interesting aspect of the novel is that all of the blacks speak in dialect while the mulattoes do not.

Summary

Rena Walden, a beautiful young mulatto woman who had grown up in a house that her white father had built for his black mistress, Rena's mother, is talking to her mother. Unknown to Miss Molly and Rena, a young man is on his way to see them. When he arrives, Molly does not recognize him at first. Then, when he speaks, she realizes this young white man is her own son. Everyone is happy to see Mr. John Warwick, as he is called. He has decided to pass the color line and has taken another name.

After a few days Rena talks to John about a problem she has. She is near white and cannot decide whether she should pass for white or remain black. John encourages her to pass and finally Rena decides to pass.

Everything works out well for a while, until Rena takes a job as a teacher and meets a handsome young white man who falls in love with her and asks her to marry him. Just when George Tryon and Rena are about to marry it is discovered that Rena is really black.

Rena is shattered by what has happened and returns to teaching. Even though he refuses to marry Rena, Tryon still wants her for his mistress. The black principal of the school where Rena teaches wants her for his mistress, however. Under the stress of all of this, Rena develops a mysterious fever. She is taken home by Jeff Wain, a mulatto she knew as a child. As the novel closes, George Tryon comes to the house behind the cedars to see Rena, only to discover that she has died.

THE HOUSE OF DIES DREAR

Kind of work: Novel for young people
Writer: Virginia Hamilton
Time: Present
Setting: Ohio
First published: 1968

Important Characters

Thomas Small—a thirteen-year-old black boy
Mr. Small—Thomas's father
Mrs. Small—Thomas's mother
Mr. Pluto—a neighbor who takes care of the Dies Drear house
Mayew Skinner—Mr. Pluto's son

Comment

Although this novel is written for young people, it can be read with pleasure and interest by adults. It is very well written and the information concerning the activities of the Underground Railroad in Ohio is accurate. The setting of the story appears to be in an area similar to Oberlin, Ohio, where a great deal of antislavery activity took place. In this semirural area many houses were used as Underground Railroad stations to help the slaves on their way to Canada or elsewhere. Many of these old houses had secret rooms where slaves were hidden until they could be moved. The author has carefully woven this historical material into the story. One important aspect of this novel is the positive image that the black central characters present. Until very recently most of the images of blacks in literature for young people have been largely derogatory and demeaning.

Summary

Mr. Small and his family, Mrs. Small, twin baby boys, and thirteen-year-old Thomas, are on their way from North Carolina to a house that Mr. Small has leased in Ohio. The house of Dies Drear is supposed to be haunted because of its connection with runaway slaves and several murders that were supposed to have taken place there. When they arrive at the house, Mrs. Small discovers that Mr. Pluto, the eccentric neighbor, has set up their furniture just as they wanted it even though she had not told him to do so. Thomas begins to search the house and discovers that it has several secret rooms. After exploring the house for some time, Thomas and his father discover the secret. The house was built over a large cavern where runaway slaves were hidden.

Dies Drear had gathered valuable antiques and kept them in the cavern. Mr. Pluto felt that they belonged to him and therefore had attempted to keep people away from the house by saying it was haunted by ghosts of murdered slaves and by Dies Drear. The novel ends as Thomas waits in the cavern for his father.

HOWARD STREET

Kind of work: Novel
Writer: Nathan Heard
Time: 1960s
Setting: Newark, New Jersey
First published: 1968

Important Characters

Gypsy Pearl—*a beautiful Howard Street prostitute*
Lonnie "Hip" Richwood—*Gypsy's pimp*
Franchot Richwood—*Hip's brother*
Rosemary—*a young black woman*

Comment

In *Howard Street* the author is writing about the lives of ghetto blacks on the lowest and meanest level. Almost all the men are pimps or drug addicts; "Hip" Richwood is both an addict and a pimp. The women are depicted as whores. In spite of the constant negative aspects of the ghetto, it does have its positive side, Franchot Richwood works for a living and refuses to become part of the sordid life around him. The author's view of ghetto life is one in which there is a complete absence of hope of escape from this harsh and unrelenting environment in which the urban blacks are trapped.

Summary

The novel begins with Gypsy Pearl, a prostitute, in bed with one of her customers. He is not satisfied with her performance and asks for his money back. She gives it to him, knowing that Hip, her pimp, is outside ready to jump the man when he leaves the building. When the customer leaves, Hip accosts him; but the man, a scrap iron worker, begins to beat him.

Gypsy tries to stop Hip from being beaten but is ineffectual. She pulls a knife from her bosom and stabs the man. She and Hip leave the scene to find "Cowboy," the local pusher, so Hip can get the fix he badly needs.

Later that evening in a local bar Gypsy Pearl is introduced to Franchot Richwood, Hip's brother, whom she has never met. They are immediately attracted to one another. Hip and Gypsy continue their activities while Franchot continues to work at his job as a brick mason but they cannot forget each other. Eventually she tells Franchot that she is in love with him. When she is jailed by the vice squad, it is Franchot who gets her out of jail. Although Hip knows that his brother Franchot loves him, he thinks Franchot is a square and continues his dissolute way of living.

One evening Hip brings two of his junkie friends home to get a fix. They are busted in a drug raid and are jailed. When Franchot finds out that Hip is being sent up for possession of heroin, he decides to take the rap himself. Gypsy Pearl, who knows that Franchot is innocent, hesitates to tell the police because she knows Hip will go to jail for several years. Before she can decide, Franchot notices her hesitation. Hip finally takes the rap himself when he discovers that he can be put on probation.

Franchot calls a cab to take Gypsy Pearl home, but he realizes that she will never belong to him alone. As the novel ends, Franchot drops Gypsy Pearl off on Howard Street and goes home.

HURRY HOME

Kind of work: Novel
Writer: John Wideman
Time: Present
Setting: U.S.A.; Africa; Spain
First published: 1970

Important Characters

Cecil Braithwaite—*a highly educated black janitor*
Esther—*Cecil's wife*
Aunt Fanny—*Esther's aunt*
Estrella—*a Spanish girl*

Comment

In *Hurry Home* the protagonist is trapped between worlds, one white, one black; and he feels he has no place in either world. In his travels toward Africa Cecil Braithwaite is really trying to find a place where he belongs. His struggle is futile because in each experience he feels a peculiar sense that something is missing. He cannot say why he began the affair with the white woman tenant in the building where he worked or why he had the affiar with Estrella, the Spanish prostitue. The problem of racism or race is not dealt with directly in *Hurry Home*. It emerges indirectly in Cecil's search for his identiy, but even here the focus is on the protagonist's personal struggle with a problem he does not solve.

Summary

Cecil Braithwaite, a trained lawyer, works as a janitor in an apartment building. He is at odds with himself. He has a brief affair with a white female tenant and periodically shuts himself up in his room to brood. His wife, Esther, whom he married while in law school, does not really understand why he has these moods.

One evening Cecil quietly leaves the apartment and sails for Europe on his way to Africa. On his journey toward his destination Cecil meets assorted individuals, each of whom he becomes involved with in some manner. In Madrid he has a brief love affair with a beautiful prostitute named Estrella, then moves on. After completing his journey and solving nothing, Cecil returns one night to Esther as quietly as he had left.

IDLE HEAD

Kind of work: Play
Writer: Willis Richardson
Time: 1920s
Setting: A southern town
First published: 1929

Important Characters

Mrs. Broadus—*a washerwoman*

George Broadus—*Mrs. Broadus's twenty-eight-year-old son*

Alice Broadus—*Mrs. Broadus's twenty-five-year-old daughter*

Brother Harris—*a black preacher*

A chauffeur

A policeman

Comment

The author in *Idle Head* is concerned with a rebel. The title comes from the saying "an idle head is the devil's workshop." George refuses to be submissive just to get work. His mother wants him to grin and bow to whites, but he refuses. He loses his job as a waiter because he will not play this role and demean himself by doing so. When he discovers a diamond and pawns it to give the women the money they need, George Broadus is merely doing what he feels he must do.

During the period when *Idle Head* was written, black men were generally depicted as grinning, shuffling clowns. George Broadus provides a startling exception to this rule. Although there is no direct statement about race problems, it is obvious that if George were to play the "darky" role he would not be unemployed.

Summary

George Broadus, a young black man, is sitting asleep in a rocking chair in the living room of the Broadus home. Mrs. Broadus enters the room and George wakes up. His mother asks him if he is going out to look for work. In the course of the conversation it is disclosed that George has not been able to get any work for some time. While George and Mrs. Broadus are talking, Alice enters. George wants to leave town and look for work elsewhere, but his mother does not want him to go.

She tells George if he will be more submissive he would not have so difficult a time finding work. George says he will not bow and scrape for anyone. Mrs. Broadus asks George to go to the house of one of her customers to pick up a load of washing. Before George leaves, he tells his sister Alice to stop searching his pockets. After George goes, Alice and Mrs. Broadus talk for a while, then there is a knock at the door. Brother Harris, the local black preacher, enters. He tells the women that they must pay their church dues or be stricken from the rolls. Mrs. Broadus explains that she has no money but Brother Harris is adamant. As Brother Harris is leaving, George comes with a large basket of clothes. When Mrs. Broadus tells George about the church dues, he tells her not to worry.

George begins looking through the clothes for anything of value to be returned to the customer. While he is sorting the clothes, he finds two pins, one gold and one containing a diamond. He examines them closely and puts the diamond pin in his pocket. He calls his mother to tell her that he has found a gold pin on one of the dresses. He gives her the pin and goes out of the room. Mrs. Broadus calls her daughter and tells her about the pin that George has found. While the women talk there is a knock at the door and a policeman and a chauffeur come into the room. The chauffeur tells Mrs. Broadus that a diamond pin is missing and asks if she has found such a pin. When Mrs. Broadus says no, they leave.

George returns, hangs up his coat and tells his mother that he has been able to scrape up some money while he was out. He gives her several bills and leaves the room. When George has gone, Alice goes through his coat pockets and finds a pawn ticket. There is a knock at the door. It is the policeman and the chauffeur again. They have come about the diamond pin that they were searching for earlier. The policeman asks where George is. When Mrs. Broadus tells them he is sleeping, they start toward George's room to wake him. At this point George comes into the room. The policeman attempts to search George's coat that is hanging on a rack but George snatches it away from him. Alice has been standing aside holding in her hand the pawn ticket she had taken from George's coat. When the policeman notices this, he pulls her hand from behind her back and takes the pawn ticket. In spite of the pleading of Mrs. Broadus, George is arrested as the play closes.

If He Hollers Let Him Go

Kind of work: Novel
Writer: Chester Himes
Time: World War II
Setting: California
First published: 1945

Important Characters

Bob Jones—*a black foreman in a shipyard*
Madge—*a white woman shipyard worker*
Ella Mae Brown—*a black woman with whom Jones is having an affair*
Henry Brown—*Ella Mae's husband*
Alice Harrison—*Bob's girlfriend*
Judge Morgan—*a white judge who sends Bob Jones to the U.S. Army*

Comment

The author's concern is with the psychological damage caused by racial predjudice. Bob Jones expects racial affronts from every direction at almost every moment. Even though he is aware of what is happening to him, Jones seems trapped and unable to help himself. This protest novel is different in that it tries to expose booby traps that existed in race relations in the United States, especially during World War II. Although the protagonist is innocent, Judge Morgan assigns him to the army anyway, because Jones has violated the sacred taboo against interracial sexual relations by daring to consort with a white woman.

Summary

As the novel opens, Bob Jones is in bed with Ella Mae Brown, the wife of a coworker, with whom he is having an affair although he has a girl of his own. After breakfast he goes to his job as foreman at a shipyard where he expects to meet racial predudice at every turn. One day on the job he meets Madge, a young, voluptous white woman worker. At first she refuses to work with him. Later she makes passes at Jones, which he refuses. During a dice game a white man strikes Jones from behind during a fight and Jones has to go home for a few days. While he is off he plans to kill the man who struck him.

One evening Bob's girl, Alice, introduces him to one of her coworkers from her social work agency. The worker is a white man and Jones becomes so suspicious of Alice that he makes statements that cause her embarrassment. As a result of Bob's attitude, Alice leaves him. Jones decides that he does not have to kill the man who hit him because his threats have frightened the man badly already. Madge continues her advances to Jones. When he continues to resist them, she frames him and accuses him of trying to rape her. As a result Jones is attacked and badly beaten by white shipyard workers. After recovering from his injuries, Bob Jones is forced to resign from his job and go into the army in spite of Madge's confession that she framed him.

IF WE MUST DIE

Kind of work: Novel
Writer: Junius Edwards
Time: 1959
Setting: A southern town
First published: 1963

Important Characters

Will Harris—*a black Korean War veteran*
Mrs. Harris—*Will's mother*
Mary—*Will's girlfriend*

Comment

The author's primary intent is to show that isolated ignorance and brutality existed extensively in the South during the period covered by the novel. Although the author directs his attention to the physical violence inflicted on Will Harris, it becomes evident that a new breed of young black has emerged. It does not even occur to Will that he is not accepted as a citizen of the United States and is considered inferior by whites. On the level of propaganda *If We Must Die* is a powerful novel.

Summary

Will Harris is having breakfast with his mother. In their conversation Will mentions to her that he intends to go to the local board of elections to register to vote in an upcoming election. After breakfast Will goes to the registration office to fill out an application. He is asked many questions, most of them designed to delay the procedure required for registration. He is refused permission to register. The next day Will Harris is fired from his job. When he tries to find another job, he discovers that he has been blacklisted throughout the county. One evening while on his way home, Will is attacked and kidnapped by a group of white men who take him to a wooded area and severely beat him. He is left tied up in the woods but is able to free himself and find help. The novel ends as Will is being carried, almost dead, in a wagon to the nearest doctor.

Imperium in Imperio

Kind of work: Novel
Writer: Sutton Griggs
Time: 1880
Setting: Virginia; Texas
First published: 1899

Important Characters

Belton Piedmont—*a young brilliant black man*
Bernard Belgrave—*Belton's friend*
Mrs. V. M. King—*a newspaper publisher*
Antoinette Nermal—*a beautiful black woman whom Belton loves*
Viola Martin—*a woman whom Bernard loves*

Comment

Imperium In Imperio is a rather bizarre and astonishing novel about a black nationalist organization that is remarkably modern. There are numerous melodramatic episodes. In one of them Belton Piedmont is kidnapped, hanged, shot, and left for dead in a doctor's office to be dissected. He awakens, kills the doctor, and escapes. Griggs discusses all aspects of the problems from Jim Crow to miscegenation that the blacks faced in the South during this period. The blacks were at the nadir of their fortunes, politically and otherwise. The author presents a militant viewpoint that is far ahead of its time. Implicit in the characters of Belton and Bernard is the old problem of color discrimination among blacks themselves. Belton Piedmont is black and Bernard is near white, and it is Belton who goes before the firing squad.

In spite of its militant tone, the book tends to back away from the extreme position. Bud Trout, secretary of state for Imperium In Imperio, betrays the organization, bringing about its destruction.

Summary

Set in Virginia, the novel opens with a declaration by Bud Trout, who is awaiting execution. In the declaration he condemns

himself as a traitor to his race, the blacks, and to his friends. Belton
Piedmont is first encountered as a small black boy going to his first
day at school. His mother has dressed him in whatever clothes she
can find for him, and everything is mismatched. At the school he
meets a young mulatto friend, Bernard Belgrave. Through their
school years these two brilliant students are pitted against one
another. In their last year the two boys tie for a prize for the best
commencement speech. Unknown to Belton, the teacher, Mr.
Leonard, has rigged the judges' committee and Bernard Belgrave
wins the prize. After finishing school, Belton finds that he has no
money to continue on to college. However, he is aided by V. M. King,
who reads his commencement speech in his newspaper. He gener-
ously provides the funds for Belton to enter State College in
Nashville. Shortly after he is enrolled, Belton leads a student revolt
against the school authorities because of racial discrimination
against a black teacher at the college. He becomes known as a
brilliant student and orator and eventually graduates.

Belton's old schoolmate, Bernard, enters Harvard after graduating from the local school. Once at Harvard, he succeeds brilliantly in
his studies and is chosen valedictorian of his class. Because of his
achievements, his story reaches the news agencies; and on his
graduation night he receives a note telling him to come to Washington, D.C. Once in the city, he is taken to the mansion of a wealthy
senator, whom he is told is his father. After leaving Harvard,
Bernard goes to Virginia and enters politics and, in spite of trickery
on the part of his opponents, wins a seat in Congress. While he is
involved in campaigning, he meets a beautiful black woman, Viola
Martin. He falls in love with her, but she refuses to marry him. She
finally writes a letter telling him she can never marry a mulatto man
and then kills herself.

Belton, too, meets a beautiful woman, Antoinette Nermal, falls
in love with her, and marries her. He loses his job because he will not
support a white candidate for Congress who is prejudiced against
blacks. Belton begins to make journeys in disguise to various places
for mysterious purposes. His wife cares for herself as well as she
can while he is away. When Belton finally returns home, he discovers his wife is about to have a child. The child is born but appears
to be white. Belton accuses Antoinette of adultery, then leaves her.

After the death of Viola, Bernard Belgrave is distraught and
near his wits end, when he receives a letter from Belton Piedmont
asking him to come to Texas. When Bernard arrives in Waco, he is
first put through a series of tests, then he is invited to join *Imperium*

in *Imperio,* a secret black nationalist organization Belton had helped establish on those mysterious journeys. Bernard accepts the invitation of the group and, because of his militant views, becomes its leader. He devises a scheme where *Imperium in Imperio* will stage an open revolt against the United States and force the government to cede Texas and Louisiana to them as a haven for blacks.

Belton opposes Bernard's plan but is voted down by Imperio In Imperium's executive committee and sentenced to death. Permitted to visit his family, he goes to see his wife, Antoinette, and the child he thought was white but who has darkened considerably. He is reconciled with Antoinette but does not remain with her and the child. Instead he returns to Texas and *Imperium in Imperio,* where he is shot to death by a firing squad.

THE INVISIBLE MAN

Kind of work: Novel
Writer: Ralph Ellison
Time: 1930s
Setting: The South; New York
First published: 1952

Important Characters

The hero—*a nameless young black man*
Mr. Norton—*a white northern philanthropist*
Jim Trueblood—*a black man*
Lucius Brockway—*a black worker at the paint factory*
Brother Jack—*leader of the brotherhood*
Tod Clifton—*a young black man*
Ras the Exhorter (the Destroyer)—*a black nationalist*
Rhinehart—*a many-sided street hustler*
Mary Rambo—*a kindly black woman*

Comment

One point that is always made concerning the novel The Invisible Man is that the author was writing about blacks as human beings first and as blacks second and therefore employed a theme that was universal. To adhere to this view completely and claim that the characters are only incidentally blacks is tantamount to denying that the novel is about blacks at all. The history and culture of the blacks pervades the entire book and nothing is what it seems to be. Ray the Destroyer can very well be construed to mean "race, the destroyer of normal relations between blacks and whites in the United States."

The author has written symbolically and on many levels. Black Tod Clifton is killed while selling Sambo dolls and Rhinehart is a many-sided exploiter of his fellow blacks. The symbols the protagonist cannot throw away are a leg chain and a black Sambo castiron bank.

Although the characters in The Invisible Man may well be universal, they are in fact black and live in the United States, where race is an everyday factor and cannot be ignored. It is interesting to note that many followers of the theory of black aesthetic could not see the blackness in this novel simply because Ellison did not shout about it. He merely wrote it into his book.

Summary

The novel begins with the hero hiding in an abandoned coal cellar in an obscure part of Harlem where whites still live. His "hole in the ground," as he calls it, is ablaze with light. The story of how he came to be in his present position is told in flashbacks. The first episode pictures a white stag smoker at which the protagonist, just graduated from high school, is forced to entertain the group by boxing other black boys, all of them blindfolded. At the end of the smoker he is given a scholarship to a college for blacks.

One day during his junior year at the school the hero is assigned by Dr. Bledsoe to drive a white philanthropist, Mr. Norton, around the area near the college. He makes several mistakes on the sightseeing tour. First he allows Norton to meet Trueblood, a black farmer who had committed incest with his daughter. When Norton asks for a drink of water, he is taken to a saloon where the black inmates of a mental institution are taken for recreation. While the attendant, Supercargo, is drunk upstairs, the inmates riot and

Norton is slightly injured. Because of these episodes, the narrator is expelled from school. Dr. Beldsoe gives him a letter of reference and a lecture on how to get along with whites. When the hero arrives in New York and goes to get a job, he discovers that the letter really says not to employ him. The plant owner's son sends him to a job at the Liberty Paint Company. He is given work in a department where the paint is mixed but he puts too much black in the white paint. He is moved to another department, where he works with Lucius Brockway, a subservient black worker. Eventually the narrator and Brockway fight. The hero is injured, treated, and released from the hospital; but he cannot remember who he is. He moves to Harlem and lives at the "Y" for a while. Finally he rents a room from Mary Rambo, a kindly black woman who tries to help him establish his identity.

While going about Harlem, he stops to watch the eviction of an old black couple. Suddenly he begins to harangue a bystander and soon the people gather and force the marshal to return the furniture to the apartment where the old people had lived. The few whites who participated in the actions are members of the brotherhood, a communist-like organization. The protagonist is asked to join. The narrator is hired to be a speaker for the Brotherhood and takes part in their activities. One of the goals of the brotherhood is to fight Ras the Exhorter, a black nationalist leader. In the fights Ras is aided by Tod Clifton, a black youth leader of the brotherhood. Shortly after one battle Tod discovers that he can no longer work with the brotherhood. One day he strikes a policeman and is shot to death. The brotherhood sees Clifton as a traitor and tells the narrator to say this at Clifton's funeral. He refuses.

At the funeral Ras, now the Destroyer, incites the crowd to riot and tries to catch the narrator. He is not able to do so because the protagonist disguises himself by putting on a large hat and sunglasses. He is mistaken for Rhinehart, a many-sided street hustler, a pimp, a number runner, a man who pays off the police, a gambler, and a storefront preacher. Later Ras spots the narrator and trys to kill him. While he is escaping from Ras and his men the narrator falls into an abandoned cellar, where he remains.

IRON CITY

Kind of work: Novel
Writer: Lloyd L. Brown
Time: 1930s
Setting: Iron City, Minnesota
First published: 1951

Important Characters

Lonnie James—*a black prisoner awaiting execution*
Lucy Jackson—*a woman trying to help free Lonnie*
Crazy Peterson— *a white prisoner*
Paul Harper—*a prisoner*
Henry Faulcon—*a prisoner*
Issac Zachry—*a Communist*
Arnold Winkler—*Lonnie's lawyer*

Comment

Iron City purports to be a novel about prison life, but much of it fails in its efforts to portray this. The story contains a great deal of propaganda about the Communist party as a positive force working in behalf of the blacks. In the effort to save Lonnie tactics similar to those used by the Party in the actual Scottsboro and Angelo Herndon cases are employed. In fact, in some respects, *Iron City* is a remarkable parallel to the story of Angelo Herndon and the problems he faced as a black Communist organizer in the South. At one point both the Herndon and Scottsboro cases are discussed in some detail.

The author has written a propaganda and protest novel in which it is shown in no uncertain terms that justice in the United States as far as the blacks were concerned was racist and they could expect to be lynched with impunity. Justice for Lonnie is blocked by the actions of the same policeman who framed him in the first place and even the Supreme Court upholds the sentence of death.

Summary

Lonnie James, who has been unjustly accused of murder, sits in a prison cell awaiting execution. Most of the novel concerns the efforts of three black Communist prisoners to free Lonnie James and save his life. Flashbacks tell the stories of Lonnie, Paul Harper, and Henry Faulcon. Interwoven with their stories are the day-to-day details of prison life.

Lonnie's case becomes a *cause celebre*. Letters are written, meetings are held, and petitions are circulated in his behalf. As the novel ends, the Mutual Benefit Society, an organization similar to the NAACP is holding a rally. Lonnie remains in his cell waiting for the death that will come in spite of the fact that there is a witness who can prove his innocence.

JOURNEY ALL ALONE

Kind of work: Novel
Writer: Deloris Harrison
Time: 1970s
Setting: Harlem, New York
First published: 1973

Important Characters

Mildred Jewell—a *a thirteen-year-old black girl*
Izola Jewell—*Mildred's mother*
Michael Jewell—*Mildred's brother*
Nat Jewell—*Mildred's father*
Aunt Vi—*Mildred's aunt*

Comment

Journey All Alone bears a remarkable similarity to Louise Meriwether's novel, *Daddy Was a Number Runner*. In both novels the protagonist is a young girl of thirteen; in both novels the family is broken up when the father leaves home. However, the two novels differ in several respects. In *Journey All Alone* the author deals with the process of a young girl's path to maturity, while in *Daddy Was a Number Runner* the concern is primarily with the soul-crushing aspects of black ghetto life.

Summary

On a winter night thirteen-year-old Mildred Jewell is awakened from her sleep by the loud voices of her parents arguing. Her father plans to leave the family to become a jazz musician. Within a short while Nat Jewell leaves to pursue his dream and there is nothing Mildred can do to stop him. She and the rest of the family are left to care for themselves. Mildred continues in school but thinks of her father.

Summer finally comes and with it the end of school. Mildred spends the long days wandering the city. She goes to Riverside Park and daydreams about Angel Rivera, the tennis court attendant. Mildred retreats into a kind of dream world. One day when she comes home, her father is there. He talks to her and leaves a few dollars for the family. The next day they go to the beach and when they return Nat is home again. Although he remains only a short while, in a fit of anger he beats Mrs. Jewell badly.

Near the end of summer Mildred meets another boy and they become friends. For a moment she is happy and forgets the harshness of the ghetto where she lives. However, she is brutally reminded of its violence when she is assaulted and raped by three teenagers. As the novel ends, she is at her aunt's house, lonely, and with her illusions rudely shattered.

JUBILEE

Kind of work: Novel
Writer: Margaret Walker
Time: 1840-1865
Setting: The South: Georgia; Alabama
First published: 1966

Important Characters

Vyry Ware Brown—*a young black slave woman*
John Morris Dutton—*a white plantation owner and Vyry's father*
Salina Dutton—*John's wife*
Randall Ware—*Vyry's first husband*
Innis Brown—*Vyry's second husband*

Comment

Jubilee is a historical novel in which the heroine, Vyry, is a kind of black female "Uncle Tom." She is the enduring black woman who survives and accommodates herself to the position the whites have given her. She does this in spite of the fact that she has suffered various indignities at their hands. Even her own father, the plantation owner John Dutton, stands by while she is whipped. Vyry's first husband, Randall Ware, is what can be called a race man. He is representative of the black men who served in the Reconstruction governments of the southern states following the Civil War. The author believes that by accommodating completely to the role that has been given them the blacks may become nonentities and lose their identities entirely.

Summary

Hetta, one of John Dutton's slaves, is dying and asks to see Vyry, her daughter by Dutton. Vyry is only two years old and does not understand what is happening. She grows up a slave on the Dutton plantation and eventually becomes a house servant to Mrs. Dutton, who hates her because Mr. Dutton is Vyry's father. At every opportunity Mrs. Dutton torments Vyry and one time hangs her by the thumbs in a closet. When she grows older, Vyry is put to work helping in the kitchen of the big house. She takes over the task of running the entire kitchen when the head cook is sold away.

One evening Vyry is told to take some supper to the blacksmith, who is shoeing the plantation horses. In this way Vyry meets Randall Ware, a free black man who has his own blacksmith shop. Randall and Vyry become lovers and eventually she has a child by him. However, when she tries to gain her freedom from Dutton, she is unable to do so. Randall Ware, because he is a free black, is forced to leave the state of Georgia. He asks Vyry to leave with him but she is caught and whipped for running away while her father, John Dutton, stands by and watches.

When the Civil War begins and the white men leave the plantations, Vyry, with Ware gone, must look out for herself. She decides to stay on the plantation and look after the Dutton family. When the war ends and Randall Ware does not come back, Vyry thinks he is dead. She marries a former slave, Innis Brown. They begin farming, but they are forced by the whites who want their land to move from farm to farm. Randall Ware finally returns; he has become prominent and well-to-do. When he meets Vyry again and talks to her, he decides that she is too passive for him and that their life together would be unhappy. Ware leaves Innis Brown's farm, taking his son by Vyry with him.

THE LAST DAYS OF LOUISIANA RED

Kind of work: Novel
Writer: Ishmael Reed
Time: Present
Setting: Berkeley, California
First published: 1974

Important Characters

Ed Yellings—*Owner of the gumbo works*

Street Yellings—*Ed's youngest son*
Minnie Yellings—*Ed's youngest daughter*
Wolf Yellings—*Ed's oldest son*
Sister Yellings—*Ed's oldest daughter*
Papa La Bas—*a voodoo detective*

Comment

In this wild satiric novel nothing is what it seems to be. The author's satire is hurled in all directions and his darts pierce every-one. Even the names of the characters convey something. For exam-ple, Street Yellings is a street rhetorician and jive-time hustler. There are numerous attacks on black women as well as "schuckers and jivers," whom the author refers to as "moochers."

Author Reed's erudition and knowledge of black history is much in evidence. Chapter 4 is a deft parody of the Greek play *Antigone.* Any interpretation of *Last Days of Louisiana Red* would probably be invalid, for the reader is never sure whether the joke is on him or the author. Reed is a wild, wild writer and a skillful one as well.

Summary

Ed Yellings arrives in Berkeley, where he works at odd jobs and eventually purchases a gumbo factory, which produces a wonderful healing mixture. As Ed becomes prosperous, he marries and has four children, Wolf, Street, Sister, and Minnie.

Ed's gumbo factory comes under attack by Louisiana Red, the scarlet evil that fills people with violent tendencies. When one of Ed's business associates is killed, Papa La Bas, famous voodoo detective, is sent for to find out who killed the gumbo worker and to discover what part Louisiana Red and "the moochers" had in the affair. After many trials and tribulations he is able to solve the problem. As the novel ends, Papa La Bas is on a plane bound for Chicago.

THE LAST OF THE CONQUERORS

Kind of work: Novel
Writer: William Gardner Smith
Time: World War II
Setting: Germany
First published: 1948

Important Characters

Hayes Dawkins—*a black soldier*
Ilse—*his German girlfriend*
Captain Polke—*a captain*
Murdock—*a soldier*
Steveson—*a soldier*

Comment

In *The Last of the Conquerors* the author's basic concern is the racism that black soldiers meet while serving in the United States armed forces. The protest in the novel is often expressed in bitter tones directed against the racial prejudice that black soldiers and other military personnel faced during World War II and still encounter. The author sees the Germans who produced Adolph Hitler and destroyed a large part of Europe as people who accept blacks and treat them respectfully as equals. In turn the black soldiers feel what it is like to be free. The rage and anger usually present in protest novels is muted by the hero's view, the tranquil environment, and his love affair with a beautiful German girl.

Summary

This novel is about American occupation troops in Germany shortly after World War II. The blacks among these troops are accepted as human beings by the Germans and there is no prejudice against them. Hayes Dawkins, a clerk, has a love affair with Ilse, a German Girl. This affair is abruptly interrupted when white American troops arrive. The blacks have discovered what is it like to be freely accepted. When the white troops appear, they bring their American racial prejudice with them and the black troops soon find themselves bearing the brunt of it. When the black soldiers are transferred from Berlin, they come under the command of Captain Polke, who hates blacks and plans to see to it that those under his command are sent home with dishonorable discharges.

Dawkins attempts to thwart Polke by letting his fellow blacks know what the captain has planned for them. Polke suspects him but cannot prove anything. One of the black soldiers goes berserk and shoots several whites. Dawkins helps him escape but in doing so ends his effectiveness in fighting Captain Polke. The captain places Dawkins in a position where he must return to the United States or face a court martial. Dawkins has no choice. He tells Ilse good-bye, saying that he plans to come back, and is sent home as the novel ends.

THE LAST RIDE OF WILD BILL

Kind of work: Poem
Writer: Sterling Brown
Time: 1950s
Setting: a city
First published: 1975

Important Characters

Wild Bill—*a black number runner*
A chief of police
A crowd of devils

Comment

In this poem the author has produced an urban folk hero in the character of Wild Bill, who is kin to Shine and others like him. He knows his environment well, and in his way, is respected by black ghetto inhabitants. As a number runner, Wild Bill has a special standing and lives by certain rules. When he is challenged by the new chief of police, he knows he must make his run whatever happens.

Summary

This ten-part poem concerns the efforts of a new white chief of police in a southern town to stop black number runner, Wild Bill, from making his run. The chief of police tells Wild Bill that he is going to close down the numbers game and put him out of business. Bill decides to challenge the chief. News leaks out that Wild Bill will make the usual run. Bets are made and people turn out to see the contest. The chief tries to stop Bill several times but is unable to do so. Wild Bill reaches his destination, but the bag he picks up has a bomb in it and Bill is blown to pieces. He awakens in hell with a crowd of devils asking him what number fell.

THE LIVING IS EASY

Kind of work: Novel
Writer: Dorothy West
Time: 1914
Setting: Boston
First published: 1948

Important Characters

Bart Judson—*a black banana wholesaler of Boston*
Cleo Judson—*Bart's wife*
Judy Judson—*Bart and Cleo's daughter*
Lily—*Cleo's sister*
Althea Binney—*Judy's teacher*
The Duchess—*the mistress of Althea's father*

Comment

In *The Living Is Easy* the author has depicted the protagonist, Cleo Judson, as a selfish, distasteful, greedy, grasping woman who will do almost anything to reach her goal. She becomes a destructive influence upon everyone she is involved with, her friends, her family, and her husband. In the end she, too, becomes a victim of her own materialism and status seeking and finds herself alone but still an ambitious climber.

The problem of race prejudice is dealt with in a very limited way. What the author is attacking is not so much the oppression of blacks by whites, but the crass materialism of the black pseudo-middle class. Cleo is not affected by racism; she is trying to make up for the poverty she suffered in her early years. In *The Living Is Easy* it is evident that in black America there is a definite class system, with the working-class blacks on the bottom of success ladder.

Summary

Cleo comes to Boston determined to become a part of the black elite of the city. She is prepared to snatch and grab to reach her goal. She meets and marries Bart Judson, a fruit wholesaler whom she really does not love, in order to get the money she thinks she needs to climb upward in the black society of Boston.

Deciding that she needs a larger house, Cleo Judson rents one in a rather exclusive part of Boston and drives Bart Judson to work harder than ever. Her friend, Althea Binney, a fair-skinned member of the Boston black elite, tells Cleo of her father's affair with the Dutchess, a beautiful woman who only appears to be white. Cleo goes to the Dutchess to regain Thea's inheritance, which the father had signed over to his mistress. When Cleo discovers that the Dutchess is not white, she becomes friendly with her and as a result of this friendship aquires valuable furnishings for her house.

As Cleo's urge to be part of the black elite intensifies and she demands more money, the pressure on her husband, Bart, increases. As a result of her actions, their marriage begins to deteriorate. Cleo connives to bring her sisters to Boston to live with her and serve as a barrier between Bart and herself. As the novel ends, Cleo's uncanny desire to climb as high in Boston's black society as she can forces Bart into bankruptcy. He leaves her alone in Boston while he goes to New York to try to start his business over again.

LOOK WHAT THEY DONE TO MY SONG

Kind of work: Novel
Writer: John McCluskey
Time: 1968
Setting: Boston
First published: 1974

Important Characters

Mack—*a young black wandering musician*
Dupree Sledge—*an old black man with whom Mack lives*
Reba Sledge—*Dupree's wife*
Michelle—*a Portuguese woman Mack meets*
Omowale—*a young black revolutionary*
Antar—*a young black revolutionary*
Reverend Fuller—*minister of the Crumbly Rock Baptist Church*
Novella Turner—*a beautiful young black woman*

Comment

There are numerous characters who stroll through the pages of this novel, perhaps too many. However, the author is presenting the many facets of the racial conflict, as well as Mack's effort to maintain his equilibrium during a turbulent period of racial history in the United States. Reba and Dupree Sledge offer Mack a breathing space that gives him time to find out where it is he wants to go and what he wants to do. His love for music helps Mack deal with his various adversities.

Summary

Mack, the protagonist, is living in the Boston area with an old couple, Reba and Dupree Sledge, who befriended him when he first came to the community. He has traveled across the United States from Santa Fe, New Mexico. He meets various and sundry individuals in the black communities around Boston, many of them jive-time hustlers. He becomes a friend of Ubangi Jones and later of Omowale and Antar, young black revolutionaries who are intense and serious in their desire for freedom for the blacks.

Mack has several encounters with women. However, when he meets Novella Turner and Reverend Fuller, he develops a close relationship with them. He finds himself drawn to Novella and falls in love with her. Dupree dies and one of Mack's friends is shot in a racial clash, but he is able to maintain his balance through his music. He is playing his music with a combo as the novel closes.

MANY THOUSAND GONE

Kind of work: Novel
Writer: Ronald Fair
Time: 1960s
Setting: Mississippi
First published: 1965

Important Characters

Granny Jacobs—*a beloved black matriarch*
Preacher Harris—*a black minister*
Sheriff Pitch—*a white sheriff*
Josh—*the sheriff's black handyman*
Little Jesse—*Granny Jacob's grandson*
Big Jesse Black—*Little Jesse's father*
Marshall Ernest Wright—*a United States marshall*
Postal Inspector Fred Worthington—*a United States postal inspector*
Bessie James—*a black woman*
Lula Ferguson—*a black woman*

Comment

As the title indicates, *Many Thousand Gone* is a fable compounded of all the facets of racial strife in the United States. The blacks are subject to every form of oppression that existed in the South. The black women are sexually exploited and the men demeaned. If the blacks even try to protest, they are promptly lynched. When Sheriff Pitch decides to teach the blacks a lesson, a lynch mob is quickly formed.

The author has written a protest novel showing the feelings of the blacks during the 1960s when the Civil Right conflict was reaching its high point. It is interesting to note that the whites in this novel misjudge the temper of the blacks. Sheriff Pitch, who had trained Josh to be a modern-day slave driver, is killed by him and Josh goes on to lead the blacks in a fiery rebellion against their white overlords. The title is a line from a black spiritual.

Summary

The town of Jacobsville, Mississippi, located in Jacobs County, was founded in the 1830s by Samuel Jacobs, a shrewd, calculating man from Natchez. With the aid of a smart lawyer and the bribery of a judge, he manages to have himself appointed executor of a plantation worth $100,000. He promptly swindles the child heir out of the estate and sells the plantation for a large profit. With this money Sam Jacobs is able to influence important politicians to act in his behalf.

In 1832 the United States government forces the Chickasaw Indians off their land and Jacobs helps to drive them away by raiding their villages. In the process he captures black slaves for his own plantation. In 1835 Jacobs enters a claim for a large portion of the Chickasaw land as reward for aiding the government in removing the Indians. This new land is known as Jacobs' section. In 1836 Jacobs's section becomes a county, the smallest in the entire state of Mississippi. With the advent of the Civil War Jacobs County declines and after the war most of the black slaves have gone. Those blacks who remain think they are free.

Sam Jacobs, by working with Yankee officials, manages to isolate Jacobs County from the rest of the state. By the end of Reconstruction, the blacks in Jacobs County are under the complete control of Jacobs and his cohorts and are virtually enslaved. The Jacobs County line is guarded by fifty armed men who prevent the blacks from escaping. By 1920 the county line riders have been reduced to a sheriff and his three deputies and the blacks have largely forgotten they were ever free.

Among the blacks of Jacobs County, Granny Jacobs is beloved by all, both children and adults, because of her wisdom. There is a tradition among the blacks of Jacobs County that the first-born child of a first-born child will always be a pure black. The white men of Jacobs County try to destroy the tradition by raping the young black females as soon as they are of age. Two black women, Bessie James and Lula Ferguson, try to divert the attention of the white men from the young black women by providing them with the sexual gratification they desire. Bessie in particular tries to protect the first-born because as a young teenage girl she was assaulted. Her lover, Clay Lemkins, badly injured three white teenagers and had to flee northward to Chicago to escape the wrath of the whites.

Bertha, Granny Jacobs's granddaughter, comes of age and marries Jessie Black, a handsome young black man. Since Granny herself was a first-born, Bertha's child will be a first-born also. Bertha dies in childbirth; but her son, Little Jesse, lives. Big Jesse talks back to one of the sheriff's deputies and the deputy attempts to chastise him. Big Jesse breaks the deputy's arm, then kills him. He leaves Jacobsville and wants to take Little Jesse with him but Granny objects, afraid that Little Jesse will die on the journey north since Big Jesse and his friend, K.C. are on the run. The blacks hide the body of the deputy and Big Jesse heads north to Chicago.

Granny Jacobs cares for Little Jessie, who is called the "black prince." As he grows, he learns quickly and soon begins to rebel against the whites. Granny decides that he has to leave for Chicago or the whites will kill him before he grows to manhood.

She pretends that Little Jesse has sickened and died and a funeral is held for him. After the funeral Granny Jacobs and Uncle Otis sneak across the county line and carry Little Jesse to a family that is on its way to Chicago. For twenty-five years Little Jesse keeps in contact with Granny through Preacher Harris, who is the only black in Jacobs County allowed to receive mail. Finally a letter arrives saying that Little Jesse now is a grown young man and has written a book about Jacobs County and the plight of the blacks there. Jesse tells Granny in the letter that a story about him will appear in *Ebony* magazine. Preacher Harris sends secretly for a subscription. When the magazine arrives, it causes great consternation among the whites. Because the magazine describes the different life-style of blacks in the North, the blacks of Jacobsville become restive.

One night Granny and Preacher Harris decide to write a letter to the president of the United States describing the condition of Jacobsville blacks. Soon two white strangers arrive, Fred Worthington, postal inspector, and Ernest Wright, a marshall. The men question

Granny, inspect the post office, and leave Jacobsville, unknown to Sheriff Pitch, who has become suspicious of them. Worthington and Wright meet other marshalls to plan a course of action. When they return to Jacobsville, they discover the mutilated bodies of three young black girls. The sheriff has planned, along with the whites of the town, to teach the blacks a lesson and a lynch mob soon gathers. The sheriff arrests and jails the marshals. While the sheriff is planning his moves, the young black men of Jacobs County prepare to rebel. While the mob is gathering to chastise and lynch them, the Jacobsville blacks, led by Josh, who was thought to be the sheriff's man, revolt and burn the town. Josh kills the sheriff and the blacks burn part of the jail and free the marshals.

MAUD MARTHA

Kind of work: Novel
Writer: Gwendolyn Brooks
Time: 1940s, 1950s
Setting: Chicago
First published: 1954

Important Characters

Maud Martha Brown—*a young black woman*
Paul Phillips—*Maud Martha's husband*
Paulette—*Maud Martha's daughter*
Mama Brown—*Maud Martha's mother*
Papa Brown—*Maud Martha's father*

Comment

   Maud Martha is poet Gwendolyn Brooks's only novel and is structured in an unusual way. It consists of thirty-four episodes in which Maud Martha's life is presented. Some of these poetic sketches are quite short. The portrait that emerges is that of a dependable black woman who is upwardly mobile and tries to reach a level that will allow her and her family to move out of the ghetto. A romantic, Maud Martha is disillusioned and her dreams are shattered; but she continues to survive. The novel is really depicting a young woman's journey from childhood to womanhood, the disappointments she encounters along the way and the reality of life in a society where race is a negative factor. The author's skill as a poet is evident in every episode.

Summary

Maud Martha is seven in the first episode and with each of the succeeding scenes she grows from child to adult. She is shown at school, with her first beau, and finally as a young married woman. In one important episode her child is born in her small apartment in Chicago's black ghetto. Her husband, Paul, has to struggle constantly against the discrimination that frustrates his efforts to advance in the business world and has difficulty making ends meet. Maud Martha takes a job to help him. Her employers are bigots who humiliate her at every opportunity. Under the press of this humiliation she quits her job and returns home to continue her struggle out of the ghetto.

THE MESSENGER

Kind of work: Novel
Writer: Charles Stevenson Wright
Time: 1960
Setting: New York City
First published: 1963

Important Characters

Charlie—*a writer who works as a messenger*

The Messenger

Shirley—*Charlie's girlfriend*
Mitch—*a friend*
Claudia—*a homosexual friend of Charlie's*
Mrs. Lee—*Charlie's friend*
Lena—*a prostitute friend of Charlie's*
Troy—*Charlie's friend*

Comment

The Messenger is a novel of despair. Charlie, the protagonist, seems to be drowning in his chaotic existence and is unable to do anything about it. His weird friends, all seemingly unable to lead normal lives, come and go through his life. They are as lonely and desperate as Charlie himself. Charlie is an alien in a world he cannot control or understand. The various episodes tend to show that the author feels the reality of life in crowded New York is absurd almost beyond belief. A person can only try adjust to it or flee from it.

Summary

As the episodic novel opens, Charlie, a young black writer, is sitting on the stoop of his apartment watching local gypsy women pick the pockets of passing men. In one episode it is discovered that Charlie is about to lose his apartment because of his haphazard and disorganized way of life. In another important scene Charlie's girlfriend, Shirley, has come over to ask him to take her out for the evening; but he is morose and indifferent and they spend the evening in Charlie's darkened apartment. It is revealed that Charlie is living in a chaotic and uncertain environment in which the fact that he is black is always an important mark against him.

Some significant flashbacks show his childhood in his Missouri home and his life as a soldier in Korea, where he learns that everyone suffers in some way. Shirley decides to leave Charlie and marry a doctor who is in love with her. Charlie does not protest. He finally decides that he must leave New York and his friends give him a farewell party. Shirley comes to tell Charlie that she won't marry the doctor after all, but he seems past caring what she will do and returns to the wild party in his apartment.

THE MIDDLE PASSAGE

Kind of work: Poem
Writer: Robert Hayden
Time: The period of the Atlantic slave trade
Setting: The middle passage
First published: 1945

Comment

Robert Hayden's knowledge of the history of the blacks in the United States is very much in evidence in this poem; yet he has been condemned by some poets and critics for not adhering to the tenets of what has come to be known as the black aesthetic. "The Middle Passage" is related to parts of T. S. Eliot's poem, "The Waste Land," and Eliot's influence is definitely present in the poem. At one point Hayden writes "those are altar lights that were his eyes." This line echoes Eliot's line in "The Waste Land," "Those are pearls that were his eyes." Hayden's use of relatively obscure historical passages and allusions is also similar to Eliot's.

By constructing his poem in a style similar to "The Waste Land," Robert Hayden reveals that his range is very wide. Hayden's knowledge of the black experience has stood him in good stead in reporting the horrors that the black slaves encountered on the trip from Africa to the New World.

This poem sharply points out a very horrible aspect of the history of black Americans that everyone wanted to sweep under the rug until recently. Upon reflection, Hayden's "The Middle Passage" can be seen to do the same kind of thing that Alex Haley's book *Roots* does but in a more limited manner.

Summary

The poem "The Middle Passage" is arranged in three parts. The subject of the poem is the infamous third leg of the triangle of the slave trade that brought slaves from Africa to the New World. The poem opens with the names of slave ships *Jesus* (Jesus), *Estrella* (Star), *Esperanges*, (Hope), and *Mercy*. Slave ships appear again: *Desire* (the first slave ship to leave an American port for the express purpose of slaving), *Adventure*, *Tartar*, *Ann*. The poet ties the parts

117

of the poem together using documents relating to the slave trade, including testimony from the trial of Cinque of the *Amistad* mutiny and notations from the log of a slave ship officer's diary. In this way the horrors of the slave trade are presented.

THE NEGRO ART HOKUM

Kind of work: Essay
Writer: George S. Schuyler
Time: 1926
Setting: New York
First published: 1926

Comment

During the Harlem Reniassance period black writers and artists began to search their history as a positive and usable source to aid them in their quest for black self-identity in a white world. However, not all blacks believed that there was any difference between blacks and whites except for color. George S. Schuyler took this position. His essay claimed that there was no such thing as Negro art. In this respect his views are similar to those of Professor Martin Kilson in his essay condemning the theory of the black aesthetic. The basic difference between Schuyler and Kilson is that their essays appeared at different periods, 1926 and 1970, respectively.

Summary

In this essay the author contends that intrinsic "Negro art" does not exist in the United States. Negro art exists, but only in African nations. To suggest that such art has been produced by the ten million Negroes in the United States is foolish. There are those in Harlem and Greenwich Village who herald the arrival of a renaissance of Negro art that is just around the corner. The art of "Homo Africanus" was about to take the world by storm.

Those who were doubtful waited patiently and still wait. Slave songs called spirituals, it is true, came from the Negroes, but they were based on biblical texts and Protestant hymns and were not original. Also from the Negroes have come sad hard-luck songs known as the "blues" and an outgrowth of ragtime known as "jazz." The "Charleston," an unusual dance, was invented by Negro children of the marketplace in Charleston. No one can or desires to deny this. However, these are caste contributions native to certain sections of the country. They are alien to northern Negroes and African Negroes. These contributions are not any more expressive of the characteristics of Negroes than the music of the Appalachians is expressive of the characteristics of the whites. One may speak of the contributions of the southern peasantry, but it is merely coincidence that most of these peasants are black.

The literature and painting of the Negro Americans that does exist is the same as that of the whites. It, too, is influenced by the art of Europe. In drama little has been written by and about Negroes that could not have been written by whites. W. E. B. DuBois, the leader of the Negro literary group, was trained at Harvard and in Germany. The best-known Negro sculptress, Meta Warick Fuller, graduated from American art schools and studied under Rodin. Henry Ossawa Tanner, best-known of Negro American painters in Paris, has received decorations from the French government. Their work is no more expressive of the Negro soul than the writings of Octavius Roy Cohen or Hugh Wiley.

The Negro is awakened by the same alarm clock that wakes the whites, eats the same kind of breakfast, and works at the same kind of job. Negroes speak the same language, read the same Bible, and see the same Hollywood version of life as the whites. They smoke the same tobacco and read the same childish magazines as the whites do. In short, Negroes react to the same pressures as whites. Therefore, it is absurd to talk about racial differences between the two groups.

Negro newspapers are like white ones and in Negro and white homes of the same economic and cultural level can be found the same furniture, literature, and talk. How, under these circumstances, can the art of the Negro be different? E. Wilmot Blyden and Claude McKay, both English; Pushkin, a Russian; Bridgetower, a Pole; Antar, an Arab; Juan Latino, a Spaniard; Dumas Pere and fils,

Frenchmen; Charles W. Chesnutt, Paul Laurence Dunbar, and James Weldon Johnson, American, are all Negroes, who show the influence of nationality, not race. Their color is incidental. Why should Negro artists in America be different when Negro artists from other countries are not?

If it can be foreseen what whites of the future will be like by studying the kind of education they receive, it should be evident that the adults of today are what they are because of the influence of the preceding generation. If this environment was about the same for blacks and whites, what is the reason for the popularity of the "Negro art hokum"?

Nonsense such as this is very likely the last ditch effort of Negrophobists to support the myth of many years' standing that there is a basic difference between blacks and whites. On this premise, which flatters the white mob, is erected the idea that Negroes are inferior and basically different from whites. Therefore any effort to show life through the medium of art must result in strange and unusual art. Although this view may seem reasonable to most Americans, intelligent people must reject it with a loud laugh.

THE NEGRO WRITER AND THE RACIAL MOUNTAIN

Kind of work: Essay
Writer: Langston Hughes
First published: 1926 (v. 122)

Comment

During the period known as the Harlem Renaissance black writers began to write the way they wanted to and not to please the whites. Langston Hughes's essay, "The Negro Writer and the Racial Mountain", was written in reply to an essay, "The Negro Art Hokum," by George S. Schuyler. Hughes's essay became a manifesto for the young black writer of the Harlem Renaissance Period.

However, during the depression it was forgotten. In the 1960s the proponents of the black aesthetic theory discovered it and found that their ideas were not really new at all.

Summary

In this essay the author states that the young negro who wants to be a poet *per se* and not a Negro poet really means subconsciously that he wants to write like white American poets. This desire to write like white poets is an enormous mountain placed in the pathway of Negro art. It is pointed out that the home from which the would-be poet came is Negro middle class, that is to say, it consists of people who, though not rich, are able to live in relative comfort. The father has what is considered a good job and the mother helps out by doing fancy needlework. The children go to an integrated school and throughout this family there are constant attempts to emulate the life-style of white America. In such an environment it is extremely difficult for the Negro artist to present the beauty of the Negro.

Hughes also believes that the upper-class Negros are just as negative in their attitudes toward themselves as the lower-middle-class Negroes are. Here, too, there is an intense desire to be like the whites in America and to acquire the means to bring these desires to fruition. Under these conditions the Negro artist who wants to discover himself and his people has an even higher mountain to climb. Fortunately there are the masses of Negroes who are more concerned with realities. They live for the present moment, and let tomorrow take care of itself, and do not particularly care whether they are like whites or anybody else. They are just themselves. It is within this group that the Negro artist who is not afraid will find material for his art. The Negro upper class is discriminatory within its churches and does not sing spirituals. There is no support for the Negro artist from this group. The interest in the Negro artist has brought him to the attention of his own people. However, the Negro artist works against a barrage of harsh criticism of his work, a criticism that urges him to show only the best side of Negro life and ignore the realities of the lives of ordinary Negroes.

The author feels that a new theater movement will result from the writings that already exist in spite of the white-oriented Negro intelligentsia. The Negro artist must search his own surroundings for subject matter for his art. He must point out that he is a Negro and is beautiful as well. The younger Negro artists who create will express their blackness and produce artistic works that please themselves, whether or not anyone else likes them. They will scale the racial mountain and be free as artists.

NOT WITHOUT LAUGHTER

Kind of work: Novel
Writer: Langston Hughes
Time: 1918
Setting: Stanton, Kansas; Chicago
First published: 1930

Important Characters

Sandy Rodgers—a boy
Anjee Rodgers—*Sandy's mother*
Jimboy Rodgers—*Sandy's father*
Aunt Hager Williams—*Sandy's grandmother*
Harriet Williams—*Sandy's aunt*
Tempy—*Sandy's aunt*

Comment

In *Not without Laughter* Langston Hughes has written about a black youth growing up in a small midwestern town. Sandy is followed through school and watched during his growing years. The various influences, some of them corrupt, upon him are shown. The problems of race prejudice are in evidence. The author discusses them and points out the detrimental and destructive effects upon the blacks of Stanton, who are humiliated almost daily. For example, when Sandy works as a spitoon polisher and bootblack in a hotel, he is one day called a "nigger" by a drunken white man, who tries to make him dance. Sandy throws his shoe-shine box at him and runs from the hotel.

This novel is similar to Al Young's *Snakes* and James Baldwin's *Go Tell It on the Mountain* in that the characters, Sandy in *Not without Laughter*, M.C. in *Snakes*, and John Grimes in *Go Tell It on the Mountain*, live in environments that tend to hinder their attempts to break away from the hostile surroundings and find their way to maturity and success.

Summary

A violent summer storm is about to strike the town of Stanton. Aunt Hager Williams is worried about her daughter, Anjee, who has not yet come home from her job as a domestic worker for one of the local white families. She has her ten-year-old grandson Sandy with her. After the storm is over, Aunt Hager takes Sandy with her as she tries to help those injured by the storm. Sandy is momentarily separated from his grandmother and is very frightened. His mother, Anjee, finds him asleep on a porch and takes him home. While she puts Sandy to bed, she thinks of her guitar-playing, wandering husband, Jimboy, Sandy's father.

One afternoon Aunt Hager has an argument with her youngest daughter, Harriet, who feels the town is stifling her. She runs with a fast group of young people and her mother does not like it. Jimboy comes home unexpectedly and the house comes alive with his guitar playing and singing. One weekend Sandy's Aunt Harriet goes out to a dance and stays very late. When she returns home, Aunt Hager is waiting to whip her. There is a carnival in town and when it leaves Harriet leaves with it. Soon summer is gone and Sandy spends his time playing with his friends and going to school. One day Sandy comes home from school and discovers that his father has gone away again.

As Sandy grows older, he takes a succession of jobs. He works in a barber shop, in a hotel as a bellboy, and finally for a printer. Sandy's Aunt Harriet is stranded in Memphis but returns home on money that Aunt Hager and Anjee are able to send her. When she comes home, however, she moves in with a friend of hers. Jimboy finds works in Detroit and Anjee goes to him, leaving Sandy in the care of his grandmother. One day Sandy sees a notice in the local newspaper that his Aunt Harriet has been arrested as a streetwalker, but he does not know what a streetwalker is.

Aunt Hager becomes very ill and dies, but no one is home except Sandy and his Aunt Tempy. After his grandmother's death, Sandy goes to live with Tempy. He finds life very different because his aunt is considered part of the black middle class of the town.

Sandy has a room of his own and books to read. In spite of her middle-class outlook, his Aunt Tempy teaches him about his own people, W. E. B. DuBois among them. One day in a local black restaurant Sandy buys a newspaper and discovers that his Aunt Harriet has become a famous blues singer. Just before the school ends for the year, Sandy's mother sends for him to join her in Chicago. Shortly after he arrives, Sandy's mother finds him a job as an elevator boy; but he does not like it and wants to go to school. He discovers that his father has gone overseas with the armed forces and his mother does not know where he is. One day during the late summer Sandy's Aunt Harriet is booked into a Chicago theater. Sandy and his mother go to see her perform. When the show is over, they go backstage to see Harriet. She is surprised to see them, especially Sandy. When she learns that he is an elevator boy and cannot continue going to school, she offers to give him the necessary funds so that he can finish his education and help his people, the blacks.

OLLIE MISS

Kind of work: Novel
Writer: George Wylie Henderson
Time: 1930
Setting: Rural Alabama
First published: 1935

Important Characters

Ollie Miss—*a young woman*
Jule—*Ollie's lover*
Uncle Alex—*a farmer*
Slaughter—*a farmhand*
Willie—*a farmhand*
Aunt Caroline—*Alex's wife*

Nan—*a relative of Caroline's*
Della—*a woman whom Jule has jilted*
Shell—*a hired hand*
Lena—*Jule's new girl*

Comment

At first glance George W. Henderson's *Ollie Miss* appears to be no more than a black rural soap opera with the heroine bearing up under various adversities. However, the novel is really a pastoral with Ollie at its center. The routine of these black peasant farmers, for that is what they are, is broken by an occasional barbecue or a camp meeting or a dance. It is at a camp meeting that Ollie is cut. The people in the novel sit on their front porches, smoke, gossip, and, in general, work hard and live quietly. Their life-style is very well described, but it is in Ollie that one finds the strongest character. She is in control of herself and is able to surmount the difficulties she encounters.

Ollie Miss is not a protest novel, as it is really raceless. There is no overt concern about the problems of race prejudice and there are no vicious whites inflicting violences upon the blacks. In fact, there are only two white characters in the entire novel, the sheriff and the grocery store owner. What the author has done is describe, in a detached way, the life of black farmers in a small, rural Alabama community. Perhaps he has made it too idyllic in view of the harsh realities that blacks faced during this period in the South, especially in rural areas.

Summary

Ollie Miss is preparing to leave Uncle Alex's farm to visit her lover, whom she has not seen for two months. In a long flashback it is shown how Ollie came to be on the farm. She appeared one spring evening carrying her belongings in a cloth bundle. She asked Alex for work as a plow hand and said she would work for her keep. Alex hired her and the next morning Ollie began work plowing. Her coworkers were male farmhands, Slaughter, Shell, and Willie. She plowed as well as the men. Alex gave her a small cabin of her own and she moved in. She continued to do her share of the work on the farm and the hired hands were puzzled by her independence. Slaughter fell in love with her but she rejected him and had a very brief love affair with Willie.

Ollie's independence arouses the enmity of Nan, whose husband had left her several years before. Ollie takes part in activities of the surrounding community; she goes to dances, barbecues, and church meetings. One night, after she has been at Alex's farm for several months, Ollie leaves, telling Alex she will be gone for a week. She goes to visit Jule. When she arrives at Jule's cabin, she finds it empty. She also finds another woman's clothes there. After preparing a meal for herself, she goes to see Della, who owns the cabin in which Jule lives. Della is in love with Jule, but he has jilted her for a younger woman.

Ollie discovers that Jule is going to be at a camp meeting and gets there before him. She meets Jule and he spends the night with her but leaves the next morning. Ollie, despondent over Jule's leaving, goes to the camp meeting that night in hope that she will see Jule there. Jule comes to the meeting with his new girlfriend. She is angry with Jule and has drawn a razor from her skirt and demanded to know where he has been. Ollie tells the girl that he was with her. The girl, Lena, whirls and slashes Ollie badly with the razor. Uncle Alex and the hired hands take Ollie home and call the doctor to take care of her wounds. The sheriff is called but Ollie refuses to identify the girl. Jule offers to marry Ollie but she rejects him and sends him away even though she is pregnant with his child.

While Ollie is recovering from her wound, Alex comes to visit. He says she can stay as long as she wants and gives her land to work for herself for half a year. The novel ends with Ollie walking across the fields to her cabin.

ONE WAY TO HEAVEN

Kind of work: Novel
Writer: Countee Cullen
Time: 1930
Setting: Harlem, New York
First published: 1932

Important Characters

Sam Lucas—*a one-armed black con man*
Mattie Johnson—*a beautiful young black woman*
Reverend Johnson—*A Harlem minister*
Aunt Mandy—*Mattie Johnson's aunt*
Emma May—*one of Sam's girlfriends*
Constancia—*Mattie's wealthy black employer*

Comment

Countee Cullen's only novel, *One Way to Heaven*, is an accurate portrayal of the religious life of the Harlem of the 1920s as embodied in the activities of its churches. His description of the various services and individuals reveals the author's familiarity with church activities (Countee Cullen's father was an A.M.E. minister).

At one point the author ridicules his cowriters of the Harlem Renaissance period and lacerates them severely. He attacks white writers who come to Harlem to use the blacks as resource material for their books. It is interesting to note that his satire is aimed for the most part at the Harlem socialites and not necessarily at the churches and their members.

Summary

Sam Lucas, a black, one-armed con man, arrives in Harlem in the middle of winter. Sam's specialty is allowing himself to be converted at religious revivals. This act always brings him some cash. He goes to the Mount Hebron Church, one of the largest in Harlem, and prepares to go into his fake conversion. At the height of the singing and praying Sam comes to the altar, throws down a pack of playing cards and a razor and cries out that he has seen Jesus and wants to be saved. Several people come to the altar, among them a beautiful black girl at whom Sam peeks through his fingers.

After services Sam introduces himself to Mattie Johnson and she invites him to her home for dinner the next week. Eventually Sam Lucas marries Mattie because this is the only way she will give herself to him. Mattie's wedding is held at the home of her wealthy black employer. At first things go well for Mattie and Sam, but Sam soon begins to drift back to his old ways. When Mattie's child is stillborn, Sam leaves her and takes up with Emma May, a fast-living woman. While he is living with Emma May, Sam becomes ill with double pneumonia. Emma May sends for Mattie, who takes Sam

127

back home. Realizing that he will soon die, Sam pulls his best sinner to salvation act so that Mattie will believe him.

THE OWL ANSWERS

Kind of work: Play
Writer: Adrienne Kennedy
Setting Place: Harlem, New York; England
First published: 1965

Important Characters

Clara Passmore—*a young black woman*
Reverend Passmore—*Clara's adopted father*
William Mattheson—*Clara's real white father*
A black man

Comment

In this very complex play the author seems to be concerned with the problem of identity. Clara is half-white and in an attempt to find her place, she picks up a black man on a subway. She tries to seduce him in a hotel in Harlem, but her attempt is unsuccessful. Her problem of where she belongs remains. In the play Clara's story is told in time periods that change from the present to the past with various historical figures such Shakespeare, Anne Boleyn, and William the Conquerer appearing and reappearing throughout the play. The author's first play, *The Funny House of a Negro,* is also concerned with the problem of racial identity.

Summary

Clara Passmore, thirty-four, is the illegitimate child of a relationship between her mother, a black cook, and William Mattheson, the richest white man in the town of Jacksonville, Florida. After

Clara is born, her mother commits suicide and Clara is adopted by
Reverend and Mrs. Passmore. When she asks where she came from,
she is told that she came from the owls. Clara's real father dies, but
she is not allowed to go to the funeral. After she grows up, she
becomes a teacher in Savannah and marries briefly. She leaves her
job as a teacher and goes to England, the home of her real father.
While she is there, she has a mental breakdown and is placed in an
institution.

THE PURPLE FLOWER

Kind of work: Play
Writer: Marita Bonner
Time: 1900
Setting: U.S.A.
First published: 1928

Important Characters

Us's—*Old Lady Us, Young Us*
Cornerstone Us—*Average Us, Sweet Young Us*
Finest Blood Us—*Old Man*
Sundry White Devils

Comment

The author of this one-act play uses allegory to illustrate the
problems that the blacks of the United States faced during a certain
period and still face to some extent today. The Us's in *The Purple
Flower* represent the blacks of the United States and the White
Devils are symbolic of the whites of America. "Nowhere" is the
dead-end region from which there is little or no progress. "Somewhere" is the environment of white America with its various oppor-
tunities and possibilities for upward mobility. The purple flower of
life at its fullest is symbolic of economic, political, and cultural

conditions that provide the means for the White Devils to thrive and prosper. The Us's (blacks) are thrust into limbo in the valley between Nowhere and Somewhere where they struggle constantly to maintain a minimal level of subsistence. Almost every aspect of the black experience in the United States is dealt with by the author.

The Leader who urges the Us's to work hard in order to be accepted in Somewhere is a reference to Booker T. Washington and signifying that the time for an open clash with the whites of America his belief in the Protestant work ethic. In one scene a young Us brings forward a pile of books and throws them to the ground. This act is symbolic of the efforts of the blacks in America to educate themselves and perhaps to be accepted in white America.

The attempt by a White Devil to grab Sweet young Us and drag her into the bushes shows the sexual exploitation to which black women were subjected in the South during this time. The conjuring done by the old Us is indicative of the experience of the blacks in their effort to obtain equality in America. Gold, books, dust, and so forth are put into the iron pot. Finally there is a demand for blood to bind it all together. On this somber note the play ends, possibly signifying that the time for an open clash with the whites of America has come. The interesting thing about *The Purple Flower* is that it appears quite relevant to the racial conflict today although the play was written in 1928.

Summary

The Us's live in Nowhere, a valley at the base of the high hill, somewhere on the pinnacle of which grows the beautiful purple flower of life. At its fullest the Purple Flower is as tall as a pine tree and stands by itself. The eternal goal of the Us's is to get near the Purple Flower of life at its fullest in order to share some of its fragrance and be a part of Somewhere. The White Devils inhabit the sides of the hill between the Purple Flower of life at its fullest and the valley where the Us's live. They employ every means to keep the Us's from reaching the top of the hill. The Us's ask permission to come up the hill and are denied. They build roads and houses for the White Devils and cultivate the valley and the sides of the hills as well, but they are knocked back down into the valley when the job is finished.

As this drama opens, the Us's are resting by a brook that runs through the valley. As they discuss their plight, they hear the song of the White Devils from across the valley. The song tells them they are not wanted in Somewhere and to stay where they are. Old Lady Us is lamenting the fact that she will never live to see the purple flower even though she has washed clothes for the White Devils for many years. The Leader had told her and the other Us's that hard work would help them reach Somewhere and the Purple Flower. A young Us scoffs at her.

As they are talking, four other Us's arrive, a middle-aged brown man, a middle-aged plump brown man, a beautiful young brown girl, and a handsome young brown woman. The newcomers join the discussion. They feel that the Us's will reach the flower if they have the proper leadership. The plump brown woman defends the leaders. Sweet and Finest Blood join the discussion. Soon a crowd gathers and different views about the ways to reach to purple flower are offered. Some Us's have worked hard; some have earned money; some have educated themselves; and some have relied on God to help them. All these methods have failed.

As the discussion becomes heated, Sweet young Us runs crying from the edge of the crowd to her mother, saying that a White Devil tried to attack her. Her brother, Finest Blood, picks up a stone and starts off to kill the White Devil but is persuaded to remain with the group. At this point an old lady Us in the group cries out that she has had a dream of a White Devil cut in six pieces. An old man Us tells the group that the time for conjuring has come and asks for an old iron pot. The pot is brought forward and in it is put dust, bags of gold, books, and other things. The old man calls for the last ingredient, blood. Young Us's offer their blood, but Cornerstone Us points out that young Us's are needed for the future.

Someone suggests that the White Devil in the bushes might supply the blood. Finest Blood picks up a stone and goes off. Old Man Us tells him that he must lure the White Devil out of the bushes and that if the White Devil kills him, blood will be supplied all the same. The play ends with everyone listening to hear what will happen. All the Us's and all the White Devils in Somewhere are listening to see if the time for confrontation has come.

QUICKSAND

Kind of work: Novel
Writer: Nella Larsen
Time: 1929
Setting: New York
First published: 1928

Important Characters

Helga Crane—*a beautiful mulatto woman*
James Vayle—*Helga's fiance*
Robert Anderson—*a black college president with whom Helga falls in love*
Peter Nilssen—*Helga's uncle*
Mrs. Hayes-Rore—*a black business woman*
Anne Gray—*Mrs. Hayes-Rore's niece and Helga's friend*
Audrey Denney—*a beautiful black socialite*
Axel Olsen—*a Danish artist who wants to marry Helga*
Reverend Pleasant Green—*a southern preacher whom Helga marries*

Comment

At first glance *Quicksand* would seem to be a novel of the tragic mulatto genre. However, upon closer examination it becomes evident that race is merely one of several factors that are responsible for Helga Crane's actions. The confusion that she faces concerning her sexuality and the rejection of her by her father and uncle must also be considered. Helga is just as unhappy, after a while, in Denmark as she was in New York. When she is rejected by Robert Anderson, the man she really desires, she falls apart emotionally and finds herself in a situation from which there is very little hope of escape. Essentially *Quicksand* is a study of the psychological problems of a very unhappy neurotic woman trapped by her own sexual desires.

Quicksand

Summary

Beautiful Helga Crane was born illegitimately of mixed blood, her father having been black and her mother Danish and white. She is at Naxos, a black college in the southern United States where she has been teaching for two years. She is dissatisfied and unhappy with the stuffy, conservative atmosphere there although her fiance, James Vayle, fits well into the Naxos environment. Helga decides to break off her engagement and leave Naxos. In the process of leaving the college she meets Robert Anderson, the president of the school, and he tries unsuccessfully to persuade her to stay. Taking the money the college owes her, Helga leaves for Chicago to visit her uncle, Peter Nilssen. Upon arriving at her uncle's home, Helga finds that he is not there and meets instead his new wife, of whose presence she had not been told. Mrs. Nilssen, noticing Helga's color, tells her that she must not try to see Mr. Nilssen at all. She states that since Helga's mother and father were not married, Nilssen is not really her uncle. Astounded by this rebuff Helga leaves the house.

With her funds rapidly diminishing, Helga feels the pressing need to find work. She finds a job as a companion and secretary to Mrs. Hayes-Rore, a prominent black club woman and widow of an important black politician. The job with Mrs. Hayes-Rore is not unpleasant and Helga is content for a while. On a trip to New York she begins to think of trying to find work in the city. During the stay in New York Helga is introduced to Mrs. Hayes-Rore's niece, Anne Grey, and begins to explore Harlem. Anne Grey is a member of the elite of Harlem and is invited to all the prominent affairs. Helga goes with her and begins to enjoy them.

At one party she again meets Robert Anderson, whom she had known at Naxos. She is strongly attracted to him but he is with Audrey Denney, a beautiful black girl, and she is able to talk to him for only a few moments. When he finally does call her, she refuses to see him. Weary of the almost constant round of parties, Helga is nervous and uneasy when a letter arrives from her uncle, Peter Nilssen. In it he apologizes for not having told her of his marriage and explains that their relationship must end. Included in the letter is a check for $5,000. Peter suggests that Helga visit her aunt in Copenhagen for a while. Following her uncle's suggestion, she sails for Denmark.

Helga remains in Copenhagen for two years and for a time is happy there. Her mother's relatives are enchanted with her because she is considered exotic. Axel Olsen, a wealthy, prominent Danish painter, falls in love with her and asks her to marry him, but Helga refuses. She has become restless and wants to return home to her people.

Upon returning to New York, she finds that her friend Anne Gray and Robert Anderson have married and regrets this because of the strong feelings she has for him. One evening she finds herself alone with Robert and suddenly she is in his arms and kissing him. She offers herself to him but he rejects her and apologizes to her for his part in the affair. Helga becomes angry and slaps him. The next day, still smarting from Robert's rejection, she goes out for a walk to try to calm down even though it is raining. Suddenly the light rain becomes a storm and Helga is soon cold and wet. In an effort to find shelter from the rain, she stumbles into a storefront church service being conducted by Reverend Pleasant Green. After the service ends, Green escorts Helga home, where she seduces him. Having done this, she decides to marry him.

Soon he is moved to a small rural Alabama town. For a short time Helga is happy; but with seemingly endless childbearing comes the realization that she is trapped in a dull and dreary situation for the rest of her life.

RACHEL

Kind of work: Play
Writer: Angelina Grimke
Time: 1916
Setting: New York
First published: 1920

Important Characters

Mrs. Loving—*a black woman*
Rachel—*Mrs. Loving's daughter*
Tom—*Mrs. Loving's son*

John Strong—*a young black man who loves Rachel*
Mrs. Lane—*a visitor*
Ethel—*Mrs. Lane's daughter*
Edith, Nancy, Mary, Martha, Louise, Jenny—*black children*

Comment

This play was first produced in 1916 at the Myrtell Miner School in Washington, D.C. *Rachel* is first of all a protest play against lynching and the mistreatment of the blacks in the South at that time. All the characters are used to speak out against the various kinds of racial prejudice and all the concomitant humiliations. Mrs. Loving, in one of her long speeches, describes the lynching of her son and husband. Tom Loving gives voice to the bitter resentment that results from discrimination in employment. Mrs. Lane protests the racial discrimination practiced against little black children. Rachel, the heroine, expresses what is most important of all, the need to give love and warmth to little black children who can be crushed in the seemingly eternal racial conflict that exists in the United States. That Rachel is the source of hugs, kisses, and endearments is important in that it shows the need for love and affection under stress must not be ignored.

The children in the play are drawn to Rachel as to a magnet by the warmth and affection that she provides. Even John Strong, whose bitterness is least evident, speaks out about prejudice that forces him to become a waiter rather than work at the job for which he was trained.

It is possible to view Rachel from two sides, that of the whites and that of the blacks. A white audience could be made aware of the problems that the blacks faced at the time this play was written. A black audience could see themselves portrayed in a positive manner. This black family is neat, clean, and hardworking, qualities that blacks were said not to possess. The Loving family is a semi-middle-class family trying to survive under the most distressing of circumstances.

Summary

Mrs. Loving and her two teenage children, Rachel and Tom, live in an apartment on the top floor of a city tenement building. Mrs. Loving sews for a living; Rachel is in high school; Tom Loving works and goes to school. One day Rachel is late coming home from school and Mrs. Loving is worried. When Rachel, a beautiful teenage girl, comes into the room she immediately hugs her mother and tells her why she is late. On her way up the stairs to the Loving apartment she met a little brown boy named Jimmy, stopped to play with him, and lost all sense of time. Rachel is fond of children and wonders if Jimmy's mother will let him come up and spend the evening with her.

The doorbell rings. It is John Strong, who has come to pick up a garment Mrs. Loving has made for his mother. While Mrs. Loving is wrapping the item, Rachel talks to John, who is a handsome black man about twenty-eight years old. Mrs. Loving gives him the package and as he leaves he looks back at Rachel.

Rachel is interested in John and begins to talk to her mother about him. She discovers that John's mother had left the South and moved north in order to educate her son. After leaving college, however, John was unable to find employment in his field because of racial prejudice and became a waiter in order to make a living and take care of his mother. While waiting for Tom to come home from his after-school job, Rachel and her mother talk. Rachel plays the piano and sings a song about childhood for her mother. She tells her that she wants to have children of her own to love. Rachel goes out to get the necessary items to complete the supper that is being prepared. While Rachel is out, Tom Loving comes home. He greets his mother, gives her his wages, and hugs her close,—telling her that he wishes there were more money. He sets the table for supper.

Rachel returns, bringing with her the little boy named Jimmy whom she had met earlier in the day. When Rachel introduces Jimmy, Mrs. Loving immediately becomes pale and nervous. Rachel is alarmed and calls Tom. Mrs. Loving indicates that nothing is wrong and the family sits down to supper. Tom and Rachel try to cheer their mother up but are only partially successful in doing so.

After supper Mrs. Loving steels herself to tell her children what she has withheld from them for many years. Their father and half-brother had been lynched by a white mob in the South ten years earlier. Mr. Loving had been overcome in spite of his having shot and killed four members of the mob when they attacked him. When his son tried to help him, he, too, was taken out and hanged along with his father. Mr. Loving was a newspaper editor who spoke out against the oppression of his people. Mrs. Loving tells her children how she had to flee with them from the South. The emotional impact on Tom and Rachel of what their mother tells them is great. Tom condemns all whites in the South, while Rachel expresses concern for all the little black babies being born in the South and the violence and depredations they will face in the future. She is so overcome that she faints in her mother's arms.

It is four years later and Rachel is now a beautiful young woman. The little boy Jimmy's parents have died of smallpox and Rachel has adopted him. Tom Loving, who has finished school, is trying to find a job. It is early morning. Jimmy has just taken a bath by himself for the first time and this is a great occasion. Tom Loving is brooding over the fact that he cannot find a job because of the racial discrimination practiced by the various companies where he has applied for work. John Strong stops by, supposedly to see how everyone is but really to see Rachel. He offers to help Tom get a job as a waiter since he can find nothing else. Tom agrees to take the job and the two young men leave. For a moment Rachel is alone; then there is a knock at the door. Rachel answers it.

At the door she meets a poorly dressed black woman and a homely little black girl. The woman, Mrs. Lane, and her daughter Ethel, are looking at an empty apartment on the same floor as that of the Lovings. Rachel asks Mrs. Lane to come in and rest for a moment. She accepts and begins to tell Rachel of some of the difficulties that little Ethel has encountered at school.

Ethel had been harassed by the white children with the tacit approval of the teacher and at the end of the day had been called a "nigger" and chased home. She was shattered by the experience and has become withdrawn and frightened. Rachel explains that the school where her son Jimmy goes does not seem too bad. Mrs. Lane leaves and Rachel is about to return to her housework but the doorbell rings. It is a messenger bringing a box of roses for Rachel from John Strong. She had been saddened by what Mrs. Lane had told her and the roses from John relieved her sadness somewhat. While she is admiring the budding roses, Jimmy comes home from school. Jimmy begins to ask Rachel about the roses and compares them to children. His mother, sensing that something is wrong, asks him what the matter is. Jimmy answers by asking Rachel what a "nigger" is. Rachel is astounded. Jimmy goes on to tell his mother that he was called a "nigger" and chased home by some white boys who threw stones at him. Rachel soothes him, gives him some cookies, and takes him out to play.

When she returns, she is sad and laments the treatment of little Ethel Lane and her own son. Noticing the budding roses John Strong had sent her, she touches them tenderly. Then suddenly she cries out that God is mocking her and her people, especially the little black children. She declares that she can no longer believe in God if He continues to allow this racial prejudice to go on. Again she looks at the roses, she takes them from the vase, tears off the buds throws them to the floor and stamps on them and falls in a dead faint as the laughter of children comes through the window.

As the third act begins it is one week after Rachel's collapse. In the opening scene Rachel is in a bedroom playing with Jimmy, who is squealing with laughter. Tom and Mrs. Loving are worried about Rachel. Since the incident where Jimmy was chased home from school Rachel has been tense and nervous. Tom tells Rachel that John Strong is coming to see her. Suddenly there is a knock at the door and several little girls enter; they visit Rachel every day. She greets them with hugs and kisses and goes out with them to visit another little girl who is ill. While Rachel is gone, John Strong arrives. Mrs. Loving tells him that Rachel is better but not completely well. When Rachel returns, Mrs. Loving goes on an errand so that John and Rachel can be alone.

After Mrs. Loving has gone, John asks Rachel why she destroyed the roses but she cannot bring herself to tell him. She tries to entertain John by singing to him but she becomes hysterical and has to stop. John puts his arms around her and tries to soothe her. He tells her that he loves her and wants to marry her; he has furnished an apartment for them. Rachel tells John Strong that she loves him and wants to marry him but feels that she must take care of little black children, love them, and protect them from the hurts of racial prejudice. She tells John that she cannot marry him and leaves the room crying as the play ends.

RIVER GEORGE

Kind of work: Novel
Writer: George W. Lee
Time: 1918-1919
Setting: Rural Tennessee; New York; Memphis
First published: 1937

River George

Important Characters

Aaron George—*a young black man*
Uncle Amity George—*Aaron's uncle*
John King—*a plantation owner*
Sam Turner—*a plantation manager*
Frank Harding
Ada Green—*a black girl with whom Aaron falls in love*
Fred Smith—*a white postmaster*
Hanna—*Ada's aunt*
Do Pop—*a black man*
Lighting—*a local black badman and friend of Aaron's*
Annie Bell—*a beautiful black woman*
Blue Stell—*a black detective*

Comment

River George is a protest novel in the sense that the author presents the various negative aspects of the racism that the black sharecroppers encountered constantly. They are cheated and underpaid, then lynched if they protest. In Aaron George the author has presented a mildly militant black hero who is a victim of racism and lynching, not because he is given to violence, oratorical or otherwise, but because he simply wants to change the status quo. He is frustrated on all counts. He cannot have Ada Green, his girl, because a white man wants her for his mistress. He is forced to take less money when he sells a farm animal. Aaron rebels when he fights Smith the postmaster and thinks that he has killed him.

The warmest parts of the novel are those that concern Aaron's life on Beal Street. The author discusses the life of the district and depicts beautiful Annie Bell in a positive way. Interspersed throughout this part of the novel are descriptions of blues songs, blues singers, and the night life of Beal Street. At these times a particular human warmth prevails. At one point during the Beal Street episodes the author manages to bring in a voodoo priestess, to whom Annie goes to buy a talisman to protect Aaron when he leaves for the war.

There is a John Henry-like aspect about Aaron's life as steamboat roustabout and the author's admiration for this group of men can be felt. Lee shows also the "white man's nigger" aspect among the blacks. Do Pop is a good example of this. He is slain by Aaron's friend, "Lighting," because of his betrayal of Aaron. Although the author is basically concerned with the plight of the sharecroppers, he has produced a panorama of black life for that period. Aaron's mother, Hannah, is a portrait of the old plantation mammy.

Summary

Aaron George comes home from college to work his father's farm as a sharecropper. The black sharecroppers are cheated constantly, but Aaron is unable to help them. During the winter he finds work in the nearby town and persuades other blacks to follow him. The whites do not like this because they see their labor force disappearing. Aaron meets and falls in love with Ada Green but discovers that he cannot have her because she is the girlfriend of the white postmaster, Fred Smith. Eventually Aaron has a fight with Smith and when Smith draws a gun Aaron tries to take it from him. In the ensuing struggle Smith is shot. Thinking that he has killed Smith, Aaron flees from the area and goes to Beal Street in Memphis.

In Beal Street Aaron meets beautiful Annie Bell, the madame of a bawdy house, and becomes her lover. He remains with Annie for a while but joins the army and goes to France when war breaks out. Aaron survives the fighting and comes back to Annie. Shortly after his return Aaron is captured by Blue Steel, a black detective, and soon is on the way back to his hometown to be tried for murder. When Blue Steel relaxes his guard for a moment, Aaron knocks him unconscious and escapes. He takes a job as a roustabout on a riverboat. When he defeats Black Bill, a giant roustabout, in a fight, he becomes the leader of the group and is known as River George. One night Aaron is kidnapped and lynched by a group of whites from Tennessee who have recognized him.

RIVER OF EROS

Kind of work: Novel
Writer: Cyrus Colter
Time: 1971
Setting: Chicago
First published: 1972

Important Characters

Clotilda Pilgrim—*a middle-aged black woman*
Addie—*Clotilda's seventeen-year-old granddaughter*
Lester—*Clotilda's eleven-year-old grandson*
Ambrose Hammer—*a roomer in Clotilda's house*
Letitia Dorsey—*a roomer in Clotilda's house*
Dunrieth Smith—*a married drug addict with whom Clotilda's granddaughter is having an affair*

Comment

In *River of Eros* the author is not concerned with the problem of race as such. His views on the subject are evident in the activities and ideas of Ambrose Hammer and Dunrieth Smith. Hammer presents a semi-Booker T. Washington view, while Smith represents black nationalism. The author reduces both opinions to their most absurd aspects. The characters in the novel seem doomed to their fate and have no control over what happens to them. Clotilda has taken on all the guilt for the problems and tragedies of her strifetorn family. She feels guilty, too, about her own mild affair with her sister's husband. It is this sense of guilt that destroys her mental balance and leads her to commit violence herself.

Summary

River of Eros begins with Clotilda Pilgrim talking to Letitia Dorsey, a roomer in her house. Clotilda, a dressmaker, takes in roomers to augment her income. Her grandson Lester comes home from school but her granddaughter Addie goes to a friend's house instead. Clotilda prepares dinner for herself and Lester. After dinner Clotilda sits by herself, thinks of times past, and remembers that she once had a brief affair with her sister's husband. In flashback it is revealed that Clotilda's daughter had been killed by her husband because he thought she was having an affair with another man. Her granddaughter, then a child, was present at the murder.

Addie finally comes home late in the night. Clotilda finds out that Addie is involved with Dunrieth Smith, a married man and also a drug addict. She begins to worry about Addie's affair and slowly begins to feel that she is partly responsible for it. Because of her feelings of guilt, Clotilda begins to disintegrate mentally. As Addie's affair continues, Lester asks Ambrose Hammer, one of Clotilda's roomers, to help get Addie away from her lover.

As Clotilda's mental deterioration continues she begins to neglect her sewing business. Addie's affair comes to an end when she tries to commit suicide because of Clotilda's rejection of her. After she recovers from her suicide attempt, Addie matures and prepares to take over the running of the house from Clotilda. She notices Clotilda's mental deterioration and she and her brother plan to ask Mr. Hammer and Letitia Dorsey to help them decide what to do about their grandmother. Before they are able to talk to Mr. Hammer, Clotilda murders her granddaughter Addie one evening while she is asleep. As the novel ends, Lester is going to live with Ambrose and Letitia, who have married. As they drive away from the mental institution where Clotilda has been placed, they tell Lester that he will be their son.

SAVAGE HOLIDAY

Kind of work: Novel
Writer: Richard Wright
Time: 1953
Setting: New York
First published: 1954

Important Characters

Erskine Fowler—*a retired insurance man*
Mrs. Blake—*a neighbor*
Tony Blake—*Mrs. Blake's five-year-old son*
Albert Warren—*president of Longevity Life Insurance Company*

Comment

Richard Wright's *Savage Holiday* is unusual for at least two reasons. First, it is the only novel of his in which no black characters appear and, second, implicit in this novel is the philosophical idea of existentialism, which the author used in a later novel, *The Outsider*. In fact, Erskine Fowler is a kind of prototype for Cross Damon of *The Outsider*. Fowler is forced to become an outsider when he is made to retire. He eventually murders Mrs. Blake. The life he had known was directly related to his job, the church he went to, the money he had, and the exclusive neighborhood in which he lived. Fowler is unable to bear the freedom that he is forced into. In the end he becomes savage in his actions but cannot take the responsibility for them.

Summary

Erskine Fowler, an insurance executive, is being honored at a retirement dinner. However, unknown to those attending the dinner, Fowler had been forced to retire to make way for the son of the president of the company. When Fowler finds out, he resists retiring; but Albert Warren, president of Longevity Life Insurance, threatens to fire Fowler without severance pay or pension if he does not go into retirement.

The morning after the party Fowler is awakened by Tony Blake, a neighbor's five-year-old son, who is playing on the balcony below his apartment. Fowler decides to get up and take a shower. As he turns on the shower, he removes his robe to step in, but the door bell rings. It is the local newspaper boy on his weekly collecting round. Since he does not have on his bathrobe, Fowler tells the boy to come back later for his money.

When the boy leaves, Fowler peeks out the door and prepares to get his Sunday paper. It is just out of reach, so he steps out into the hall quickly to get the paper. At this instant the wind blows the door to his apartment shut. He is locked out of his apartment and stands naked in the hallway. He takes the elevator to try and find the custodian. However, then the elevator stops at the custodian's floor, two young women are waiting. He pushes the button for his own floor, but is unable to get off there because more people are waiting for the elevator to take them down.

Finally Fowler is able to get out of the elevator on the floor above his own apartment. Fowler runs out to the balcony of a nearby apartment to try to get to his own and, in the process, frightens Tony Blake, a five-year-old boy who is playing on the balcony on his hobby horse. The frightened child loses hold and plunges to his death. Fowler crawls through to his bathroom window.

Later he attends church as if nothing had happened. He had not called the police. When he returns from church, the custodian's wife tells him that Mrs. Blake saw a pair of naked male feet dangling in the air over her apartment window. Fowler panics and goes to Mrs. Blake. When he meet her, he is strongly attracted to her and later asks her to marry him. This unusual behavior after such a short meeting makes Mrs. Blake suspicious. She tells Fowler that she will consider his proposal and give him an answer later. When Mrs. Blake continues to go out with other men, Fowler quarrels with her. She threatens to go to the police with her suspicions about Fowler in relation to her son's death. In a fit of rage Fowler kills her with a butcher knife then returns to his apartment and calls the police.

Scarecrow

Kind of work: Novel
Writer: Calvin Hernton
Time: 1960
Setting: Atlantic Ocean; New York City
First published: 1974

Important Characters

Scarecrow—*a black American writer*
Maria—*a black woman who loves Scarecrow*

Oriki—*Scarecrow's daughter*
Wantman Kane—*a poet*
Dr. Yas—*a psychologist*

Comment

The author of *Scarecrow* is concerned with a problem that plagues race relations in the United States today and has done so throughout its history: sex between blacks and whites. One of the taboos is that there are to be no sexual relations between black men and white women in spite of the fact that such relations have existed since slavery between white men and black women. Author Hernton has dealt with this subject extensively in his nonfiction and this novel also concerns black and white sexual relations and their various ramifications.

Summary

Scarecrow, a black American writer, is in his apartment preparing to pack his clothes and leave his white wife. She comes home and finds him packing his bags. She berates him and tells him that she will not let him go away with Maria, a black woman with whom Scarecrow has fallen in love. In the ensuing quarrel Scarecrow strangles her, cuts up her body and packs it in a trunk for disposal at sea while on a cruise to Europe.

Using the flashback technique the author reveals that Scarecrow's past has been a savage one. He has as a child witnessed the lynching by crucifixion of his father and received other injuries, mainly psychological, as a result of white racism. As the voyage to Europe progresses, Scarecrow and Maria become passionately involved and it becomes evident that Scarecrow is losing control of his actions. A member of his party is killed and he does not realize he is the killer. Because of his internal conflict, the relationship between Scarecrow and Maria begins to deteriorate. They fight each other and both die as the result. The novel ends on this note.

THE SIGNIFYING MONKEY

Kind of work: Urban folk narrative
Writer: Unknown
Time: Anytime
Setting: a jungle
First published: 1963

Important Characters

The monkey
The lion
The elephant

Comment

The urban folktale *Signifying Monkey* illustrates a special kind of folklore. The monkey is a trickster and an agitator. He is a signifier. When the lion has been badly beaten by the elephant and returns to his lair, the monkey begins to cast aspersions upon the lion's virility. This tale is usually delivered as a ribald toast liberally sprinkled with profanity. There are several versions of this folktale.

Summary

One day in the jungle a monkey and a lion were talking. The monkey tells the lion there is another individual, the elephant, who is more powerful and can beat the lion in combat. In addition the elephant has made derogatory remarks concerning the lion's mother. Upon hearing this, the lion roars through the jungle to the place where the elephant is peacefully sleeping and challenges him to a fight. The elephant beats the lion badly and the lion drags himself back to his own part of the jungle. As soon as the lion arrives, the monkey, from his perch in the trees, taunts him, saying he is not unbeatable and he will come down from his place in the trees and beat the lion some more if he says anything. In his ardor the monkey jumps up and down on the tree limb. His foot slips and he falls to the ground. Immediately the lion leaps upon him. The lion tells the monkey that his end has come. At this point the monkey tells the lion that he has a special secret to reveal to him. The lion lets the monkey go and immediately he scoots back up in the trees and begins to taunt the lion again. The lion warns the monkey that he had better remain in the tree if he wants to stay alive. This is the reason monkeys are generally found chattering in the treetops.

SNAKES

Kind of work: Novel
Writer: Al Young
Time: 1950s-1960s
Setting: Detroit
First published: 1970

Important Characters

M. C. Moore—*a black youth*
Claudette Moore—*his grandmother*
Uncle Donald and Aunt Didi—*his uncle and aunt*
Tull—*a piano player*
"Shakes" Harris—*M.C.'s closest friend*
Champ—*a schoolmate of M.C.'s*
Donna Lee Jackson—*M.C.'s girlfriend*
Claire—*a prostitute*
Abdullah Salah—*a musician*
Jimmy Monday—*a musician*
Billy Sanchez—*a blind musician*

Comments

Structurally the novel *Snakes* is not cohesive. Various episodes in which the young protagonist is involved are presented and his friends wander in and out of his life. M.C.'s primary problem is to find his identity and to escape from a hostile and oppressive environment that will destroy him as it does his friend, Champ, whose slow destruction is evident throughout the novel. Champ does not have a goal toward which to strive and is soon trapped by drug addiction and its accompanying violence. "Shakes" Harris is trapped in a different way. He exhibits a lack of will that might help him break away from the restrictive hold of his parents. There is in M.C.'s decision to strike out on his own a degree of uncertainty of which he is totally aware. This is evident from the entry he makes in his diary for the day that he leaves for New York. The problem of racial prejudice as a factor in M.C.'s search for personal identity is apparent only once, when M.C. is involved in a fight with one of his white schoolmates. Snakes as a novel is concerned with the problem of a young boy's personal survival in an oppressive black ghetto.

Summary

M.C., the young hero of this short novel, is orphaned while he is very young and lives with his grandmother, Claudette, in a black ghetto in Detroit. The narrative, written in the first person, concerns primarily M.C.'s high school years and his relationships with his friends "Shakes" Harris, Champ, Donna Lee Jackson, Billy Sanchez, and Jimmy Monday. M.C.'s first love is music. It is awakened when he is ten years old and goes to live for a year in Mississippi with relatives whom he comes to know as Uncle Donald and Aunt Didi. Uncle Donald is a hustler and whisky runner and soon opens an illegal beer garden where people come to drink, gamble, and dance. M.C. and his cousin Jab sneak out of bed and spend their time listening to the music and watching the dancers in the front of the house.

In a deal Uncle Donald acquires a piano for his cafe so his customers who wish to play it can do so. M.C. learns to play the piano a little and is taught some techniques by Tull, an itinerant musician. M.C.'s music becomes important to him and in high school he learns to play the guitar. His friend "Shakes" Harris begins to play in the school band. M.C. does not think seriously about becoming a musician until he meets Champ, another student, who is older than he is. Champ, although he plays no musical instrument, becomes an important influence on M.C. by introducing him to various kinds of music that he has not heard before.

M.C. begins to expand his knowledge of music and to think seriously about organizing a band. He and "Shakes" Harris practice in earnest and begin to look around for other musicians. Champ, an irregular student at best, disappears, then returns to school without explanation. He meets M.C. and "Shakes" on the street one day, takes them to the apartment of three young prostitutes he knows, and introduces them to marijuana. At first M.C. is reluctant to join the pot party, but eventually he does and afterwards goes home high from his first experience.

Shortly after this episode M.C. is able to find two good musicians, Jimmy Monday and the blind Billy Sanchez, and organizes a combo. The band begins to play at dances, parties, and anywhere else they can. Although M.C. is a good student and is interested only in music and reading, his grandmother Claudette is worried about his desire to become a musician. She feels that the hostile ghetto environment will destroy him. M.C. remains in school but continues to lead the band. Eventually a song, "Snakes", which he has written, is recorded and the band becomes better known as the Masters of Ceremony. The combo enters a contest for the star of tomorrow and wins top prize. After M.C. graduates from high school, he decides to free himself from the ghetto and leaves for New York to try his skill as a musician.

THE SOUL BROTHERS AND SISTER LOU

Kind of work: Novel for young people
Writer: Kristin Hunter
Time: 1968
Setting: Philadelphia
First published: 1968

Important Characters

Louretta Hawkins—*a fourteen-year-old black girl*
"Fess" (Philip Satterthwaite)—*a leader of the "Hawks"*
William Hawkins—*Louretta's grown-up brother*
Blind Eddie Bell—*an old black musician*

The Soul Brothers and Sister Lou

Momma—*Louretta's mother*
Mr. Lucitanno—*Louretta's music teacher*
Lafferty—*a vicious white policeman*

Comment

This novel deals with the maturing of a young girl who is the product of the black urban ghetto and faces a hostile environment as she presses on toward maturity. In the process of growing up she is level-headed and with the help of Blind Eddie Bell discovers aspects of her heritage she had not known before. She is able to defuse the explosive situation after Jethro's death in spite of the opposition of "Fess," who fights against her ideas at every turn. Finally he succumbs to them. In essence, then, Louretta's love of music salvaged Louretta and the "Hawks."

In some respects *Soul Brothers and Sister Lou* is similar to Al Young's novel, *Snakes*. M.C., the protagonist, also forms a musical group consisting of high school students from the ghetto. The problem of racial prejudice is dealt with primarily in the character Lafferty, but even here the harshness is not total. Basically the story concerns the passage of Louretta Hawkins, adolescent, to Louretta Hawkins, mature youth.

Summary

Fourteen-year-old Louretta Hawkins is walking home from school when she sees a police car cruising to a stop and a big white police officer get out of the car. She runs down the alley and tells the boys the police are after them. The boys leave the alley and move out onto the street, where there are crowds of people; so if they are stopped by the police, there will be witnesses.

The boys thank Louretta and introduce themselves; they are called the "Hawks." After meeting the gang, Louretta becomes their friend and a member of the gang. One day while they are talking, they all decide that what they need is a clubhouse. Louretta's grown-up brother, William, who works in the post office, but who wants to become a printer, is able to find a place to set up a print shop. The place is large enough for the Hawks to use part of it as a clubhouse. Louretta meets Blind Eddie Bell, an old musician, and becomes interested in music through her conversations with him. Her teacher, Mr. Lucitanno, recognizes that she has a certain talent for music and is able to interest Louretta and the Hawks in singing as a group.

One evening when the Hawks are having a dance, Lafferty, a

white policeman who likes to harass the young blacks of the neighborhood, arrives with his new young partner. The two policemen enter the clubhouse and try to break up the dance. In the ensuing melee one of the Hawks is shot by Lafferty's partner. Immediately everyone in the neighborhood is angry and, led by "Fess," a brilliant but bitter black youth, plan a meeting in which they will demand revenge for the shooting. When Jethro, the Hawk gang member who was shot, dies, the demand for revenge against the police intensifies. At Jethro's funeral the Hawks sing a song that is really a poem that "Fess" has written for Jethro. The funeral only increases the anger of the neighborhood and everything seems about to explode.

When three strange white men come to the clubhouse to see Louretta and the Hawks, they are at first thought to be policemen. However, they are not from the police. They have been sent by Louretta's music teacher and represent a record company. The group sings for them and the representatives decide to record them. The group does not have a name. After some deliberation the Hawks decide to call themselves the Soul Brothers and Sister Lou. With the help of Blind Eddie Bell, several songs are arranged, recordings are made, and the group begins to perform as professional singers.

SOUTH TOWN

Kind of work: Novel for young people
Writer: Lorenz Graham
Time: 1950s
Setting: The South
First published: 1958

Important Characters

David Williams—*a sixteen-year-old black youth*
Ed Williams—*David's father*
Mrs. Williams—*David's mother*

South Town

Mr. Boyd—*a white owner of the South Town Auto Agency*
Sam McGavock—*a white mechanic*
Betty Jane—*David's sister*

Comment

This novel for young people shows the situation in which the blacks found themselves following World War II. The blacks returned home but refused to accept their prewar status. Resistance to white oppression was increasing and the blacks were making demands for the rights that were justly theirs. At one point in *South Town* someone mentions that the blacks do not act the same since World War II.

South Town depicts the beginning of a period of intense activity on the part of the blacks, a period that was to culminate in urban insurrections and overt political action.

Summary

David Williams, sixteen, is ambitious and wants to go to college to become a doctor. He lives with his family on a farm near a small southern town. His father, Ed Williams, is a mechanic and is often away from the farm working at his trade. He cannot practice it in his own town for the same wages that white mechanics earn.

One day David saves the life of the town's auto dealer and garage owner, Mr. Boyd. David gets a job at the agency garage for the summer while he waits for his father to come home from working out of town. While he is working at the garage, he becomes friendly with Sam McGavock, an old white mechanic.

When Ed Williams comes home, Mr. Boyd wants him to work at his garage but he will not pay him the same wages he pays the white mechanics. Mr. Williams refuses to work for less pay. Mr. Boyd becomes angry and decides to teach him and the other blacks a lesson. Ed Williams's house is searched and his guns taken away by the local sheriff. Later the Williams's house is attacked and the Williams family fights back with the aid of Sam McGavock, a white mechanic. Shots are fired and one person is badly injured.

Ed Williams is arrested, put in jail, and brought to trial. He is acquitted, but while he was in jail he was badly beaten by the sheriff and his men. Ed Williams recovers but decides he cannot remain in South Town. As the novel ends, the Williams family is moving away.

THE SPORT OF THE GODS

Kind of work: Novel
Writer: Paul Laurence Dunbar
Time: Early 1900s
Setting: A southern town; Harlem, New York
First published: 1902

Important Characters

Berry Hamilton—*a black man*
Fannie Hamilton—*Berry's wife*
Joe Hamilton—*Berry's son*
Kit Hamilton—*Berry's daughter*
Francis Oakly—*Maurice Oakly's brother*
Maurice Oakly—*Berry's white employer*
Hattie Sterling—*a chorus girl*
Minty Brown—*a girl from the Hamilton's hometown*
Bill Thomas—*Joe's New York friend*
Skaggs—*newsman*

Comment

The Sport of the Gods deals with the impact of an urban environment upon immigrants from rural areas, with the beginnings of the Great Migration of blacks out of the South to cities of the North and elsewhere. The author adheres to the "plantation tradition" that everything was simpler in the country. The Hamiltons are removed from their quiet southern home to an urban environment that destroys them. The all-pervading destructiveness of racial prejudice is implicit in the actions of Maurice and Francis Oakly in their framing of Berry. The deliberateness with which it is done is indicative of the hostility and exploitation that blacks faced in their quest for justice.

Structually the novel is defective. There are several melodramatic incidents, some of them quite absurd. The gambler is conveniently killed off and Berry and Fannie are reunited and return home. Joe is a most naive character and seems a bit unreal. In spite of its shortcomings, Dunbar's *Sport of the Gods* was far ahead of its

The Sport of the Gods

time. It was the first novel to try to deal with the more sordid aspect of the black ghetto environment.

Summary

The novel opens with a description of Berry Hamilton and his family, his wife, Fannie, and his children, Joe and Kitty. They live in a small, neat, house adjacent to the mansion of Maurice Oakly, Berry's employer. The Hamiltons are a church-going, money-saving, upwardly-mobile black family. One day Berry Hamilton is accused of stealing five hundred dollars from Francis Oakly. He is arrested, brought to trial, found guilty, and sentenced to ten years in prison. After Berry's imprisonment the Hamilton family is subjected to so much hostility that they move away from the small town to New York.

Upon arriving in New York, the Hamiltons find an apartment in the black ghetto and attempt to sort out their lives. Joe finds a job and with the aid of a new-found friend, Bill Thomas, he begins to explore New York. Bill first takes Joe to the Banner Club, a well-known cabaret. Here he introduces him to Hattie Sterling, one of the chorus girls. Joe becomes enamored of her and begins to make frequent visits to the club. One evening Minty Brown, a young woman from Joe's hometown, comes to the club and tells everyone, including their landlord, the story of the Hamilton family's problems. Joe leaves the apartment.

In spite of the Hamilton's troubles Hattie continues her relationship with Joe. Fannie and Kitty are evicted from their apartment and Fannie loses her job. Joe tells Hattie of their plight and she offers Kitty a job as a chorus girl at the Banner Club, which Kitty accepts. Eventually Hattie tires of Joe and breaks off their relationship. He begins to disintegrate and becomes a drunkard. One evening at the Banner Club, Skaggs, a newspaper reporter, asks Joe about his father's being in prison. Joe tells him the story. After Skaggs leaves, Joe goes to Hattie's apartment and in a drunken rage chokes her to death. He is arrested, tried, convicted, and imprisoned.

Skaggs investigates Berry's case and discovers he had been framed by Maurice Oakly to protect his brother, Francis. When Skaggs confronts Maurice, he admits everything and has a mental breakdown. Berry is freed and returns to find his family in a state of complete disarray. Joe is in jail for murder; Kitty has become a singer and chorus girl; and his wife has married Gibson, a gambler who beats her periodically. Berry wants Fannie to come away with him but she refuses. He finds a job and remains near her. Finally

Gibson is killed in a fight and Fannie is free. She and Berry return to their home in the South. The novel ends with Fannie and Berry sitting on their porch listening to the screams of insane Maurice Oakly.

STRANGER AND ALONE

Kind of work: Novel
Writer: J. Saunders Redding
Time: 1920s-1940s
Setting: The South
First published: 1950

Important Characters

Shelton Howden—*a black college official*
Perkins Wimbush—*president of Arcadia College*
Nan Marriot— *a young woman whom Shelton marries*
Dr. Hubert Posey—*a white professor*
Valerie Tillett—*a girl with whom Shelton falls in love*
Professor Matthew Clarkson—*a black professor*
Gerry Wimbush Rudd—*Perkins's daughter*
Judge Reed—*a white judge*

Comment

In this novel the author explores a subject that has not been dealt with to any great extent. The only other novel that concerns itself with black education in the South prior to 1950 is O'Wendell Shaw's *Greater Need Below*.

Stranger and Alone is a study in betrayal. Shelton Howden not only betrays his people but himself as well. Shelton also destroys his relationship with Valerie Tillett, a girl he falls in love with but cannot win because of his own defective sense of self-worth.

155

Throughout his life Shelton has been brainwashed into thinking of blacks as inferior. Thus when white professor Posey says in his class that blacks are by nature inferior to whites, Shelton either cannot or will not make the effort to find material to contradict him. This subtle racism affects Shelton in such a way that he comes to dislike both ordinary blacks and those who demand their rights. In the end he becomes much like his mentor, Wimbush, and ends in betraying his own people to save himself.

Summary

Shelton Howden enters New Hope College, a black southern college, to prepare for medical school. Since he is of only average intelligence, Shelton is urged to go into a field in line with his abilities.

When he graduates from college, Howden takes a job as a Pullman porter for the summer. He finds that he cannot associate easily with the other porters. He becomes alienated from them and they ridicule him. One evening he is forced by them to drink rotgut whiskey and, in the attempt to avoid his fellow porters, he jumps from a moving train and is badly injured.

Shelton is hospitalized and while he is there a friend of his, Professor Clarkson, arranges for him to get a scholarship to complete his graduate work in New York. Later Shelton takes a teaching job at Arcadia State College in the South. At the college he is strongly influenced by Perkins Wimbush, president of the college, and becomes his assistant. While working with President Wimbush, Shelton meets and falls in love with Gerry Wimbush Rudd the president's beautiful, but slightly wild, daughter. As he continues to work with Wimbush, he is placed in progressively higher positions. Finally he is placed in charge of all of the black schools in the state.

In this capacity he is able to discover what the blacks are planning and doing. He finds out that they are secretly organizing in an attempt to secure voting rights. Shelton discovers when they plan to act. Since he wants to maintain his own position, he goes to the office of Judge Reed to tell the plans that the blacks have made.

THE STREET

Kind of work: Novel
Writer: Ann Petry
Time: 1943
Setting: Harlem, New York
First published: 1946

Important Characters

Lutie Johnson—*a beautiful young black woman*
Mrs. Hedges—*Lutie's neighbor*
Bub Johnson—*Lutie's son*
Boots Smith—*a black musician*
Mr. Jones—*the super in the building where Lutie lives*
Junto—*the white owner of the building where Lutie lives*

Comment

The Street concerns the pressure of ghetto living that keeps those who live there in relentless poverty and, in some instances, completely devoid of hope. No one is exempt from this inexorable pressure. Mr. Jones's lust is a kind of borderline madness that comes to the surface when he tries to drag Lutie into the basement. Mrs. Hedges sees Lutie as a prospective prostitute and Boots Smith views seducing her as a way of getting back at Junto. As a result of all these pressures upon her, Lutie resorts to violence, not so much because she hates Boots Smith but because he is representative of the control of the black ghettos by the whites, in this case by Mr. Junto. On another level Lutie is a stereotype of the black matriarch who survives every adversity while her men are destroyed. Symbolically The Street is not just about beautiful Lutie Johnson being crushed by the ghetto environment; it is also representative of blacks as a group trying to survive under enormous pressure that takes a daily toll.

Summary

Lutie Johnson, a beautiful black young woman, is searching for an apartment in Harlem. She is separated from her husband, whom she had caught with another woman. Lutie finds a shabby apartment consisting of two rooms. Since she is attractive, Lutie soon receives the attentions of hustlers and assorted pimps who live in the ghetto. Three men in particular want her: Mr. Jones, the building super, who has an intense and distasteful lust for her; Mr. Junto, a white man who owns the building where Lutie lives; and Boots Smith, a black musician. Boots Smith offers Lutie a job with a band, but Lutie soon finds out that the band is controlled by Junto and that he intends to have her for his mistress. Lutie's son Bub has gotten into trouble. He winds up in reform school while Lutie is with the band. Boots Smith, the band leader, tries to seduce her. Enraged, Lutie grabs a candlestick and savagely beats Boots to death. As the novel ends, Lutie is on board a train heading for Connecticut to escape from the police.

SULA

Kind of work: Novel
Writer: Toni Morrison
Time: 1920-1965
Setting: Medallion, Ohio
First published: 1974

Important Characters

Sula Peace—*an attractive black woman*
Nel Wright—*Sula's friend*
Jed Greene—*Nel's husband*
Eva Peace—*Sula's grandmother*
Albert Jacks—*one of Sula's lovers*

Comment

The author has managed to compress into this short novel the life of an entire black community in a midwestern town during a forty-five-year-span. The carefully drawn characters live in surroundings of poverty where hope for a better life is almost nonexistant. And yet *Sula* is not a protest novel in the direct sense. The protest that is found is in the disordered lives and environment of the doom-laden characters, from Sula's one-legged grandmother to Nel, who walks behind Sula's coffin and mourns her.

Summary

Preceded by a prelude, the central narrative of the novel concerns Sula's childhood, her meeting with Nel Wright, the beginning of their friendship, and their lives in the town of Medallion, Ohio. One tragic thing that binds them together is that they cause the drowning of a young boy. Nel marries Jed Greene, a handsome young black. Sula leaves Medallion to go to college and eventually move to the West. When she returns to Medallion after ten years, she has become a hardened and somewhat loose woman.

Shortly after her return Sula puts her grandmother in a nursing home for no real reason. She systematically has sexual relations with just about every black husband in Medallion, including Jed, Nel's husband. Gradually the blacks begin to look on Sula as an evil presence. Jed leaves her and she takes Albert Jacks as a lover. Their relationship lasts until she dies. Only Nel mourns her when she is buried.

A Sunday Morning in the South

Kind of work: Play
Writer: Georgia Douglas Johnson
Time: 1924
Setting: The South
First published: 1974

A Sunday Morning in the South

Important Characters

Sue Jones—*a seventy-year-old grandmother*
Tom Griggs—Sue's nineteen-year-old grandson
Bassie Griggs—*Sue's seven-year-old grandson*
Liza Triggs—*Sue's sixty-year-old friend*
Matilda Brown—*Sue's fifty-year-old friend*
A white girl
Two policemen

Comment

This grim little play has a greater impact than one would suspect because of the validity of its statement against lynching. During the period with which the play is concerned there was an almost constant practice of lynching blacks, innocent or not. Even in recent times, as late as 1970 in Augusta, Georgia, during a riot six black men who were not involved in the melee were shot down by the police. One knows from the moment that the police arrive what is going to happen to Tom. The author's message is too close to reality for comfort.

Summary

Sue Jones is in the kitchen of her house cooking Sunday breakfast for her grandsons. She calls them to breakfast. While they are having their meal, Sue's friend, Liza Triggs, comes in. Sue offers her something to eat. Liza mentions that a young white woman had been attacked and the local whites were searching for the black man whom they said was the rapist. While they are talking, there is a knock on the door. When the door is opened, two policemen and a white girl are standing there. One of the policemen asks for Tom Griggs, Sue's grandson. When he comes forward, he is asked where he was the night before.

Tom tells them that he was home and that his grandmother can vouch for him. The police say her word does not count. The girl is brought forward and, in spite of the fact that she is not sure whether Tom is the man who attacked her, she identifies him. Tom is taken away and Sue begins to pray for him. As she is doing this, her friend Matilda comes in to tell Sue that she had seen a mob trying to take Tom away from the police to lynch him. Liza Triggs suggests that Sue send to the good whites of the community to try to get help to

160

save Tom. Sue hears the singing coming from the church nearby and rocks in her rocking chair while her friends try to help by telling her not to worry, that Tom will be coming back any moment. Matilda leaves on the run, then suddenly returns with the news that Tom has been lynched.

TEACUP FULL OF ROSES

Kind of work: Novel for young people
Writer: Sharon Bell Mathis
Time: 1970
Setting: a large city
First published: 1972

Important Characters

Joe Brooks—*a seventeen year-old black youth*
Isaac Brooks—*Joe's father*
Mattie Brooks—*Joe's mother*
David Brooks—*Joe's younger brother*
Paul Brooks—*Joe's older brother*
Ellie—*Joe's girl*
Warwick—*a black gangster*
Aunt Lou—*Joe's aunt*

Comment

This short novel illustrates the positive and negative aspects of love among the members of a black family in an urban ghetto. The positive aspects of love and affection are displayed in Joe's love for his brilliant younger brother, David; the negative aspects are revealed in the love Mattie Brooks shows for Paul, love given at the expense of Joe and David.

The strength and weakness that the Brooks family displays and the obstacles they must face almost daily are shown. Paul is trapped by heroin and is helpless when Joe tries to regain the money that Paul had given to Warwick, the pusher. The Brooks family is catapulted into a tragic situation when David, the bright star, is lost. In a very real sense the entire family is severely diminished by the loss.

Summary

Joe Brooks, who is about to graduate from high school, is waiting with his father and David, his fourteen-year-old brother, for Mrs. Brooks to come home with the oldest son, Paul, who has been in the hospital for heroin addiction. A special meal is being prepared for him. Joe is not sure Paul is cured and he leaves the house to find Warwick, a local cheap gangster and drug pusher, to warn him to stay away from Paul. He meets some of the young blacks that hang around Warwick and has to fight one of them. He manages to get away and head for home. On the way he meets Paul. After talking to Paul he goes to visit his girl, Ellie. When he returns home, he hears his mother arguing with Mr. Brooks and condemning Joe because he did not bring Paul home. When he talks to his brother again, Joe is convinced that he is not cured.

He is very fond of his younger brother, David, and wants to see that he gets a good start in his young life. Mrs. Brooks gives all her attention to Paul so Joe tries to guide Davey and give him advice. Mrs. Brooks has an argument with Joe. He decides to leave home to join the navy. Joe goes to the bank and draws out what money he has to buy gifts for everyone before he goes into the navy. His mother refuses hers because Joe refuses to stay and look after Paul. Ellie and David go to Joe's graduation ceremony. While they are there, Paul finds the remaining money that Joe had hidden and goes to Warwick. Joe and David go to find Warwick to get the money back but in the gun fight that follows David is shot and killed. Joe stands crying as the novel ends.

THEIR EYES WERE WATCHING GOD

Kind of work: Novel
Writer: Zora Neal Hurston
Time: 1930s
Setting: Florida
First published: 1937

Important Characters

Janie Starks—*a beautiful black woman*
Logan Killicks—*Janie's first husband*
Joe Starks—*Janie's second husband*
Virgil Woods (Teacake)—*Janie's lover and third husband*
Phoebe Watson—*Janie's closest friend*
Nanny—*Janie's grandmother*

Comment

The story of Janie Starks is basically the story of a woman's attempt to fulfill herself and the men who either hinder or help her in this effort. Logan Killicks, Janie's first husband, sees her only as a woman to care for him and help him farm his land. He wants her to work in the fields as he does. He cares nothing for her feelings and makes no effort to understand her as a person. When Janie meets Joe Starks, she thinks she has found someone who will want her for herself. However, she discovers that even though she lives with him for twenty years, Joe sees her as the mistress of his house and the mayor's wife and nothing else. Janie's opinion is never sought and is often rejected when it is offered. It is only when Joe dies and Janie meets Teacake that she begins to fulfill herself as a person.

Teacake is a happy-go-lucky, itinerant farm worker and gambler. He leads a haphazard existence. He is ten years younger than Janie, yet he accepts her for what she is. He makes no demands upon her and provides the love and understanding she is seeking. She in turn loves him desperately and goes with him wherever he goes. She is shattered when she has to shoot him in self-defense. The problem of race in this novel is not prominent, but rather subordinate to the story of Janie and her quest for love and understanding.

163

Their Eyes Were Watching God

Summary

Janie Starks returns to her hometown after a two-year absence. Everyone wonders what happened to her during that time. It is known only that Janie left town with a new lover much younger than herself. Janie has only been back in town a short while when her friend Phoebe Watson comes to her house to bring her some food. After the meal the two women sit on Janie's back porch and Janie tells Phoebe about her life and what has happened to her since she left the town.

Janie begins with her life with her grandmother, who cared for her since she was a baby. Janie's mother was only seventeen when Janie was born and abandoned her soon after. One day when Janie was sixteen her grandmother saw her kissing a young boy and called her in the house to tell her about her mother. Nanny is afraid that Janie will follow the same path. She urges her to marry a local farmer, Logan Killicks, who is in love with her. Janie marries Killicks but remains with him only a short time. She meets Joe Starks and in a short while leaves Logan Killicks to marry Starks. She goes with him to a small, all-black town in Florida. Joe Starks becomes involved in the life of the town as its leading citizen and businessman and finally, mayor. Janie lives the respectable life of Mrs. Starks for twenty years. Then Joe dies and she is left alone. She continues to operate Joe's general store for a while. One day she meets Virgil Woods, better known as "Teacake," and in a short time he becomes Janie's lover.

Teacake asks her to leave town and come to him in Jacksonville because he has found work. Janie leaves her home of twenty years and goes to him. She takes with her two hundred dollars emergency money. She arrives in Jacksonville, where Teacake is waiting for her, and they are married. One morning she wakes to find her money and Teacake gone. She thinks that he has stolen it and run away. Teacake had used the money to give a huge party. Next day after the party Teacake tells Janie that he is going to give her the two hundred dollars back. He is able to do this from his winnings in a dice game. Although Teacake wins the money in the game, he gets into a fight with one of the players and is hurt. He gives Janie the two hundred dollars that he borrowed and she dresses his wounds. After his injuries are healed, Teacake tells her that they are going to the Everglades in southern Florida to work as migrant workers.

By the time they reach the farming region, Janie and Teacake have become almost inseparable. Teacake teaches Janie how to shoot a rifle, hunt, and fish. They work in the fields together and go hunting and fishing often. One evening the workers notice the animals around the farming regions are leaving because of an impending hurricane. A number of workers leave but Teacake decides to stay. He and Janie are caught in the storm. Janie is attacked by a mad dog. Teacake kills the animal but not before he is bitten on the cheek. Janie tries to get medical attention for Teacake. They reach the city of Palm Beach but Teacake and other blacks are pressed into service to clean up after the storm and bury the dead. The wound on his face goes untreated. After he returns to Janie, Teacake becomes steadily worse because the dog that bit him was rabid. Janie tries to take care of him and finally Teacake allows a doctor to look at him. He is given medicine but it is too late. He becomes delirious and tries to kill Janie. She shoots and kills him in self-defense. Janie is put on trial and acquitted. She buries Teacake and returns to her home town.

They That Sit in Darkness

Kind of work: Play
Writer: Mary Burill
Time: 1919
Setting: The rural South
First published: 1919

Important Characters

Malinda Jasper—*the mother*
Linda, Miles, Aloyius, Mary Ellen, Jimmie, John Henry (a week-old infant)—*Malinda's children*
Elizabeth Shaw—*a visiting nurse*

Comment

In this unusual little drama the author is dealing with a subject that was taboo during the period the play was written. It is a play for

women, and in fact the only males in it are the boy children. Mr.
Jasper never appears. The basic point of this piece is that poor
people should be taught how to practice birth control rather than
have many more children than they can properly care for. Several of
the Jasper children are not as healthy as they should be and are often
hungry. The subject of race is not discussed at all.

Summary

Mrs. Jasper, thirty-eight years old, and her oldest child, Linda,
seventeen, are washing tubs of clothes, which Mrs. Jasper takes in
to help Mr. Jasper care for the seven children. Mr. Jasper works hard
to care for his family but barely makes ends meet. While they are
washing clothes, Mrs. Jasper complains of having pains and takes
tablets prescribed for her by her doctor. The children are hungry
and there is no money to buy milk for them. They go to bed hungry.
Elizabeth Shaw, a visiting nurse, arrives and is immediately alarmed that Mrs. Jasper has gotten up from bed so soon after giving birth
to her latest child, who is only a week old. The nurse wants her to get
to bed immediately, but Mrs. Jasper refuses. She tells Elizabeth
Shaw about her daughter's going to Tuskeegee. Linda has been
packing her trunk to leave the next day.

Miss Shaw tells Mrs. Jasper that she must not perform so many
heavy tasks because childbearing has weakened her heart, but Mrs.
Jasper says that she must work because they need the money. Miss
Shaw explains that she must be careful about having more children
and apologizes for not being able to tell her about birth control
because of the law of the state. Finally the nurse is able to get Mrs.
Jasper to bed. Linda continues to pack her trunk. While she is doing
this, the children come in and Linda tells them of her plans after
college and everyone is happy. Suddenly the nurse rushes into the
room and calls for Linda to go for the doctor because Mrs. Jasper's
condition has grown quite serious. Before she can leave, Miss Shaw
calls to tell her it is too late. Mrs. Jasper has died. Linda tells her
brother to go and meet the father and realizes that she will not need
her trunk now.

THE THIRD LIFE OF GRANGE COPELAND

Kind of work: Novel
Writer: Alice Walker
Time: 1960s
Setting: Rural Georgia, Greene County
First published: 1970

Important Characters

Grange Copeland—*a black sharecropper*
Josey—*Grange's wife*
Margaret—*Grange's first wife*
Brownfield Copeland—*Grange's son*
Mem—*Brownfield's wife*
Daphney, Ornett, Ruth—*Brownfield's children*
Shipley—*a white man*

Comment

This novel is about survival, both spiritual and physical. Although Brownfield Copeland brutalizes his wife, Mem, he cannot break her spirit. He literally kills her trying to do it. It is Mem who finds the house in the town and a job to support everyone. The men, too, are concerned with survival. When Grange Copeland goes to New York as a young man, he is forced to do almost anything to survive. Until the child Ruth comes to live with him, Grange is a selfish man whom one would not expect to change. He has abandoned his own children; and even when he returned home from New York, he continued to ignore his son, Brownfield, as he had always done. When Ruth arrives, Grange undergoes a change and becomes more compassionate. He tries to do for her what he did not do for his son, Ruth's father, Brownfield. This change helped negate some of the hatred he felt for himself and those around him.

Summary

Grange Copeland is entertaining relatives from the city on his farm. He is a hardworking sharecropper but he is taciturn and has no positive relationship with his son, Brownfield, who stands in

167

awe of him. Grange continues to eke out a living as a sharecropper until he and his wife fight and part company for good. Margaret poisons herself and her illegitimate child. Grange goes to New York to live for awhile. He does almost anything to survive. After Grange leaves, Shipley, a white landowner persuades Brownfield to become a sharecropper, but he decides to run away. He wanders until he meets and marries Mem, a pretty young woman, who is much better educated than he is. He then becomes a sharecropper permanently. Under the stress of sharecropping Brownfield becomes brutal and mean. he beats Mem horribly and neglects her and his children. He continues in this manner until Mem threatens him with a shotgun.

Grange Copeland returns, buys a small farm, and marries again. Mem finds a house in the nearby town and takes a job since Brownfield does not have any income. Brownfield resents her superiority over him and continues to brutalize her. Finally he murders her and is sent to prison. His father takes the little girl Ruth to live with him and a warm relationship develops between the two. While in prison Brownfield broods over the fact that his father is raising his child. When he is finally released, he sues Grange for custody of Ruth; but she does not want to live with him. However, he insists that she do so. Grange shoots Brownfield right in the courtroom.

THIS CHILD'S GONNA LIVE

Kind of work: Novel
Writer: Sarah E. Wright
Time: 1930s
Setting: Tangierneck, Maryland
First published: 1969

Important Characters

Jacob—*a farmer*
Mariah—*Jacob's wife*

Vyella—*Jacob's sister*
Rabbit, Skeeter, William—*Jacob and Mariah's children*
Al Jefferson—*Jacob's friend*
Miss Bonnie—*A landowner*

Comment

This Child's Gonna Live is a protest novel that emphasizes the intense racial prejudice that the blacks have encountered. Jacob meets discrimination at almost every turn and the unrelenting poverty combined with the race prejudice takes its psychological toll from Jacob and Mariah. Nightriders visit Jacob and his father is lynched, but he and Mariah continue to survive. The author portrays Mariah as the strong-willed character who sees Jacob as a "going nowhere man"; yet it is Jacob who saves her.

The novel is very well written and the author uses stream of consciousness to provide a view of the emotional upheaval in the minds of the characters, especially Mariah and Jacob. It leaves a distinct awareness of the barren, unsavory existence they and other blacks face in Tangierneck, where there is a complete absence of hope in escaping grinding poverty.

Summary

Jacob and Mariah are awakening. Jacob gets up to begin chores on the small plot of land from which they try to earn a living. Mariah is pregnant, yet she works in the fields in spite of Jacob's insistance that she is not to do so. Mariah wants Jacob to leave the farm and move to the city, but he refuses to do this even though his brothers have all abandoned the land. Jacob's ownership of the land is in doubt; and he owes money to Miss Bonnie, who says that Jacob's father's land belongs to her. Since he cannot earn money from his farm, Jacob takes Mariah and his children and tries to find work in the factories that might hire blacks.

While he is going from place to place trying to find work, his father is arrested and charged with the murder of Miss Bonnie, even though there is no real proof that this is true. Mariah in her pregnant condition stays with Jacob though all the turmoil that he faces. She is determined that the child she is carrying will survive even though she has lost one child. Her son, Rabbit, dies on Jacob's travels in search of work. Mariah and Jacob return to Tangierneck poorer than before, but they have the land because Miss Bonnie left a will

Tired

returning the land to Jacob's father. Jacob's sister dies and Jacob takes in her children.

Mariah becomes despondent and tries to drown herself. She finds that the water is too cold, and before she can drown Jacob rescues her and scolds her for wading in that water when she is unable to swim. He does not know that she tried to commit suicide. Wet and cold, Mariah returns to the cabin to fix breakfast for Jacob and the children. They both continue to try to eke out a living from their land and to escape from the relentless poverty that faces them.

TIRED

Kind of work: Poem
Writer: Fenton Johnson

Comment

In the poem "Tired," a new and very desolate tone is sounded. The poet does not write in dialect about happy times on the plantation; there is a note of complete dispair throughout the entire poem. Fenton Johnson's poetry was no doubt influenced by the work of Edgar Lee Masters and Carl Sandburg of the Chicago School.

Summary

Written in free verse, the poem illustrates the poet's attitude of disillusion and despair with American civilization as black Americans know it. The protagonist and his wife will stop working for whites, abandon their home, and toss the children in the river because it is better for them to die than grow up and face the intense racial prejudice that awaits them. They will then spend their days and nights drinking at the local gin mill to escape the misery, poverty, and wretchedness that surrounds them.

THE TRUE AMERICAN

Kind of work: Novel
Writer: Melvin Van Peebles
Time: The present
Setting: Heaven; Hell; the United States
First published: 1976

Important Characters

George Abraham Carver (Abe)—*a black chain-gang prisoner*
Dave Stock—*a fur trapper*
The Devil—*ruler of Hell*
Dogface—*Abe's friend in Hell*

Comment

This ribald satire pokes fun at almost every American attitude, racial, political, or ethical. There is a United States section of Hell where all the negative racial attitudes directed against the blacks are in evidence. The Devil is portrayed as a swinging, calculating director of Hell and is constantly seeking ways to expand the misery of those under his control. He smokes oparajuana, a mixture of opium and marijuana, and organizes orgies for his department heads. He creates a riot by parading beautiful naked white women before black males.

The meals are all soul food, which the blacks love and whites hate. Neither Jesus nor Heaven are immune from the author's savage attacks. When Abe Carver dies the first time, his last words are "Jesus Christ"; and Christ, in the form of an office manager who checks the new arrivals into Heaven or sends them to Hell, answers, "yea." Abe gets to know Christ well since he is killed three times and goes to Heaven each time to be checked in. The portrayal of Dave Stock is almost savage. He is seen as progressing from an ignorant, illiterate lout to a money-grabbing businessman in the American tradition. As he progresses, he picks up all the worst traits of this breed of man. Dave even acquires a psychiatrist; he becomes "a true American."

The True American

Summary

As the novel opens, George Abraham Carver, an ignorant, rural black man, is sent to the chain gang as the result of a fight. Shortly after he is imprisoned, he and a fellow inmate, Dogface, attempt to escape; but Dogface is killed and Abe is returned to the chain gang. One day while working in a rock quarry, Abe is killed in a rock slide. He wakes up in Heaven. When it is discovered that he does not belong there, he is sent to Hell.

Upon arriving in Hell, he meets his old friend, Dogface, and a white man, Dave Stock, who had been a fur trapper on earth. Dave and Abe become friends. After being in Hell a while, Abe Carver decides that he wants to return to earth. The Devil, who is always trying to reorganize and modernize his realm to increase the misery of Hell's inhabitants, discovers that Abe Carver's hymn-singing made all the denizens of Hell feel so bad that the misery meters set a new record.

Dave Stock and Abe have a conference with the Devil and the Devil agrees to allow Abe and Dave to return to earth. Illiterate and dumb, Dave arrives in Chicago in the middle of the Great Depression. Abe Carver goes back to Georgia; but after an encounter with a white man, he flees to Chicago to find Dave.

Dave finds a job as a dishwasher in a restaurant. He meets a beautiful girl names Suzannita and falls in love with her. Abe arrives in Chicago and finds his way to the black ghetto. He goes to a house rent-party, where he meets a beautiful black woman. Her boyfriend objects to Abe's attention to her and he and Abe fight. Abe is stabbed to death and wakes up in Heaven again. He is promptly sent back to Hell. The Devil has modernized Hell to the extent that its inhabitants are more miserable than ever and after a short stay Abe is ready to give earth another try. Abe teaches the Devil a new dance and makes another deal to return to earth; however, the Devil tricks him and sends him back just as World War II begins. Abe is drafted and fights all the way through the war facing racism and prejudice on every side.

After the war ends, Abe returns to Chicago and accidentally meets Dave Stock, who by this time has educated himself, become a businesman, made a fortune, and married Suzannita. He thinks Abe is trying to blackmail him over some crooked business deals he has made. Dave gives Abe a large sum of money. Abe does not know what the money is for but he takes it and leaves for the South to become a freedom rider. When the civil rights struggle begins, Abe joins it and winds up in jail. One morning a white sheriff arrives, takes Abe out of his cell, and turns him over to a mob, which promptly kills him. As the novel ends, Abe is on his way to Hell again.

TRUMBULL PARK

Kind of work: Novel
Writer: Frank London Brown
Time: 1950s
Setting: Chicago
First published: 1959

Important Characters

Louis Buggy Martin—*a black worker*
Helen Martin—*Buggy's wife*
Carl Burton, Arthur Davis, Harry. Harvey, Kevin Robinson—*Buggy's friends and heads of the various black families in Trumbull Park*

Comment

Trumbull Park depicts the psychological development of Buggy Martin as he lives under the constant pressure of racism and white mob harassment. Buggy Martin grows stronger psychologically and becomes less fearful, although at times he shows signs of weakness. He breaks down and cries at one point when the white mob jeers at him while he is being taken to work in a police patrol wagon. Buggy's fears disappear as he and the other men walk through the white mob to work.

Summary

A child falls to its death from the fourth floor porch of the shabby tenement house where Louis Buggy Martin lives. He decides to move his family out of the tenement and into Trumbull Park, a public housing project on the South Side of Chicago in an area largely inhabited by whites. As soon as black families move into the project, trouble begins.

The white inhabitants do not want the black families to stay in Trumbull Park and try to drive them out. Rocks and even bombs are thrown through the windows of the homes of these families. Under the pressure of this kind of attack, Buggy Martin and the other black men are taken to their jobs in police patrol wagons and their homes are under police guard twenty-four hours a day. As a result of the almost continuous violence, some of the blacks move from Trumbull Park; but Buggy Martin and his friends choose to remain. Buggy becomes the leader of the group of blacks who choose to stay. At a meeting of the black men of Trumbull Park it is decided that they will not go to work in the police patrols; they will walk. As the novel ends, Buggy and his friends walk through a hostile white mob on their way to work.

Two Love Stories
(Basketball Game)

Kind of work: Novella
Writer: Julius Lester
Time: 1956
Setting: Nashville, Tennessee
First published: 1972

Important Characters

Allen Anderson—*a fourteen-year-old black youth*
Reverend Anderson—*Allen's father*
Mrs. Anderson—*Allen's mother*
Rebecca Van—*a fourteen-year-old white girl*

Comment

In *Basketball Game* Allen and Rebecca become friends, only to be forced apart by something they cannot control. At the time the story takes place, integration was unheard of in the South and humiliation and intimidation of blacks was a matter of course. Allen is able to integrate the local public library; but he cannot do anything about his relationship with Rebecca, which is destroyed by the racial climate that existed at that time.

Summary

As the novella *Basketball Game* begins, Reverend Anderson and his family have just moved to Nashville, Tennessee. Soon after they arrive, Allen meets a fourteen-year-old white girl who is his next-door neighbor. Allen and Rebecca become friends and he tells her about his desire to become an artist. When Reverend Anderson buys Allen a basketball hoop, Allen and Rebecca play basketball with one another. One day Allen goes to the public library but is told he cannot use it. A librarian who is a northerner gives him a card anyway.

One afternoon Rebecca and Allen walk to the nearby university, where he will paint a picture. An old black man working there calls Allen aside and tells him that he should not be seen with a white girl because it will cause him nothing but trouble. Rebecca's father comes to Allen's house to warn Allen's father that he must stop his son from seeing Rebecca.

As the summer wears on, Allen and Rebecca continue to see each other and play basketball. One day Rebecca tells Allen that they are moving away because her father does not want Allen to see her anymore since he is a black youth. Allen is hurt but tells her that he will not forget her. While shopping for Christmas, Allen sees Rebecca again in a department store. He calls to her but she does not answer him. He goes home and asks his father to take down the basketball hoop. As the hoop is being taken down, Allen bursts into tears and the story ends.

UNDERTOW

Kind of work: Play
Writer: Eulalie Spence
Time: 1929
Setting: Harlem, New York
First published: 1929

Important Characters

Dan Peters—*a black man*
Hattie—*Dan's wife*
Charley—*Dan and Hattie's son*
Clem Jackson—*the other woman*
Mrs. Wilkes—*a boarder*

Comment

Undertow is a play in which the problem of race is not involved. The author presents a universal love triangle. The triangular relationship exists between Dan Peters, an incredibly downtrodden man, so downtrodden as to seem unreal; his wife, Hattie, a stubborn, stern, vicious, and awfully mean woman; and Clem, who is gentle and loving. In the end Dan vents his rage by killing Hattie, but he destroys his relationship with Clem and seals his own fate in the process. He gets Clem out of the house before he presumably turns himself in.

Summary

Hattie is sitting in the dining room of her boardinghouse in Harlem. She is talking to her somewhat scapegrace son, Charley, who needs five dollars. Charley notices that his father, Dan Peters, has not come home for supper. In the ensuing conversation Charley hints that he knows why Dan is late and that if Hattie will give him five dollars he will tell her something about Dan. Hattie gives him the money and Charley tells her that he saw Dan meet a woman he knew on the street about a week before. Hattie has an idea who the woman is. Charley laughs at her and leaves. Dan comes home and asks for his supper, but Hattie tells him there is none for him. He goes out to get something to eat.

After Dan leaves the house, a boarder, Mrs. Wilkes, comes in to tell Hattie that there is a woman waiting for her in the living room. Hattie takes off her apron and goes in. The woman is Clem, who has loved Dan before he married Hattie. She asks Hattie to divorce Dan so she can marry him and make him happy. Hattie refuses. While the women are talking, Dan comes in and sees Clem. Clem wants Hattie to free Dan because she can no longer just run away with him because of the effect it will have on her own daughter's coming marriage. Dan asks Clem to leave the house with him. At this point Hattie threatens to tell Clem's daughter everything. Dan becomes angry and tells Hattie to be quiet. However, when Hattie not only will not be quiet but begins to call Clem harsh names, Dan grabs Hattie by the throat and chokes her violently. Finally he throws Hattie to the floor. In the process Hattie strikes her head on the base of a mantlepiece and dies. Dan hurries Clem out of the house. He returns and discovers that Hattie is dead. As the play ends, he stands looking at Hattie's body.

THE VULTURE

Kind of work: Novel
Writer: Gil-Scott Heron
Time: 1969
Setting: New York
First published: 1970

Important Characters

John Lee—*a seventeen-year-old black youth*
Eddie Shannon ("Spade")—*an eighteen-year-old black youth*
Tommy Hall ("Afro")—*a seventeen-year-old black youth*
Ivan Quinn ("I.Q.")—*a nineteen-year-old black youth*
Junior Jones—*a sixteen-year-old black youth*
Ricky Manning—*a friend of I.Q.'s*

The Vulture

Comment

The Vulture is about drugs, their sale and use. Implicit in the portrayal of the four young black men is the knowledge of the extent to which drug pushers, users, and assorted other dissolute individuals pervade the black ghettos to prey upon those who live there. The tendrils of the drug business are spread through the ghettos, numbing the spirit of the young and taking their lives. Each of the protagonists is in some way involved with drugs, either as a user or a dealer. The portraits of these young men are uncomfortably close to reality and cannot be lightly brushed aside.

Summary

The police are examining the corpse of a young black man lying in an alley. Using flashback techniques the ideas of each of four protagonists are revealed and tell the story of the young black man lying dead in an alley. "Spade" Eddie Shannon at eighteen is "The Man" or leading dope pusher in the area where he lives. His friends are "Afro" Tommy Hall, a college-educated black man who is a part-time black nationalist with a plan to corner and establish a monopoly over the drug business in the black ghetto, "I.Q." Ivan Quinn, a student at Columbia University and one of the street gang, and Junior Jones, seventeen, who burns a police car to prove that he has heart.

The dead young black man, John Lee, made the mistake of trying to play both ends against the middle by being both a pusher and a blackmailer. The novel follows each protagonist in his daily pattern of living to show the savage obstacles they each encounter. It is I.Q. who sees the destruction that is rampant in the ghetto but even so is caught up in it. One day in the park I.Q. meets a beautiful young white girl and eventually they become lovers. This relationship upsets I.Q.'s friend, Ricky Manning, who then kills a drug pusher and frames I.Q. Junior Jones becomes suspicious of Ricky and tricks him into revealing the truth. As Junior Jones is trying to decide what to do next, Ricky jumps eight floors to his death. It is revealed that John Lee was killed because he tried to hold out on his payment to his supplier.

White Face

Kind of work: Novel
Writer: Carl Offord
Time: 1940s
Setting: Rural Georgia; Harlem, New York
First published: 1943

Important Characters

Chris Woods—*a sharecropper*
Nella Woods—*Chris's wife*
Harris—*a white overseer*
Cousin May—*Chris's relative in New York*
Chester May—*Cousin May's husband*
Manny—*an agitator*
Baby Love—*Chris and Nella's child*
Marvin Wallman—*a lawyer*

Comment

One thing that is pointed out immediately in *White Face* is that the transition from rural to urban life for poor blacks is extremely difficult. Chris and Nella discover that life in the North is not as easy for blacks as it seems to be. The hostility of the ghetto environment causes Chris to become intense, embittered, and violent. He rebels against all the injustices perpetrated upon him by lashing out in all directions. Even his wife, Nella, is not immune from his anger.

Chris becomes the stereotype of the mean brute black running amuck in the city. Nella becomes a portrait of the enduring black woman who is the soul of patience while Manny is representative of evil incarnate. Chris does not really understand that Manny, in his way, is abusing him just as the whites do. The effects of the savage racism strips Chris of his manhood with no chance for redress. He becomes a kind of rural Bigger Thomas striking out in all his savagery in an attempt to regain a positive self-concept.

Summary

Chris Woods is on his way to see Mr. Harris, the white overseer of the plantation on which he is a sharecropper. Chris asks Harris for his fair share and an accounting because he feels he has been cheated. Harris strikes Chris with a whip and Chris beats him very badly and flees. He gathers his family, Nella, his wife, and their baby daughter and Tommy, his brother-in-law, and runs away to his cousin May's. They are taken in, but this arrangement does not work. Problems arise, and Chris and his family move to a small shabby apartment. Chris is unable to find work; and because he is afraid the authorities are searching for him for what he thinks is his killing of Harris, he goes out only at night. Nella finds work as a domestic in the Bronx and Chris remains home to care for Baby Love, who is ill.

As a result of this situation Chris becomes embittered. In his nocturnal rovings he meets Manny, a black fascist agitator, and feels that Nella will betray him. Although she is really trying to help him, he plans to kill her. One day he follows her and attacks Marvin Wallman, a Jewish lawyer to whom Nella had gone for help. He beats Wallman severely and tries to escape but is captured and imprisoned. Manny and the black fascist group claim that Chris was merely protecting Nella from Wallman, who was trying to rape her. But Chris is also charged with the murder of Harris, who died after Chris ran away from the Georgia plantation.

Nella decides to tell the truth about the Wallman incident in spite of threats on her life by Manny and his group. She enlists the help of the Colored Congress, an NAACP-like organization. In prison Chris becomes even more embittered and his hatred for Nella intensifies. When she visits him, he curses her. He tries to grab a guard's pistol and is shot dead on the spot.

WHITE MARBLE LADY

Kind of work: Novel
Writer: Roi Ottley
Time: 1938-1945
Setting: Harlem, New York
First published: 1965

Important Characters

Jeff Kirby—*a young black, highly trained musician*
Deborah Comstock—*a beautiful, wealthy, young white woman*
Perky Sparhawk—*the owner of the Back Door Lounge*
Knox Gilbert—*a friend of Deborah's*
Abbie Comstock—*Deborah's mother*

Comment

White Marble Lady shows the intense pressures under which a black and white marriage exists. Both Jeff and Deborah begin to feel the pressures even before they are married. Deborah is forced to move from her apartment when it is discovered that her boyfriend is a black man. The author examines the psychological as well as the social ramifications of the mixed marriage and finds that racism pervades every aspect of such a relationship.

Summary

Jeff Kirby is visiting with his friend, Perky Sparhawk, the owner of the Back Door Lounge, a Harlem nightclub, where both blacks and whites go. Jeff, a Julliard Music School graduate, is a musician and composer who sometimes plays at the Back Door. As the evening wears on, Jeff begins playing the piano. While he is playing, he notices a beautiful young white woman enter with Knox Gilbert, an agent and promoter for black entertainers who work at the Back Door.

Gilbert goes to talk to Perky Sparhawk and leaves the young woman alone. Thinking that she is completely alone, a young black man tries to pick her up. Jeff Kirby sees what is going to happen and intercedes. He introduces himself and talks to Deborah Comstock until her escort returns, then he returns to his piano.

Deborah Comstock is strongly attracted to Kirby and later they meet again when Knox Gilbert becomes Jeff Kirby's agent. Jeff and Deborah fall in love and marry; their respective families try to break up their relationship. Jeff Kirby becomes famous as a singer and composer and is known as the Tan Troubador. Deborah's family practically disowns her. When World War II breaks out, Jeff goes into the army to entertain the troops. Very often Deborah is left alone and her family prevents her from trying to contact Jeff. Under the stress and pressures of her family, Deborah has a mental breakdown and dies. As the novel closes, the war is over and Jeff Kirby returns to the Back Door Lounge to see his old friend, Perky.

PART II

A Short Companion
for Afro-American Literature and History

AFRICAN FREE SCHOOLS   Blacks in the early United States encountered difficulties in educating their children. In many instances it was necessary for the blacks to establish their own schools because they were prevented from sending their children to the schools for whites. One of the best known of these separate school systems was the African Free Schools of New York. African Free School #1 was opened in 1787 at 245 Williams Street. There were forty children in the first class. The subjects taught were reading, writing, arithmetic, and the manual and domestic arts. A class in navigation was taught as well. During the first ten years, the number of students was never greater than sixty. However, by 1820 African Free School #1 had enrolled over five-hundred children and a second school, African School #2, was opened. These schools were established and controlled by the New York Manumission Society. In 1834, when it became necessary for the society to affiliate the African Free Schools with those under the control of the Public School Society, there were fourteen hundred black students in the schools.

AFRICAN GROVE, THE   In 1816-1817 there were over ten thousand free blacks in New York City. They had nearly all been freed when New York State abolished slavery in 1790. Because of racial prejudice, the blacks did not have places of entertainment to which they could go in their leisure moments. To remedy this situation, Mr. Henry Brown, a retired steward on a Liverpool liner, rented or leased in 1817 a house on Thomas Street. He renovated it and established a small tea garden at the rear of the property. Here the blacks were able to relax and were entertained by singers and musicians. Various foods and drinks could be purchased as well. This tea garden became known as the African Grove. A rather negative and somewhat racist description of this place of amusement for blacks appeared in the *National Advocate,* a New York City newspaper, on August 3, 1821. The African Grove was closed around 1822 or 1823.

AFRICAN SURVIVALS   During the transition from freedom in Africa to slavery in the United States, the blacks were separated from their African cultural tradition and many of their former customs were obliterated. However, some scholars believe that traces of these customs and traditions have survived in the form of words and stories. Others believe that all cultural traces have been completely lost. Two scholars who represented opposing views on this subject were E. Franklin Frazier (1894-1962), who believed that all African traditions had failed to remain intact under the pressure of slavery, and Melville J. Herskovitz (1895-1963), who represented the opposite view. Herskovitz felt that African culture did survive and that these survivals were clearly evident in the black oral tradition. This particular controversy is still very much alive today.

AFRICAN THEATER, THE   In 1816-1817 Mr. Henry Brown established in New York City a tea garden for free blacks. It was located on Thomas Street and was a successful business venture. The African Grove, as the establishment was called, became so popular as a center of entertainment that Mr. Brown decided to open a regular theater with black actors playing the parts in the plays. The small theater that seated three-hundred to four-hundred people was built in 1821 at Mercer and Bleeker streets. It was known or came to be known as the African Theater. Its success was immediate and whites began to attend in large numbers. However, they did not wish to be seated with the blacks, so Mr. Brown consented to set aside a section for whites. The African Theater and the African Grove were both closed during the early 1820s. The reason given for the closing of the little theater was that the whites in the audiences became so riotous that they were a public nuisance. An article that appeared in *The American,* a New York City newspaper, on January 10, 1822, indicates that the African Theater was closed because it had become a successful rival for the white-owned Park Theater that had been established in 1790.

AFRO-AMERICAN LEAGUE   During the last quarter of the nineteenth century the blacks felt the need to find some way to combat the racial prejudice that they encountered almost everywhere in the United States. On May 28, 1887, in the *Freeman,* a black newspaper, in an editorial T. Thomas Fortune issued a call to prominent blacks urging them to meet in convention to try to devise a means by which the blacks could fight more effectively for their rights. Because of the elections of 1888, the convention was not held. However, in November 1889, a second call was sent out and on December 22 a conference was held in Chicago. As a result of the conference deliberations, the Afro-American League was organized for the express purpose of fighting for the rights of the blacks in the United States.

AFRO-AMERICAN PUBLISHING COMPANY, INC.   Established in 1965 and based in Chicago, this company is concerned with educational publishing; and their output is geared to schools on both the elementary and secondary levels. Its purpose is to produce and publish materials for Afro-American and African studies. The company publishes both paperbacks and hardcover books as well as various kinds of multimedia kits using pictures, tapes, filmstrips, and records.

ALBANY MOVEMENT, THE (1961-1962)   During a period of five days, December 12-16, about seven hundred and fifty blacks were arrested as a result of a series of mass marches on city hall in Albany, Georgia. These street demonstrations were in protest against the trial of several "freedom riders" who had attempted to desegregate the white waiting room of the Georgia Central Railway station. Among those arrested on December 16 was one of the protest leaders, Dr. Martin Luther King. The demonstration leaders called off the December 18 march as the result of an agreement with the city officials on a plan to release, temporarily, those who had been arrested and to desegregate bus and railroad facilities. Included in the plan were meetings to discuss other integration measures. Blacks agreed to halt mass protests for sixty days while the city undertook to carry out its part of the agreement. On July 10, Dr. King was sentenced to forty-five days in prison for taking part in the protest. King had rejected the alternative of paying a fine. However, an unknown person paid the fine and Dr. King was released on July 12, 1962. Protest demonstrations that began because of Dr. King's arrest led to further mass arrests of blacks. On July 16, the officials of the Albany City Commission stated that there would be no further negotiations with the demonstration leaders. Dr. King was arrested on July 27 while leading a "prayer vigil" in public. He was released on August 10. At King's trial the judge stated that segregation would not be enforced in public places. The day after the trial of Dr. King, the blacks set out to test this statement. They tried to use public libraries and parks reserved for whites. The police promptly closed these facilities. A long stalemate followed these last demonstrations and the city refused to negotiate or to open public facilities. In turn the blacks organized a boycott of public buses that forced the Cities Transport Company of Albany to cease operations on March 7, 1962. As late as July 10, 1964, attempts were still being made to desegregate the public parks and swimming pools of Albany, Georgia.

ALDRIGE, IRA (1807-1867) This actor and playwright was born in New York City of free parents. He was educated at the African Free Schools of New York and Schenectady College. Later he attended the University of Glasgow, where he was the roommate of James McCune Smith. Aldrige became interested in the theater as a boy and worked for a time as a stagehand at New York's Chatham Theater. In his youth he had an opportunity to act in plays at the African Theater, which had been organized by blacks for their own entertainment. In 1824, at the age of seventeen, Ira Aldrige went to England, where for two years he went to school and worked in the Coburg and other theaters. In 1826 he married Margaret Gill, an English woman, and began his professional career. His profession carried him throughout the British Isles and Europe and in the process he became an accomplished and skillful actor. Among the many roles he played were King Lear, Shylock, and Othello. During his career he received numerous tributes and awards, including the Cross of Leopold from the Tsar of Russia and a Maltese Cross. A close friend, Taras Shevchenko, painted his portrait, which hangs today in the Moscow Art Gallery. Throughout his career Aldrige kept in contact with his friend James McCune Smith by letter. He was aware of the problems that the blacks in America faced. Although he became a British citizen and did not return to the United States, Aldrige contributed to the abolitionist cause. In 1867 he decided to return home but died in Lodz, Poland, on August 7. His tomb in that city is cared for today by the Society of Polish Artists of Film and Theater. In 1932, when the Memorial Theater at Stratford upon Avon was opened, one of the thirty-three memorial chairs honoring great actors was named for him.

ALEXANDER, MARGARET WALKER (1915-   ) This poet, novelist, and essayist was born in Birmingham, Alabama. She was educated at private schools and at Northwestern University and the University of Iowa. In 1942 her first book of poetry was published by the Yale University Press in its Younger Poets Series. Ms. Walker has taught and lectured at many colleges and universities, including Livingston College, West Virginia State College, and Jackson State College. She has received several awards for her work, among them the Yale Award for Younger Poets and the Houghton Mifflin Literary Fellowship. Her poetry and other writings have been published in many magazines, including *Poetry Magazine, Phylon, New Challenge, Negro Digest, Freedomways,* and the *Virginia Quarterly.*

ALLEN, "BLIND BOY" FULLER (1903-1940)   This blues singer and guitar player was born in Rockingham, North Carolina. His education was limited, but he learned to play the guitar as a boy. When he was in his twenties, he was blinded in an accident in a mill. He left the mill region and moved to Durham, North Carolina, where he became a street singer and earned a fair living this way. He continued singing for several years and earned enough money to get married. When he was thirty-one years old, in 1934, "Blind Boy" Fuller, as he was generally called, met a young harmonica player named Saunders Terrell, better known as "Sonny" Terry, and became his partner and friend. The two blues singers sang and played at the parties and social functions in the Durham area until 1935, when they were taken to New York by their manager, J. B. Long, to audition for the American Recording Corporation. The audition was a success and Fuller made his first records that year. He continued recording off and on until the summer of 1940, when he died of a kidney ailment.

ALLEN, SAMUEL ("PAUL VESEY") (1917-   )   This poet, lawyer, and essayist was born in Columbus, Ohio. He was educated in local schools and at Fisk University and the Harvard Law School. He completed further work at the New School for Social Research and the Sorbonne in Paris, France. As a lawyer, Mr. Allen has worked as deputy assistant district attorney for New York; assistant general counsel for the United States Information Agency; chief counsel, Community Relations Service, Department of Commerce; and associate of law at Texas Southern University. In addition to these activities, Samuel Allen has taught English at several universities, among them Wesleyan University (1970-1971) and Boston University (1971 to the present). While studying at the Sorbonne, he began writing poetry, and his poems were published in the French journal

Presence Africane. He has lectured at universities in Canada and Africa, as well as the United States. He has read his poetry at many colleges and universities throughout the United States.

AMENIA CONFERENCE (1916)   With the death of Booker T. Washington, those who favored the accommodationist views in race relations were left leaderless. W. E. B. DuBois, leader of those blacks who disagreed with the ideas espoused by the group, suggested that both factions meet and solve their differences and develop one single program for the progress of blacks in the United States. A meeting was held in August 1916 at the estate of Joel Spingarn in Amenia, New York. As a result of the various group discussions, the participants drew up a series of resolutions stating: that all forms of education were desirable for the blacks, that blacks must have political freedom, and that all black leaders must work together toward the same goal and forget the old controversies and factional alignments.

AMERICAN NEGRO ACADEMY   Founded in 1897, this organization was the result of the ideas of Alexander Crummell, who dreamed of gathering a group of young black scholars who would use the methods of scholarship to aid in the progress and elevation of the blacks in America. In March 1897, Crummell's idea became a reality and the American Negro Academy was established. The organization was composed of black scholars and their number was limited to forty. The purposes of the academy were the promotion of science and art, the cultivation of a form of intellectual taste, the fostering of higher education, and the defense of the Negro against vicious assaults. This last objective was the most important of all, and the academy members found themselves embroiled in intense scholarly polemic against written racist attacks on the blacks. Between 1897 and 1920 a series of twenty-two occasional papers was published by the academy, all in defense of the blacks in some way. These papers are now available in a reprint edition.

AMERICAN SOCIETY FOR AFRICAN CULTURE, THE   Established in 1957, this cultural group's purpose was to provide a more extensive knowledge of African cultural traditions. The ASAC came into existence as a result of the First International Congress of Negro Writers and Artists, which was held in Paris in 1957. The organization sponsored lecture series and produced several publications, including a magazine, the *African Forum.* In the mid 1960s, allegations were made that the U.S. Central Intelligence Agency provided funds for ASAC, and the society began to decline and eventually ceased to exist.

AMISTAD, I, II   Published in a paperback format, this journal contains well written essays, poetry, short stories, and other prose selections of the younger black writers. Among the contributors are Ishamael Reed, John A. Williams, and C. L. R. James. Thus far two volumes have appeared. The title of the journal is a reference to the slave mutiny that occurred aboard the Spanish slaver *Amistad* in 1839. *Amistad* is the Spanish word for friendship.

AMSTERDAM NEWS, THE   Begun in 1909 by James Anderson, this general black newspaper has had several owners. In 1936 it was bought by two doctors, Clelan B. Powell and Philip M. H. Savoy. Dr. Savoy died in 1965, and Dr. Powell became a sole owner.

ANDREWS, BENNEY (1930-   )   This painter, a mixed-media artist, was born in South Madison, Georgia. His parents were sharecroppers. He was educated in local schools, the University of Chicago, and the Art Institute of Chicago. Andrews has taught at Queens College, at the New School for Social Research in New York, and at the University of California in Hayward. A prolific artist, his work is found in many private collections as well as public ones, among them the Museum of Modern Art, the Slater Memorial Museum, the Norfolk Museum, and the Butler Institute of American Art in Youngstown, Ohio.

ANGELA MURRY   This is a character in Jessie Fauset's novel, *Plum Bun.*

AN IDYL OF THE SOUTH   This last volume of the poetry of Albert A. Whitman published in 1901 consists of two long poems, *The Octroon,* 1248 lines divided into 161 *ottava rima* stanzas, and *The Southlands Charms,* arranged in 74 *ottava rima* stanzas and having 582 lines.

ANTISLAVERY SOCIETIES   In the mid 1830s, when the Abolitionist Movement increased its pace, antislavery societies organized for the express purpose of bringing an end to slavery in the United States began to appear. In 1833 the American Anti-Slavery Society was founded. Soon there was a sizable network of such societies in existence in the northern United States. Almost every major city had its antislavery organization. There were state and regional societies as well.

ARVAY HENSON   This is a character in Zora Neal Hurston's novel, *Seraph on the Suwanee.*

ASHLEY EXPEDITIONS, THE   In the early part of the nineteenth century the fur industry began to expand. Fur-trading expeditions up the Missouri River and into the Rocky Mountains were organized by William H. Ashley, lieutenant governor of Missouri, between 1822 and 1826. In 1822 Lt. Governor Ashley established the Rocky Mountain Fur Company for the purpose of developing a fur trade with the Indians in the Rocky Mountains. One of the most important results of these expeditions was the exploration of the vast area of the northwestern United States. Many mountain men, trappers and traders, were employed. These men were fearless and possessed great knowledge of the Indians, their customs and language. Two black mountain men who were employed by the Rocky Mountain Fur Company and served as guides for the Ashley expeditions were James P. Beckwourth and Edward Rose.

ASIENTO DE NEGROS   *Asiento* is a Spanish word meaning contract or agreement. The *Asiento de Negros,* or contract for the blacks, was an agreement made by the Spanish government with individual Spaniards or subjects of other countries giving, for a fee, the exclusive right to supply black slaves and some manufactured goods to Spanish colonies in the Americas. One of the first companies to hold the *Asiento de Negros* was a trading company of Genoa, Italy, which held it in 1517. This lucrative contract was highly prized and was held at various times by different countries. In 1528 a German firm agreed to supply four thousand slaves to Spanish colonies. Portugal, France, and England all held the *Asiento* at one time or another.

ASSOCIATION FOR THE STUDY OF NEGRO LIFE AND HISTORY (SEPTEMBER 9, 1915)   For very many years the part played by the blacks in the history of the United States was either ignored or minimized and generally downgraded. On September 9, 1915, the Association for the Study of Negro Life and History was established by Carter Godwin Woodson to counteract negative views toward the history of the blacks of the United States. This organization is still quite active and has several thousand members. The scholarly journal, the *Journal of Negro History,* associated with it has a worldwide reputation and thousands of subscribers.

ASTRAL HERNDON   This is a character in Sutton Grigg's novel, *Overshadowed.*

ATKINS, DOROTHY (1936-   )   This painter, designer, sculptor, and jeweler was born in Brooklyn, New York. She was educated in local schools and at the University of California at Berkeley. Her work has been exhibited at the California State Exposition, the Space Art Show, the Scranton Museum, and the Oakland Museum.

ATKINS, RUSSEL (1926-   )   This poet, playwright, composer, and editor was born in Cleveland, Ohio, and educated in its public schools. He attended the Cleveland Music School Settlement, the Cleveland Institute of Music, and the Cleveland Institute of Art. Mr. Atkins has worked as a consultant for writers' conferences, as a lecturer and director of poetry workshops, as poet in residence and instructor at Cleveland's famed Karamu House, and as a member of the Cleveland State University Forum. Russel Atkins is the founder of *Free Lance Magazine,* the oldest black little magazine in the United States. His poetry has appeared in many periodicals, including *Free Lance, Beloit Poetry Journal,* and the *Ohio Poetry Review.*

ATLANTA DAILY WORLD   Established in 1928 by William Alexander Scott, this newspaper became a daily publication in 1932. Scott was assassinated in 1934 and the paper came under the leadership of Cornelius A. Scott.

ATLANTA UNIVERSITY RESEARCH CENTER   The Trevor Arnett Library of Atlanta University is the main library of the university. It contains over two-hundred thousand cataloged volumes. Among the important collections is the Countee Cullen Memorial Collection, established by Cullen's friend, Harold Jackman, in 1942. This collection contains the papers and manuscripts of several contemporary black writers, including James Baldwin and Gwendolyn Brooks. Also noteworthy is the Henry P. Slaughter Collection, which, among other items, contains the John Brown letters.

ATTAWAY, WILLIAM (1911-   )   This short story writer and novelist was born in Greenville, Mississippi, but grew up in Chicago. He was educated in Chicago public schools and at the University of

Chicago. After completing his education, Mr. Attaway worked at a variety of jobs from labor organizer and salesman to actor. Finally he became a writer.

ATTITUDE   A writer's attitude toward his subject decides the tone of his work. It may be sad, satiric, angry, or happy. The novels of Ishmael Reed, for example, are generally satiric in attitude; the tone of Richard Wright's novels is realistic and harsh. The attitude of many black poets of the 1960s tends to be one of anger.

AUNT SARA   This is a character in Mercedes Gilbert's novel, *Aunt Sara's Wooden God.*

AVEY   This is a character in Jean Toomer's collection of writings, *Cane.*

BALDWIN, JAMES (1924-   )   A novelist, critic, essayist, screenwriter, and playwright, James Baldwin was born in Harlem, New York, and educated in its public schools. After leaving school, he worked at various jobs and wrote at night. In 1945, when he was twenty-one years old, Baldwin won a Saxon Trust Award and in 1948 he received a Rosenwald Fellowship, which enabled him to go to Europe, where he remained for ten years. He published his first novel, *Go Tell It on the Mountain*, in 1952 and has continued to write almost constantly since that time. Mr. Baldwin has written novels, essays, and screenplays. His reputation has become international. He has lectured all over the world and has appeared on many television and radio programs. There have been numerous critical studies of his work.

BALTIMORE AFRO-AMERICAN, THE   John Murphy, Jr., bought the paper in 1892 for $300 and ran it until his death in 1922. After his death, the *Afro-American* was operated by his sons. Carl Murphy was publisher until his death in 1967. John Murphy III became president of the Afro-American Publishing Company and Carl Murphy's daughter, Frances Murphy, became the publisher of the paper.

BAMBARA, TONI CADE (1939-   )   This short story writer, critic, and editor was born in New York City. She was educated in the New York public schools and at Queens College and the City University of New York. She studied further at the University of Florence, Italy; the Ecole de Mime Etienne Decroux, Paris; New York University; the Katherine Dunham Dance Studio; and the New School for Social Research. Ms. Cade Bambara has worked as a welfare investigator for the State of New York and an instructor of English at City College and Rutgers University, where she is now associate professor of English. She has lectured at several colleges and universities. Her work has appeared in many publications, among them the *Massachusetts Review, Black World, Prairie Schooner, Umbra,* and *Redbook.*

BARAKA, IMAMU AMIRI (LEROI JONES) (1934-   )   This poet, playwright, editor, short story writer novelist, music critic, essayist, and black nationalist leader was born in Newark, New Jersey. He was educated in the public schools and at Rutgers, Howard, and Columbia universities. Baraka began writing during two years spent in the air force. After leaving the air force in 1955, he moved to New York, where be became an important member of the beat generation group of writers centered in Greenwich Village. His poetry began to appear in the early 1960s; plays and music criticism followed. In 1965 Mr. Baraka moved to Harlem and founded the Black Arts Repertory Theater, a cultural workshop. In 1966 he moved to Newark, New Jersey, and established Spirit House, a cultural center. Since 1969 he has been intensely interested in political action in Newark and directs much of his energy toward that end. He has won numerous awards for his writing, including a Whitney Fellowship in 1963 and a Guggheim Fellowship in 1965. His poetry and other writings have appeared in many periodicals and magazines such as the *Beloit Poetry Journal, Black World, the Nation, Massachusetts Review, Umbra, the Village Voice, Negro Digest,* the *Journal of Black Poetry, Poetry Magazine, Paris Review,* and *Freedomways.*

BARRACOON   The term barracoon is derived from the Spanish term *barracon,* which is a form of the word *barraca,* meaning a hut or storage shed. When slaves were brought to the staging or holding areas in Africa, often there were not enough slaves on hand to supply the ships waiting in the ports. It was necessary to keep the slaves in an encampment until enough of them were brought in to supply the waiting ships. An encampment of this kind was called a *barracoon.*

BARRAX, GERALD WILLIAM (1933-   )   This poet was born in Attala, Alabama. However, he grew up in Pittsburgh, Pennsylvania, and was educated in the public schools of that city. Later, while serving in the air force (1953-1957), he attended the University of the Philippines. After his term of service was over, he completed his education at Duquesne University, the University of Pittsburgh, and the University of North Carolina at Chapel Hill. Mr. Barrax has worked at many jobs. He has been a mail carrier, postal clerk, a steel mill worker, a substitute teacher in public schools, and a college teacher. He has taught at North Carolina Central University (1969-1970) and at North Carolina State University (1970-1972). His poetry has been published in various magazines and journals, among them *Poetry*, *Black World*, the *Journal of Black Poetry*, *Poetry Northwest*, *Southern Poetry Review*, *Four Quarters*, and *Colloquy*. He has been awarded the Bishop Carroll Scholarship for Creative Writing and the Broadside Press Award for Poetry in 1972.

BARTHE, RICHMOND (1901-   )   This sculptor and painter was born in Bay St. Louis, Mississippi, but grew up in New Orleans. He was educated in local schools and at the Art Institute of Chicago. He studied further at the Art Students' League in New York. He began his career as a painter but turned to sculpture, at which he excelled. Mr. Barthe's work has been exhibited many times in places such as the James A. Porter Museum, the Whitney Museum, the University of Wisconsin, and the Pennsylvania Academy of Fine Arts. His work can be found in various collections, including the Metropolitan Museum of Art, the Whitney Museum of American Art, and the New Theater of London. Richmond Barthe has received many awards for his work, including the Eames McVeagh Prize; the Rosenwald Fellowship, the Guggenheim Fellowship and the Edward Alford Award.

BECKWOURTH, JAMES P. (1798-1866?)   This mountain man, trapper, guide, explorer, and chief of the Crow Indians was born in Fredericksburg, Virginia, on April 6, 1798. In 1805 or 1806 Beckwourth's father moved his wife and thirteen children west and settled on land about twelve miles from what is now St. Charles, Missouri. When he was ten years old, Jim Beckwourth's father sent him to St. Louis to school. His education lasted about four years; and when he was fourteen, he was apprenticed to a blacksmith to learn the trade. Beckwourth remained with George Casner, his employer, for about three years. As a result of an altercation with Mr. Casner, he left the job and became a hunter with a keelboat expedition headed up the Mississippi River to Illinois. He was assigned the task of supplying meat for the entire crew of the expedition. The job lasted about eighteen months. In this way Beckwourth began his career as a mountain man. In 1823 he went to work for the Rocky Mountain Fur Company. Soon his abilities as a trapper, hunter, and guide became widely known. He led various expeditions through the Rocky Mountain region and became friendly with numerous Indian tribes. He fought and served as a scout in the second Seminole War (1835-1842). Later he led several expeditions through the Rocky Mountains. On one of these explorations he discovered a pass through the Sierra Nevada Mountains that today is called Beckwourth Pass. When he died, around 1866, Beckwourth was a chief of the Crow Indians, who, it was said, poisoned him rather than let him leave them and return to live among the white men.

BIBB, HENRY (1815-1854)   This editor and abolitionist was born a slave in Shelby County, Kentucky. He escaped from slavery in 1837 but returned South to get his wife. He was recaptured but managed to escape a second time and went west to Detroit, Michigan. In Detroit he became an active abolitionist lecturer, traveling widely through several states from Michigan to Massachusetts. About 1849 or 1850, Henry Bibb moved to Sandwich, Ontario, where he began to publish an antislavery newspaper, the *Voice of the Fugitive*, and continued his abolitionist activities.

BIGGER THOMAS   This is a character in Richard Wright's novel, *Native Son*.

BIG SEA, THE   This is the autobiography of poet Langston Hughes first published in 1940. It is important for the information it provides about the Harlem Renaissance and the writers and artists who participated in it.

BIRMINGHAM MARCHES   On April 3, 1963, the blacks in Birmingham, Alabama, began an intense drive to end segregation in lunch counters and public places and to bring a halt to discrimination in employment. In the two months this campaign lasted, over three thousand persons, most of them black, were arrested. International attention was directed toward race problems in the United States when on Sunday, September 15, 1963, a bomb explosion killed four little black girls attending a Sunday school class at the Sixteenth

Street Baptist Church. The bomb blast injured fourteen other blacks and blew large holes in the church. This incident is the subject of Dudley Randall's poem, *"The Ballad of Birmingham."*

BITA PLANT   This is a character in Claude McKay's novel, *Banana Bottom.*

BLACK   This is a term that not only describes a particular group of people of the United States but indicates a radical change in the self-identity pattern of that group. During the 1960s the blacks began to view themselves in different ways, therefore the name they were originally called changed drastically. The term "Negro" began to indicate a negative and inferior self-image, while the term "Black" implied the new sense of pride this group had come to feel. News-papers, magazines, and media in general have come to refer to this group, formally called Negroes, Afro-Americans, and so forth, as blacks. For example, the *Negro American Reference Book,* in its second edition, has the title the *Black American Reference Book.*

BLACK ACADEMY OF ARTS AND LETTERS, THE   Established in 1969 with a three-year grant of $150,000 from the Twentieth Century Fund, this organization's purpose was to promote and motivate those persons active in arts and letters pertaining to blacks in the United States. This organization ceased to exist in the 1970s.

BLACK ACADEMY REVIEW, THE   Founded in 1970, this quarterly journal is concerned with the history and literature of the blacks in Africa and the United States. Each issue is about eighty pages long and usually contains five or six articles on subjects ranging from poetry to problems of Africa. Many of the articles are about Africa, but some of them are about black writers such as Richard Wright. The essays are well written and well researched.

BLACK AESTHETIC   When the term "aesthetic" is used, the refer-ence is to a concept of the beautiful. Black aesthetic, then, can be said to refer to the intrinsic beauty in the history and literature of the blacks in the United States. The civil rights activities of the 1960s and the incipient cultural nationalism that resulted from this struggle has caused the blacks to search, in a somewhat romantic way, their own history and the history of Africa for its best ele-ments. Some poets, novelists, playwrights, and critics such as Don L. Lee, Hoyt Fuller, Addison Gayle, and Imamu Baraka feel that any art or literature produced by a black artist must reflect intensely the black experience in the United States. In a very simple sense the black aesthetic demands that art and literature of black artists serve the black people above all else and whatever is produced must be done in the context of the aspirations of the blacks.

BLACK ANIMA   This is a long poem by N. J. Loftis.

BLACK CODES (1865-1966)   Following the end of the Civil War practically all of the ex-Confederate States passed laws that placed many restrictions upon the newly freed blacks. For the most part these laws, generally called "black codes," were designed to give the whites control over the blacks and in many ways were quite similar to the old slave codes. Blacks were usually referred to in these laws as "persons of color." The codes legalized slave marriages but prevented interracial marriage. Labor contracts had to be signed even though many ex-slaves could neither read nor write. Blacks could testify only in court cases that involved blacks. Blacks could not move readily from place to place. No blacks were permitted to vote, serve on juries, or send their children to public schools. The codes varied from state to state but all were restrictive.

BLACK CULTURAL NATIONALISM   Throughout the history of blacks in the United States there has been an interest on the part of various blacks in writing, in a positive manner, about the experience they have undergone. There have been and still are efforts being made to create a body of literature for blacks by blacks. The "black cultural nationalism," as it is sometimes called, had its beginnings in the work of J. W. C. Pennington's *Textbook of the Origin and History of the Colored People* (1841), William Wells Brown's *The Black Man: His Antecedents, His Genius, and His Achievements* (1863), and George Washington Williams's *History of the Negro Race in America from 1619 to 1880.*

BLACK DIALOGUE   This is an irregularly published journal begun in 1965 as an off-campus magazine for San Francisco State College students. Its issues contain essays, stories, poems, book reviews, drawings, and photographs.

BLACK LITERARY SOCIETIES   During the nineteenth century, as early as 1828, black literary societies were established by the free blacks in New York, Pennsylvania, Massachusetts, Connecticut,

Rhode Island, New Jersey, Maryland, Washington, D.C., Ohio, and Michigan. The primary purpose of these organizations, which were also known as debating or reading societies, was to provide the blacks with an opportunity to improve their education and expand their intellectual horizons. Some of these societies were the Demosthenian Institute of Philadelphia (1837), the Phoenix Society of New York City (1833), the Boston Philomathean Society (1836), and The Convential Society of Washington, D.C. (1834).

BLACK MILITANT   In their quest for civil rights, justice, and equality of opportunity, a number of blacks have expressed the idea that black Americans must have something to say about what is happening to them and they demand that the various inequalities directed against the blacks be corrected. The attitude of such blacks is characterized by a seeming hostility and agressiveness. Black militants, as they are often called, are not a new phenemenon. These aggressive views have always existed among the blacks in the United States in their fight against slavery and oppression during their four-hundred-year stay in the Americas. Leaders who could be called black militants in their time are Richard Allen in the eighteenth century; Henry Highland Garnet, Frederick Douglass, and David Walker in the nineteenth century; and W. E. B. DuBois, Malcolm X, and Stokeley Carmichael in the twentieth century.

BLACK OPALS   Established in 1927 in Philadelphia, this literary journal contained poems, stories, and essays by black writers living in the Philadelphia and New York areas. In the first issue there was one poem by Lewis Alexander, three poems by Langston Hughes, and an essay by Alain Locke. All the other poems, stories, and essays were by writers from the Philadelphia area, including Arthur Huff Fauset, Beatrice Miller, and Loraine Chambers.

BLACK POETRY   During the severe civil rights struggles and the several innercity insurrections that took place in the latter part of the 1960s, there emerged a new kind of poetry among the blacks. Earlier black poetry, written between 1930 and 1950, tended to be cast in a traditional manner. However, some poets, such as Langston Hughes and Ray Durem especially, wrote poetry that was strident in tone and gave an indication of the direction black poetry was to take. The new black poetry uses as reference points urban street language, black music, and black folklore and is harsh and noisy. Sonia Sanchez's poems *A Coltrane Poem* and *To Chuck* are excellent examples of the use of black music and black street language to achieve the effect that the poet desires. The use of urban folklore is clearly evident in Ethridge Knight's poem *Dark: I Sing of Shine.*

BLACK POSITION, THE   Published on an irregular basis, this small magazine is edited by the well-known poet, Gwendolyn Brooks. Each issue usually contains several short articles on various aspects of the culture of black Americans.

BLACK PREACHING   Religion has played an important part in the lives of the blacks in the United States, both slave and free. The ministers or preachers of the various churches the blacks established were often social and political as well as religious leaders. Many preachers were known for the sermons they preached to their congregations since many of them adopted an emotional and poetic style in their sermons and became famous for the elaborate imagery incorporated in their preaching. Some of these preachers were educated and some were not, but each one served his people. John Jasper, a semieducated minister, became widely known for his sermon, *The Sun Do Move*, which he preached over two hundred and fifty times. References to black preaching are found in much of the writing of Afro-Americans. James Weldon Johnson's collection of poetry, *God's Trombones*, is written in a style based on the sermons of the black preaching of the nineteenth century. In his novel, *The Autobiography of An Ex-Colored Man*, Johnson describes in some detail a black minister preaching to his congregation. In *The Invisible Man*, Ralph Ellison constructs a portrait of the black preacher in the character Homer Barbee.

BLACK REVIEW, I, II   This magazine is similar to *Amistad* in its use of a paperback format, but here the similarity ends. Whereas *Amistad* tends to express support of the black revolution, *Black Review* is somewhat more general in its range. While it does express concern for the black revolutionary view, it is less ardent in its support than *Amistad*. Each issue contains literary essays, poetry, stories, and literary criticism; and its writers include Nikki Giovanni, Ed Bullins, and Julius Lester.

BLACK SCHOLAR   First published in 1969, this journal is concerned with the academic world as it affects blacks. At the same time it pays close attention to the problems faced by both the average and the radical blacks. The articles are scholarly and well documented and often deal with the works of black authors. In addition to articles, each issue usually contains book reviews, some poetry, and sometimes short stories.

BLACK THEATER   This journal is concerned with the black theater movement. It was first published in 1968. Each issue usually contained reviews of scripts of new plays, articles on black playwrights, and news of the activities of the various black theatrical and cultural organizations in the United States. *Black Theater* ceased publication in 1972.

BLACK TOWNS   During the last quarter of the nineteenth century many blacks left the South because of the numerous problems they faced and moved into the Midwest. Some of them settled in Kansas, Oklahoma, Nebraska, and Missouri. In several instances, all-black towns were developed, some of which are still thriving today. Two of these towns are Boley and Langston, both located in Oklahoma.

BLACK WORLD (NEGRO DIGEST)   Founded by John Johnson in 1942 as the *Negro Digest*, this monthly publication changed its name to *Black World* in 1970. Each issue contains seven or eight signed articles covering all aspects of black American cultural and political life. Special issues on poetry, theater, and black history are published annually. Included also are book reviews, poetry, and short stories. The view generally expressed is that of black cultural nationalism, however, the articles are well written. Articles by Imamu Baraka and critics Darwin Turner and Houston A. Baker have appeared in *Black World*. Very often articles pertaining to Africa appear as well. *Black World* ceased publication in 1976.

BLUEBOY   This is a character in Robert D. Pharr's novel, *The Book of Numbers*.

BONA   This is a character in Jean Toomer's collection of writings, *Cane*.

BONTEMPS, ARNA (1902-1973)   This poet, novelist, short story writer, essayist, editor, teacher, and critic was born in Alexandria, Louisiana, but grew up in Los Angeles. He was educated in the Los Angeles public schools, at San Fernando Academy, and at the University of Chicago. He taught and lectured at many colleges and universities, including Fisk University, the University of Illinois, and Yale University. Mr. Bontemps received several awards for his work, among them the Guggenheim Fellowship, the Rosenwald Fellowship, the Dow Award, and grants from the Endowment for the Humanities. His writings have appeared in numerous magazines and journals, such as *Crisis, Black World, Negro Digest, Library Quarterly, Saturday Review,* and *Phylon.*

Boxleys Conspiracy (1816)   Early in the year 1816 Virginia planters were startled by the plans of George Boxley. A governor's reward notice in the *Richmond Enquirer* of May 22, 1816, describes him as having "a thin visage of a sallow complexion, thin make, his hair light or yellowish, thin on top of his head and tied behind—he stoops a little in shoulders, has large whiskers, blue or gray eyes, pretends to be very religious, is fond of talking and speaks quick." He was in his mid-thirties and a little over six feet tall. During the winter of 1815, Boxley decided to attempt to free the slaves of Virginia and organized a conspiracy that involved Louisa, Spotsylvania, and Orange counties. He and his followers obtained guns, swords, and clubs. The rebels were to meet at harvest time at Boxley's farm, bringing weapons and horses. Their plan called first for an attack on Fredericksburg, Virginia, and then a direct assault on Richmond. The plot was aborted when a female slave belonging to Ptolemy Powell betrayed the plan. The police and the military were alerted and arrested about thirty of the rebel slaves. Boxley attempted to rescue his followers but his efforts failed and he was forced to flee. Eventually Boxley surrendered and was imprisoned. However, with the aid of a candle and a file smuggled to him by his wife, he escaped from jail in May 1816. Although a reward of $1,000 was offered, he was apparently never recaptured. Six or seven of the rebel slaves were hanged; others were banished from the state.

Branch, William (1927-   )   This playwright, television writer, producer, and director was born in New Haven, Connecticut. He was educated in public schools and at Northwestern, Columbia, and Yale Universities. Mr. Branch has been involved in theater activities since his early years in college. During his freshman year at Northwestern University, he joined the national black cast of *Anna Lucasta.* He has written for television as well as motion pictures. For television he has written the documentaries "The City," "What is Conscience?," "Still a Brother: Inside the Negro Middle Class," and others. William Branch has won several awards for his work, among them the Robert E. Sherwood Television Award, the Blue Ribbon

Award of the American Film Festival, and a Guggenheim Award for Creative Writing.

BRAWLEY, BENJAMIN GRIFFIN (1882-1937)   This teacher, poet, critic, historian, short story writer, and clergyman was born in Columbia, South Carolina. He attended the public schools of Nashville, Tennessee, and Petersburg, Virginia. He obtained degrees from Morehouse College, the University of Chicago, and Howard University. He taught English at Morehouse, Shaw, and Howard. Brawley's writings were primarily literary and social history, although he did write several books of poetry and some short stories. His work is characterized by Victorian overtones, but much of it is still useful for the historical information it provides about the cultural history of black America.

BROADSIDE PRESS, THE   Established in 1965 by poet Dudley F. Randall, this Detroit-based company concentrates on the publication of poetry. Recently, however, it has published some critical studies and reference books, most of which are about poets or poetry. The company began with the production of broadsides with one or more poems on a single sheet. Since 1965, Broadside has published both paperback and hardcover books.

BROOKS, GWENDOLYN ELIZABETH (1917-   )   This poet, editor, novelist, critic, essayist, and teacher, was born in Topeka, Kansas. Her parents moved to Chicago shortly after she was born; she grew up in Chicago and still lives there. She was educated in the Chicago public schools and at Wilcon Junior College. Ms. Brooks began writing poetry as a child and had her first poem published in the magazine *American Childhood* when she was only fourteen years old. When she finished college, she began work as a journalist. In 1945 her first book of poetry, *A Street In Bronzeville*, was published. In 1949 she was awarded a Pulitzer Prize for her second collection of poetry, *Annie Allen*. She was the first black person to receive this award. Gwendolyn Brooks has lectured and read her poetry at many colleges and universities, among them the University of Chicago, Columbia College, and Cuyahoga Community College of Cleveland, Ohio. Her poems have appeared in numerous magazines and journals, including *Common Ground, Black World, Ebony, Freedomways, Poetry Magazine: the Journal of Black Poetry,* and *Harpers Magazine.*In addition to the Pulitzer Prize, Ms. Brooks has received the Gugghenheim Fellowship for creative writing and a 1947 grant for the American Academy of Arts and Letters. In 1968 she was chosen poet laureate of Illinois and in 1976 she became the first black woman elected to the National Institute of Arts and Letters.

BROWN, FRANK LONDON (1927-1962)   This editor, novelist, essayist, and short story writer was born in Kansas City, Missouri, and received his early education there. He graduated from Wilberforce University and completed work at Roosevelt University and the Chicago Kent College of Law. Mr. Brown worked as a machinist, union organizer, and associate editor of *Ebony Magazine*. At the time of his death, he was director of the union leadership program at the University of Chicago. His many articles and short stories appeared in *Downbeat, Southwest Review*, the *Chicago Review*, the *Negro Digest*, the *Chicago Sun Times*, the *Chicago Tribune*, and other publications.

BROWNSVILLE RIOT (1906)   On a night in August 1906, a group of unidentified black soldiers of two companies, B and C, of the twenty-fifth United States infantry stationed at Fort Brown near Brownsville, Texas, came into Brownsville and shot up the town, killing one person and wounding a policeman. For some time these troops had endured the insults and racial prejudice inflicted upon them and this violent outbreak was the result. The officers of these black troops investigated but obtained no information. President Theodore Roosevelt ordered a full-scale investigation, which proved that the soldiers were from companies B and C. No identification was made because none of the soldiers would testify against their comrades. On November 5, President Roosevelt ordered 159 privates and noncommissioned officers from companies B and C dishonorably discharged and barred from the army and navy because of the silence maintained concerning the riot. A number of people felt these soldiers were being treated unfairly. Senator Joseph Foraker from Ohio demanded the accused men be given a full and fair trial before being subjected to such harsh punishment. In January 1907 a full Senate investigation began; however, after several months of study, the committee voted to uphold President Roosevelt's order. In 1909 Senator Foraker persuaded the government to establish a court of inquiry concerning the entire Brownsville incident. The results of the inquiry did nothing to remove the charges against the discharged soldiers. In 1973 the army removed the charges against the survivors of the Brownsville incident and they or their heirs received a monentary compensation

of approximately $25,000 from the government. In 1971 black play-
wright Charles Fuller's play *The Brownsville Raid* was produced in
New York City.

BUCKS OF AMERICA   During the American Revolutionary War
blacks served as soldiers and sailors in the Continental Army. In at
least two instances all-black or majority black regiments or companies were organized. One such unit was the Bucks of America, as
they called themselves. This company, formed in Boston and led by
a black colonel named Middleton, fought throughout the war. At the
end of the conflict, this unit was presented with a flag as a tribute to
their courage and devotion by John Hancock, then governor of
Massachusetts. The banner is now in the care of the Massachusetts
Historical Society.

BUFFALO SOLDIERS   Following the Civil War, two units of black
cavalry men, the ninth and the tenth regiments, were organized for
service in the American West. The black troopers developed an
outstanding record as fighters, although they constantly faced violence and racial prejudice from the white population. These soldiers
fought Indians, outlaws, and cattle rustlers. Their Indian advers-
aries called them "buffalo soldiers" because of the similarity between the tightly-curled hair of the blacks and the hair of the
buffalo. To the Indians, the buffalo was a sacred animal. The name
caught on and finally the buffalo became part of the military
insignia of these units. White soldiers derisively referred to the
black troopers as "brunets." The famous artist of the American
West, Fredric Remington, sketched and painted many of these black
soldiers. English author John Prebble wrote a novel about them,
entitled *Buffalo Soldiers*.

BULLINS, ED (1935-   )   This playwright, poet, editor, critic,
producer, and short story writer was born in Philadelphia, Pennsylvania. He was educated in local schools and at the William Penn
Business School of Philadelphia, Los Angeles College, and San
Francisco State College. He has worked extensively in the theater as
associate director of the New Lafayette Theater, and founder and
director of the community and experimental Theater, Black Arts
West, located in San Francisco, California. Ed Bullins's essays have
appeared in many magazines and journals, such as *Negro Digest*, the
Drama Review, Black Theater, Black World, and *Manhattan Re-*

view. He has received several awards for his plays, including the Obie Award and the Vernon Rice Award (1968).

BURNS, ANTHONY, FUGITIVE SLAVE CASE, THE   In 1850 the United States government passed a strict fugitive slave law. The Anthony Burns case was a direct result of this law. On May 24, 1854, an escaped slave named Anthony Burns was arrested and put under guard in a federal jury room of the Boston Courthouse. This was done at the request of Burns's former owner, Colonel Charles Suttle of Alexandria, Virginia. The news of the escaped slave's arrest spread quickly in spite of the authorities' efforts to keep it secret. On the morning of May 26 three prominent Boston lawyers; Charles M. Ellis, Richard Henry Dana, Jr., and black attorney Robert Morris, arrived in court to defend Burns. On the evening of May 26, a meeting was held at Faneuil Hall to protest Burns's arrest and the use of special deputies many of whom were thugs and ex-convicts to guard him. Fiery speeches were made by abolitionists Wendel Phillips and Theodore Parker. At the end of the meeting those in attendance were urged to go to the courthouse and rescue Burns by force if necessary. The crowd rushed from the hall to the courthouse, where they found others, led by black leader Lewis Hayden and white abolitionist leader Thomas W. Higginson, battering down the doors. Once inside, the rescuers were met by constables and deputies armed with pistols and clubs. In the fighting, Thomas Higginson was wounded and Marshall Batchelder was shot and killed. The police were reinforced by soldiers; the abolitionists were driven from the building and many were arrested on the spot. When Burns's trial was held, soldiers and policemen surrounded the courthouse, lined the stairways to the courtroom, and guarded each window and door. When the trial ended, Burns was sentenced by United States Commissioner Edward G. Loving to be returned to his former owner. In order to get Burns to the dock, the Fifth Regiment of Artillery and twenty-two other military units were called out. The Boston police, a contingent of marines, and fifteen-hundred dragoons surrounded Burns and marched him to the revenue cutter *Morris* that was to return him to Virginia. A crowd of fifty-thousand gathered along the line of march and hooted and jeered at the soldiers and police. At one point the crowd clashed with the police and several persons were injured. On June 2, when the cutter departed, thousands lined the docks and prayed for Burns. In 1855 sufficient money was raised and Burns's freedom was bought.

CARR, LEROY (1905-1935)   A blues singer, musician, and recording artist, Carr was born in Nashville, Tennessee, and attended the public schools of that city. When he graduated from high school, he took a job in a clothing store. He learned to play the piano as a young man and by the time he was twenty-four he was playing nightclub engagements on weekends in the Nashville area. In 1925 Carr began singing as well as playing and soon became popular as a blues singer. In 1928 he left Nashville for Chicago to record for the first time. In Chicago he met guitarist Frances "Scrapper" Blackwell, and the two men recorded together. They were sucessful and Carr moved to Indianapolis, Indiana, where he lived quietly, visiting Chicago only to make new records. In 1934 Carr moved to a new recording company but in the process broke with his partner, "Scrapper" Blackwell, over contract agreements. Leroy Carr died in Nashville in 1935. "Scrapper" Blackwell became relatively obscure after his break with Carr but continued to play in and around Indianapolis. In 1958 he began to make a number of public appearances before large audiences. Between 1959 and 1962 he made several recordings and was gaining in popularity when he was killed in an alley in Indianapolis on October 6, 1962.

CATLETT, ELIZABETH (1919-   )   This sculptor, painter, and lithographer, was born in Washington, D.C. She was educated in local schools and at Howard University. She completed graduate work at the University of Iowa, where she studied under Osip Zadkine and Grant Wood. She studied further at the Art Students' League of New York and the Art Institute of Chicago. Ms. Catlett has taught at Dillard University, Hampton Institute, Prairie View College, and the University of Mexico. She has been awarded the Rosenwald Fellowship, a prize for sculpture in the biannual exhibition of Mexico City, and an honorable mention in the second Latin American Print Exhibit, Havana, Cuba. Ms. Catlett's work can be found in many museums, including the Museum of Modern Art, New York; the Library of Congress; the Museum of Modern Art, Mexico; and the Howard University Museum.

CHARLES TAYLOR, PROFESSOR   This is a character in Chester Himes's novel, *The Third Generation.*

CHASE RIBOUD, BARBARA (1936-   )   This sculptor was born in Philadelphia, Pennsylvania. She was educated in local schools and at the Tyler School of Art at Temple University, in 1957. In 1960 she completed graduate work at Yale University. Ms. Chase-Riboud has traveled widely and has visited Siam, China, Mongolia, France, and Egypt. She has received the John Hay Whitney Fellowship (1957-1958), the Philadelphia Alliance Purchase Prize, and a National Endowment for the Arts Award. Chase-Riboud's work can be found in the Newark Museum, the Museum of Modern Art, New York; and the Bertha Shafer Gallery, New York.

CHESNUTT, CHARLES (1858-1932)   This novelist, short story writer, and poet was born in Cleveland, Ohio. His parents had moved to Cleveland from Fayetteville, North Carolina, in 1856. In 1866 Chesnutt's father returned his family to North Carolina. Chesnutt was educated at Howard School, where, upon graduation, he became first a teacher then later the principal. In 1883 he moved his family to New York, where he worked as a reporter on the *New York Mail and Express*. Later that year he moved back to Cleveland and became a legal stenographer for the Nickle Plate Railroad. He passed the Ohio bar examinations and became a lawyer. He practiced law and wrote for about fifty years. In 1928 Mr. Chesnutt received the Spingarn Award for his writing.

CHICAGO DEFENDER, THE   Founded in 1905 by Robert Sengstacke Abbott, this Chicago-based paper is one of the best known black newspapers in the United States. The *Chicago Defender* is published in both daily and weekly editions. It became a daily newspaper in 1956. Abbott ran the *Chicago Defender* until his death in 1940, when his nephew, John H. Sengstacke, took over the business. Today the *Defender* is the centerpiece of the Sengstacke group of papers, which includes the *Michigan Chronicle*, the *New Pittsburgh Courier* and its branches, and the *Tri-State Defender*.

CIVILIAN CONSERVATION CORPS (CCC)   This was established in 1933 to meet the employment needs of young men between the ages of eighteen and twenty-five. Young people in the CCC lived in work camps under the direction of army officers. They performed a variety of tasks, such as reforestation, fire prevention, road construction, bridge and dam building, and mosquito control. By the end of 1943, when the CCC was placed under the Federal Works Agency, over two million young men had served in it. Many of the youths employed were black and from urban areas.

CLA JOURNAL   In this journal, founded in 1957, much space is devoted to black American literature, one of the very few scholarly journals to do so. It also includes in its articles and bibliographies materials on all aspects of English and American language and book reviews. Since it is the official house organ of the College Language Association, a certain amount of business news of the CLA is included in each issue. From time to time an entire issue may be devoted to the work of one writer.

CLARE KENDRY   This is a character in Nella Larsen's novel, *Passing*.

COFFLE   The word "coffle" derives from the Arab word quafilah and refers to a line of men or animals chained together. When moving groups of slaves from one place to another, both slave owners and slave traders chained the slaves together in a coffle. In the pre-Civil War South and Washington, D.C., coffles of slaves were a common sight. Washington was an important center of the domestic slave trade until 1850. Many slave coffles appear in William Wells Brown's novel, *Clotel*.

COLTER, CYRUS (1910-   )   This lawyer, novelist, and short story writer was born in Noblesville, Indiana, and attended the public schools. He obtained his advanced education at Youngstown College in Ohio and at Ohio State University. He completed studies at Chicago Kent College of Law and was admitted to the bar in Illinois in 1940. In 1942 he entered military service, where he reached the rank of captain. In 1946 Mr. Colter returned to the practice of law in Chicago. In 1950 he was appointed assistant commissioner of the Illinois Commerce Commission. In 1951 he became a full member and is at present its senior member. Cyrus Colter began writing stories as a hobby when he was fifty years old and since that time has continued to produce stories and novels. He is a member of numerous committees, clubs, and boards of trustees. including the Chicago Symphony Orchestra. He has won several awards for his short stories, including the Iowa School of Letters Award for short fiction.

COLTRANE SYNDROME   John Coltrane (1926-1967) was a jazz musician whose music strongly influenced the work of several black poets. Michael Harper, Imamu Baraka (LeRoi Jones), Sonia Sanchez, and Langston Hughes have employed the jazz motif in their writings. In Michael Harper's poetry, especially, the Coltrane syndrome, as it can be called, is clearly evident. He uses titles from some of Coltrane's pieces of music and one volume of his verse bears the title *Dear John Dear Coltrane.*

COMMITTEE FOR IMPROVING INDUSTRIAL CONDITIONS OF NEGROES IN NEW YORK   This organization was established in May 1906 to improve the economic conditions of the blacks in industrial New York. Its emphasis was on industrial education for blacks. A number of black leaders who participated in the activities of the CIICNY were Reverdy C. Ransom, T. Thomas Fortune, and Fred R. Moore, an editor of the *New York Age.*

COMMISSION ON CIVIL RIGHTS   Established by the Civil Rights Act of 1957, this federal agency was designed to investigate the real or supposed violations of the civil rights of all United States citizens. Among these rights were voting, free speech, and free assembly. This commission has investigated numerous instances of the infringements of the civil rights of black and other minority citizens.

CONCRETE POETRY   Poets who write concrete poetry substitute the basic parts of language, syllables, letters, and words for the usual parts of a poem such as rhyme, stanza, meter, and sometimes even regular sentence structure. The poems are organized in such a way as to provide a visual effect as well as an auditory one. Guillume Apollinaire, an early twentieth-century French poet, used this form in his book *Calligrammes.* Norman Henry Pritchard writes concrete poetry extensively. He is one of the few black American poets who use this form to any great extent. In one of his poems he uses the capital letter Z arranged on the page in such a way that it forms the shape of a large *A.*

CONTRABAND OF WAR   Anything or anyone that would be of aid to the Confederacy could be legally confiscated by the Union. Runaway slaves who came into the Union lines were usually put to work for the Union armies. Such slaves were often called "contrabands."

CORNBREAD   This is a character in Ronald Fair's novel, *Hog Butcher.*

CORTER, ELDZIER   (1915-   )   This painter was born in Richmond, Virginia; but when he was a year old, his family moved to

Chicago. He was educated in local schools and attended the Art Institute of Chicago. He completed further study at the Institute of Design, Columbia University, and the Pratt Graphic Center. Cortor has taught at the South Side Community Art Center of Chicago and worked on the Illinois Art and Crafts Project. Mr. Cortor's work has been exhibited at the James Porter Gallery of Howard University, the South Side Community Art Center, City College of New York, the Boston Museum of Fine Arts, the Albany Institute of History and Art, and the Metropolitan Museum of Art, New York. Eldzier Cortor has won many awards for his painting, including the Carnegie Award, the Bertha Aberie Florsheim Award, the Guggenheim Travel Award, the Rosenwald Fellowship, and the William H. Bartel Award. His work can be found in the Rosenwald Collection and the Musee Du Peuple Haitian, Haiti, among others.

COTTER, JOSEPH SEMON, SR. (1861-1949)   This poet, short story writer, and teacher was born in Bardstown, Kentucky, in 1861. He was forced to leave school in the third grade and was unable to return until he was twenty-two years old. He had worked at many jobs, including tobacco stemmer, brickyard worker, whiskey distiller, and prizefighter. When Cotter finally completed his education, he became a schoolteacher and eventually a principal. His poetry is at times didactic and at times militant on the question of the rights of Afro-Americans.

COTTER, JOSEPH S., JR. (1895-1919)   This poet was born in Louisville, Kentucky. He was educated at Fisk University but had to leave in his second year because of tuberculosis. In 1918, one year before his death at twenty-four, he published a small book of poems that showed great promise. His father was the well-known poet and teacher, Joseph Semon Cotter Sr.

COTTON KINGDOM, THE   The so-called "cotton kingdom" was the land that extended from South Carolina to the Mississippi River. The economy of this large region was based primarily on the plantation, which produced cotton on a very large scale by using slave labor extensively. Between 1830 and 1850 cotton planters extended their holdings beyond the Mississippi River and into Texas. This expansion of the cotton industry led to a direct increase in the domestic slave trade. The term "cotton kingdom" was made popular by Frederick Law Olmstead, who used it in a two-volume study of southern slavery.

Cox, IDA (1889-1967)   A blues singer, recording artist, and composer, Ida Cox was born in Knoxville, Tennessee. She began singing early and by the time she was fourteen she was singing in minstrel shows. In 1923 she made a series of recordings for Paramount Records that sold well and assured her success. She continued to record for Paramount until 1929. All through the 1930s, Ida Cox continued working. She established her own well-organized show that traveled the black vaudeville circuit until well into the 1950s. In 1939 she made several successful recordings with a band that included such jazz men as "Hot Lips" Paige and J. C. Higginbotham (Higginbottam). She retired around 1960 but was persuaded in 1961, when she was in her seventies, to make one last record. She was backed on this record by Coleman Hawkins, Roy Eldrige, and Sammy Price.

CROSS   This is a poem by Langston Hughes.

CROSS, DAMON   This is a character in Richard Wright's novel, *The Outsider*.

CRUMMEL, ALEXANDER (1819-1898)   This clergyman, scholar, and essayist was born free in New York City. His early education was obtained at African Free Schools there. When he was twelve years old, his parents sent him to an academy in New Canaan, New Hampshire. With him were three other black youths, one of them the future leader, Henry Highland Garnet. Although the school was supposed to be interracial, the four black students were received with extreme hostility by the citizens of New Canaan and driven from the town. The school building was destroyed. Crummel was able to complete his education at Oneida Institute in New York. Desiring to become an Episcopal minister, he applied at the General Theological Seminary in New York City; but his application was rejected when it was discovered that he was a black man. Aided by the abolitionist, John Jay, he was able to enter a seminary in Boston, where he completed his studies and was finally ordained a minister in Philadelphia in 1842. He did not serve as a priest in the Philadelphia area, however, because the chief Episcopal church official, Bishop Onderdonk, wanted him to accept a nonparticipating role in church affairs of the diocese. Finding this course unacceptable, Crummel left Philadelphia for New York, where he found a small parish he served for ten years. In 1852 Alexander Crummel left the United States for England and enrolled in Queens College at Cambridge University, receiving his degree in 1853. Instead of returning to the United States, he went on to Liberia, where he remained for twenty years. Finally, in 1873, he returned to Washington, D.C. where he became pastor of St. Mary's Mission. Later he was the leading figure in the building of St. Luke's Protestant Episcopal Church. He became the minister of St. Luke's and remained in that capacity for over twenty years. His sermons and speeches became widely known for their eloquence. When he retired in 1894, Alexander continued to write and speak about the problems of the blacks. In 1897 he founded the American Negro Academy. Although he was known primarily as a minister, he was one of the best black writers of the nineteenth century.

CURVING ROAD   This is a collection of ten short stories by John Stewart published in 1975. "Blues for Pablo" is set in San Francisco and concerns the relationship between Pablo, a middle-aged slaughterhouse owner who dreams of bullfighting, and a vibrant young woman whose way of life is very uninhibited. "The Pre-Jail Party" is a bittersweet story of a prostitute who buys one of her sister prostitutes a clock as a gift and gives it to her at a party held for her just before she goes to jail for six months.

DARK SYMPHONY   This is a long poem by Melvin B. Tolson.

DASEIN   Established in 1961, this literary journal appeared irregularly. The first issue had as its editor Walt Delegall, with Percy Johnson as publisher. The advisory board of the publication consisted of Sterling Brown, Arthur P. Davis, Owen Dodson, and Eugene C. Holmes. The art editor was William White. Contributing editors were W. Alfred Fraser, Oswald Govan, Lance Jeffers, Leroy Stone, and Joseph White. The first issue of *Dasein* contained four short stories, one play, nineteen poems, and four paintings, three by Joseph White and one by Lois Mailou Jones. This issue also contained a memorial to Richard Wright.

DAUGHTERS OF THE AMERICAN REVOLUTION, THE   Established in 1890, this organization has as its purpose the perpetuation of the spirit and memory of the early patriots of the United States, especially those of the American Revolution. The DAR as this organization is generally called, has a membership of approximately two hundred thousand and has national headquarters in Washington, D.C., in Constitution Hall. It is intense in its efforts to identify historic places and preserve national mementos and monuments. At times the group's reactionary and conservative outlook and actions have placed it in a negative light. The best example of this is the refusal, in 1939, of the DAR to allow world-renowned singer Marian Anderson to appear at Constitution Hall. Secretary of the Interior Harold Ickes arranged for Ms. Anderson to give a concert on the steps of the Lincoln Memorial. This concert was attended by seventy-five thousand people. There are few if any black members of this organization.

DAVE   This is a character in Robert D. Pharr's novel, *The Book of Numbers*.

DAVIS, FRANK MARSHALL (1905-   )   This poet, newsman, and editor was born in Arkansas. He received his education at Kansas City State College. Mr. Davis has had an extremely active career as a newspaperman and an editor. He was one of the founders of the *Atlanta Daily World* and later became the executive editor and administrator of the Associated Negro Press, a wire service based in Chicago. He has received awards and fellowships for his poetry. In later years Mr. Davis moved to Hawaii, where he now lives. He is still relatively active in the field of literature and occasionally lectures on the mainland.

DAVIS, OSSIE (1917-   )   This actor, playwright, editor, and screenwriter was born in Cogsdell, Georgia, grew up in Waycross, Georgia, and attended the schools of that city. After graduating from high school, Davis hitch-hiked to Washington, D.C., and entered Howard University. He left Howard at the end of his junior year and went to New York to gain practical experience in the theater and to try his hand at writing plays. Inducted into the army in 1942, Davis spent much of his military service in Liberia, West Africa, as a surgical technician in the Medical Corps. Eventually he was transferred to the Special Services Branch, where he was able to write and produce several shows. Mr. Davis returned to the theater in 1946 in the principal role of Jeb in Robert Ardrey's play of the same name. He continued to be active in the theater and studied play writing at Columbia University in 1948. During the 1950s, Ossie Davis appeared in a number of plays, among them *Green Pastures, The Royal Family, The Wisteria Trees,* and *No Time for Sergeants.* Along with his theatrical work he managed to appear in several motion pictures, including *Fourteen Hours* and *No Way Out.* In 1961 his play *Purlie Victorious* opened at the Cort Theater. Later this play was made into a successful motion picture and a musical version of it was produced in New York in 1971. Davis has continued his work in both theater and motion pictures and has branched out into other facets of the industry. His latest films are *The Slaves*, *Scalphunters*, and *Sam Whiskey*. He has appeared in and written many television plays and received an Emmy Award for his part in *Teacher, Teacher*. In addition, Mr. Davis finds time to be active in the civil rights movement and to write numerous critical articles on the theater. Recently he has become a motion picture director, having directed *Cotton Comes to Harlem* and other films. He often works with his wife, Ruby Dee, whom he married in 1948.

DEACONS FOR DEFENSE AND JUSTICE (1964)   During the early 1960s, civil rights workers and protesters in the South were often attacked by whites who were opposed to their activities. In order to provide protection for the civil rights groups operating in Mississippi and Louisiana, a group was organized in Jonesboro, Louisiana, in 1964 to defend the black community against the Ku Klux Klan and its allies. Some of the members who were inclined toward religion may have been responsble for the group's unusual name. The Deacons, as the loosely organized, armed group was usually called, were involved in the Bogalusa, Louisiana, disturbances of April 8, 1965, in which they exchanged gunfire with the Ku Klux Klan.

DEMBY, WILLIAM (1922-   )   A novelist, screenwriter, and teacher, William Demby was born in Pittsburgh, Pennsylvania, and grew up there and in Clarksburg, West Virginia. He attended local schools and West Virginia State College, Fisk University, and the University of Rome. Demby served two years in the army, spending most of his time in Italy. While he was in the army, he wrote for the army newspaper, *Stars and Stripes*. In 1947 Mr. Demby returned to Rome, where he lived for twenty years and worked as a jazz musician, screenwriter, and translator for Italian and European film producers. He returned to the United States sometime later.

DEMOSTHENIAN INSTITUTE   In several northern cities during the first half of the nineteenth century, free blacks organized reading, debating, and literary societies in order to broaden their intellectual horizons. The Demosthenian Institute was one of these societies. Organized in the home of John P. Burr on January 10, 1837, the main purpose of the institute was to train its members as public speakers.

By 1841 the Demosthennian Institute had forty-two members and its library contained over one hundred historical and scientific works. A weekly newspaper, the *Demosthenian Shield*, began publication on June 29, 1841. Approximately one thousand people subscribed to the paper before its first issue appeared.

DEMOSTHENIAN SHIELD   First published in June 1841, this weekly newspaper was the publication of the Demosthenian Institute, a black literary society established in 1837.

DETECTIVE STORY   Some short stories or novels are about a crime, often a murder, that is solved by a detective logically examining available evidence. Sometimes the detective is a member of a police force; sometimes he is a private detective. Black writers who have written detective stories are Rudolph Fisher, who wrote *Conjure Man Dies*, and Chester Himes, who wrote *Cotton Comes to Harlem* and several other crime novels. In 1958 Chester Himes received the coveted French prize, *Grand Prix Policier* for his detective novels.

DIALECT POETRY   The term "dialect" refers to the language of a particular group, class, or district; its meaning is derived from the Greek word, *Dialektos*, to discourse. During the latter part of the nineteenth century, a number of black American poets wrote using the dialect of the southern blacks. James D. Corrothers, Daniel Weberster Davis, James Edwin Campbell, and Paul L. Dunbar used this form to some extent. The success of these poets in using black dialect varied. The poet who used this form with the greatest degree of skill was Paul Laurence Dunbar, whose fame rested largely on the dialect poems he wrote. All of the poets mentioned wrote a substantial amount of work in standard English.

DIXECRATS, THE   In 1948 the States Rights Democratic party was organized by a group of southern Democrats in protest against the plank in the party's political platform that favored civil rights for blacks. Popularly known as the Dixiecrats, the party nominated J. Strom Thurmond of South Carolina for president. He carried four states, Alabama, Louisiana, Mississippi, and South Carolina, acquiring a total of thirty-nine electoral votes.

DODSON, OWEN (1914-   )   This poet, playwright, novelist, short story writer, and essayist was born in Brooklyn, New York. He was educated in local schools and at Bates College and Yale

University. While at Yale, two of his plays, *Divine Comedy* and *Garden of Time*, were produced. He has been head of the Department of Drama at Howard University and director of drama at Atlanta University, Spellman College, Hampton Institute, and Lincoln University. In addition to these posts, he has been poet in residence at the University of Arizona and has lectured and read his poetry in many parts of the United States and Europe. His essays have appeared in many magazines and journals, such as *Color, Common Ground, the New Republic, Harlem Quarterly,* and *Negro Digest*.

DOGGEREL   Sometimes poets produce poorly written, unimportant verse, characterized by trite subject matter, monotonous rhyme patterns, and trivial sentiment. Verse of this kind is usually referred to as doggerel.

DOMESTIC SLAVE TRADE, THE   Very soon after slavery began in the American colonies, a domestic slave trade emerged, especially in the southern English colonies. All of those buyers who did not purchase slaves directly from the slavers did business with local slave markets. Those involved in the domestic trade obtained their merchandise in various ways. Some slave holders sold their surplus slaves. The estates of planters who died without heirs were disposed of through sales by the courts. Often the property of these estates was in the form of slaves. Planters frequently used local newspapers to advertise the sale of slaves. Public auctions were often held, generally in or near the local courthouses. When the domestic slave trade started, most of the slaves sold were American born, but there were some Africans sold as well. Although the trade was small when it first began, by the middle of the eighteenth century it had increased enormously. When the African slave trade was closed by government order in 1808, the domestic trade increased even more. The trade in slaves between the upper and lower South was brisk and had become well organized by 1800. As a result of the increased demand, slave trading firms were established. The long-distance domestic trade was systematically organized and firms involved in it had assembly points in the upper South and markets for distribution in the lower South. One of the best-known domestic slave trading firms was that of Franklin and Armfield. This firm had an assembly area in Alexandria, Virginia, and sold slaves in the markets of Natchez and New Orleans. The Alexandria division of the company was equipped with a brick office building and residence.

Included also were a hospital and stockades with sleeping and eating quarters for the slaves. John Armfield ran the Alexandria division of the company and Isaac Franklin was in charge of the Southwest division.

DORIS   This is a character in William Demby's novel, *The Catacombs*.

DOUGLAS, AARON (1899-   )   This painter, teacher, illustrator, and printmaker was born in Topeka, Kansas. He was educated in local schools and at the University of Kansas, the University of Nebraska, Columbia Teachers College, and L'Academie Scandinave. He studied further under artist Winold Reiss. For a short period of time he taught art at Lincoln High School in Kansas City, Kansas. In 1923 he moved to New York, where he became known as the most prominent painter of the Harlem Renaissance period and produced numerous illustrations for books and journals. He illustrated the works of James Weldon Johnson, Langston Hughes, and Countee Cullen. In addition to his work as an illustrator, Aaron Douglas produced many paintings and murals using scenes from the history of the blacks of the United States. His work has been exhibited at the Baltimore Museum, the Art Institute of Chicago, and the Omaha Gallery of Modern Art. Aaron Douglas's work can be found in the Fisk University Library Murals, the New York Public Library, and Bennet College.

DOUGLASS, FREDERICK (1817-1895)   This editor, journalist, publisher, orator, and black leader was born a slave in Talbot County, Maryland. He was taught to read by his owner's wife when he was a boy. Later he continued to educate himself. In 1838 Frederick Douglass, whose real name was Augustus Washington Bailey, made his escape from slavery. In 1841 he became an agent for the Massachusetts Anti-Slavery Society and was one of their best speakers. In 1845 Douglass published an autobiography, *The Narrative of Frederick an American Slave;* and he was forced to flee to England where he spoke against slavery. While he was in England and Europe, money was collected and his freedom was purchased. In 1847 he began to publish the North Star, a newspaper, and rapidly became the leader of the blacks in the United States. At the beginning of the Civil War, Frederick Douglass recruited blacks to serve as soldiers in the Union forces. Following the war, he became deeply involved in Republican politics, becoming United States marshal and minister to Haiti. Douglass continued to fight for the rights of the blacks until his death.

DRED SCOTT CASE, THE   During the decade of the 1850s a series of incidents occurred that propelled the United States toward the Civil War. One of the most important of these was the famous Dred Scott case in 1857. In 1834 Dred Scott, the slave of army surgeon Dr. John Emerson, was taken by Emerson to an army post in Rock Island, Illinois. In 1835 Dr. Emerson was transferred to a post at Fort Snelling, Wisconsin. In 1838 Emerson returned to St. Louis and brought Scott and Scott's wife and child with him. In 1844 Dr. Emerson dies, leaving Scott to his widow. During the 1840s Mrs. Emerson moved to New York and left Scott in the care of Henry and Taylor Blow, the sons of Scott's first owner. Henry T. Blow was an antislavery activist and a well-to-do lawyer. In 1846 he brought suit in the Missouri courts to obtain Scott's freedom on the grounds that any slave who had lived in free territory was automatically free. The lower Missouri court ruled in Scott's favor. However, the case was appealed to the Missouri Supreme Court, which reversed the lower court. It held that Scott voluntarily returned to Missouri, and as a resident of Missouri he was still a slave as a result of his return since slavery was legal in that state. Scott's lawyer appealed the case to the U.S. Supreme Court in 1856. In 1857 the Court decided against Scott. The majority opinion of the Supreme Court was delivered by Chief Justice Roger Brooke Taney. The opinion indicated that Scott was not a citizen and thus could not bring suit in federal court. Concerning the blacks, the opinion held that blacks were inferior to whites and had no rights that had to be respected. The opinion further stated that Congress had no power to exclude slavery from any territory in the United States. The outcry against the court was great and the Dred Scott decision only served to widen the existing gap between the North and South on the issue of slavery.

DUBOIS, W. E. B. (1868-1963)   This novelist, short story writer, historian, poet, critic, editor, sociologist, and civil rights leader was born in Great Barrington, Massachusetts. He received his early education in the local schools and at Fisk and Harvard universities. He was the first black person to receive a Ph. D. from Harvard. He later spent two years at the University of Berlin. After his return from Germany he became an instructor at Wilberforce University. In 1894 he was instructor in sociology at the University of Pennsylvania, then in 1897 DuBois became professor of economics and history at Atlanta University. In 1905 he organized the Niagara Movement, which in 1908 merged with the newly formed NAACP. Dr. DuBois became the founder and editor of the Crisis magazine, the house publication of the NAACP, and the spokesman for the blacks. His views supported those blacks who wanted complete equality rather than those who adhered to the accommodationist outlook of Booker T. Washington. Dr. DuBois continued to speak out on the race issue until he left the United States to live in Ghana in 1962. During his long career, Dr. DuBois wrote many essays, books, and poems; his work has appeared in many journals, including *Phylon,* which he founded, the *Crisis, Arts Quarterly,* and *Freedomways.* He was elected to the National Institute of Arts and Letters in 1943. He has received an LL.D. from Harvard University and one from Atlanta University. Dr. DuBois lived in Ghana until his death in 1963.

DUNBAR, PAUL LAURENCE (1872-1906)   This poet, novelist, essayist, and librettist was born in Dayton, Ohio. He was educated in the Dayton public schools, graduating with honors from Central High School. He took a job as an elevator operator, since there was no money available for him to continue on to college. Dunbar began writing poetry very early while in elementary school, and continued to write while he worked as an elevator boy. In 1892 he published, at his own expense, a slender book of poetry, only sixty-two pages, containing fifty-two poems. Three years later another small volume of poems, *Majors and Minors,* was published, again at his own expense. On June 27, 1896, William Dean Howells wrote a favorable review of *Majors and Minors* in *Harper's Weekly;* and as a result of Howells' review, Dunbar was suddenly famous. A new collection of his poems was published in 1896, and in 1897 he went to England on a reading tour. Upon his return, he moved to Washington, D.C., and went to work at the Library of Congress. In 1898 Dunbar left the Library of Congress to continue writing. In 1900 he became ill. He returned to his home in Dayton, Ohio, in 1903 and remained there until his death in 1906.

DUREM, RAY (1915-1963)   This poet was born in Seattle, Washington. His formal education ended when he was fourteen, when he ran away from home and joined the navy. During the Spanish Civil War, he served as a soldier with the International Brigade. He began writing poetry in the early 1940s; his writing appeared in numerous magazines and journals, among them *Phylon, Umbra,* and *Venture.* He attended the University of California and worked at various jobs, including his trade of television technician. In 1954 Ray Durem moved his family to Mexico. He tried commuting between Guadelajara and Los Angeles until 1962, when he moved his family back to Los Angeles. He died of cancer on December 17, 1963.

DUST OF SILENCE   This is a novel by Oliver Pitcher, published in 1960.

EBONY   Established in 1945, this monthly publication is the most widely circulated and the best known of all black magazines. It is similar to the now-defunct magazine, *Life,* except that its primary concern is with the world of the blacks. Its writers discuss all aspects of black life in the United States and the lives and problems of blacks in other parts of the world such as Africa, South America, Canada, and Cuba. Over the years *Ebony* has published articles about many black writers and their work.

EDMONDS, RANDOLPH S. (1900-   )   This playwright and drama critic was born in Lawrenceville, Virginia. He was educated at St. Paul's Normal School and at Oberlin College and Columbia and Yale universities. He completed advanced work at the University of Dublin and the London School of Speech and Drama. He has taught drama at Hampton Institute, Dillard University, Florida A & M College, and Atlanta University. Mr. Edmonds has written over forty plays and numerous articles concerning drama. His writings have appeared in the *Crisis, Phylon,* and *Negro Digest.*

EDWARDS, JUNIUS (1929-   )   This novelist and short story writer was born in Alexandria, Louisiana. He was educated in local schools, in Chicago, and at the University of Oslo in Norway. Mr. Edwards has worked in the advertising field and is the director of an agency in New York. His short stories have appeared in several magazines and journals, including the *Transatlantic Review* and the *Urbanite.* He has won several awards for his work, including the Eugene Saxon Fellowship (1959).

ELDER, LONNE, III (1931-   )   This playwright and screen and television writer was born in Americus, Georgia. He was educated in public schools and at the Yale University School of Drama. Mr. Elder has served in the United States Army; worked on the docks and as a waiter; has been a professional gambler; and has been employed in the theater, motion pictures, and the television industry. From 1970 to 1971 he was a writer for the television series "McCloud" and in 1968 for the series "N.Y.P.D." In 1972 he wrote the screen play for the film *Sounder*. Lonne Elder has received the Vernon Rice Award (1970), the John Hay Whitney Fellowship (1965-1966); the Outer Critics' Circle Award (1970); and the Stella Holt Award (1970).

ELEGY   An elegy is a poem that laments or mourns the death of someone. Black leader Malcolm X's death elicited numerous elegies from black and white poets all across the United States. Many of these poems of mourning were collected in an anthology, *For Malcolm*, edited by poet and publisher Dudley Randall. The word elegy comes from the Latin word *elegia*, which in turn is derived from the Greek term, *elegia*, which means a lament.

ELGAR ENDERS   This is a character in Kristin Hunter's novel, *The Landlord*.

ELLISON, RALPH WALDO (1914-   )   This novelist, short story writer, and essayist was born in Oklahoma City, Oklahoma. He was educated in local schools and at Tuskeegee Institute. He has worked in the Federal Writer's Project and during World War II served in the Merchant Marine. He has taught and lectured at Bard College, the University of Chicago, Rutgers University, and the Salzburg Seminar in American Studies in Salzburg, Austria. Mr. Ellison's writings have appeared in a great many magazines and journals, among them *Partisan Review*, *Negro Digest*, *Harper's*, the *Saturday Review*, the *New Republic*, *Crisis*, and *Esquire*. He has received the Rosenwald Fellowship (1945-1947); he was a Fellow at the Academy in Rome (1955-1957), the National Book Award for *The Invisible Man* (1953), and the Chevalier de l'Ordre Arts et Lettres of the French government (1960).

ELSPETH   This is a character in W. E. B. DuBois's novel, *The Quest of the Silver Fleece*.

EMERSON-HALL PUBLISHERS, INC   This company was established in 1963 by Harper and Row editor Alfred Prettyman, who felt that the book industry's interest in blacks as employees and black material was momentary. It operates out of New York and publishes paperback and hardcover books. The emphasis has been on books concerned with the social sciences; however, they have published poetry, fiction, and children's books as well.

ERMA WYSONG   This is a character in Sutton Griggs's novel, *Overshadowed*.

ESTHER KENNEDY   This is a character in Elizabeth Vroman's novel, *Esther*.

EXODUSTERS   This is a term that referred to those blacks who left the South and migrated to Kansas, Nebraska, and other midwestern states during the great exodus of blacks from the South in 1879. Because of the many difficulties they faced in the South, (the loss of political power, crop failure, and unfair and often cruel treatment by landlords and merchants), thousands of blacks left the South in search of better conditions. This large migration resulted in a debate between Frederick Douglass and Richard H. Greener, two black leaders of that period. Douglass wanted the blacks to stay in the South, while Greener urged them to leave. One of the most unusual leaders of these migrants was Benjamin "Pap" Singleton, an ex-slave.

FABIO, SARAH WEBSTER (1928-   )   This poet, critic, and playwright was born in Nashville, Tennessee. She was educated in local schools and at Spellman College and Fisk, Wichita State, and San Francisco State universities. Her writings have appeared in several magazines and journals, including *Black World* and *Negro Digest*.

FACTOR   The captains of slave ships did not want to remain in the slave ports any longer than they had to. The amount of money they could earn depended upon how quickly they could get their full complement of slaves and set sail for the West Indies to reach there with as complete a cargo as possible. The slave-trading companies created a middleman called a factor to live permanently on the company post and keep an adequate supply of slaves on hand for the slaving ships that came to port.

FAIR, RONALD (1932-   )   This novelist and short story writer was born in Chicago, Illinois. He was educated in the public schools of Chicago and at business college. Mr. Fair served as a hospital corpsman in the navy and has worked as a court reporter. His writings have appeared in such magazines as *Essence* (July 1971) and *Negro Digest* (July 1965).

FANNY COPEE   This is a character in Kristin Hunter's novel, *The Landlord.*

FAUCET, JESSIE REDMOND (1886-1961)   This novelist, short story writer, poet, and essayist was born in Philadelphia, Pennsylvania. She was educated in the public schools of Philadelphia, at Cornell University, the University of Pennsylvania, and the Sorbonne in Paris. In 1906 Ms. Faucet became a teacher of Latin and French at KM High School in Washington, D.C., which later became Dunbar High School and was famous for the high level of teaching practiced there. She remained at Dunbar until June 1919, when she resigned her position and became a literary editor on *Crisis* magazine, where she worked under W. E. B. DuBois. Jessie Faucet remained at *Crisis* until 1926, when she gave up her post and returned to teaching. She became a teacher in the New York public school system, where she remained until 1944. Even while teaching, Ms. Faucet continued as a contributing editor for the *Crisis*, writing many poems, essays, and short stories. After her retirement, she was visiting professor at both Hampton and Tuskeegee institutes. She died in her native city Philadelphia in 1961.

FAUSET, ARTHUR HUFF (1899-   )   This anthropologist, critic, short story writer, and essayist was born in Flemington, New Jersey. He was educated in public schools and at the University of Pennsylvania. He has studied the folklore of the blacks in Nova Scotia, Philadelphia, the British West Indies, and the southern United States. He is a fellow of the American Anthropological Association and has received several awards for his work. His book *Black Gods of the Metropolis* has become a classic in its field. In 1931 Arthur Fauset won a prize for his story *Symphonesque.*

FEELINGS, TOM (1933-   )   This painter, designer, writer, and illustrator was born in Brooklyn, New York. He was educated in public schools and at the School of Visual Arts of New York City. Mr. Feelings has traveled extensively in Africa and for a short time worked as staff illustrator for the *African Review.* He has illustrated many books, among them *To Be A Slave, A Quiet Place, Tales of Temba,* and *Black Pilgrimage.* His work has been exhibited at Morgan State College, Atlanta University, and the Brooklyn Art

Felton, B.

Fair. He has received the Certificate of Merit from the Society of Illustrators.

FELTON, B. (ELMER BUFORD) (1934-   )   This poet, essayist, and short story writer was born in Cleveland, Ohio. He was educated in the Cleveland public schools and at the University of Miami in Oxford, Ohio, and the Cleveland Bible College. His writings have appeared in various magazines, including *Black Ascension* and *Black Opinion*. B. Felton's poetry can also be found in the Broadside Press anthology, *A Broadside Treasury*, edited by Gwendolyn Brooks.

FIFTEENTH AMENDMENT (1870)   The third of three post-Civil War amendments, it gave the blacks the right to vote. Before the passage of this amendment, blacks could not vote in several southern states, including Georgia and Louisiana.

FIRE   First published in 1926, this literary journal made its appearance in Harlem. Its editors were Wallace Thurman, Langston Hughes, Gwendolyn Bennet, Zora Neal Hurston, Aaron Douglas, and Richard Bruce. The first issue of this quarterly contained drawings by Aaron Douglas and Richard Bruce and poems by Langston Hughes, Countee Cullen, Edward Silvera, Helene Johnson, Waring Cuney, Arna Bontemps, and Lewis Alexander. Included also were a play by Zora Neal Hurston; stories by Wallace Thurman, Zora Hurston, and Gwendolyn Bennet; an essay by Arthur Huff Fauset; part of a novel by Richard Bruce; and an editorial comment by chief editor Wallace Thurman. The reception of this new journal was extremely hostile and it went out of existence after the initial publication.

FIRST REGIMENT OF SOUTH CAROLINA VOLUNTEERS   In August 1862, a change in the Union War Department policy brought about the official sanction of the recruitment of blacks to serve as soldiers in the Union Army. General Rufus Saxon of the Department of the South was ordered to arm and provide equipment for five thousand volunteers. Immediately a regiment, all black except for officers, was organized. In January the First Regiment of South Carolina Volunteers was mustered into service. Early in 1863 the regiment fought in South Carolina and Florida and gained a reputation as a hard fighting unit of the Union Army.

FISHER, RUDOLPH (1897-1934)   This physician, novelist, and short story writer was born in Washington, D.C. He grew up in Providence, Rhode Island, and was educated in the public schools there. A brilliant student, he graduated with honors from Classical High School in 1915. He attended Brown University, from which he graduated with high honors, having been elected to three honor societies. In 1920 he received a master's degree, also from Brown, and entered Howard University Medical School, graduating in 1924. In 1925 Fisher moved to New York and studied at the College of Physicians and Surgeons of Columbia University for two years. He began the practice of medicine in 1927, specializing in X-ray treatments. He began writing short stories while still in medical school and his stories appeared in several magazines, including *Atlantic Monthly* (February 1925 and August 1927) *Crisis* (#30, 1925); *Opportunity* (February and March 1931) and *Story Magazine* (June 1933). He was awarded the Spingarn Short Story Prize for 1925.

FISK JUBILEE SINGERS   In October 1871 Fisk University, a black university located in Nashville, Tennessee, sent out a group of ten young student singers under the direction of Reverend George White. Their task was to raise funds for the expansion of the institution. The group was called the Fisk Jubilee Singers. After an uncertain beginning, the young singers won acclaim at Oberlin, Ohio, and at the White House. They sang the religious songs that had been sung by slaves. This group went on many tours to raise funds for Fisk University. They sang before the royal courts of several European countries and gained a worldwide reputation. As a result of their concerts, the Fisk Jubilee Singers raised $150,000, which was used in 1875 to build a dormitory for women, appropriately called Jubilee Hall. October 6, the day on which the young singers set out on their first tour, is known as Jubilee Day and is still celebrated at Fisk University.

FISK UNIVERSITY SPECIAL COLLECTIONS, THE   Fisk University Library has over twenty special collections of materials on the history and culture of the blacks of America. Included in those collections are the W. E. B. DuBois Collection, the Edwin R. Embree Collection, the Jean Toomer Papers, and the Charles S. Johnson Papers. There are almost three-hundred thousand cataloged items in the Fisk University special collections.

FLORENCE DESSAU   This is a character in Arna Bontemps's novel, *God Sends Sunday*.

FOR MY UNBORN AND WRETCHED CHILDREN   This is a poem by A. B. Spellman.

FORTEN, CHARLOTTE (1838-1914)   This translator, short story writer, teacher, and poet was born in Philadelphia, Pennsylvania. She was the granddaughter of James Forten, a wealthy black business-man and abolitionist. She was educated privately and at the Higginson Grammar and the Salem Normal Schools in Salem, Massachusetts. After finishing her education in 1856, she taught for two years at Epps Grammar School in Salem. However, ill health forced her to return to Philadelphia in 1858. During the time she spent in Salem, she lived in the home of the Charles Lenox Redmond family. Here she became acquainted with many of the leading abolitionists of the period and, as a result, became dedicated to the struggle against slavery. Five years after the outbreak of the Civil War, Charlotte Forten volunteered to serve the Port Royal Relief Association at Port Royal, South Carolina. She was assigned to St. Helena Island, where she taught illiterate slaves to read and write and served in other capacities such as nursing the sick and caring for the children. She remained in the South until 1864, when her health failed and she was forced to return home to Philadelphia. When she was well again, she went to work with the New England Freedman's Aid Society. During her stay in South Carolina, she wrote articles for the *Atlantic Monthly* and other magazines. After her return home she wrote many short stories and translated a French novel, *Madame Therese,* for Scribners Publishing Company. In May 1854, when she was sixteen years old, Charlotte Forten began to write a journal. She kept it for many years, even when she was in South Carolina. It is for this journal that she is best known. It was in the manuscript collection of Howard University's Moorland Library until 1953, when it was edited and published by Ray Allen Billington.

FORT PILLOW MASSACRE   On April 12, 1864, Confederate troops under Nathan Bedford Forrest attacked Fort Pillow, Tennessee, about fifty miles north of Memphis. The result of this attack was one of the worst atrocities to occur during the Civil War. The fort was commanded by Major L. F. Booth with a detachment of 557 men, of whom 262 were blacks from the Sixth United States Heavy Artillery Regiment. Major Booth was killed early in the attack. The new commander withdrew his troops into the fort proper and refused to surrender the garrison. The Confederates attacked the fort a second time and captured it. The Union troops were given "no quarter," especially the black troops. As soon as the fort surrendered, its defenders were killed. Some were shot, others were buried alive, and still others were bayoneted to death. The killing continued from three in the afternoon until midnight. Of the 262 black troopers in the fort, 238 were slaughtered.

FORT WAGNER, THE BATTLE OF   On July 18, 1863, Union Army units were ordered to attempt to capture a heavily fortified Confederate strongpoint that was a key position in the defense of Charleston, South Carolina. Located on Morris Island was one of the strongest earthworks built during the Civil War. It was almost immune from frontal assault. The soldiers of the black Fifty-Fourth Massachusetts Regiment played a prominent part in the attack on the position. The fort was bombarded by the Union naval forces and the Union Army artillery units before the attack began. The Union forces were ordered forward with the Fifty-Fourth Massachusetts Regiment in the forefront. The black soldiers made a gallant charge toward the parapets of the fort and managed to reach the first before they were forced to withdraw under the intense fire of the defenders. The casualties suffered by the regiment were severe; of the 600 men who began the assault, only 353 lived through the attack; 247 men were killed outright. This battle helped to reverse the feeling on the part of many whites that blacks would not make good soldiers.

FOURTEENTH AMENDMENT (1868)   The second of three post-Civil War amendments, it gave citizenship to blacks and it is the most detailed of the Civil War amendments. It also abolished the three-fifths clause, which counted the slaves as three-fifths of a person. It solved the problem of dual citizenship by making persons born in the United States citizens of both the nation as a whole and the state in which they lived.

FRANKLYN GORDON   This is a character in Mercedes Gilbert's novel, *Aunt Sara's Wooden God*.

FRAZIER, FRANKLIN (1894-1862)   This sociologist was born in Baltimore, Maryland. He was educated in public schools and at Howard and Clark universities and the University of Chicago. He was a research fellow at the New York School of Social Work and completed further study as a fellow of the American-Scandinavian Foundation. Mr. Frazier became an authority on the sociology of the blacks of the United States and wrote numerous articles and several books. His study *The Negro in the United States* has become a classic in its field. The publication of *Black Bourgeoisie,* his controversial study of the black middle class, caused him to be even more widely known. Franklin Frazier received the Guggheim Fellowship (1940) and the McIver Award of the American Sociological Society.

FRED MERRIT   This is a character in Rudolph Fisher's novel, *The Walls of Jericho.*

FREE AFRICAN SOCIETIES   In 1787 black leader and minister Richard Allen and several of his friends were pulled from their knees while praying in St. George's Church in Philadelphia. Shortly, after this incident, Allen led the blacks from St. George's and established a self-help organization, the Free African Society of Philadelphia, "to support one in sickness and for the benefit of widows and orphans." Soon free African societies were organized in other cities, the African Society of Boston in 1796 and the New York African Society in 1809. Although the Free African Society of Philadelphia was prominent, it was not the first of its kind. As early as 1780 the African Union Society of Newport, Rhode Island, was in existence. Its papers are presently on loan to the Newport Historical Society.

FREE BLACKS, THE   In 1790 the first census in the United States showed that there were approximately sixty-thousand free blacks in the nation or 7.9 percent of the total population. There were free blacks both in the northern and southern parts of the United States. By 1830 there were three-hundred twenty thousand free blacks and by 1830, nearly five-hundred thousand. Forty-one percent lived in the South and 46 percent lived in the North. Some had been manumitted by their owners; some had bought their own freedom; still others had been born of free mothers both white and black. Another category of free blacks were those who hade made good their escape from slavery. In the South the presence of free blacks embarrassed the planters and tended to undermine the slave system. Free blacks lived a precarious existence in the North as well as in the South. Often they were kidnapped and sold into slavery or claimed as runaway slave by slaves catchers. The southern planters carried out programs specifically designed to diminish and darken the character of the free blacks. Controls over them increased each year. Two well-known leaders of the free blacks were Frederick Douglass and William Wells Brown.

FREEDMENS BUREAU (1865-1874)   Although the northern victory in the Civil War reunited the northern and southern parts of the country, the South was left in a devastated condition. Black ex-slaves and poor whites found their existence extremely precarious. Blacks especially were in great difficulty because many of them had no homes, no jobs, and no job skills. The federal government established the Bureau of Refugees, Freedmen, and Abandoned Lands to help the people, both blacks and whites, dislocated by the war. This agency, better known as the Freedmens Bureau, placed officials in each southern state. The bureau aided the blacks and other refugees by furnishing medical services and general supplies, by opening schools, and by managing abandoned lands and supervising labor contracts between the freedmen and their employers. Between 1865 and 1869 the Freedmens Bureau issued twenty-one million food rations, five million for whites and sixteen million for ex-slaves. Schools were established on all levels, day schools, night schools, Sunday schools, and colleges. The teachers in these schools were usually from the North and worked under hostile conditions. Freedmens courts and arbitration boards were established as well. The bureau was constantly under attack from its beginning. Its functions were sharply curtailed in 1869 and in 1872. Congress withdrew its financial support and the agency began to die, although it continued to exist feebly until 1874.

FREEDOM NOW PARTY   During the decade of the 1960s severe opposition to civil rights legislation existed in Congress. Because of this resistance, some blacks felt that a third, all-black, political party should be formed. As a result of this feeling, it was announced on August 28, 1964, that the Freedom Now Party, an all-black national political party, would be organized. It would run candidates for the 1964 congressional and local elections.

FREEDOM RIDERS (1961)   During the week of May 14-16 racial rioting occurred in Alabama and ceased only after federal marshals were sent to that state. The riots began as a result of a demonstration protesting the discrimination against blacks in interstate travel. A group of black and white demonstrators who referred to themselves as "freedom riders" chartered buses and set out to ride from Washington, D.C., to New Orleans to challenge segregation at bus stops, restaurants, and stations. Teams of freedom riders were attacked and beaten in Annistion, Birmingham, and Montgomery, Alabama. In the Anniston attack one bus was destroyed by a fire bomb. This tour was sponsored by the Congress of Racial Equality.

FREEDOMS JOURNAL (1827-1829)   Before 1827 there was no newspaper or magazine in the United States that was published by blacks. In March 1827, in New York City, a group of free blacks met in the home of Boston Cromwell and decided to establish a newspaper for the black people of the city. Samuel Cornish, a Presbyterian minister, and John B. Russwurm were chosen to be editors. The new publication, *Freedoms Journal* gave the blacks in New York City a platform from which to voice their views on matters that concerned them, matters often ignored by the white press. After the first issue of the paper, Samuel Cornish resigned as editor and until 1829, when he left for Liberia, John Russwurm was sole editor. After Russwurm's departure, Samuel Cornish again became editor.

FREEDOMWAYS   This quarterly journal was founded in 1961. Each issue usually contains poetry, fiction, nonfiction, and book reviews. Articles are well written and are about ten pages long. A regular feature in each issue is the annotated bibliography of recent books about blacks in the Americas and abroad compiled by Schomburg bibliographer Ernest Kaiser. Occasionally special issues on a particular topic are published.

FREE VERSE   Free verse, sometimes called *verse libre,* is different from standard verse in that there is usually no regular metrical pattern. Although free verse does not have the regular rhythm pattern of conventional poetry, there are many possibilities for the poet to achieve the desired effect. Even the shape of the poem on the printed page can be employed to elicit the response that the poet wants. Many black American poets use this form. Among those who write free verse extensively are Gwendolyn Brooks, Margaret Walker Alexander, and Ethridge Knight.

FULLER, META VAUX Warick (1877-1967)   This sculptor was born in Philadelphia. She was educated in local schools and at the Pennsylvania School of Industrial Art, the Pennsylvania Academy of Fine Arts, Academic Colorossi Paris, and the Ecole des Beaux Arts, Paris. She studied under famous sculptor Auguste Rodin. Her work has been exhibited at the Boston Art Club, Howard University, the Art Institute of Chicago, the New York Public Library, and City College of New York. Meta V. Warick Fuller's work can be seen in the Cleveland Art Museum, the Schomburg Collection, Palmer Institute, and the San Francisco Museum of Fine Arts.

GAMMON, REGINALD (1921-   )   This painter and photographer was born in Philadelphia. He was educated in local schools and at the School of Fine Arts of Philadelphia. During World War II, Mr. Gammon served in the navy and spent several years in the Pacific on the island of Guam. A prolific artist, his work has been exhibited in the Minneapolis Institute of Art, the Boston Museum of Fine Arts, the Harlem Cultural Center, the Rhode Island School of Design, and the Philadelphia Print Club. Mr. Gammon's work can be found in the Chase Manhattan Fine Arts Collection, the Dennison College Collection, and the Benny Andrews Collection. He has received fourth prize for his work in the Jazz/Art Exhibit at the Detroit Art Institute.

MR. GARIE   This is a character in Frank Webb's novel, *The Garies and Their Friends.*

GARNET, HENRY HIGHLAND (1815-1882)   This abolitionist, orator, editor, minister, diplomat, black leader was born a slave in Maryland. In 1824 his father took his family and escaped to New Hope, Pennsylvania, where they remained until 1825, when the family name was changed and Mr. Garnet moved to New York. Henry Garnet was educated at the African Free Schools of New York and at Oneida Institute. While he was still studying, he became involved in antislavery activities. In 1840, after graduating from Oneida Institute, Garnet moved to Troy, New York, and taught in the school for black children. In 1843 Mr. Garnet was ordained a Presbyterian minister. He quickly gained a reputation as an orator of the first rank. He increased his participation in the antislavery movement despite the fact that he had only one leg. Some abolitionists considered him a radical. In 1843 he addressed the Convention of Free Colored People in Buffalo, New York. In his speech he urged the slaves to revolt openly against their owners. This speech caused a clash between Garnet and Fredrick Douglass, and Henry Garnet lost the support of the convention. Douglass was captapulted into the position of national leader of the blacks. Garnet served as a minister to several churches in New York and Washington, D.C. While he was at the Fifteenth Street Church in Washington

(1864-1866) he preached a sermon in the House of Representatives. In 1881 President Garfield appointed him minister to Liberia, but he did not serve out his term. He contracted a fever and died from a severe attack of asthma in Monrovia on February 13, 1882.

GENE BROWNING   This is a character in John A. Williams's novel, *The Sons of Darkness and the Sons of Light.*

GEORGE WASHINGTON   This is a character in Cecil Brown's novel, *Life and Loves of Mr. Jiveass Nigger.*

GERRYMANDER   This word was first used in 1812 during the second term of Elbridge Gerry as governor of Massachusetts. It refers to the redistricting of voting areas so that the voting advantage is in the favor of a particular political party. One February 11, 1812, a bill was passed in the Massachusetts state legislature redistricting the voting units of the state so as to give a partisan advantage to Jeffersonian Republicans. Essex County was reorganized in such a way that it resembled a salamander. The newspapers were quick to name this new district a "gerrymander." Since 1812, this method has been used to gain partisan political advantage in city, state, and congressional districts. Under this procedure, minority voting strength can be confined to a few districts. Gerrymandering has often been used to prevent blacks from gaining political strength or advantage both in the northern and southern states. The best example of the use of gerrymandering to restrict the black voter occurred in Tuskeegee, Alabama, in 1957 when a state law was passed that reset the city boundaries so as to exclude all but ten of the city's four hundred black registered voters. In 1960 the Supreme Court ruled that this law violated the Fifteenth Amendment by depriving black voters of their rights and was therefore unconstitutional.

GHANA, ANCIENT (750-1077 A.D.)   The West African empire of ancient Ghana dates from 300 A.D. Ghana was ruled by Berber invaders from North Africa from 300 A.D. to 700 A.D., when the Sonike people regained local political control from their Berber conquerers. Old Ghana consisted of parts of the present-day countries of Mali, Senegal, Guinea, and Mauritania. The first group to hold great political power in the area of the Senegal and Niger rivers, were the Sonike people. The Sonikes were a group of related tribes, each tribe especially named and divided into clans. The division of labor was related to the division of the tribes or clans.

The Sisse were the ruling clan; they produced most of the government officals. The Kante clan were metal workers and blacksmiths. Other clans produced farmers, cow herders, fishermen, and clothing makers. In approximately 700 A.D. a local warrior, Kaya Maghan, led a successful revolt against the ruling Berbers and Ghana began a period of immense growth and development. Two kinds of metal were very important in the expansion of Ghana, gold and iron. The Sonikes were probably the first, and for a very long time the only, people who used iron in their part of Africa. The troops of Ghana's army used iron weapons. This gave them superiority over their neighbors, whom they conquered. The kings of Ghana were powerful figures with great influence and the empire was complex. Most of Ghana's wealth depended on trade. The twin cities Koumbi-Selah were located at the crossroads of all the trade routes. The centers of these cities were six to ten miles apart and were connected by a long avenue. As a result of its strategic location, Koumbi-Selah became the busiest marketplace of its time in West Africa. The most important items of trade were gold and salt, but wheat, cloth, leather, gum arabic, copper, ivory, pearls, slaves, and seashells were traded as well. Ghana reached the zenith of its power in the mid-eleventh century. In about 1050 the Almoravids, a stern and austere Moslem religious sect, began the invasion of Ghana from North Africa. Under the leadership of Ibn Yacin, an acetic Moslem reformer, the Almoravids continued their attacks for seven years, until Ibn Yacin's death in 1057. A new leader, Abu Bakr, was chosen and after a short pause the attacks on Ghana increased sharply. By 1067 the Almoravids were hammering at the gates of Koumbi-Selah and the city was put under a siege that lasted off and on for ten years. In 1076-1077 the city fell and Ghana began a decline from which it never recovered. Abu Bakr died in battle while suppressing a revolt and the Almoravids withdrew from Ghana, but the Sonikes were never able to regain control of their former subjects. The Songhay and Mandingo people declared themselves independent. The descendants of the Sonikes still live in the same region as their ancestors had; however, this area today is part of several different countries.

GILBERT LYCEUM   This black literary and scientific society was organized in Philadelphia on January 3, 1841. The membership was opened to both sexes. Lectures were delivered to the group at various times. There was a membership of forty-one at one time.

GOD IS FOR WHITE FOLKS This is a novel by Will Thomas, published in 1947.

GOODMAN, SCHWERNER, CHANEY INCIDENT, THE On June 21, 1964, three young civil rights workers disappeared after having been held for five hours in jail on a speeding charge in Philadelphia, Mississippi. The three young men were Andrew Goodman, twenty years old, a white college student from Queens New York; Michael Schwerner, twenty-four years old, a white member of the Congress of Racial Equality; and James Earl Chaney, twenty-one years old, a black member of CORE from Meridian, Mississippi. The young men had worked with the Council of Federated Organizations (COFO) in a summer campaign to register black voters. When the three civil rights workers did not call in to their headquarters on June 22, Attorney General Robert F. Kennedy ordered a full-scale FBI investigation; and on June 25, 1964, President Lyndon Johnson authorized the use of naval personnel from the naval air station at Meridian to help in the search for the missing men. On August 4, 1964, the bodies of the three young men were found in a newly built earth dam about five miles from Philadelphia, Mississippi. The autopsies on the bodies revealed that all three men had been shot to death and that Chaney had been savagely beaten before being shot. On December 4, 1964, nineteen men, including a sheriff of Neshoba County and his deputy, were arrested on federal conspiracy charges in relation to the murders. On October 9, 1967, eighteen of the men were put on trial before a federal court in Meridian, Mississippi. On October 20, an all-white jury found seven of the accused guilty and sentenced them to prison.

GORDONE, CHARLES (1925-   ) This playwright was born in Cleveland, Ohio. He was educated in public schools of Elkhart, Indiana, and at Los Angeles State College, where he majored in drama. Mr. Gordone has worked in many phases of the theater and motion picture industry including acting and screen writing. He has directed many plays, among them Erskine Cadwell's *Tobacco Road*, Sidney Kingsley's *Detective Story*, Eugene O'Neill's "Sea Plays", Hatcher Hughes's *Hell Bent Fer Heaven*, and Gothe's *Faust*. Mr. Gordone has won numerous awards as a playwright: The Pulitzer Prize (1970), the New York Drama Critics Award (1970), the Vernon Rice Award (1970), and a National Institute of Arts and Letters grant (1971). He has also received an Obie Award for best actor of the year 1964.

GRAHAM, LORENZ B. (1902-   )   This short story writer, critic, poet, and children's author was born in New Orleans. He was educated in local schools and at the University of Washington, the University of California, Virginia Union University, and the New York School of Social Work. Mr. Graham has taught at Monrovia College in Liberia, and worked for the Los Angeles county Probation Department, and served as professor of English at California State University at Pomona. He has won the Thomas A. Edison award. His writings have appeared in several journals and newspapers, such as *Elementary English,* the *New York Times,* and *Players Magazine.*

GRANDFATHER CLAUSE   In the attempt to disenfranchise black voters and circumvent the requirements of the Fifteenth Amendment, several southern states passed statutes that exempted from suffrage requirements those and their lineal descendants who had possessed the right to vote as of January 1, 1867. Since blacks could not vote at that time, they were effectively excluded from voting in any election. However, poor and illiterate whites could vote. Several southern states provided grandfather clauses in their constitutions: South Carolina, 1895; Louisiana, 1898; North Carolina, 1900; Alabama, 1901; Virginia, 1902; Georgia, 1908; and Oklahoma, 1910. In 1915 the grandfather clause was declared unconstitutional by the United States Supreme Court in the case of *Gwin and Beal* vs. *United States.*

GRAPEVINE TELEGRAPH   Very often it was necessary to send information along the Underground Railroad escape routes, information indicating that fugitive slaves were on the way. A clandestine method or code called the "grapevine telegraph" was used to convey the messages. One such coded message sent in 1859 by an Underground Railroad agent read as follows: "By tomorrow evening's mail you will receive two copies of The Irrepressible Conflict bound in black. After perusal, please forward and oblige." The agent who received the message knew immediately that it meant two black slaves were on their way to the station. They were to be cared for and sent on to the next station.

GREAT SOCIETY   This term was used in a speech by President Lyndon Johnson at the University of Michigan in 1964. The ideas he expressed were later developed by his administration into the goals toward which it should aim. In the Great Society, education would

237

be expanded, assaults on various diseases would be made, crime and delinquency would be suppressed, civil rights would be protected, and a campaign against waste and inefficiency would be undertaken. In general "the quality of life" for all would be improved. Only parts of this ambitious program were achieved.

GREENLEE, SAM (1903-   )   This poet, short story writer, novelist, and essayist was born in Chicago. He was educated in the public schools and at the universities of Wisconsin, Chicago, and Thessalonikki in Greece. He has served as an officer in the United States Army and as a foreign service officer for the United States Information Agency. He has won several awards: the Meritorious Service Award, USIA, and the Book of the Year Award by the British press. Mr. Greenlee's articles have appeared in *Black World* and *Negro Digest*.

GRENADA RIOTS, THE   On September 12-13, 1966, black children attempting to attend two all-white schools of Grenada, Mississippi, were attacked by mobs of whites armed with ax handles, chains, clubs, and iron pipes. At the Lizzie Elementary School black children were beaten by a mob while the police stood by and watched. Three of the children were severely injured; one of them suffered two broken legs.

GRIGGS, SUTTON E. (1872-1930)   This novelist and minister was born in Chatfield, Texas, and educated at Bishop College, where he was a superior student, and Richmond Theological Seminary (today part of Virginia Union University). He was ordained in 1893 and became the pastor of a church in Berkley, Virginia, where he remained for two years. In 1895 Griggs became corresponding secretary of the education department of the National Baptist Convention and retained his post for twenty years, leaving it in 1915 to become a minister again. He held several posts as pastor in different parts of the country. In 1930 Mr. Griggs moved to Texas to work on the establishment of a national religious and civic institute. He died while working on this project.

GRIMKE, ANGELINA WELD (1880-1958)   This poet, playwright, and teacher was born in Boston. She was educated at Carleton Academy in Minnesota, Cushing Academy in Massachusetts, the Girls Latin School in Boston, and the Boston Normal School of Gymnastics. After completing her education, she went to work as a teacher at the Armstrong Manual Training School in Washington, D.C. In 1916 she became a teacher of English at Washington's famous Dunbar High School. Eventually she moved to New York.

GUARDIAN, THE This newspaper was established in November 1901 by Monroe Trotter and George Moore. It continued publication until the 1920s, when it ceased to exist. The *Guardian* served as a platform from which the blacks could voice their militant protest against the racial prejudice directed against them during the early part of the twentieth century. As editor of the paper, Monroe Trotter was unalterably opposed to the views of Booker T. Washington and fought him at every turn. Trotter demanded full rights for the blacks.

GUNN, WILLIAM HARRISON (BILL) (1934-   ) This actor, playwright, and novelist was born in Philadelphia, Pennsylvania. He was educated in Philadelphia public schools and spent some time in the army. Mr. Gunn's work has appeared in *Drama Review*. He wrote filmscripts for the motion picture *Angel Levine, Don't the Moon Look Lonesome,* and *The Landlord*.

GUY, ROSA (CUTHBERT) (1928-   ) This short story writer and novelist playwright, and essayist was born in Trinidad, West Indies, and came to the United States when she was four years old. She has traveled widely in the West Indies to study the languages and customs of the region, especially Haiti and Trinidad. Ms. Guy speaks Creole and French fluently.

HAIKU In Japan some poets write haiku, a form of poetry that employs seventeen syllables arranged in lines of five, seven, and five syllables. This form of poetry is organized to provide a precise picture and at the same time to elicit a special emotion and a particular spiritual understanding. Alice Walker and Richard Wright have written poetry using the haiku form.

HALEY, ALEX PALMER (1921-   ) This novelist and essayist was born in Ithaca, New York. When he was six weeks old, he was taken to Henning, Tennessee, by his mother while his father completed work on a graduate degree. He was educated in local schools and at Elizabeth City Teachers College. In 1939 Alex Haley joined the coast guard and served until his retirement in 1959. He began writing while in the coast guard and when he retired he began a career as a professional writer. Mr. Haley's work has appeared in many maga-

Hamer, Martin J.

zines such as *Reader's Digest, Playboy,* and *American History Illustrated.* For his book, *Roots,* he received the National Book Award and the Pulitzer Prize in 1977.

HAMER, MARTIN J. (1931-   )   This poet, editor, and short story writer was born in New York City. He was educated in the public schools and at City College. He has worked as an editor for a major publishing company and as an electromechanical designer. Hamer's poetry and short stories have been published in various magazines, including *Negro Digest* and *Atlantic Monthly.* His stories have also appeared in several anthologies.

HAMILTON, VIRGINIA (1936-   )   This writer of children's books was born in Yellow Springs, Ohio. She was educated in local schools, at Antioch College, Ohio State University, and the New School for Social Research. She has won the Edgar Allen Poe Award, the Ohioan Book Award (1969), the Newbery Honor Book Award for 1971, the National Book Award (1975), and the Newbery Medal (1975).

HAMMON, JUPITER (1720-1806)   This poet was born a slave. He belonged to Henry Lloyd of Lloyds Neck, Long Island, near Queen's Village; and very little is known about him. Hammon was thought to be known and respected as a slave preacher. He learned to read and write and began to write poetry. His poetry is largely religious in nature, being patterned after the work of the Methodists of the period. In his poems he urged the acceptance of one's lot, whatever it was. Hammon did not like slavery but seemed unable to do much about his condition. He remained a slave all of his life. His poetry antedates Phillis Wheatley's by several years.

HARLEM   A section of upper Manhattan, Harlem is the area where most of the blacks of New York City live. Harlem was originally a Dutch village established on land purchased by Henry and Isaac DeForest in 1637. In the early 1800s wealthy New Yorkers organized large estates in the area. In the early 1900s blacks began to move into Harlem. During and after World War I blacks began to migrate northward in great numbers. Many of them settled in Harlem, which was soon known as the black capital of the United States. Many black writers, including Rosa Guy, James Baldwin in *Go Tell It On The Mountain,* Countee Cullen in *One Way to Heaven,* and James

Weldon Johnson in *The Autobiography of an Ex-Colored Man,* have written about Harlem.

HARLEM RIOTS (1964)   On July 18-19 one of the most serious riots in Harlem for several years occurred as the result of a fifteen-year-old black youth being shot to death by a white policeman. On July 16 a group of black pupils of a Manhattan school were splashed with water by a white man who was hosing down the sidewalk. The students promptly attacked the man and in the melee a policeman shot fifteen-year-old James Powell. A riot in which white and black students fought the police with rocks and bottles began. On July 18 a peaceful protest demonstration turned violent when an unruly crowd attacked a Harlem police station. When the police tried to break up the crowd, one black man was killed and twenty-five people, including six policemen, were injured. Further rioting occurred on July 19. Whites were attacked and passing cars stoned. Black ministers and civil rights leaders who tried to calm the crowd were shouted down. The entire police force of New York City placed on an emergency footing and policemen, wearing steel helmets, cordoned off the riot area and dispersed the crowd by firing their guns in the air. In addition to the one man killed, 119 people were injured and 108 arrested. Martin Hamer has written a novel for young adults about these riots. It is called *The Sniper.*

HARLEM WRITERS GUILD, THE   Organized in 1950 by writers John O. Killens and Rosa Guy, this group was set up to train young blacks to be writers and to promote their work. John O. Killens became chairman of the guild and held this post until 1960. The Harlem Writers' Guild is still in existence and meets today in the Countee Cullen branch of the New York Public Library.

HARLEM WRITERS' WORKSHOP   Established in 1945 by John Henik Clarke and others interested in writing, this workshop was based at the Harlem YMCA. The group met on Sunday evenings. Its basic purpose was to aid black writers in improving their work. An important member of the workshop was the late Langston Hughes.

HARPER, FRANCES ELLEN WATKINS (1825-1911)   This poet, novelist, and lecturer was born free in Baltimore, Maryland. Her parents died when she was very young and she was cared for by her aunt. She was educated in a school for free blacks operated by her uncle,

William Watkins, a minister. When she was fourteen years old, she left school and went to work as a housekeeper for a Baltimore bookstore owner. While there she read extensively and began to write poetry. In 1850 she went to Union Seminary, not far from Columbus, Ohio, where she taught classes for two years. Then she taught elementary school in Pennsylvania. While in Pennsylvania, Ms. Harper began to work in behalf of the antislavery movement. Her first book of poetry was published in the fall of 1854. She went to work as a lecturer for the Maine Antislavery Society, covering over eight states in her travels. In 1860 she retired to marry Fenton Harper of Columbus, Ohio. Mr. Harper died in 1864 and Ms. Harper began lecturing again. After the Civil War, she continued to write and lecture. Her works were published as late as 1895. Frances Harper died in 1911 at the age of eighty-seven.

HARPER, MICHAEL S. (1938-   )   This poet and teacher was born in Brooklyn, New York; but he grew up in Los Angeles, California. He was educated at California State College and at the University of Iowa, where he acquired an M.A. degree. Mr. Harper has taught at several colleges and universities, among them Los Angeles City College, Clark College, where he was poet in residence, the University of Illinois, and Brown University. His poems have appeared in many anthologies and periodicals, including *Poetry Magazine*, *Black World*, and the *California Quarterly*. He is included in anthologies such as *The Poetry of Black America* and *To Gwen with Love*. He has lectured on poetry and read his works in many parts of the country and has received numerous awards and fellowships.

HARRY AMES   This is a character in John A. Williams's novel, *The Man Who Cried I Am.*

HAYDEN, ROBERT E. (1913-   )   This poet, anthologist, and essayist was born in Detroit, Michigan. He was educated in the local schools of Detroit and at Wayne State University and the University of Michigan. Mr. Hayden has worked mainly as a teacher of English literature at Fisk University and the University of Michigan. He has read his poetry at many universities and colleges, including the University of Washington, the University of Louisville, and Case Western Reserve University in Cleveland, Ohio. Robert Hayden has received the Hopwood Award for Poetry (1938-1942); a Ford Foundation Fellowship (1954-1955); and the grand prize of the World Festival of Negro Arts, Dakar, Senegal; (1966). His poems have been

published in many journals and magazines, such as *Black World,*
Atlantic Monthly, Phylon, and the *Midwest Journal.* In 1976 Mr.
Hayden became poetry consultant to the Library of Congress.

HENDERSON, GEORGE WYLIE (1904-   )   This short story writer
and novelist was born in Warriors Stand, Alabama. He was educated in local schools and at Tuskeegee Institute. After leaving
school, he moved to New York and worked as a printer for the *New*
York Daily News. His short stories appeared in several magazines
and newspaper, including *Redbook* and the *New York Daily News.*

HENDERSON, STEPHEN E. (1925-   )   This poet, short story writer, critic, and painter was born in Key West, Florida. He was
educated in local schools and at Morehouse College, the University
of Wisconsin, and Harvard University. Presently professor of Afro-
American studies and director of the Institute for the Arts and
Humanities at Howard University, Dr. Henderson has taught at
Virginia Union University and has been Spencer Research Fellow at
the Institute of the Black World. He has lectured at Atlanta Univer-
sity, Clark College, the University of Virginia, and the University of
North Carolina. He has won the Mervill European Travel Grant, a
grant-in-aid from the Council of Learned Societies, and Howard
University faculty research grants. His book, *Understanding the*
New Black Poetry, was submitted as a Pulitzer Prize entry for 1973.
Stephen Henderson's writings have appeared in many journals and
magazines, such as *College English, Black World, Phylon,* the *New*
York Times Book Review, and *Ebony.*

HENRY, JOHN   Every group of people has its folk heros; among the
blacks in America John Henry is such a hero. John O. Killens has
written a book about him. Other materials concerned with the John
Henry legend are available.

HENRY PATMORE   This is a character in Rudolph Fisher's novel,
The Walls Of Jericho.

HERNTON, CALVIN (1934-   )   This poet, essayist, and novelist
was born in Chattanooga, Tennessee. He attended Fisk University
and Talladega College. His poems have been published in numerous
journals and magazines both here and in Europe. Several anthologies have included his work. Some of his well-written essays
have been a source of controversy. Hernton has lectured in Sweden,

England, and other countries. He has served as professor of Afro-American studies at Oberlin College in Ohio.

HILL, BERTHA CHIPPIE (1905-1950)   A blues singer, Bertha Hill was born in Charleston, South Carolina. When she was about twelve or thirteen years old, her family moved to New York. By the time she was fourteen, she was singing in a nightclub. For several years she worked in Harlem, then moved on to Chicago, where she sang with King Oliver's band for a short time. In the fall of 1925 she recorded her first record under the Okeh label with Louis Armstrong on the cornet and Richard Jones on piano. She made several more recordings, all of them very successful. in 1929, when she was about twenty-four years old, Bertha Hill retired to raise a family. In 1944 she made several records for Circle, Inc., and in 1948 she participated in the Paris Jazz Festival and was immensely successful. Her comeback was short-lived, for she was struck by a hit and run driver and died of severe injuries in a Harlem hospital on May 7, 1950.

HIMES, CHESTER (1909-   )   This novelist, short story writer, critic and essayist was born in Jefferson City, Missouri. His early education was obtained in the schools of Augusta, Georgia; Pine Bluff, Arkansas; and St. Louis, Missouri. He graduated from high school in Cleveland, Ohio, and attended Ohio State University. When he was nineteen years old, Chester Himes was sentenced to prison for twenty years for armed robbery. He served seven years in the Ohio State Penitentiary and was released in 1935. While he was in prison, he began writing and his stories were published in various magazines. In 1930 his account of the Ohio State Penitentiary fire was published in Esquire magazine. After his release from prison, Mr. Himes worked at various jobs and kept writing. In 1954 he went to Europe and has remained there since, in France and Spain. He received the 1958 Grand Prix Policer for his detective novels. His work has appeared in numerous magazines, among them Coronet, Esquire, Negro Story, Opportunity, and Abbotts Illustrated Weekly.

HOLLOWAY, JOHN WESLEY (1865-   )   This poet was born in 1865 in Flat Shoals, Georgia. His father, a former slave who had learned to read and write and had become one of the first black teachers in the state of Georgia, saw to it that his son was well educated. Mr. Holloway was educated at Clark and Fisk Universities. While at

Fisk University, he sang for a short while with the famous Fisk Jubilee Singers. Though Holloway was trained as a teacher, he was a trained minister as well. He worked as both teacher and clergyman. He was ordained in 1900 and for several years served as a minister in churches in Georgia, New Jersey, Oklahoma, and Alabama. In spite of his very busy life, he found time to write poetry. His verse generally follows the plantation genre and was patterned after the dialect poems of Paul Lawrence Dunbar.

HOPKINS, SAM "LIGHTNIN" (1912-   )   A blues singer and musician, Hopkins was born in Centerville, Texas, and grew up in that farming region. His education was limited. He learned to play the guitar before he was eight years old and once had a lesson from "Blind" Lemon Jefferson, a blues singer of note. As he grew up, he began playing for social functions in the area around Centerville. Two or three times Hopkins played with Jefferson when Jefferson came to visit the town. During the Great Depression, Hopkins worked a farm near Centerville. Eventually he married and hired out as a farmhand on a large farm near Dallas. He continued playing and singing earning some money while doing so. In 1945 Hopkins's uncle persuaded him to leave farming and earn his living singing. For a while he sang and played in the nightclubs in and around Houston with his cousin "Texas" Alexander, also a blues singer. in 1946 Alexander and Hopkins went to Hollywood to record. The venture was a limited success and by early 1947 "Lightnin" was back in Houston. That year he met a young war veteran named Bill Quinn, who was in the record business; his company was Gold Star Records. Hopkins recorded several very successful songs with this company over a two-year-period. However, in 1948 or 1949 he recorded several songs for another company and in the process duplicated songs he had recorded for Gold Star Records. As a result of this Quinn fired him. Since 1948 Sam "Lightnin" Hopkins has recorded hundreds of blues songs and sings and plays at concerts in the United States, England, and Europe.

THE HOUSE OF FALLING LEAVES   This is a poem by William Stanley Braithwaite.

HOUSE SLAVE   On the larger plantations, the slaves were divided into two main groups: those slaves who worked in the fields, or field hands, and those slaves who worked in the plantation house and around the grounds. The house slaves were butlers, maids, cooks, and nursery attendents or mammies who looked after the plantation owner's young children. Often these slaves received somewhat better treatment than the field hands and their food and clothing was of better quality. Some of these house slaves displayed loyalty to their owners; others did not. The character Vyry in Margaret Walker's *Jubilee* is a house slave.

HOWARD UNIVERSITY PRESS, THE   Established in 1970, this Washington, D.C., company is a scholarly press and publishes chiefly literary criticism, poetry, and academic studies, although novels have been published.

HUGHES, LANGSTON (1902-1967)   This poet, editor, novelist, essayist, and song lyric writer was born in Joplin, Missouri. He was educated in the public schools of several cities, including Topeka and Lawrence, Kansas; Lincoln, Illinois; and Central High School in Cleveland, Ohio. He later attended Columbia and Lincoln universities. He began writing poetry in grammar school; by the time he reached high school, he was writing regularly. After graduating from high school in 1920, he went to Mexico, where he lived with his father for a summer before entering Columbia University. At twenty Langston Hughes signed on as a seaman on a freighter going to Africa. Mr. Hughes traveled in many parts of the world and visited Russia, France, Italy, Mexico, Cuba, and several African countries. His writings have appeared in many magazines and journals, among them *Fire*, the *Crisis*, *Opportunity*, *Phylon*, *Negro Digest*, and the *Messenger*. He received the Harmon Gold Award for Literature and a Guggenhiem Fellowship in 1935. Mr. Hughes made his home in Harlem, New York.

HUNTER, ALBERTA (1897-   )   A blues singer, actress, recording artist, and composer, Alberta Hunter was born in Memphis, Tennessee. Without her mother's permission she went with an aunt to Chicago when she was about twelve or thirteen years old. By the time she was fifteen, she was singing in a Chicago nightclub, where she remained until she was seventeen. As her reputation grew, she worked at other clubs. In 1922 she wrote a song, "Down Hearted Blues," and recorded it. The record was a success for Alberta Hunter; but it was even more of a hit for Bessie Smith, who recorded it in 1923. Ms. Hunter left Chicago for New York, where she was able to join a Broadway show. During the 1920s and 1930s, she made many recordings and spent several years in Europe as a singer and actress. During World War II, she made numerous trips to Europe and the South Pacific, entertaining troops. In 1954-1955 she returned to Broadway as an understudy for three roles in the play *Mrs. Patterson*. In the late 1950s Alberta Hunter became a nurse and gave up acting and singing completely. In the late 1970s she resumed her career at the age of 80.

HUNTER, KRISTIN (1931-   )   This novelist, short story writer, poet, and children's author was born in Philadelphia. She was educated in local schools and at the University of Pennslyvania. Ms. Hunter has worked as a copywriter, teacher, and information officer for the city of Philadelphia. From 1972 to the present she has lectured in English at the University of Pennsylvania. She has received the Philadelphia Athenaeum Literary Award, the Lewis Carroll Shelf Award, the Council on Interracial Books for Children Award, and the Chicago Tribune Book World Fair Award in 1975. Her work has appeared in several magazines and journals, among them *Essence, Black World,* and *Negro Digest.*

HURSTON, ZORA NEAL (1903-1960)   This novelist, short story writer, folklorist, playwright, and essayist was born in the all-black town of Eatonville, Florida. She was educated in the public schools of Eatonville, Morgan Academy in Baltimore, and Howard University. She studied further at Barnard College and Columbia University. While at Columbia, Hurston studied anthropology under Franz Boas. She was awarded a Guggenheim Fellowship in 1936-1938, which enabled her to live in Haiti and the British West Indies to study the folklore of those areas. She worked at various jobs while in school, including a job as a maid. At one time in her career Zora Hurston was secretary to writer Fannie Hurst. She received the Ainsfield award. Morgan State University awarded her an honorary doctor of literature degree. Her essays appeared in numerous magazines, including *Negro Digest,* the *Saturday Evening Post,* the *Journal of American Folklore,* and the *Journal of Negro History.* Zora Neal Hurston died poor and obscure in Florida in 1960.

INDENTURED SERVANT   During the colonial period of American history in the English settlements many people, usually white males, bound themselves out to labor for several years in order to gain passage to the New World. There were three classes of these servants: the free willers, who came to the colonies of their own free will, those who were kidnapped off the streets and shipped to the

New World, and those who were political prisoners. A contract was written, signed, and torn in such a way that there were deep indentures on the parchment or paper on which it was written. The term "indentured" was derived from this practice. The servant kept one half of the contract and the employer the other half. The term of indenture was usually from five to seven years, at the end of which the servant was provided with a gun, clothing, and a small tract of land. When the blacks first arrived in the English colonies, their status was that of indentured servants. However, within a relatively short time the terms of indenture for black servants were extended, which could be done legally for various infractions of the law. Many blacks had their terms of service extended for life. By 1640 blacks had for all intents and purposes become slaves permanently.

INSTITUTE FOR COLORED YOUTH The problems faced by blacks in acquiring an education were enormous, but in some instances efforts were made to help them. This was particularly true among the Quakers of Pennsylvania. The Institute for Colored Youth came into existence as a result of the actions of a Quaker named Richard Humphreys. At his death in 1832 he left $10,000, which he said was to be used for the education of the black slaves who had been freed. Because of the general negative attitude toward the education of the blacks, nothing was done to carry out this plan until 1839. The Quakers then appointed a board of trustees to carry out this provision of Humphreys' will. Land was purchased in Philadelphia County and a number of black youths were taught the skills of farming and shoe making. In 1842 the school received other monies, including an $18,000 gift from a Quaker named John Zane. The emphasis, as far as the education of the blacks was concerned, continued to be vocational until 1846, when all the industrial training equipment was sold and the money received put into a fund to establish an evening school for academic subjects. In 1852 a day school was organized and a building was erected on Lombard Street in Philadelphia. The school opened under the name of the Institute for Colored Youth. It was coeducational and Charles L. Reason, a black man from New York, was the director. Many black youths received their secondary education at this school. It later became known as Cheney State College.

INSTITUTE OF THE BLACK WORLD Established in 1969, the purpose of this organization is to research and write about all aspects of the black experience in America. It is based in Atlanta, Georgia. A number of pamphlets and other materials have been published by this organization.

IN THESE DISSENTING TIMES   This is a long poem by Alice Walker.

IOLA LEROY   This is a character in Frances E. W. Harper's novel, *Iola Leroy*.

IRONY   At various times writers try to convey an attitude that is opposite of what is literally intended; this technique is called irony. One poem that is ironic in tone is Countee Cullen's *Yet I Do Marvel*.

I THOUGHT IT WAS TANGIERS I WANTED   This is a poem by Langston Hughes.

J. PENNINGTON PORTER   This is a character in Rudolph Fisher's novel, *The Walls of Jerico*.

JAKE JOHNSON   This is character in Richard Wright's novel, *Lawd Today*.

JAMES WELDON JOHNSON COLLECTION, THE   Housed at Yale University, this collection was established in 1950 by Carl Van Vechten. Included in the collection are manuscripts, letters, photographs, and autographed copies of works of black writers of the 1920s and 1930s, many of whom Van Vechten knew personally.

JAZZ   The term "jazz" describes a distinctly American kind of music that is very strongly influenced by the music of blacks. The origin of the word is somewhat obscure; it is thought to have originated in the Creole dialect of the New Orleans area, however, other indications are that its origin is either French or Arabian. The components of this form of music can be traced well back into the nineteenth century. The rhythms and melodies of jazz are found intermittently in the minstrel songs, spirituals, blues, and work songs of the southern blacks of the pre-Civil War era. The influence of jazz on American popular music in general did not begin until the 1890s, when it began to influence the ragtime piano music that was being played in New Orleans. Jazz did not become widely known until after World War I, when the navy closed the Storyville area of New Orleans and jazz men began to drift north. Among them were such musicians as Joe "King" Oliver, Jelly Roll Morton, and Louis Armstrong. Today the influence of this musical form is evidence in most American music.

JEFFERS, LANCE (1919-   )   This poet and critic was born in Fremont, Nebraska. He was educated in the public schools of Stromsberg, Nebraska, and at Columbia University, where he was an honor student and graduated *cum laude* in 1951. He has worked as a teacher at Morehouse College, Tuskegee Institute, Howard University, California State College, Long Beach, Bowie State College, and Federal City College. His work has appeared in many magazines, including *Phylon*, *Freedomways*, *Negro Digest*, *Darein Quarto*, and The *Tamarack Review*. Mr. Jeffers's poetry has been published in numerous anthologies as well.

JEFFERSON, "BLIND" LEMON (1897-1930)   A blues singer and guitarist, Lemon Jefferson was born blind in Wortham, Texas, a small market town in a rural community. His education was practically nonexistent. By the time he was fourteen, he was quite large, weighing over two-hundred pounds. He learned to play the guitar and began singing at local functions in and around Wortham before he was twenty years old. In 1917 Jefferson left Wortham for Dallas. Because his reputation as a singer was unknown, he encountered financial difficulties and for a short while became a wrestler in local theaters. As his reputation as a blues singer became established, he began to earn money by singing. "Blind" Lemon left the theater and began to sing for dances and parties in Dallas and the surrounding areas. When Jefferson was in Dallas, he sang in the red-light district and soon was able to purchase an automobile and hire a driver. In the early 1920s he married; his son was born around 1925 or 1926. "Blind" Lemon Jefferson's singing engagements kept him traveling. They carried him to Alabama, Tennessee, and along the southern coast of Texas. By 1924, recording firms had become interested in Jefferson's singing and in 1925 he went to Chicago to record for the Paramount Record Company and Okeh Records. In the four years that he recorded for these companies, Jefferson made over seventy-nine records. One evening in February 1930, after a recording session, Jefferson left Paramount studios on a singing engagement; he did not reach his destination. Early the next morning "Blind" Lemon Jefferson was found frozen to death on the sidewalk of a Chicago street, his body covered with drifting snow and his guitar beside him.

JET   A pocket-sized news magazine, this publication is one of the Johnson Publishing Company's group of periodicals, which include *Ebony, Ebony Jr., Tan*, and, until 1976, *Black World. Jet* provides current information on almost every aspect of the lives of the blacks in America. There are sections on art, religion, literature, entertainment, politics and sports. Often the articles have sensational titles, but this is misleading; the magazine is well written and very readable.

JIHAD PUBLISHING COMPANY   Organized by poet, playwright, novelist and essayist Imamu Amiri Baraka (LeRoi Jones) in 1967, this company is based in Newark, New Jersey. It was designed to provide an alternative apparatus for young black writers who might find it difficult to have their work published. At the present time, the company published various kinds of pamphlets, and books about history, drama, and poetry. In 1974 the Jihad Publishing Company changed its name to the Vita Ya Watu Publishing Company.

JIM CROW SYSTEM, THE   Following the end of the Civil War Reconstruction Period, after 1876, most southern states enacted laws and established policies designed to keep blacks and whites apart. These laws and practices were known as the Jim Crow laws or the Jim Crow system. The term "Jim Crow" itself is said to have originated with the minstrel act of Thomas Dartmouth Rice, a famous white "black faced" minstrel, better known as "Daddy Dan" Rice. In 1828 or 1839, he saw a ragged black street urchin dancing and singing a song called "Jim Crow." Rice copied the song and dance and included it in his act. By 1833 he had become famous for this skit. The words "Jim Crow" from the song slowly came to refer to the blacks and the practice of segregating them from the white population. Most of the Jim Crow laws appeared in the South during the last quarter of the nineteenth century. However, the system operated in the North as well, although there were only a few instances where segregation was legally enforced. One such instance was the Massachusetts "Jim Crow" law of 1841, which segregated blacks and whites in railroad cars. Tennessee enacted a similar law in 1881. By 1888 every southern state had enacted such laws; and by 1908 blacks were segregated not only in public transportation, but also in courtrooms, hospitals, barber shops, asylums, cemeteries, prisons, and orphanages. The Jim Crow system remained intact well into the twentieth century, both in the northern and southern states. Pro tests against the laws and practices of Jim Crow intensified in the 1950s and continued through the 1960s, when the system collapsed.

JIM FARREL   This is a character in Curtis Lucas's novel, *Flour is Dusty*.

JIM ROBINSON   This is a character in A. Q. Jarrette's novel, *Beneath the Sky*.

JOE Kelp   This is a character in Zora Neal Hurston's novel, *Seraph on the Suwanee*.

JOHN BUDDY   This is a character in Zora Neal Hurston's novel, *Jonah's Gourd Vine*.

JOHN CARTER   This is a character in Mercedes Gilbert's novel, *Aunt Sara's Wooden God*.

JOHNNIE ROANE   This is a character in Ann Petry's novel, *Country Place*.

JOHNSON, FENTON (1886-1958)   This poet, playwright, and editor was born and educated in Chicago. He attended both the University of Chicago and Northwestern University. Most of Fenton Johnson's poetry appeared during and after World War I. In addition to writing poetry, Johnson wrote and produced his own plays, which were staged at the Pekin Theater. Johnson edited and published several little magazines. After 1920 he published very little and was not involved in the Harlem Renaissance. When the depression hit, Johnson's family suffered from it. He worked for a time for the Federal Writer's Project in the Chicago area.

JOHNSON, GEORGIA DOUGLAS (1886-1966)   This poet was born in Atlanta, Georgia, and was educated in the schools there. She attended Atlanta University and studied music at Oberlin Conservatory in Ohio with the idea of becoming a composer. She soon gave up this ambition. When her husband was appointed recorder of deeds, she moved to Washington, D.C. Later she worked for the federal government. Her writings, however, became her main occupation. Ms. Johnson's home became a famous as a meeting place for black artists. Her poems are minor, although a few of them display strong emotion and intense feeling.

JOHNSON, JAMES WELDON (1871-1938)   This poet, novelist, editor, critic, essayist, lyricist, teacher, diplomat, and executive secretary of the NAACP was born in Jacksonville, Florida. He was educated in public schools and at Atlanta and Columbia universities. After college he became a teacher in Jacksonville, Florida, and eventually the principal of the only high school for black children, which he developed by adding a grade each year beyond eighth grade to the elementary school. He was admitted to the Florida bar. Shortly after becoming a lawyer, James Weldon Johnson and his brothers went to New York, where they had some success as songwriters. He remained in New York to live and write. He worked as an editor, and he wrote song lyrics. Later he was asked to become the executive secretary of the NAACP, a post he held for several years. Johnson's essays appeared in many magazines and journals, such as *Century, Survey Graphic,* and *Crisis.*

JOHNSON, JOHN HAROLD (1918-   )   This publisher and journalist was born in Arkansas City, Arkansas. He obtained his early education in Arkansas City and when his family moved to Chicago in 1933, he attended the University of Chicago and Northwestern University's School of Commerce. After completing his education, he worked for the Supreme Liberty Life Insurance Company. In 1942 Johnson borrowed $500 on his mother's furniture and launched a magazine, the *Negro Digest.* In 1945 he established *Ebony* magazine and began to organize the Johnson Publishing Company, which is still expanding today.

JOHNSON, LONNIE (1894-1970)   A musician and blues singer, Lonnie Johnson was born in New Orleans. He had ten brothers and sisters, most of whom died young in an influenza epidemic in 1915, leaving only Lonnie and an older brother, James. He was educated in public schools, and as a youth he was carefully taught to play both the guitar and the violin. He later learned to play the banjo as well. During the early years of World War I, the Johnson brothers played in and around New Orleans. In 1917 he left for London and did not return to the United States until World War I ended. He and his brother took jobs playing in a band on the Mississippi River steamer *St. Paul.* He played with the Charlie Creath band until 1922, when he and Creath had a bitter disagreement and Johnson left the band. For three years he did not play at all. During this time he earned money by working first in a tire factory in Illinois and later in a steel mill in East St. Louis. In 1925 Johnson won a blues contest and was contracted by an agent of the Okeh Record Company and asked to record for them. He and his brother made their first records in St. Louis and achieved some success. Lonnie Johnson continued to record until well into the 1950s, although his success during these latter years was limited. When the blues revival began in the 1960s, he returned to England and achieved a marked degree of success. In 1963 at various concerts he continued to impress audiences with his skill as a guitarist. He continued playing until his death in 1970.

JOHNSON PUBLISHING COMPANY, THE   In 1961, the Johnson Publishing Company, publishers of *Ebony, Jet, Tan, Ebony Jr.* and *Negro Digest (Black World)*, established a book division. The firm specializes in publishing books on black history.

JONES, GAYL (1940-   )   This poet, novelist, and short story writer was born in Lexington, Kentucky. She was educated in local schools and at Connecticut College and Brown University. Her writing has appeared in several magazines and journals, including *Essence, Ms. Magazine, Laureate,* and *Silo.* She has received the Connecticut College Award, the best original poem, 1969 and 1970, the Frances Steloff Award for Fiction and a Breadloaf Writer's Conference Scholarship, 1971.

JONES, LOIS MAILAU (1906-   )   This painter, designer, teacher and illustrator was born in Boston, Massachusetts. She was educated in local schools and at the Museum School of the Boston Museum of Fine Arts. She completed work at the Academy Julian in Paris and at Howard University. Ms. Jones has traveled widely in Haiti and the Caribbean. Her paintings are in the permanent collections of the Brooklyn Museum, the Corcoran Galley of Art, the Palais National in Haiti, the University of Purjah, and the American Embassy in Luxembourg. She has won the Lubin Award and the Washington Society of Artists Award. Lois Mailau Jones is an art teacher as well as a practicing artist. She is associate professor of design at Howard University, where she has taught since 1930.

JONNA MARSHALL   This is a character in Jessie Fauset's novel, *There Is Confusion.*

JOPLIN, SCOTT (1868-1917)   This musician and composer was born in Texarkana, Texas. His father was an ex-slave, and his mother was a laundress. His parents were interested in music; his father played the fiddle and his mother sang and played the banjo. Several of his five siblings either played musical instruments or sang. Joplin learned to play the piano when he was a boy and displayed such talent that he was able to continue his piano studies under a local teacher named Louis Chaurin, who taught him to play ragtime. When he was fourteen years old, he left home after an altercation with hs father and went on his own. He played in honky-tonk cafes and bordellos and led a nomadic life as a traveling musician. In 1896 Joplin settled in Sedalia, Missouri, where he obtained employment as a piano player. In 1908 Scott Joplin moved to New York and continued writing music until his death in 1917. His music was used as the score for the motion picture *The Sting* and his opera, *Treemonisha*, was performed in Atlanta in 1972. Several more productions of this opera have been staged since that time.

JORDON, JUNE MEYER (1936-   )   This poet, children's writer, essayist, editor, and novelist was born in Harlem, New York. She was educated in New York public schools and at Barnard College and the University of Chicago. Ms. Jordon has taught writing at Yale University (1974-present); and Sarah Laurence College in Bronxville, New York (1969-1970) and 1973-1974). She has been a Fellow of the American Academy in Rome (1970-1971). Her writings have appeared in numerous magazines and journals, among them *Essence*, *Black Creation*, *Black World*, *Freedomways*, *Harper's Bazaar*, the *Library Journal*, *Encore*, the *New York Times Magazine*, the *Village Voice*, *Partisan Review*, and *Esquire*.

JORDON, NORMAN (1938-   )   This poet and playwright was born in Ansted, West Virginia and was educated in Cleveland, Ohio. Mr. Jordon has worked at many jobs. He has been in the navy (1955-1959) a shipping clerk, dishwasher, youth leader, outreach worker, director of a youth center, technical writer, and writer in residence at Karamu House (1970-1971). He has read his work at Case Western Reserve University, Cleveland State University, and Cuyahoga Community College. His poems have been published in numerous journals, including *Umba*, *Cricket*, *Confrontation*, *Black World*, and the *Journal of Black Poetry*. He has been awarded the Hamet Ells Performing Arts Fellowship at Cleveland, Ohio, Karamu House.

JOSHUA "SHINE" JONES   This is a character in Rudolph Fisher's novel, *The Walls of Jericho*.

JULE   This is a character in George W. Henderson's novel, *Jule*.

KANSAS-NEBRASKA ACT (1854)   In 1854 Stephen A. Douglas, U.S. Senator from the State of Illinois, introduced in the Senate a bill intended to ease the tensions in the political struggle between the northern and southern states. The bill contained provisions that would allow the residents of the Kansas and Nebraska territories to decide for themselves, using the principle of popular sovereignty, whether they wanted slavery. A clause in the Kansas-Nebraska Act eliminated the Missouri Compromise agreement of 1820, which prohibited slavery north of Missouri's southern border.

KECKLY, ELIZABETH (1825-1905)   She was born at Dinwiddie Court House, Virginia. Her parents were slaves. When she was fourteen years old, she was sent to live with her owner's son, a Presbyterian minister, and remained there four years. She was sold to another owner in Hellsboro, North Carolina. Her new owner raped her and as a result a son was born to her. She was sold back to her former owners and served the daughter of the family. She became an expert seamstress and was able to buy freedom for herself and her son in 1859. She moved to Washington in 1860 and found employment as a dressmaker with Mrs. Jefferson Davis. She met Mrs. Lincoln, became her personal dressmaker, and moved into the White House. She founded in 1862 the Contraband Relief Association to help the ex-slaves.

KELLEY, WILLIAM MELVIN (1937-   )   This essayist and novelist was born in New York City. He was educated at the Fieldston School and at Harvard University, where he attended the classes of John Hawkes and poet-playwright Archibald MacLeish. Mr. Kelley has taught classes at the New School for Social Research and has been writer in residence there.

KENNEDY, ADRIENNE (1931-   )   This playwright was born in Pittsburgh, Pennsylvania, but grew up in Cleveland, Ohio. She was educated in the Cleveland public schools and at Ohio State University, from which she graduated in 1952. She completed additional work at Columbia University and at American Theater Wing and Circle in the Square Theater School. Ms. Kennedy has taught drama and play writing at Yale University. She has received the Ohio Award for her play *The Funnyhouse of a Negro*; a Guggenheim

Fellowship, grants from the Rockerfeller Foundation, the Stanley Drama Award and a grant from the Endowment for the Arts.

KENNETH HARPER   A character in Walter White's novel, *The Fire in the Flint*.

KILLENS, JOHN O. (1916-   )   This novelist short story writer, editor, essayist, playwright, and screenwriter was born in Macon, Georgia. He was educated in local schools and at E. Waters and Morris Brown colleges; Howard, New York, and Minnesota universities; and the Terrell Law school. Mr. Killens has worked for the National Labor Relations Board and served as director of the Harlem Writer's Workshop and the Black Arts Program at the Columbia University School of the Arts. He has been writer in residence at Fisk and Howard universities. His essays have appeared in *Library Journal, Black World, Arts in Society,* and *African Forum*.

KINCH   This is character in Frank Webb's novel, *The Garies and Their Friends*.

KNIGHTS OF THE WHITE CAMELIAS   During the Reconstruction Period following the Civil War, numerous secret societies whose purpose was to wrest political control of their communities from the northerners and the blacks were organized. The Knights of the White Camelias, established in New Orleans in 1867, was such an organization. It differed from a similar secret society, the Ku Klux Klan, in that its members were more conservative in outlook. Their organizational structure was relatively simple. Each member referred to the other as "brother" and their leaders were addressed as commander. This group ceased to exist in 1870. Frank Yerby describes the actions of this group in his novel, *The Vixens*.

LADIES OF THE RACHMANINOFF EYES   This is a novel by Henry Van Dyke published 1965.

LAND BEYOND THE RIVER   This is a play by Loften Mitchell, published in 1963.

LANDRY THAYER   This is a character in Paul Laurence Dunbar's novel, *The Love of Landry*.

LAUENTINE STRANGE   This is a character in Jessie Fauset's novel, *The Chinaberry Tree*.

LEE, DON L. (Mwalimu HAKI R. MAGAHABUTI) (1942-   )   This poet and essayist was born in Little Rock, Arkansas. He was educated in Chicago public schools and at Chicago City College and Roosevelt University. Haki Magahabuti (Don L. Lee) has worked for the United States Postal Service (1964-1965), as an executive for the Speigel Company (1965-1966), and since 1968 has lectured at various colleges and universities: Columbia College (1968), Cornell University (1968-1969), Northeastern Illinois State College (1969-1970), University of Illinois (1969-1971), and Howard University (1971-present). Mr. Magahabuti's writings have appeared in *Black World, Black Scholar, Ebony, Evergreen, Freedomways, Journal of Black Poetry, The New York Times,* and *Scholastic Magazine.* He has received several awards for his works, including a National Foundation of Arts Award in 1970.

LEE, GEORGE W. (1894-1976)   A novelist, insurance executive, and political leader, George Lee was born in Indianola, Mississippi. He was educated in local schools and at Alcorn A and I College. Although Mr. Lee spent much of his life as an insurance executive and politician, he found time to write several books. One of them concerned Beal Street in Memphis, Tennessee, famous for its blues singers and nightclubs. Mr. Lee died in August 1976.

LESTER, JULIUS (1939-   )   This folksinger, novelist, short story writer, poet, editor, essayist, teacher, and children's author was born in St. Louis, Missouri. He was educated in public schools and at Fisk University. Julius Lester is a man of many talents. He has also taught black history at the New School for Social Research. Lester has received the Nancy Black Award for 1969 and was runner-up for the Newbery Award for 1969. His essays have appeared in the *New York Times, Evergreen Review, Ebony,* and many other magazines and journals. During the years of the civil rights movement, Mr. Lester was a full-time worker for SNCC.

LEWIS, EDMONIA (1843-1900)   This sculptor was born near Albany, New York. Her mother was a Chippewa Indian and her father, a free black. Since both parents died when she was a child, Edmonia lived with her mother's people and was raised according to Chippewa traditions. Later she was adopted by an abolitionist group and sent to Oberlin College in Ohio. She studied in Boston, Massachusetts, under Edmonia Brackett. After completing her studies in Boston, Edmonia Lewis left the United States and lived in Rome, where she continued to study. For many years some of her work was lost, however, much of it has been uncovered recently. Her works are in the collections of the Federick Douglass Institute of Negro Art and History, Harvard College Library, the Fogg Museum, and the San Jose (California) Public Library.

LEWIS, NORMAN (1909-   )   This painter and teacher was born in New York and educated at Columbia University. He studied further under Augusta Savage and Raphael Soyer from 1936 to 1939. He taught at the Harlem Art Center as part of the Federal Art Project Program. He has had exhibitions of his work at Atlanta University, the Baltimore Museum of Art, and the Albany Institute.

LIBERATOR, THE   Founded in 1961 and edited by Daniel H. Watts, this New York-based magazine represents the militant wing of the blacks. A large part of each issue is devoted to civil rights, and political, economic, and other problems. Some poetry is published, as well as photographs. There are reviews of films, television, and books.

LIBERATOR, THE   Established and edited by William Lloyd Garrison, this antislavery newspaper was published in Boston from January 1, 1831, to December 29, 1865. The annual subscription price was two dollars and its circulation was never more than three thousand. Blacks contributed financially to the paper and many black leaders wrote articles for it. The Liberator was helpful to Garrison in his efforts to change the direction of the antislavery movement from advocating the gradual freeing of the slaves to demanding uncompensated emancipation.

LIBERTY PARTY   In United States political history at various times third political parties have emerged for specific purposes. The Liberty party was the first antislavery party formed in the United States. It was organized in Albany, New York, in 1839. Its candidate for the presidency in the 1840 election was James G. Birney. Birney won 62,300 votes in the election and the Liberty party was successful in splitting the Whig party. As a result of the split, James K. Polk, the Democratic dark horse candidate, became president. In 1848 the Liberty party merged with the Free Soil party. Some blacks were active in the Liberty party.

LIDA LAURISTON   This is a character in Joshua Henry Jones's novel, *Sanction of Law.*

LILLIAN TAYLOR   This is a character in Chester Himes's novel, *The Third Generation.*

LINDA YOUNG   This is a character in Rudolph Fisher's novel, *The Walls of Jericho.*

LITTLE AUGIE   This is a character in Arna Bontemps's novel, *God Sends Sunday.*

LITTLE MAGAZINES   Magazines that have a small circulation, limited funds, and sometimes very short lifespan are generally called little magazines. Their purpose is usually to expound on or foster advanced theories concerning the writing of poetry and prose. As far as black writers are concerned, the black little magazines serve a dual purpose. They offer a platform from which black authors can express their ideas and serve also as outlets for the publication of their writings. Since many black writers encountered difficulty having their essays and articles published in little magazines during the early part of the twentieth century, it was necessary for the blacks to produce their own. Since the 1920s, black little magazines have been published and have continued to appear. In the 1960s and 1970s, their numbers increased sharply. There is a high turnover, although a few of these publications have had quite long lives. *Free Lance,* a little magazine published in Cleveland, Ohio, by black poet Russel Atkins, has been in existence for over twenty-five years.

LOCKE, ALAIN L. (1886-1954)   This editor, literary critic, and philosopher was born in Philadelphia, Pennsylvania. He was educated in the public schools of Philadelphia and the Philadelphia School of Pedagogy. He earned degrees from Harvard University, the University of Berlin, and Oxford University in England, where he was a Rhodes Scholar from 1907 to 1910. In 1916 Mr. Locke was appointed assistant professor of philosophy and education at Howard University. Although he taught and lectured at many universities in numerous countries, Dr. Locke remained at Howard University until 1953. In 1925, with the publication of the classic anthology, *The New Negro*, he became widely known as an authority on the cultural history of blacks in America. In addition to this classic work, he produced many essays on almost every aspect of the blacks of the United States, including their art, music, literature, and drama. His writings appeared in *Opportunity*, *Survey Graphic*, the *English Journal*, *Crisis*, and *Phylon*.

LOOSE PACKERS   Some slave ship captains purchased only as many slaves the ship was designed to carry. The slaves on these ships were, in some cases, allowed freedom of the deck in good weather and were adequately fed, on the theory that this procedure would keep most, if not all, of them alive and therefore bring a large profit at the slave markets. These ships were usually kept cleaner than the regular slave-trading ships.

LYNCH   Sometimes punishment and even death are inflicted upon an individual by extralegal means and without due process of law. Those persons who participate in this kind of activity are said to lynch their victim. The term is possibly derived from the actions of Colonel Charles Lynch of Virginia (1736-1796), who used extralegal methods of trial and punishment to secure information from the Tories in Virginia during the American Revolution.

LYNCHING   Very often extralegal punishment and death were inflicted upon the blacks in the United States by mobs of whites. This was especially true in the southern states, where thousands of blacks from the latter part of the nineteenth century to the 1960s were killed by methods that varied from shooting to burning to hanging. Often white mobs broke into local jails, took the victim out, and lynched him. In most cases the lynchers were not brought to trial at all, were quickly freed, or were given extremely light sentences when a trial was held. John Wideman's novel, *The Lynchers*, concerns a lynching attempt that failed.

MC CLUSKEY, JOHN (1944-   )   This short story writer, novelist, essayist, and editor was born in Middletown, Ohio. He was educated in public schools and at Harvard and Stanford universities. He has taught at Miles College, Valparaiso University, Case Western Reserve University, and is presently professor of English at the University of Indiana at Bloomington. Mr. McCluskey's writings have appeared in *Black World*, the *Cleveland Plain Dealer*, *Studies* in Black Literature, Journal of Black Studies, and Negro Digest. His short story "John Henry's Home" was selected for inclusion in Best American Short Stories 1976.

McCONE COMMISSION, THE   During the period of August 11-16, 1965, very serious rioting occurred in the Watts black ghetto area of Los Angeles, California. Thirty-four persons were killed and millions of dollars worth of property was destroyed. On August 19, 1965, Governor Edmond H. Brown appointed a special commission headed by John A. McCone, former chairman of the Atomic Energy Commission and director of the Central Intelligence Agency, to investigate the causes for the Watts riots and to recommend action to prevent the recurrence of such outbreaks. The commission issued its report on December, 16, 1965. It stated that the Watts riots were caused by intense frustration on the part of the blacks about the inequalities practiced against them and not by outside influence, as had been suggested. The Watts Writer's Workshop was organized after the Watts riots.

McKAY, CLAUDE (1890-1948)   This poet, novelist, short story writer, and essayist was born in Sunnyville, Jamaica. His education was irregular. He was largely self-educated, with help from an older brother and an English folklore collector. When he was fourteen years old, he left his village for Kingston, where he eventually became a police constable. While in Kingston, he became a writer. By the time he was twenty-two, two books of his poetry had been published and he received an award from the Institute of Arts and Sciences that carried with it a sum of money. In 1912 Claude McKay left Jamaica for the United States. He entered Tuskegee Institute but soon transferred to Kansas State College, where he completed two years work. In 1914 he left Kansas for New York City, where he earned his living working at various jobs while he continued writing. In 1917 his poetry began to be published; Seven Arts Magazines published two of his poems under the pseudomyn Eli Edwards. In 1918 a number of his poems were published in Pearsons Magazine and in 1919 his poetry began to appear in the Liberator. In 1919 McKay left the United States for Holland, Belgium, and England and did not return until 1934. He traveled to many parts of the world but wrote his novels mainly in France. In 1944 he was baptized as a Catholic and spent the remaining four years of his life teaching in Catholic schools in Chicago.

MacPherson, James A. (1943-   )   This editor, short story writer, and lawyer was born in Savannah, Georgia. He was educated in local schools and at Morgan State College, Harvard Law School, and the University of Iowa. He has worked as an editor, janitor, teacher and waiter. He has received a Rockefeller grant and grants from the National Institute of Arts and Letters. His articles have appeared in magazines such as the *Atlantic Monthly*.

Major, Clarence (1936-   )   This poet, novelist, essayist, critic, and editor was born in Atlanta, Georgia, and grew up in Chicago. He was educated in the Chicago public schools, at Art Institute of Chicago, and the University of Wisconsin. Major has spent most of his working life in the field of writing; he has been a writing instructor for the Harlem Education Program, an instructor at Columbia University, visiting writer at the University of Wisconsin, guest lecturer at Queens College, and lecturer at Sarah Lawrence College. He has also been an editor of *Journal of Black Poetry* and the *Coercion Review*. His essays and poems have appeared in the *American Poetry Review, Soulbook, Essence, Journal of Black Poetry, Black World, New York Quarterly,* and the *Nickle Review*. Clarence Major has received the National Council Award, the Arts Prize, and a New York Cultural Foundation Award.

Mali, Ancient (1230 A. D.-1481)   The empire of Mali originated in the tiny state of Kangaba, West Africa, around 1000 A. D. In the twelfth century the once-proud empire of Ghana decayed and fell apart and its former subjects broke away and declared themselves independant. Among these subjects were the Mandingo people. This group was a tribal branch of the Sosso and Sonike peoples, and all three of these groups spoke the Mande language. The Mandingoes differed from the other groups, however, in that they had accepted the Moslem faith of their own accord; the Sonikes had had the Moslem religion forced upon them by the Almoravids and the Sossos had rejected Islam completely, retaining their own tribal religion. Various groups struggled for the remains of Ghana's empire. In 1180 the southern group of the Sonike people established a kingdom in the area around the city of Sosso and attempted to recreate the Ghanian empire. In 1203 the twin cities of Koumbi-Selah were overrun by Sumanguru, the most powerful of the Sosso kings. He held the city for a short time, then abandoned it. He tried to consolidate his political position by removing any rivals. He simply killed them off, including his own brothers. One of his rivals was a young boy, a cripple, and not considered dangerous; therefore his life was spared. Sumanguru made a mistake, however, in sparing the life of Sundiata Keita, for he overcame his fragile health and became a skilled warrior and leader. In 1230 he became the king of Mali, a small state with the city of Kangaba as its capital. After becoming king, Sundiata rallied the Mandingo leaders around him, raised an army, and staged a revolt against Sumanguru. Savage fighting continued for five years. The final test of strength between the armies of Sosso and Mali came in 1235 at Karina in western Africa. Sumangurus's forces were defeated and he was killed in the fighting. After the battle of Karina, Sundiata was able to conquer the remaining Sosso cities without much difficulty. By 1240 Mali was the strongest state in the western Sudan. Sundiata moved his capital from Kangaba to Niani, further down the Niger River, and began the organization of the Mali empire on a large scale. He appointed governors responsible to him in the newly conquered regions and established a central government. He introduced new methods of farming and new crops such as millet, cotton, and peanuts. Mali became the richest farming region in western Africa under his reign. In 1255 Sundiata Keita was wounded by a stray arrow at a festival and died of his wound. The people of Mali still conduct special ceremonies to honor Sundiata. After the death of Sundiata the throne went to one of his sons, Mansa Wali I, who held the empire together from 1255 to 1270. Upon his death the throne went to another of Sundiata's sons, Mansa Karifa. He was very unpopular and somewhat unbalanced. Beginning with the rule of Karifa, Mali underwent a confused period in which a severe struggle for power took place. In 1312 Mansa Musa the Magnificent emerged as a remarkable and very able leader. He brought stability to Mali at a crucial period and reestablished law and order in the empire. He managed to extend Mali's borders to the Atlantic Ocean. Being a devout Moslem, he made a pilgrimage to Mecca in 1324. He carried so much gold on this journey to Mecca that the price of gold in Egypt fell when he arrived there. This pilgrimage became legendary and was talked about for many years. Musa I was the first African king to appear on maps of Europe; he was called "The Lord of the Negroes of Guinea." Upon his return to Mali, he brought with him scholars and architects to build new buildings in the major city of Timbuctu. He established the University of Sankore, which became famous through the Moslem world. When Musa I died in 1337, the empire of Mali began slowly to decline. The Songhai city of Gao revolted and broke away from the empire and grew stronger. Mali lingered on and did not completely lose its political identity until the seventeenth century, although the empire was overrun by the Songhai people in 1481.

MANUMISSION   This is a process whereby slaves were given their freedom. The term "manumission" derived its meaning from the Latin words *manus* and *mittere*, free from the hand. Deeds of manumission or free papers were given to slaves for various reasons, usually for some meritorius service but sometimes because of guilt on the part of the slave owner. In the 1780s thousands of black soldiers and their families received deeds of manumission for their services in the Continental Army during the American Revolution.

MARCH ON WASHINGTON, D.C., 1941   In 1941 the United States was preparing its industries for war and jobs were plentiful; yet blacks were hired, if at all, only in menial capacities even in industries with government contracts. Because of this discrimination against blacks in employment, black leaders felt a drastic plan of action was needed. A. Philip Randolph, president of the Brotherhood of Sleeping Car Porters, suggested that a march on the capital by thousands of blacks demanding redress and guarantees of employment, especially in the defense industries, be organized. The idea was well received among blacks, but President Roosevelt attempted to circumvent the movement by speaking out against racial discrimination. Eleanor Roosevelt and Fiorella La Guardia, mayor of New York, tried to persuade black leaders to abandon the project. They refused to do this. The march was to take place on July 1, 1941. In late June government officials were intensely concerned about the march. President Roosevelt appealed to Randolph and other black leaders to give up the entire plan. After several conferences with Randolph and other black leaders, President Roosevelt stated that if the march were called off, he would issue an order prohibiting discrimination in employment in defense industries. The march on Washington was cancelled and on June 23, 1941, President Roosevelt issued executive order 8802, which prohibited discrimination in employment by industries holding government contracts.

MARGE PERKINS   This is a character in Kristin Hunter's novel, *The Landlord*.

MAROONS, THE   In the mid-seventeenth century, when the British took control of Jamaica, many of the black slaves availed themselves of the opportunity to escape into the mountain regions of the island. These runaway slaves were called Maroons. The term is derived from the Spanish word *cimarron*, meaning wild or unruly. The fugitive slaves organized themselves into communities and conducted guerilla warfare against the planters. Plantations were raided, and arms and ammunition were taken, along with other provisions. The British government employed both army and navy forces against the Maroons but were defeated. Indians brought in by the English to hunt down the group were themselves hunted by the Maroons. The British government finally signed a treaty with the Maroons in 1738. In the United States similar groups of runaway slaves conducted the same kind of limited warfare against the southern planters during the eighteenth and nineteenth centuries.

MARSHALL, PAULE (1929-   )   This short story writer and novelist was born in Brooklyn, New York. Her parents were West Indian immigrants who came to the United States after World War I. She was educated in the New York public schools and at Brooklyn College. Ms. Marshall has worked as a librarian in various New York libraries and as a journalist. In her career as a journalist she has traveled throughout the West Indies and to Brazil, Guyana, and other South and Central American countries. Ms. Marshall's writings have appeared in *Harper's* and *Freedomways*. She has won several awards for her work, including the Guggenheim Fellowship (1960) the Rosenthal Award (1961), the Ford Foundation Grant for Poets and Fiction Writers (1964-1965), and the National Endowment for the Arts and Humanities Award (1967-1968).

MARY DALTON   This is a character in Richard Wright's novel, *Native Son*.

MATHEUS, JOHN (1892-   )   This linguist, playwright, short story writer, and drama teacher was born in Keyser, West Virginia. He was educated in local schools and at Western Reserve and Columbia universities. He completed graduate work at the University of Chicago and the Sorbonne in Paris. Mr. Matheus has had a distinguished career as a teacher; he was head of the Department of Romance Languages at West Virginia State College from 1922 until 1953. He has traveled widely and lectured at universities and colleges and in Europe, Africa, Cuba, Mexico, and various countries in

South America. Professor Matheus's writings have appeared in *The Crisis, CLA Journal, Opportunity, Modern Language Journal,* and the *Arts Quarterly.* He has received the Officer de L'Ordre Nationale Honneur et Merite from the Haitian government.

MATHIS, SHARON BELL (1937-   )   This teacher, critic, short story writer, and children's author was born in Atlantic City, New Jersey. She was educated at local schools and at Morgan State College. She has worked as a special education teacher and has been writer in residence at Howard University (1972). Ms. Mathis has won the Council on Interracial Books for Children Award for *Sidewalk Story* (1970), Breadloaf Writer's Conference Award (1970), and an ALA Notable Book Award for *Teacup Full of Roses* (1972). Her writings have appeared in *Black World, Essence,* and *Ebony Jr.*

MAX   This is a character in John A. Williams's *The Man Who Cried I Am.*

MAYFIELD, JULIAN (1928-   )   This actor, short story writer, novelist, journalist, and screenwriter was born in Greer, South Carolina. He was educated in the local schools and at Lincoln University in Pennsylvania. Mr. Mayfield has worked as an aide to the former president of Ghana, Kwame Nkrumah, and lectured at Cornell and New York universities. He has edited the papers of the Accra Assembly and the magazine the *African Review,* which he helped found. Julian Mayfield's writings have appeared in *Commentary,* the *African Review, Black World,* and *Black Scholar.*

MELODRAMA   The term "melodrama" comes from the French word *melodrame,* which in turn is derived from the Greek word *melos,* meaning song. Originally melodrama referred to a play having songs and music dispersed through it; however, the term as it is used today indicates a situation in a novel, poem, or play in which excessive emotion or sentiment is used at the expense of the law of cause and effect.

MEREDITH MARCH, THE   On June 5, 1966, James Meredith and four companions began a two-hundred twenty-mile demonstration walk from Memphis, Tennessee, to Jackson, Mississippi, in order to encourage the blacks in Mississippi to register and vote. On June 6, Meredith was shot and wounded by a shotgun blast from ambush near the town of Hernando, Mississippi. He was taken to a hosptial

Meriwether, Louise

in Memphis, where it was found that his wounds were not serious. He was released from the hospital on June 8, 1966.

MERIWETHER, LOUISE This novelist, and short story writer was born in Haverstraw, New York. She was educated in local schools and at New York University and the University of California, Los Angeles. She has worked as a newspaper reporter on the *Los Angeles Sentinel*, as a legal secretary, and as a story analyst for Universal Studies.

MERRY GO ROUND This is a poem by Langston Hughes.

METAPHOR Writers often describe one object by comparing it with another. The term "metaphor" refers to the application of words or phrases to an object or idea to imply a comparison with another object or concept. In the poem *Four Glimpses of Night*, poet Frank Marshall Davis says that "Night is a wandering child creeping between earth and sky." The word metaphor comes from the greek word *Metaphora*, which means a transfer.

METER Most poetry has a certain rhythmic structure generally known as its meter. The term "meter" is from the Greek word *metron*, meaning measure; it refers to any kind of rhythm in poetry caused by the number and kind of metrical feet in a stanza or line of verse.

MILLER, MAY (MRS. JOHN SULLIVAN) This poet, teacher, playwright, and lecturer was born in Washington, D.C. She was educated in local schools and at Howard, American, and Columbia universities. Ms. Miller worked for some time as a drama teacher at Frederick Douglass High School in Baltimore, Maryland. She has lectured on and read her poetry at Monmouth College, the University of Wisconsin, and Phillip Exeter Academy. May Miller's poetry has been published in the *Antioch Review*, *Common Ground*, *Poetry Magazine*, the *Crisis*, and *Phylon*.

MILNER, RONALD (1938-   ) This playwright, drama critic, and editor was born in Detroit, Michigan. He was educated in the Detroit public schools and at Columbia University. He has been writer in residence at Lincoln University in Pennsylvania and has also taught at Michigan State University at East Lansing. He has been the recipient of a Rockefeller Foundation Award and the John Hay

Whitney Fellowship. His writings have appeared in *Negro Digest* and *Black World.*

MIMI DAQIN   This is a character in Walter White's novel, *Flight.*

MINERVA LITERARY ASSOCIATION, THE   Established on October 3, 1834, this organization was for black women. There were thirty ladies at its first meeting. The group produced numerous programs, which consisted of readings and recitations of various pieces of literature, some original. The ladies of this association produced both poetry and prose.

MISCEGENATION   At various times men and women of different races have lived together with or without the benefit of wedlock. Those persons involved in such a relationship are said to practice miscegenation; in the United States this often means marital or other relationships between black women and white men or white women and black men. Black authors have produced several poems, stories, plays, and novels on this subject. Among them are *Mulatto,* a play by Langston Hughes; *Cross,* a poem by Langston Hughes; *Blood Burning Moon,* a story by Jean Toomer; and *White Marble Lady,* a novel by Roi Ottley.

MIDDLE PASSAGE   This term refers to that part of the triangular slave trade route in which slaves were carried from Africa to the West Indies or to the North American colonies. The slaves were transported under inhuman conditions. During the passage the slaves were often packed into the ships on shelves with no more than twenty-four inches head room. The slaves could neither stand nor sit upright; for most of the trip they were chained together in a prone position. If the slaver was a loose packer, the slaves were sometimes allowed on deck for exercise and food. In bad weather they were kept in the hold. In general most slave traders showed very little or no feeling for their human cargo. During the infamous middle passage, slaves died by the hundreds of thousands from ill treatment, disease, and suicide. Alex Haley describes the middle passage in some detail in his book, *Roots.*

MISSISSIPPI MARCH, THE   On June 6, 1966, James Meredith was shot and wounded from ambush near Hernando, Mississippi, and was unable to continue a demonstration march from Memphis, Tennessee, to Jackson, Mississippi. Begun on June 5, the march was made to encourage the blacks in Mississippi to register and vote. On June 7, Martin Luther King and other civil rights leaders continued the march begun by Meredith. Several incidents occurred along the line of march. In Philadelphia, Mississippi, on June 21 a mob of whites stoned the marchers. On the same day blacks and whites exchanged gunfire in the black ghetto section of that town. On June 23, state highway patrolmen attacked the marchers with tear gas, clubs, and rifle butts when they attempted to pitch a tent on a school ground in Canton, Mississippi. The march ended on June 26, 1966, when fifteen thousand people marched through Jackson. Among the march leaders in addition to Dr. King were Stokely Carmichael of SNCC, Floyd McKissick of CORE and Walter Reuther of UAW. This march was the third largest march, after the March on Washington on 1963 and the Selma to Montgomery march of 1964.

MISSISSIPPI PLAN, THE   During the last quarter of the nineteenth century in the southern United States, white political leaders developed various ways systematically to deprive the blacks of their voting rights. One such plan, developed in Mississippi, required all citizens between the ages of sixteen and sixty years old to show a poll tax receipt and to be able to read and interpret the state constitution before they could vote. This practice allowed the election officials to discriminate between black and white voters with the result that blacks were stripped of their votes. Black citizens were also disenfranchised for minor crimes. This plan was adopted by the Mississippi Constitutional Convention in 1890 and upheld by the United States Supreme Court in the case of *Williams* vs. *Mississippi* in 1898. Six other southern states adopted constitutional changes similar to the Mississippi Plan.

MISSOURI COMPROMISE   The controversy over the entrance of the Missouri Territory into the United States as a full state began in 1817 and lasted until 1821, when Missouri was finally admitted to the Union. From 1817 to 1819, the Missouri Territorial Assembly petitioned Congress for statehood. In 1819 the number of slave and free states was equal. When the House of Representatives passed a bill authorizing Missouri to frame a constitution, a New York Congressman James Tallmadge proposed an amendment keeping slavery out of the new state. The amendment passed in the House but failed to pass in the Senate, and Congress adjourned. In December 1819, the Territory of Maine petitioned to enter the Union as a free state; a political compromise was arranged. Maine was to be admitted as a free and Missouri was to come into the Union as a slave state with the provision that there would be no slavery north of Missouri's southern border. After bitter debate, Missouri was admitted to the Union on March 6, 1820. A constitutional convention was called and met on June 12, 1820. The convention immediately authorized the state legislature to pass laws keeping blacks and mulattoes out of the new state. This action caused another bitter congressional debate; a second compromise was reached on March 22, 1821. Missouri would not be admitted to the Union until it was agreed that the new constitution would not infringe upon the rights of anyone. On August 10, 1821, Missouri was finally admitted to the United States. The Missouri Compromise, as these agreements were called, remained intact until the Kansas-Nebraska Act was passed in 1854.

MITCHELL, LOFTEN (1919-   )   This playwright was born in Harlem, New York, and obtained his education through high school in New York City schools. He was further educated at Talladega College in Alabama and attended City College of New York and Union and General Theological seminaries as well. He worked for a time for the New York City Welfare Department as an investigator specializing in cases concerning Gypsies. Mitchell began writing plays early and continued to do so even while he was attending school. He has won the John Simon Guggenheim Award for creative writing in drama. His play *Land Beyond the River* had a long successful run off-Broadway in 1957 and has appeared in several anthologies. His critical writings have been published in *Freedomways* and the *Crisis*.

MONODRAMA   Sometimes plays are written in which there is only one performer. Such a dramatic piece is called a monodrama. Three monodramas by playwright Ed Bullins are *The Theme is Blackness*, *The American Flag Ritual*, and *A Short Play For A Small Theater*.

MONTGOMERY ALABAMA BUS BOYCOTT, THE   For many years blacks were "Jim Crowed" on public transportion facilities in almost all the southern states. Blacks could not ride in the front part of the public buses and were segregrated on railway coaches. On the evening of December 1, 1955, in Montgomery, Alabama, a highly respected black woman, Mrs. Rosa Parks, refused to give up her seat on the bus to a white and was arrested for violating the Jim Crow laws. Her arrest galvanized the black community into action and catapulted

271

into a leadership position a young Baptist minister named Martin Luther King, Jr. An organization was formed and committees were activated. On Monday, December 5, a boycott of the public buses of the Montgomery transportation system began. The blacks refused to ride the buses for a year while black lawyers developed court cases to test the constitutionality of the Jim Crow laws. During this period the homes of the boycott leaders were bombed and their lives were threatened. Car pools formed to take blacks to and from their destinations were harassed, but the boycott continued. Finally the various law cases concerning the Montgomery incident reached the U.S. Supreme Court, which ruled on November 13, 1956, that Alabama state and local laws requiring segregation by race on public transportation systems were unconstitutional.

MONTGOMERY IMPROVEMENT ASSOCIATION, THE   In 1955 on December 5, a boycott of the public buses by the blacks of Montgomery, Alabama, was begun. In order to coordinate the boycott, the Montgomery Improvement Association was organized that same day with Martin Luther King, Jr. as its chief officer.

MORGANFIELD, MCKINLEY ("MUDDY WATERS") (1915-   )   This blues singer and musician was born in Rolling Fork, Mississippi, near Clarksdale. His mother died when he was three years old and he went to live with his grandmother in Clarksdale and attended the public schools there. When he reached his teens, he went to work as a farmhand; it was during this time that he made a recording for the Library of Congress. "Muddy Waters" learned to play the guitar when he was twenty-two and began playing for dances on weekends. He left the farm and joined a road show for a short time but soon returned to Clarksdale. In 1943 Morganfield left Mississippi for Chicago. From 1943 to 1946 he worked at various jobs and played in nightclubs in the evenings. In 1946 he made his first commercial record. His popularity grew. "Muddy Waters" has sung and played in England and Europe as well as the United States.

MORRISON, TONI (1931-   )   This teacher, novelist, editor, and essayist was born in Lorain, Ohio. She was educated in local schools and at Howard and Cornell universities. She has taught at Texas Southern University and Howard University. Ms. Morrison has been an editor for the Random House Publishing Company since 1965. She has lectured at writers' conferences, including the Cuyahoga Community College Writers' Conference (East Campus)

Cleveland, Ohio, in 1976. Her essays have appeared in several journals, including *Black World*.

MOTLEY, WILLARD (1912-1965) This novelist was born in Chicago and educated through high school there. After graduating from high school, he worked as a ranchhand, cook, shipping clerk, radio scriptwriter, and writer for the Office of Civil Defense and the Chicago Housing Authority. Mr. Motley traveled throughout the United States. In 1941, when he was twenty-nine years old, he returned to Chicago and began writing his novel, *Knock on any Door*, which was published in 1947. Eventually it was made into a successful film. Willard Motley died in Mexico City in 1965.

MURRY, ALBERT (1916-   ) This short story writer, teacher, novelist, literary critic, and essayist was born in Nokomis, Alabama. He was educated in the public schools and at Tuskeegee Institute to the Masters level. He has completed work at Ohio State, Michigan, and Norwestern universities. Murry has also studied at the University of Paris and the Air Force Academy. As an air force major, now retired, Mr. Murry served in North Africa and the Middle East. In addition to his air force career, he has taught literature at Colgate, University of Missouri, University of Massachusetts, and the Columbia University School of Journalism. Albert Murry's articles have appeared in the *New Leader, Life, Bookweek,* and *Book World*.

MYERS, WALTER DEAN (1937-   ) This editor, short story writer, essayist, children's writer, and lecturer was born in Martinsburg, West Virginia. He was educated in local schools and at New York City College and served in the army (1954-1957). Mr. Myers has worked at various jobs, including employment supervisor for the New York State Department of Labor (1966-1969). Since 1970 he has worked as an editor for the Bobbs Merrill Publishing Company. His essays have appeared in *Black Creation* and *Black World*. He has lectured at Case Western Reserve University in Cleveland, Ohio. Mr. Myers has received the Council on Interracial Books for Children Award for *Where Does the Day Go*.

NATIONAL LEAGUE FOR THE PROTECTION OF COLORED WOMEN Established in 1906 by Frances A. Kellor, a wealthy white social worker, this organization was founded for the express purpose of helping to protect black women sent north by various agencies from exploitation and to provide respectable housing and training schools for them. Attempts were also made to find suitable employment for the new arrivals. Later this agency merged with another, the Committee for Improving the Industrial Conditions of Negroes in New York, to form the National League on Urban Conditions Among Negroes in New York, better known as the Urban League.

NATIONAL YOUTH ADMINISTRATION, THE (NYA)   In 1935 the Roosevelt administration established the, NYA which gave young people between sixteen and twenty-five part-time jobs in high schools, universities, and colleges. In this way the young people remained in school and did not enter the already overcrowded job market. The Negro Affairs section, as it was called, of this organization was directed by Mary McLeod Bethune.

NEGRITUDE   The term negritude describes the concept of a shared cultural experience on the part of the Black Africans, especially those in the former French colonies. Intrinsic in this concept is the belief that there is an innate unity in the culture of the blacks, wherever they may be in the world. The Negritude Movement was begun in 1932 or 1933 by black French-speaking poets Amie Ceasaire, Leon Damas, and Leopold Senghor. These writers, influenced to some extent by the works of Langston Hughes, Countee Cullen, and Claude McKay, felt that their African culture was being overwhelmed by that of the French and that they must fight against the encroachment and return to their African cultural roots. This, in a limited way, is similar to the Afro-American idea of Soul, which supposes that there is a common cultural experience native to all blacks in the United States. Negritude can be said, in a very simplistic sense, to be Soul with an African beat.

NEGRO HISTORY BULLETIN, THE   Established in 1937 in Washington, D.C., this small magazine is published by the Association for the Study of Negro Life and History. It is designed to promote the study of the history and literature of the blacks of the United States and elsewhere. Each issue is about thirty pages long and contains articles on various aspects of the life of the blacks. Very often there are articles particularly concerned with literature. Book reviews appear in almost every issue and occasionally poetry is published. All articles are well written and carefully researched.

NELL, WILLIAM COOPER (1816-1874)   This historian and abolitionist was born in Boston. He obtained his early education at an elementary school for black children. He later read law in the law office of a prominent Boston lawyer. Nell became deeply involved in the antislavery movement and served on the Boston all-black vigilance committee. In 1851 he helped Frederick Douglass with the publication of his newspaper, the *North Star*. Much of his time was spent in providing public schools for black children. In addition to these activities, Mr. Nell collected and preserved materials pertaining to the part played by blacks in the American Revolution. In 1855 he published a small book on this subject, *Colored Patriots of the American Revolution*. He also wrote numerous abolitionist pamphlets.

NELSON, ALICE DUNBAR (1875-1935)   This poet, playwright, short story writer, and editor was born in New Orleans, Louisiana. She was educated in local schools and at Straight College, the University of Pennsylvania, and the Cornell University School of Industrial Arts. She became a teacher in the New Orleans public schools Later she taught at Howard School in Wilmington, Delaware, and also in New York. In 1898 she married Paul Laurence Dunbar. Dunbar died in 1906 and she remained a widow until 1916, when she married Robert J. Nelson. Her writing appeared in the *Crisis, Opportunity*, and the *A.M.E. Church Review*.

NEW PITTSBURGH COURIER, THE   Established in 1910, this newspaper is one of the oldest black general papers. It began as a small news sheet published by a Methodist church. Robert L. Vann, a lawyer with some experience in journalism, was brought in to keep the small paper solvent. From this small operation the *Pittsburgh Courier* was developed. Robert L. Vann ran the *Courier* until his death in 1940, then his widow conducted operations for several years. The *Pittsburgh Courier* was sold and became a part of the Sengstacke group of newspapers under the name the *New Pittsburgh Courier*.

NEWT WINGER   A character in Gordon Parks's novel, *The Learning Tree*.

NEW YORK PHILOMATHEAN SOCIETY, THE   Established in 1830 in New York City, this literary society was limited to male member-

275

ship. The purpose of this organization was to provide black New Yorkers the opportunity to expand their general knowledge and to increase their knowledge of literature in particular. By 1837 the society had developed a circulating library of six hundred or more volumes for its members. In 1843 the Philomathean Society became an Old Fellow Lodge and changed its name to Philomathean Lodge #646.

NIAGARA MOVEMENT, THE   In June 1905 a group of prominent blacks, responding to a call sent out by W. E. B. DuBois, met on the Canadian side of Niagara Falls to develop plans for protesting against the inequalities that black Americans faced in the United States. The group met in Canada because no white hotel on the U.S. side of Niagara Falls would accept them. Their deliberations resulted in a platform that, among other things, called for the restoration of voting rights for the blacks, an end to racial discrimination, equality in human rights and freedoms, and support of basic principles of brotherhood. The conference participants incorporated themselves as the Niagara Movement and met in the following years at Harpers Ferry, Virginia, (1906); Boston, Massachusetts (1907); and Oberlin, Ohio (1908). The movement functioned through its various committees. The Health Committee called for a national campaign to eradicate tuberculosis among blacks; the Education Committee recommended the production of a pamphlet on the education of blacks in the South for the Legislatures and the public at large. State and local branches were established, but they were limited in their progress by the lack of money. Booker T. Washington, the leader of the blacks at this time, was opposed to the Niagara Movement's program and used his powerful influence to thwart its progress at every opportunity. By 1909 the organization was dying and in 1911 it merged with the newly founded National Association for the Advancement of Colored People and ceased to exist as a separate organization.

NO-QUARTER POLICY, THE CONFEDERATE   When the Civil War began, the federal government refused to enlist blacks, free or otherwise, in the Union armies. However, in late 1862 some blacks were given military training and after January 1, 1863, when the Emancipation Proclamation was issued, blacks were recruited for the northern armies. The Confederate response to the Union action was immediate. On May 1, 1863, the Confederate Congress gave President Jefferson Davis authority to execute the white officers of black troops. Black soldiers who were captured were to be treated according to the laws of the state in which they were captured. At this time many southern states imposed the death penalty for insurrection and the black soldiers were considered rebels. Some reports indicated that black Union troopers captured in battle were given no quarter and not allowed to surrender; they were executed on the spot. On July 30, 1863, President Lincoln issued a proclamation stating that for every Union soldier executed or in any way mistreated, a Confederate prisoner in Union hands would be similarly treated. This proclamation served to curtail somewhat the mistreatment of black Union troops in battle, but there were reported instances where the Confederate no-quarter policy continued.

NORFOLK JOURNAL AND GUIDE, THE   Begun as a house organ for the Knights of Gideon, a Norfolk lodge, this newspaper was purchased by Plummer Bernard Young and changed into a regular black newspaper. In 1911 Young organized the Guide Publishing Company and continued to publish the *Norfolk Journal and Guide* until his death in 1962. The newspaper is still run by a member of the Young family. The *Norfolk Journal and Guide* is sometimes referred to as the black *New York Times.*

NOT A MAN AND YET A MAN   This is a long poem by Albery Whitman.

OCTOROON, THE   First published in 1901 in *An Idyl of the South,* Albery A. Whitman's last collection of verse, *The Octoroon,* tells the story for the love of Sheldon Maury for his beautiful octoroon slave, Lena. Sheldon Maury, the handsome son of a prominent plantation owner, falls deeply in love with Lena. The two lovers enjoy a brief happiness, but Sheldon's father finds out about the relationship and, for the sake of the family honor, sells Lena to another plantation owner without telling his son. When Sheldon discovers that Lena has been sold, he immediately rides to her rescue. When he arrives at the plantation where Lena has been taken, he finds that she has escaped from her uncouth and brutish new owner, who had also fallen in love with her. Sheldon finally finds Lena dying in a woodsman's cottage. He reaffirms his love for her and Lena dies in his arms. Sheldon in his grief and anger over what he considered his father's betrayal of him prepares to leave the plantation but is persuaded to remain.

OFFORD, CARL RUTHVEN (1910-   )   This novelist, poet, essayist, and short story writer was born in Trinidad, West Indies, and was educated upon coming to the United States. Mr. Offord has also worked as an insurance executive and publisher.

OTTLEY, ROI (1906-   )   This journalist, editor, biographer, and novelist was born in Harlem, New York. He was educated in the public schools and attended St. Bonaventure College, the University of Michigan, Columbia University, New York University, and St. John University School of Law. Ottley began his career as a journalist, columnist, reporter, and editor on the *Amsterdam Star News.* He served as editor of the Federal Writer's Project study of blacks in New York. Although he was best known as a journalist, Roi Ottley was involved in many other activities. In 1943 he was publicity director of the National CIO War Relief Committee.

OVERSEER, THE   Each plantation had one individual who supervised the work of the plantation slaves and operated the complex when the owner was absent. The overseer's or supervisor's job was to secure as much work as possible from the slaves. To do this the overseer used whatever methods he felt were necessary. Very often a whip, the symbol of the office of overseer, was employed against those slaves who did not work fast or well enough.

OWEN, CHANDLER (1809-1967)   This editor, political leader, and labor leader was born in Warrenton, Virginia. He was educated in the Warrenton public schools and at Virginia Union and Columbia universities. Although he gave up editing for politics, Chandler Owen is best known as coeditor of the magazine the *Messenger.* He worked with A. P. Randolph in this publication from 1917 until 1923, when he moved to Chicago and became involved in the politics of that city. He continued to write for the *Messenger* for about a year after leaving New York. Even though Owen and Randolph were in different cities, they maintained their close friendship and often wrote or visited one another. When Chandler Owen died in Chicago in 1967, his lifelong friend A. Philip Randolph came to bury him.

PARKS, GORDON (1912-   )   This poet, motion picture director, and composer was born in Fort Scott, Kansas. He was educated in Kansas and in the public schools of St. Paul, Minnesota. He worked at a variety of jobs while attending high school; as a piano player, a waiter, and a janitor in a flop house. In 1933 he joined the Civilian

Conservation Corps. He became interested in photography in 1938, bought a twelve-dollar camera, taught himself photography, and began to earn his living as a commercial photographer. In 1941 he was awarded a Rosenwald Fellowship, which enabled him to study photography at his leisure. Mr. Parks has won the American Society of Magazine Photographers Award, the Frederick W. Brehm Award, and the Spingarn Award (1972).

PASSING There are found among the black population of the United States persons whose skin color is such that they cannot be distinguished from members of the dominant white population. Some blacks who are in this position choose to escape from the poverty, the racial distress, and the economic inequalities by pretending to be white. Such persons adopt the cultural pattern and value system of the white majority. Blacks who take this action are said to be "passing." Several novels by black writers have dealt with this subject including *Passing* by Nella Larsen, *Plum Bun* by Jessie Faucet, *The House Behind the Cedars* by Charles Chesnutt, *Flight* by Walter White, and *Alien Land* by Willard Savoy.

PATTERSON, RAYMOND R. (1929-   ) This poet and lecturer was born in New York. He was educated in local schools and at Lincoln and New York universities. Mr. Patterson has worked as a children's supervisor at the Youth House for Boys in the Bronx (1956-1958). He has taught English and literature at Benedict College (1958-1959) and City College of New York (1968-present). His poetry has appeared in the *Chicago Tribune Magazine*, the *Minnesota Review*, *Negro Digest*, *Scholastic Voices*, *Phylon*, and *Presence Africaine*. His poems appear in anthologies such as *New Black Voices*, *Soul Book*, and others. He has won the Barestone Mountain Poetry Award (1950), the National Endowment for the Arts Award (1970) and the Library of Congress Poetry Reading Award (1970).

PAWLEY, THOMAS (1917-   ) This editor and playwright was born in Jackson, Mississippi. He was educated at Virginia State College and at the University of Iowa. Mr. Pawley has taught at Prairie New State College, Atlanta University, Lincoln University, and the University of California at Santa Barbara. His writings have appeared in *Crisis* and *Phylon* magazines.

PECKING ORDER, THE This is a novel by Mark Kennedy published in 1953.

PETER BYE   This is a character in Jessie Fauset's novel, *There is Confusion*.

PETRY, ANN (1911-   )   This novelist, short story writer, and critic was born in Old Saybrook, Connecticut, and obtained her early education there. After completing high school, she entered the College of Pharmacy at the University of Connecticut, following the family tradition since several members of her family have been pharmacists. Ms. Petry began writing early, while she was still in high school. In 1938 she married and moved to New York City, where she was employed as an advertising writer on the *Amsterdam News*, a prominent black newspaper. Later she worked with another paper, the *People's Voice*, as a general reporter. In 1945 she was awarded a Houghton Mifflin Scholarship and in 1946 her first novel, *The Street*, was published. She has received the Best American Short Story Award (1946) for "Like a Winding Sheet."

PHARR, ROBERT DEAN (1916-   )   This novelist and short story writer was born in Richmond, Virginia. He was educated in local schools and at Virginia Union and Fisk universities. His writings have appeared in *New Black Voices* (anthology) and *New York Magazine*.

PHOENIX SOCIETY, THE   One way that blacks in the United States broadened their educational outlook during the early nineteenth century was through literary and debating societies. The organization of this kind that exerted a very great influence on the black community and had the largest membership was the Phoenix Society of New York City. Established in 1833, the Society had as its main purpose the improvement of the blacks in morality and literature. Anyone of good "moral character" could become a member of the Phoenix Society, however, applicants had to be accepted by its board of directors. The Society was integrated to the extent that there were some whites on its board of directors. On this board were black men of prominence such as Theodore S. Wright, clergyman; Samuel Cornish, newspaper editor; David Ruggles, writer; and Charles B. Ray, school official. One important white member of the board was Arthur Tappan. The Phoenix Society undertook to carry out an extensive program that included the raising of $10,000 for erecting a building to house a library, reading rooms, lecture rooms, and a small museum. Ward societies were begun. The task of the members of these ward groups was to visit the different families in the wards and register every black person according to age, sex, occupation, and the ability to read and write. Blacks both young and old were to be persuaded to become members of the societies. Adults were to be encouraged to attend meetings and to see to it that their children got to school each day. In addition to these activities, the ward societies were to organize and maintain circulating libraries that blacks could use for a small fee.

PIPPIN, HORACE (1888-1946)   This primitive painter was born in West Chester, Pennsylvania. When he was still very young, his family moved to Goshen, New York, where he went to school. When his father died, Pippin was forced to leave school to help support his mother. When she died in 1911, he left Goshen and moved to Paterson, New Jersey, where he worked for a moving and storage company. In 1916 he volunteered for duty in the United States Army and was sent to France the next year. He was involved in severe combat in extended trench warfare while his unit was attached to the French army. He was badly wounded and lost the use of his right arm. In 1929 he devised a method of painting and drawing by holding up his useless right arm with his left hand. In 1933 Pippin's work was discovered and his paintings appeared in an exhibit at the Museum of Modern Art. With this exhibit his reputation grew and Horace Pippin became famous. He continued to paint until his death from a stroke in 1946.

PLANTATION, THE   A large farm or estate, this unit was the mainstay of southern agriculture. The plantation was often practically self-sustaining. There were generally orchards, fields, smoke houses, slave quarters, barns, and work facilities surrounding the planter's residence, usually known as the "big house." Some of these plantations consisted of thousands of acres of land with thousands of slaves as a work force. The very large plantations, however, were few in number. The ideal plantation consisted of about one-thousand acres of land and one-hundred slaves to work it. Often the estate produced its own food and had its own stables and craft shops (such as blacksmith, carpenter, shoe shops, and, in some cases, spinning facilities). Early plantations often had their own docks from which to ship their crops. The plantation setting appears in the work of George W. Lee, Ernest Gaines, and other black writers.

PLANTATION SYSTEM, THE This economic system as it developed in the southern English colonies was a group agricultrual economy of the original "plantings" or new settlements in the tidewater region of Virginia and other parts of the South. The labor force for the farm units or plantations created by this system consisted of black slaves provided by foreign and domestic slave traders.

POLITE, CARLENE (1932-   ) This novelist and essayist was born in Detroit, Michigan, and was educated there. Ms. Polite has been a professional dancer and a teacher of dancing. She has been active in politics as a member of the Michigan Democratic State Central Committee, 1962-1963.

PORTER, DOROTHY BURNET (1905-   ) This bibliographer, historian, librarian, and essayist was born in Warrenton, Virginia. She was educated at Howard and Columbia universities. She has worked in many phases of library work but is best known for her work as bibliographer of materials pertaining to the history and literature of black Americans. In addition, Dorothy Porter has written numerous historical essays and her work has been published in the *Journal of Negro Education,* the *Journal of Negro History,* and *Phylon.* For many years she was curator of the Moorland-Spingarn Collection of materials concerning black literature located at Howard University.

PORTER, JAMES A. (1905-1971) This artist, art critic, art historian, painter, and teacher was born in Baltimore, Maryland. He was educated in public schools and at Howard and New York universities. He studied further at the New York Art Students' League, Columbia, and the Institute de'Arte et Archeologie in Paris. After completing his studies he returned to Howard University, where he became profsssor of art. He is an expert in the historical background of the black American artist. His work in this field has yet to be surpassed. Even though new critics are active today, they often base their work on Porter's writings. James A. Porter was in almost constant demand as a lecturer and his many articles have appeared in numerous journals.

PRICHARD, N. H. II (1939-   ) This poet and short story writer was born in New York City. He was educated in the public schools, at Washington Square College, the Institute of Fine Arts, and New

York and Columbia universities. Prichard has read his work at numerous colleges and universities, for literary societies, and for television. Mr. Prichard has been poet in residence at the Friends' Seminary (1968-present) and an instructor in the poetry workshop at the New School for Social Research (1969-present). His writing has been published in *Negro Digest, Umbra, East Village, Hudson Review, Poetry Northwest,* and in many other publications.

PRIDGETT, GERTRUDE ("MA" RAINEY) (1886-1939)   This blues singer was born in Columbus, Georgia, and went to school there. She began singing in nightclubs and cabarets in the early 1900s. When she was eighteen, she married William "Pa" Rainey, a dancer and singer with a minstrel show known as the Rabbit Foot Minstrels, and spent many years on the road playing the black vaudeville circuit in towns in various parts of the South. On one occasion when the show stopped in Chattanooga, Tennessee, "Ma" took under her care a young singer named Bessie Smith, who became her protege and eventually a well-known singer in her own right. In 1923 "Ma" Rainey recorded a series of blues for Paramount Records. The songs were very successful and between 1923 and 1929 she made many recordings. Her fame as a singer declined during the Great Depression and by 1930 she had ceased to record. She retired completely from show business in 1933 when her mother and sister died. She spent the remainder of her life in Columbus, Georgia, and died on December 22, 1939.

PROLETARIAN FICTION   In some novels and short stories the primary emphasis is placed not upon characters as such but on their condition as members of the working class and the various problems they encounter as part of this group. Fiction of this kind is generally characterized by an attempt on the part of the author to describe the adverse and negative economic environment that stifles the progress of the working man. There has been little fiction of this kind written by Afro-American writers. Three writers who produced what can be called proletarian fiction at some time in their careers are Alden Bland, *Behold a Cry;* William Attaway, *Blood On the Forge;* and Chester Himes, *The Lonely Crusade.*

PROSE POEM   A prose poem is prose characterized by a distinct rhythm and the extensive use of poetic imagery or symbols. Some of the best examples of prose poetry by a black writer of the United

States is to be found in the writing of W. E. B. DuBois, especially in *The Souls Of Black Folk*. The entire short essay "Of the Passing of the First Born" from this volume can be called a prose poem.

PROSODY   A poet very often must use the vowels and consonants of words in various ways. The term "prosody" refers to the science of metrics and the principles involve the use of metrical patterns, stanza forms, rhythm, and word syllables. It is, in essence, a grammar of versification.

PROTEST WRITING   Black writers in the United States from the eighteenth to the twentieth centuries have engaged in writing books, articles, pamphlets, speeches, and letters in which they protested against the conditions that both enslaved and free blacks have had to live under. This protest writing, as it is sometimes called, is not confined to polemics. Protest against the racial prejudice directed toward blacks in America is evident in novels, plays, poems, and short stories. The writers protesting the inequalities inflicted upon the blacks in the United States vary greatly. They range from Richard Allen and Absolom Jones in the eighteenth century to Ishmael Reed and James Baldwin in the twentieth.

PSYCHOLOGICAL NOVEL   Sometimes novelists are mainly concerned with why the characters act as they do. There is great involvement with interior characterization of what goes on in a character's mind rather than a description of what happens in the novel. Prose fiction or novels of this kind are usually called psychological novels and not only report the action but explain why it happens. In this sort of writing, characterization is of extreme importance. Ernest Gaines's *Catherine Carmier* can be said to be a psychological novel.

PYRRHIC VICTORY   Pyrrhus of Epirus (318-272 B.C.) was a brilliant military leader who conducted a series of campaigns against the Roman armies in Sicily from 280-275 B.C. The term "pyrrhic victory" refers to a statement Pyrrhus is supposed to have made after the Romans lost the Battle of Asculum. In this battle the Romans were defeated but the best part of Pyrrhus' own army was destroyed. He is said to have exclaimed, "One more such victory and we are lost." Any victory that is gained at great cost is said to be a pyrrhic victory. The fifth part of Wallace Thurman's *The Blacker the Berry* is called "pyrrhic Victory."

QUATRAIN, THE   The quatrain is a stanza of poetry that consists of four lines. There are almost endless varieties of this form of poetry. The rhyme arrangements in the quatrain vary but the most familiar is the pattern in which the first and third and the second and fourth lines rhyme. This is represented by the symbols *a b a b*. Countee Cullen's poem "In Memory of Colonel Charles Young" is written in quatrains. The term quatrain comes from the Latin word *quattuor*, which means four.

RACE MAN   The term "race man" was used during the early part of the twentieth century to describe those black leaders who were concerned with the welfare of the blacks above anything else. The ideas they expounded were closely related to those expressed by today's Black Nationalist or Black Militant Movement. Black leaders of the past who would be characterized as race men are W. E. B. DuBois, Monroe Trotter, T. Thomas Fortune, and, on occasion, Booker T. Washington.

RACHEL   This is a character in Angelina Grimke's play, *Rachel*.

RALPH KABNIS   This is a character in Jean Toomer's collection of writings, *Cane*.

RANDOLPH EXCITEMENT, THE   When John Randolph, former congressman from Virginia and member of the famous Randolph family of Virginia, died in 1833, he left a will that freed his five-hundred slaves. The will also provided money for the purchase of land in Ohio upon which the ex-slaves could settle. In 1846 the executor of Randolph's will, Judge Leigh, bought thirty-two hundred acres of land in Mercer County, Ohio, to be divided into forty-acre lots and distributed among about three-hundred of the five-hundred ex-slaves. When the blacks arrived in southern Miami County on their way to their land in Mercer County in the middle of summer in 1846, they encountered intense hostility from the local white population. Their camp was surrounded and armed men drove the ex-slaves out of Miami County and across the border into Mercer County. Their reception in Mercer County was equally hostile. They were harassed and tormented until they were unable to settle on the land that had been set aside for them. Gradually the blacks scattered, settling in various places such as Piqua, Montezuma, and Milton, Ohio.

RAPE OF FLORIDA, THE   This long poem of 2,313 lines and 251 spenserian stanzas was first published in 1884 and reissued in 1885 and 1889 as *Twasinta's Seminoles*. Black poet Albery A. Whitman relates incidents in the Seminole Wars, which the army fought intermittently from 1816 to 1842 against the Seminole Indians and their black slave allies in an attempt to remove them from Florida. In the poem while Osceola sits brooding about his enemies, the government dragoons attack a neighboring Seminole chief, Palmecho, and his followers. The army troops are defeated and driven off by Atlassa, a handsome noble warrior who is in love with Ewald, Chief Palmecho's beautiful daughter. Under a flag of truce Palmecho is tricked by the Americans, put in chains, and imprisoned. When Palmecho is captured, Ewald rides to Atlassa and urges him to attempt a rescue. Atlassa returns to camp to find that Ewald has been captured and imprisoned by the army. After fierce resistance, the Seminoles are overwhelmed and Atlassa, along with his warriors, is sent into exile in Mexico. Just before the ship carrying the Seminoles away departs, Ewald is freed, joins Atlassa, and sails into exile with him.

RAS THE DESTROYER   This is a character in *The Invisible Man* (1954) by Ralph Ellison. In an early part of the novel this character is known as Ras the Exhorter because of his intense and vivid black nationalist speeches exhorting blacks to follow him.

RAY DOUGLAS   This is a character in Herbert Simmons's novel, *Man Walking on Eggshells*.

RAYMOND TAYLOR   This is a character in Wallace Thurman's novel, *The Infants of the Spring*.

REDDING, J. SAUNDERS (1906-   )   This critic, editor, novelist, and short story writer was born in Wilmington, Delaware. He was educated in local schools and at Brown and Columbia universities. He has taught at Morehouse College, Louisville Municipal College, Southern University, Hampton Institute, and Cornell University. Mr. Reddin's essays have appeared in the *American Scholar*, *Negro Digest*, *Contemporary Literature*, *Phylon*, *Massachusetts Review*, and the *Boston University Journal*. He has received the Rockefeller Foundation Grant (1940), the Guggenheim Fellowship (1945-1946 and 1959-1960), and the distinguished service award of the National Urban League.

286

REDMON, EUGENE (1937-   )   This poet, critic, teacher, and editor was born in St. Louis, Missouri, but grew up in East St. Louis, Illinois. He was educated in local schools and at the University of Southern Illinois and Washington University. He served three years in the Marine Corps and has been editor of the *East St. Louis Beacon* and the *East St. Louis Evening Voice*. Mr. Redmon has taught and lectured at Southern Illinois University, Webster College, Southern University, Oberlin College, and California State University at Sacramento. Eugene Redmon's work has appeared in the *Activist, American Dialog, Freelance, Journal of Black Poetry, Black World,* and *Oberlin Review.* He has received several awards for his writing and his scholarship. In 1963 he was selected one of the outstanding college students in the United States. He has received the first prize in the Annual Free Lance Poetry Contest (1968) and a writing grant from California State University.

RED RECORD   In the last quarter of the nineteenth century many blacks were lynched in the southern United States. In 1892 Ida Wells (Barnett) compiled a statistical pamphlet on lynching that she called the *Red Record.*

RED SUMMER, THE   During the period between June and December of 1919, seventy-six blacks were lynched and twenty-five race riots occurred. Because of the intense violence and bloodshed, this period of racial strife came to be known as the "Red Summer". Major race rioting took place in Chicago and in Washington, D.C.

REED, CANNON, AND JOHNSON   Based in Berkeley, California, and established in 1974 by novelist and poet Ishmael Reed and his associates, this company was organized to publish the work of relatively unknown writers who showed promise. Both poetry and prose are published in paperback and hardcover editions.

REED, ISHMAEL (1938-   )   This poet, essayist, editor, publisher, and novelist was born in Chattanooga, Tennessee. He was educated in local schools and at the University of Buffalo for a short time, but he is mainly self-educated. He has taught at the University of Seattle and the University of California at Berkeley. His writings have appeared in the *Nickle Review, Arts Magazine, Black World, Umbra, Poetry India, Cricket, Liberator Essense,* and *Scholastic Magazine.* Mr. Reed has received the University of California at Berkeley Outstanding Instructor Award (1968) and in 1975 he won the Ainsfeld Wolf Award.

RENAISSANCE   Meaning "rebirth," this term generally refers to the transition from the Middle Ages or Dark Ages to the modern period in Western Europe. The intense cultural activities of black artists during the years 1908 to 1926 in Harlem, New York, earned the name "Harlem Renaissance."

RHYME   This term refers to an identity in sound of some part, usually the end, of words or lines of verse.

RICHARDSON, WILLIS (1889-   )   This playwright, critic, poet, and short story writer was born in Wilmington, North Carolina. He was educated in Washington, D.C., and graduated from the famous Dunbar High School. He studied drama and poetry by a correspondence course. He worked for the Bureau of Printing and Engraving from 1911 to 1954, when he retired. Mr. Richardson began writing in 1920. In 1923 his play *The Chip Women's Fortune* was produced in New York. He became the first black playwright to have a serious play produced on Broadway. His essays have appeared in the *Crisis* and *Opportunity*. He was awarded the Spingarn Medal for 1925 and 1926 and the Edith Schuarh Cup from Yale University Theater in 1928.

RINEHART   This is a character in *The Invisible Man* by Ralph Ellison. Rinehart is a cynical and sinister opportunist who adapts to any situation or activity he finds advantageous to him. In the novel he is by turns a pimp, a number runner, and a spurious minister of a storefront church.

RIOTS   These are violent outbreaks of public disorder by a group or groups of people. They may be spontaneous or planned. Riots often involve hundreds and sometimes thousands of people and result in large-scale property damage. Often numbers of people are killed or injured.

RIVERS, CONRAD KENT (1933-1968)   This poet was born in Atlantic City, New Jersey. He was educated in the public schools and at Wilberforce and Indiana universities; he also completed work at Chicago Teachers College. At the time of his sudden and unexpected death he was a teacher in the Gary, Indiana, public school system. His poetry appeared in *Black World, Negro Digest, Antioch Review,* and the *Kenyon Review.* Rivers wrote his poems in a traditional manner, and his unfortunate death ended his poetic career while it was still developing. His poems are characterized by a sadness and bitterness.

ROBERT BURRELL ("BLOOD")   This is a character in Hari Rhodes's novel, *A Chosen Few.*

ROGERS, JOEL AUGUSTUS (1883-   )   This essayist, journalist, novelist, and historian was born in Jamaica and was largely self-educated. Mr. Rogers's articles have appeared in the *Messenger*, the *Baltimore Afro-American*, the *Pittsburgh Courier*, and *American Mercury Magazine*. In addition to the many articles and books on black American history, Rogers published two novels, *Blood Money* (1923) and *the Golden Door* (1927). Until recently Joel Rogers published much of his own work. It was to be found primarily in the black communities across the United States. However, since the 1960s, his work has been available in public libraries.

ROMANTIC TRADITION   In the latter part of the eighteenth century in Europe and England a literary movement emerged that rejected the classical concepts of form and order. This movement lasted until the mid-nineteenth century and was characterized by a style of literature that emphasized emotion rather than reason and inspiration or imagination instead of logic. This Romantic Movement, as it was referred to, called for the full expression of emotions and spontaneous action rather than order and restraint. It resulted in a "Romantic Tradition" that influenced the work of poets Countee Cullen, Anne Spencer, Angelina Grimke, and others.

ROOTS   In 1976 Alex Haley's book, *Roots*, was published and immediately became a best-seller. In 1977 a television production based on the book was shown and the impact on the television audience was enormous. The reason for the *Roots* "phenomenon" has been the subject of many articles.

ROYAL AFRICAN COMPANY, THE   Established in 1672, this London-based trading company was active until 1750, when it was dissolved. From 1672 until 1697 the Royal African Company enjoyed a complete monopoly of the African slave trade, the greater part of which involved North America and the West Indies. Beset by a series of financial problems, the company was unable to retain its monopoly of the African slave trade after 1697.

ROSIE FLEMING   This is a character in Kristin Hunter's novel, *God Bless the Child.*

RUNNING THE NEGROES   During the Civil War southern planters lost many slaves. As soon as the Union forces appeared in any area of the South, the slaves ran away and slipped through the Union lines to freedom. To prevent this constant escape, southern plantation owners began to remove their slaves from the vicinity whenever it was known that northern armies were near. Often the slaves had to be dragged away and in some cases those slaves most reluctant to leave were shot as a lesson to others.

RUSH LIBRARY AND DEBATING SOCIETY   Established in December 1836, this organization was incorporated in March 1837. Its purpose was basically the same as that of the Philadelphia Library Company. The members of the society paid dues with which books were purchased; the member could then borrow the book free or for a very small fee. By 1838 the Rush Library and Debating Society had over forty members and 132 books in its library. By 1841 the number of books had increased by 200.

SALAAM, KALAMU JA (VAL FERDINAND) (1947-   )   This poet, short story writer, playwright, drama critic, and publisher was born in New Orleans. He was educated in local schools and completed business college. He is director of *BLKARTSOUTH,* co-editor of *Nokmbo,* a journal. He is also editor of *Black Collegian.* Kalamu Ja Salaam has received the Wright Award for his drama criticism. His work has appeared in *Black World, Journal of Black Poetry, Black Theater,* and *Negro Digest.*

SALEM WITCHCRAFT TRIALS, THE   Witchcraft, the practice of evil or unholy acts by witches or people who are said to have evil powers, was in evidence in the early American colonies. Persons suspected of practicing witchcraft were severely persecuted and, in some instances, killed in Massachusetts, Connecticut, and Virginia. The pinnacle of this kind of persecution was reached in Salem, Massachusetts. In March 1692 began a series of witchcraft trials that resulted in the execution of twenty persons as witches, one of them, Giles Cary, being pressed to death. The trials started with the arrest of Tituba Indian, a black female slave, and two white women. By the time the trials ended, a hundred and fifty persons were imprisoned in addition to those executed. A key figure in the Salem witchcraft trials of 1692, Tituba Indian was the slave of Samuel Parris, who had purchased John and Tituba Indian in Barbados, West Indies, in 1688. He remarried them on board the ship *Blessing* on November 10, 1688. In the spring of 1692, when the Salem witchcraft trials began, Tituba was one of the first persons arrested. She was accused of practicing evil arts upon four young girls, causing them to act in a hysterical manner. In prison Tituba was whipped until she implicated others in the practice of witchcraft.. Even when the trials ended, Tituba remained in prison until she was purchased by Samuel Conklin, who paid her fees to the jailer and employed her in his weaving business. In November 1693 Conklin purchased Tituba's husband, John Indian. In 1964 Ann Petry wrote a book about this unusual woman.

SATURDAY EVENING QUILL THE   Published in Boston in 1928, this literary journal, which was the annual publication of the Saturday Evening Quill Club, lasted for at least two issues, 1928 and 1929. The first issue contained forty-two poems, two essays, two short plays, and two articles in seventy-two pages. Among the eighteen authors whose work appeared in the first issue were Waring Cuney, Dorothy West, and George Reginald Margetson. The second issue was much like the first. The work of Helene Johnson, Joshua Henry Jones, Jr. and Lois Maliou Jones appeared in this issue. The Saturday Evening Quill Club was organized in 1925. Although most of the members were black, it had an open membership.

SCAB   During the early twentieth century, when labor unions were attempting to organize, plant owners often used nonunion workers to take the place of the union workers on strike. Such nonunion men were known as scabs. Both Alden Bland's novel, *Behold A Cry,* and William Attaway's novel, *Blood on the Forge,* are about black workers who work as scabs to survive.

SCHUYLER, GEORGE S. (1895-   )   This novelist, and short story writer, editor, and journalist was born in Providence, Rhode Island. He was educated in the public schools of Syracuse, New York. When he was about seventeen years old, he joined the army and remained there until 1920. During World War I he served as a lieutenant. He was editor of the *Messenger* from 1923 to 1928. He was also on the editorial staff of the *Crisis,* the *Nation, Opportunity, New Masses,* the *Pittsburgh Courier, The Messenger, Common Ground, American Mercury,* and *Negro Digest.*

SCOTT-HERON, GIL (1949-   )   This poet, novelist, teacher, pianist, singer, and lyricist was born in Chicago but grew up in Jackson, Tennessee, where he lived with his grandmother. He attended the public schools until he was about thirteen years old, when he moved to New York to live with his mother. After graduating from a private high school, Scott-Heron entered Lincoln University and later completed graduate study at Johns Hopkins University. His writing has appeared in *Ebony Magazine*. He received the Langston Hughes Creative Writing Award in 1968. Although he is best known as a musician and leader of the eight-piece band, Midnight, he is also a professor of English at Federal City College.

SELMA-MONTGOMERY DEMONSTRATIONS, THE   On January 18, 1965, Martin Luther King, Jr. led demonstrations in Selma, Alabama, to assert the right of blacks to register and vote. Dallas County, in which Selma is located, had a black population of almost 90,000 and about 50,000 whites. However, only 904 blacks were registered as voters, compared with almost 25,000 whites. In other adjoining counties the situation was just as bad as far as black registered voters were concerned. Election officials employed a complicated "literacy test" that included an examination paper on the Constitution to keep the blacks from registering to vote. Demonstrations began outside the county courthouse in Selma and numerous arrests were made on various charges. Dr. King was arrested on February 1, 1965, along with 800 others for parading without a permit. On March 5, Dr. King announced that he would organize a march from Selma to Montgomery, the state capital. He planned to present to Governor Wallace a petition demanding the right to register and vote and to protest also against the brutality employed against the marchers in Selma. Governor Wallace banned the march and ordered the police to stop the group from marching on March 7, about 600 blacks attempted to cross the Pettis Bridge and begin the march to Montgomery. They were attacked by state troopers using whips, clubs, tear gas, and cattle prods. A number of the marchers were arrested.

SHARECROPPER   After the Civil War many farmers, both black and white, who did not own land became tenant farmers and worked the land for the landowners, receiving a share of the crop in return for their labor. The landowner generally supplied land, a cabin, tools, working stock, fuel, feed for the stock, and about half the fertilizer. Very few sharecroppers had any money and the landowner often had a commissary on the premises to provide the basic necessities such as food and clothing for the tenants. The cost of all supplies came out of the tenants' share before they received anything. Very often the sharecroppers were never able to get out of debt and were taken advantage of by the landowner. This was especially true in the case of black sharecroppers. At one time it is estimated that about three million people were involved in sharecropping. The central characters are involved in sharecropping in the novels *Blood on the Forge* by William Attaway, *River George* by George Lee, and *White Face* by Carl Offord.

SHE WALKS IN BEAUTY   This is a novel by Joel Rogers published in 1936.

SHINE   The character "Shine" appears as the hero figure in many ballads or verse narratives in the black urban oral tradition; he is witty, adroit, and street wise. The best known of the "Shine" black urban folklore narratives is *Shine and the Titanic*, which exists in many different versions.

SHINE, TED (1936-   )   This editor and playwright was born in Baton Rouge, Louisiana. He was educated in local schools at Howard University, the State University of Iowa, and the University of California at Santa Barbara. He has taught and lectured at Prairie View A & M College, Prairie View, Texas.

SHORT STORY, THE   A short fictional prose narrative, the short story usually consists of from five hundred to about fifteen-thousand words. Several authors who wrote powerful short stories are Charles Chesnutt, Rudolph Fisher, Paul Lawrence Dunbar, and Langston Hughes, whose story "A Good Job Gone" has become a classic. Alice Walker's collection of stories, *In Love and Trouble,* is powerful in impact. Some black authors were better known for their stories than for other writings, as in the case of Eric Waldron, who is best known for his collection of stories, *Tropic Death.*

SIT-IN MOVEMENT.   The "Sit-in Movement" began in Greensboro, North Carolina, on February 1, 1960, when four students from North Carolina Agricultural and Technical College quietly sat down at the lunch counter of the Woolworth Variety Store of Greensboro. The students were refused service and asked to leave. When they did not leave, the police were called and the students were arrested. Other black students took their places and expanded the sit-in protest to another store, the Kress store. This form of protest against the local custom of refusing service to blacks at lunch counters expanded rapidly. By February 8-9, the movement had spread to the cities of Charlotte, Durham, and Winston-Salem. By mid-February, the sit-in project had spread to fifteen southern cities. At the beginning of the movement, the main targets were the F. W. Woolworth and Kress stores, but soon libraries, drive-in restaurants, and other public places came under attack. Thousands of blacks were arrested and fighting broke out between blacks and whites. On April 19, 1960, the home of black civil rights lawyer and Nashville city councilman Alexander Looby was blown up by a dynamite bomb. The sit-ins continued throughout the summer and there was some desegregation of eating facilities. The first integration of lunch counters in a large southern city took place in San Antonio, Texas, on March 16, 1961.

SKALAWAGS   During the Reconstruction Period after the Civil War, this term was applied to those southerners who worked with the freedmen in local and state governments in those states that had been readmitted to the Union at the war's end. The attitude of the southerners toward the skalawags was one of contempt. Some skalawags were sincere in wanting to help the ex-slaves; others wanted only personal gain.

SLAVE DRIVER   On many plantations one or more slave drivers assisted the overseer. These men were slaves who were given the authority to whip their fellow slaves. Their assignment was to keep order among the slaves in their quarters and to see to it that they got out of the quarters and into the fields each day. If a driver refused to whip his fellow slaves, he himself would be whipped. The slave drivers were sometimes given better quarters than other slaves and often better food.

SLAVE JAILS AND PENS   Domestic slave traders often found it necessary to have on hand a supply of slaves to sell to their customers; these slaves were kept in pens or jails in order to prevent their escape. Sometimes local jails were used to hold the slaves until enough were acquired for a sale. The large slave trading firms such as Franklin and Armfield had pens or jails attached to their places of business. One such pen this company utilized was located between Washington, D.C., and George Washington's home in Mt. Vernon,

Virginia. The conditions of these holding areas varied; some were clean and well kept while others were dirty and unpainted. All of these confinement areas had one thing in common; the doors and windows were secured by many heavy bolts and padlocks. One of the most unusual of these facilities, which stood until 1922, was located just behind the slave market in Charleston, South Carolina. This jail was known as "Ryan's Nigger Jail." It was a four-story double house with heavily barred windows and heavy padlocks and bolts on every door. The house was on a lot sixty feet wide and one-hundred and seventy-five feet long. The slaves kept here were sold at the slave market near the jail.

SLAVE LABOR, THE GANG SYSTEM OF Slaves who worked under the gang system of labor were divided into groups of twenty or thirty and worked as a unit. The supervisor of the gang was an overseer or a slave driver. Often he was on horseback because from this position lazy or careless workers could be spotted easily. The overseer used various methods to get the slaves to work: beatings, verbal abuse, and ridicule were all employed, but most often a whip was used to drive the slaves to work harder. It was the symbol of authority on the plantation.

SLAVE LABOR, THE TASK SYSTEM OF The main concern of the plantation owner was the production of a profitable crop using slave labor. One way to raise this crop was to assign each slave a certain amount of work to complete each day. When the task was finished and the work checked, the slave was free for the rest of the day. This system was supposed to give the slaves an incentive to work hard and do their jobs well, but it was not used extensively. In the cotton- and hemp-growing regions there was always work for the slaves to do and they began to slow down on their tasks because generally they did not receive the time off even if the work was well done. The system seemed to work best in the rice-growing areas, where the fields were relatively small and work assignments could be better organized and defined.

SLAVE MARKETS, THE SOUTHERN In the South during the pre-Civil War period thousands of slaves were bought and sold in the domestic slave trade. Slave markets were found in several cities and various towns and villages. Some market facilities were built for the express purpose of slave sales. In Charleston, South Carolina, practically all the buying and selling of slaves was done on the street near the old Exchange or Custom House, located on East Bay Street. When an auction was in progress, a red banner was flown so all who were interested would know of it. In 1856 Charleston passed a city ordinance prohibiting the sale of horses, carriages, or blacks anywhere near the Exchange; slave traders then held their sales on their own premises. After July 1856 Thomas Ryan & Son, slave traders, opened a slave market on Chalmers Street; and by the end of the 1850s almost all public sales of slaves were held there. In Richmond, Virginia, during this period slaves were bought and sold in and around Fifteenth Street between Main, Franklin, and Broad streets. One of the busiest slave markets of all was in the basement of Odd Fellows Hall, a building that was still in use in 1930. In New Orleans, slaves were sold regularly in the two main hotels, the St. Charles and the St. Louis, as well as in various public places. One of the best-known auction sites was the French Exchange, located in the rotunda of the St. Louis Hotel.

SLAVE NARRATIVE, THE   Between 1703 and 1865, hundreds of slave biographies were published. These biographies or "slave narratives," as they were called, presented the slave's view of slavery rather than the master's view. In this respect valuable information concerning the slave trade, the plantation operations, and the planter class is provided. After 1831, when the antislavery activities increased, a great many slave narratives were published. Occasionally it was charged that the abolitionists themselves had either written the narratives or had rewritten them extensively. Some of the ex-slaves who wrote their own biographies were Frederick Douglass, *My Bondage My Freedom*; John Malvin, *North into Freedom*; J. W. C. Pennington, *The Fugitive Blacksmith*; and Solomon Northrop, *Twelve Years a Slave*.

SLAVE SMUGGLING   On March 2, 1807, Congress passed a law that prohibited the African slave trade to the United States. The law took effect in January 1808. The immediate result of this new law was a sharp increase in slave smuggling. Very little effort was made to enforce the law and slave traders were able to bring many slaves into the South illegally. The main ports of entry for the smugglers were St. Augustine, Florida, and Savannah, Georgia.

SLIM GREER   This is a character in Sterling Brown's poem, "Slim in Hell."

SMITH, BESSIE (1897-1937)   This blues singer, recording artist, and songwriter was born in Chattanooga, Tennessee. Her education was limited and when she was in her teens she joined Ma Rainey's Rabbit Foot Minstrels, a road show that passed through Chattanooga. She traveled with Ma Rainey and other shows and worked in various taverns for several years. The recording director of Columbia Records heard her sing in a nightclub in Selma, Alabama, and had her brought to New York City to record. Bessie Smith made her first record in 1923 and from 1924 to 1928 she gained wide recognition as a blue singer. She was known as the Empress of the Blues. When the depression began, she declined in popularity as a recording artist and by 1931 she stopped recording. She continued to travel with vaudeville shows until 1937, when she was injured in an automobile accident in Clarksdale, Mississippi, and died on her way to the hospital.

SMITH, CLARA (1895-1935)   This blues singer was born in Spartanberg, South Carolina. Nothing is known of her childhood. By the time she was twenty-three years old she was a feature attraction on the black vaudeville circuit. She appeared in St. Louis, Nashville, and New Orleans. She made her first recording around 1923. In the fall of that same year she recorded several duets with Bessie Smith. Clara Smith made many recordings, some with such artists as Don Redman, Fletcher Henderson, and Louis Armstrong. She died of a heart attack in Detroit in 1935.

SMITH, WILLIAM GARDNER (1927-1974)   This novelist and essayist was born in Philadelphia. He was educated in the public schools of Philadelphia and at Temple University. He worked as a reporter for several black newspapers, then moved to France, worked for French newspapers, and continued to write.

SOCIETY FOR THE PROPAGATION OF THE GOSPEL IN FOREIGN PARTS   Chartered by William III to help the Anglican Church, the SPG, as it was called, was organized in England for work in the American colonies by Reverend Thomas Bray in 1701. Its activities in the colonies were generally missionary; it founded churches and schools. In the Carolinas the society suggested to slave owners that slaves should be taught to read and write and be given time off to study the Scriptures. Where the owners permitted it, the SPG missionaries taught the slaves. In one unusual case the SPG promoted the establishment of a school for blacks in Charleston, South Carolina, in which the teachers were slaves owned by the society. While their missionary work helped ease the lot of slaves somewhat, the SPG generally accepted the basic idea of slavery and this gave the planters and other slave holders a sense of security. In spite of its avowed purpose to help the Anglican Church and raise the standard of living for both blacks and whites, the SPG had a spotty record. The activities of the society extended from Maine to Georgia. The SPG ceased operations after the outbreak of the American Revolution.

SOCIETY OF THE FRIENDS OF THE BLACKS, THE   In France near the middle of the eighteenth century, writers such as Voltaire and Rousseau began to denounce slavery and the slave trade with special emphasis on slavery in the French colonies. The Society des Amis des Noir (The Society of the Friends of the Blacks), a French abolitionist organization, was established in 1788. Unlike the English abolitionist societies, it demanded an immediate halt to the slave trade as well as the abolition of slavery itself. The president the Society of the Friends of the Blacks was the famous French philosopher, Condorcet; and its membership included social reformer the Duc de la Rochefoucauld and the Marquis de Lafayette.

SONGHAI   Today there are about six-hundred thousand Songhai people who live near the banks of the middle Niger River between Timbuktu and the western border of Nigeria. They are now citizens of the Mali Republic and play a part in the political life of five countries: Mali, Mauritania, Dahomey, Nigeria, and Upper Volta. For a very long time the Songhai have had no state of their own. In the sixteenth century the Songhai State or Empire was the largest in all of West Africa with the exception of Kanem-Bornu. The rise of the Songhai coincided with the decline of the Mali Empire. As the Empire of Mali began its slow and steady collapse after the death of Mansa Musa the Great in 1337, the Songhai city of Gao broke away from the dying empire and declared its independence. By 1420 the Songhai people had become strong enough to extract tributes from some of their neighbors, among them the powerful Bambarba people. By 1464 they had conquered Mema, one of the strongest neighboring provinces, which had gained its independence from Mali. These conquests laid the groundwork for the victories of the man who was to become one of Songhai's greatest rulers. Sunni Ali emerged as the leader of the Songhai in 1465. He increased the size of his army and immediately began the formidable task of expanding Songhai's borders. Sunni Ali Ber or Sunni the Great, as he was called, was a brilliant military leader and was almost constantly at war. By 1468 he had fought off attacks by the fierce Mossi warriors, who attempted to extend their control from northern Songhai to the entire kingdom. That same year Timbuktu, which had been controlled by the Tauregs since 1393, fell before his attacks. Shortly after the fall of Timbuktu Sunni Ali centered his assault on the city of Jenne. The capture of Jenne was difficult and the city was under seige for eight years. Since Jenne was located on wet, marshy land, it was necessary for Sunni Ali to develop an amphibious force to capture the city. He organized a fleet of four hundred canoes to blockade the city and cut off any water approaches by which it could be supplied. Jenne was finally captured in 1475. In spite of almost constant warfare, Sunni Ali was able to establish a stable government. In 1483 Sunni Ali's forces encountered the Mossi armies at Jiniki To'oi and soundly defeated them, thus greatly reducing a serious threat to his power. Sunni Ali died by drowning in 1492 while returning from a successful campaign against the Fulani of Gurma. In all of his military career Sunni Ali never lost a battle. Although he was a Moslem, Sunni Ali was not devout and was classed as an infidel by religious officials whom he forced to obey the laws. Because of this he made many enemies among them.

After the death of Sunni Ali the throne went to his son, Sunni Baru, who tried to carry out his father's plans. However, he soon encountered opposition from the Moslems, who resented what they considered Baru's repressive measures. Moslem religious leaders began to search for someone to champion their cause. In 1493 power was seized by Muhammad Toure, who had been one of Sunni Ali's chief ministers and a general in his army. Sunni Baru resisted, but his army was defeated in 1500 and he was forced into exile. Askia (General) Muhammad Toure was a shrewd ruler. To overcome the Moslem opposition, he invited them to participate in the cultural and political life of the empire. He invited more scholars, artists, and doctors to his capital Timbuktu; its universities became known through the Moslem world to a greater extent than ever before. Between 1497 and 1498 Askia Muhammad made a pilgrimage to Mecca that because of its elaborateness was talked about for many years. In general he maintained the traditional Moslem ceremonies and practices. Under Muhammad Toure's rule the governmental structure of Songhai was altered considerably. The empire was divided into five single provinces ruled by governors appointed by and responsible directly to Muhammad Toure. A court system was organized as well. All officials of towns and villages were also appointed by the Askia and reported only to him. He extended the borders of the empire to the Hausa states in what is now northern Nigeria. In 1513 he ordered his forces into the Hausa states and captured the cities of Gobir, Zaria, and Katsina. Muhammad Toure also attacked the powerful city of Kano but was unable to capture it. In 1528 Askia was ousted from power by a *coup d'etat* led by his son, Musa. He was placed under house arrest and then exiled to an island in the Niger River. In 1531 Askia Musa was overthrown by one of his own generals, Muhammad Began. Askia Began was deposed by another of Askia Muhammad's sons in 1537. The aged Muhammad Toure was allowed to return to the palace but his ruling days were ended. He died in 1538 and was buried in the city of Gao, where his tomb is often visited today. Between 1528 and 1591 at least eight different kings held the throne, but most of them had to spend much of their time suppressing the numerous revolts of their subjects. Under these conditions the empire began to decline. Its collapse was hastened by military incursions from Morocco in North Africa. Moroccan troops led by Judar Pasha armed with guns badly defeated the Songhai forces, who were armed with spears, bows, and arrows, in October 1591 at the battle of Tondibi. As a result of this battle the Songhai Empire ceased to exist.

SORROW SONGS, THE   black spirituals, because of the sadness and longing for freedom expressed in them, are often called "sorrow songs." W. E. B. DuBois in *The Soul of Black Folk* wrote an essay about black spirituals called "Of Sorrow Songs."

SPIRITUALS, BLACK   During the period of slavery the blacks developed a particular variety of religious folk songs, often retelling biblical stories. Although there is a long tradition of religious or spiritual singing in the United States among the population in general, the songs of the blacks have characteristics that set them apart from others of this kind. In very many cases the black spirituals served as a form of emotional release for the oppressed blacks. They were also used to convey messages to slaves preparing to run away from their owners. These songs are still an important part of the culture of the blacks.

SPIVEY, VICTORIA (1910-1977)   This blues singer, musician, and recording artist was born in Houston, Texas, and grew up there. She recorded her first blues song, "The Black Snake Blues," in 1926 when she was only sixteen years old. Between 1926 and 1937 she composed and recorded numerous blues songs. Her records sold well and she was quite successful as a recording artist. In 1936 Victoria Spivey recorded "The Black Snake Blues" a second time, but the record had few sales. In the 1940s and 1950s she did only a limited amount of recording. However, when the "blues revial" began in the 1960s, Victoria Spivey established her own recording company, Spivey Records, which is today a successful business venture.

STONO REBELLION, THE   On September 9, 1739, twenty slaves, at Stono, South Carolina, killed the two guards at an arsenal. They obtained arms and began to march toward the Florida border. Along the way they killed all the whites in their path, with the exception of one man whom they considered good, and burned several buildings. The lieutenant governor of the province, who was returning home to Charleston, sighted the group and alerted the local militia. The blacks had a twelve-hour head start but stopped to rest and were attacked by the government troops. Although the slaves fought fiercely, they were defeated and the revolt was suppressed. Forty-four blacks and twenty-five whites were killed in this uprising. Sometimes this revolt is called the Cato Conspiracy.

STOREFRONT CHURCHES   These churches have the common characteristic of being housed in rented stores or movie theaters. They are usually found in the poorer areas of the black urban ghetto. The ministers of these churches are often semiliterate and generally have little or no training for the ministry. Most of these organizations are Baptist in denomination, although some adhere to the tenets of holiness and spiritualist doctrines. Much of the action in James Baldwin's *Go Tell It on the Mountain* occurs in a storefront church. Baldwin, Ellison, and Hughes used storefront churches in their novels.

STREAM OF CONSCIOUSNESS   The term "stream of consciousness" refers to a technique employed by some writers to indicate what goes on in the mind of a character. The assumption of a writer using this method is that the activities of the mind are fluid rather than static. The indication is that at any given time in the mind of any person or character there is a constant stream of consciousness that operates on all levels of awareness at the same time and involves thoughts, sensations, and memories. One important twentieth-century writer who perfected the stream of consciousness method was

the Irish writer James Joyce. Black novelists Owen Dodson and
William Demby have both employed this method in their work,
Dodson in *Boy at the Window* and Demby in *The Catacombs*. In
William Demby's highly experimental novel the stream of con-
sciousness technique is only one of several that he employs.

STUDENT NONVIOLENT COODINATING COMMITTEE (SNCC)   Begun by
southern black students, this protest organization was established
at the close of a two-day conference held April 15-17, 1960, on the
campus of Shaw University in Raleigh, North Carolina. The meeting
was sponsored by the Southern Christian Leadership Conference
and was attended by 132 black and 10 white students from eleven
states and the District of Columbia. The expressed purpose of SNCC
or "Snick," as it was popularly known, was to coordinate the
activities of students working in the civil rights movement.

STYLE   From the Latin word *stilus,* which means a writing instrument, the term style refers to the way in which words are written or
arranged so that the ideas and personality of an author are con-
veyed. An author's style will vary depending upon the intent he or
she has in mind. In Ralph Ellison's *Invisible Man* one finds several
styles of writing all by the same author. Poet N. H. Pritchard writes
both in the style of concrete poetry and in free verse. On the other
hand, Ishmael Reed, a poet and novelist, uses satire in both his
poetry and his novels.

SUBLIME   In many instances poetry is of such high quality and the
language employed so lofty in nature the poem stands out as supreme. Anything that impresses the mind with its beauty or power
is often said to be sublime.

SUBPLOT   A subplot is a minor or secondary plot that runs
through a novel or other fiction. A novel may have more than one
subplot, especially if there are many characters involved. James
Baldwin's *Another Country,* for example, has several subplots in
addition to the main story line that involves Rufus Scott and his
white mistress, Leona. A second plot or subplot shows the relationship of Ida and Vivaldo Morre, her brother's white friend. A third
minor plot has as protagonists Eric Jones, an actor, and other
assorted characters.

SYMBOL   A symbol is an image or word that stands for more than itself and has added or implied meaning. The leg chain, the cast iron bank, and a diploma that the protagonist in Ralph Ellison's *The Invisible Man* carries in his briefcase and that he seems unable to discard are symbols of the present as well as the past historical status of the blacks in the United States. Symbols in poetry can be more intense perhaps but serve a similar purpose. In Langston Hughes's "Mother to Son," life is symbolized as a stairway in varying degrees of disrepair that one must continue to ascend.

TAFFY JOHNSON   This is a character in Phillip B. Kaye's novel, *Taffy*.

TAKE A GIANT STEP   This is a play by Louis Peterson published in 1954.

THEODORE HALL   This is a character in William Gardner Smith's novel, *Anger at Innocence*.

THESE LOW GROUNDS   This is a novel by Waters E. Turpin published in 1937.

THIRD PRESS, THE   Established in 1970 by playwright and critic Joseph Okpaku, this company publishes scholarly works, autobiographies, biographies, critical essays, poetry, and children's books by both black and white writers. In 1975 the *Third Press Magazine* began publication.

THIRD WORLD PRESS, THE   Founded in 1967 by poet Don L. Lee, this Chicago-based company publishes poetry, criticsm plays, and children's books. Many of their recent publications have been educational and historical. Both paperback and hardcover books are published.

THIRTEENTH AMENDMENT, THE   The Thirteenth Amendment, which was the first of the post-Civil War amendments concerning blacks to be passed, officially ended slavery. Slavery in the rebel states was abolished by the Emancipation Proclamation, but its legal status had never been decided. Sponsored by the radical

Republicans, this amendment became a part of President Andrew Johnson's reconstruction program. The Confederate States were required to ratify the Thirteenth Amendment as one of the conditions of their return to the Union. By December 1865, enough votes had been obtained to assure passage and the amendment became a part of the Constitution.

THOMAS, ALMA (1895-   )   This painter was born in Columbus, Georgia. She began school in Columbus. When her family moved to Washington, D.C., she continued her education in the local schools and at Howard University, where she became the first black student to receive a degree in fine arts from Howard's art department. She completed graduate work at Columbia University. In 1925 Ms. Thomas became a teacher in the District of Columbia and taught art for thirty-five years. In addition to teaching, she studied at American University. Upon her retirement she began painting full time. Her first show was held at the DuPont Theater Art Gallery in 1964, and most of her paintings were sold. Since 1966, her work has been shown in the George Washington Art Gallery, the Bing Art Gallery, and at the Whitney Museum in New York.

THOMPSON, ERA BELL (1911-   )   This journalist and critic was born in Des Moines, Iowa. She was educated in local schools and at Morningside College and the Medill School of Journalism. Ms. Thompson has worked as associate editor (1947-1951), co-managing editor (1951-1964), and international editor for Ebony Magazine. Her articles have appeared in Ebony and Chicago and New York newspapers. She has received honorary doctorates from Morningside College and the University of North Dakota.

THORNTON, WILLIE MAE ("BIG MOMMA" (1925-   )   This blues singer and musician was born in Montgomery, Alabama. By the time she was fourteen years old, she had begun traveling with Sammy Green's Hot Harlem Review out of Atlanta. She won first prize as a singer in an amateur show. The Hot Harlem Review needed a singer and hired her. She remained with the show, traveling in various parts of the South on the black vaudeville circuit, until 1948. When Ms. Thornton left Sammy Green's show, she settled in Houston, Texas, and sang in nightclubs there. She worked with the late Johnny Ace, Johnny Otis, Roy Milton, and others during the decade of the fifties. Since the advent of the "blues revival" of the 1960s and 1970s, "Big Momma" Thornton has remained very active in the blues field. She also performed in England and Europe.

THURMAN, WALLACE (1902-1934)   This novelist, critic, editor, playwright, and essayist was born in Salt Lake City, Utah. He was educated in local schools and at the University of Utah and the University of California. After leaving the University of California, he remained in Los Angeles to work as a journalist. He attempted to start a movement similar to the Harlem Renaissance but was unsuccessful. He left for Harlem, New York, in late summer 1925. Almost as soon as he arrived in New York, he became involved in various literary activities. He edited the literary magazines *Harlem* and *Fire* and A. P. Randolph's magazine, the *Messenger*. He became a reader for the Macauly Publishing Company. He died of tuberculosis on Welfare Island on December 22, 1934.

TIGHT PACKERS   The captains of some trading ships acquired as many slaves as possible and packed them spoon fashion in the cargo holds as tightly as they could, therefore carrying more slaves than the ship was designed to hold. In this way, even if a large number of slaves perished, and very often under this system many of them did die, there would still be enough of them left to provide sufficient profit for the trader. If, by chance, the number of deaths was small, the profit was even greater.

TOLOSA   In 1898 James Weldon Johnson and his brother, J. Rosmond Johnson, wrote a light opera called *Tolosa*, for which they hoped to find a producer in New York. Although they did not find one, they did meet people who were helpful to them in furthering their musical careers.

TOLSON, MELVIN B. (1900-1966)   This poet, teacher, and political leader was born in Moberly, Missouri. He was educated at Fisk, Lincoln, and Columbia universities. Tolson taught at Wiley College, Tuskegee Institute, and Langston University in Oklahoma, where he remained for a number of years and became professor of creative literature. In addition to his teaching and writing, Melvin Tolson was active as a politician. He served as mayor of Langston, Oklahoma, several times. His poetry is complex and shows the poet's wide range of intellectual interests. In 1953 he was commissioned to write a poem for the Liberian Centennial and International Exposition. When he died in 1966, he was writer in residence at Tuskegee Institute.

TOOMER, JEAN (1894-1967)   This poet, short story writer, novelist, playwright, and essayist was born Nathan Eugene Toomer in Washington, D.C., and educated in the public schools of that city, at the University of Wisconsin, and at the City College of New York. The grandson of P. B. S. Pinchback, a prominent black politician of the Reconstruction Period, Tooner was one of the most brilliant of the Harlem Renaissance "writers". He is known mainly for one book, *Cane,* a mixture of poetry, short stories, and prose sketches. It is generally thought that Toomer did not write much after his first book, but he left a large amount of unpublished material. He wrote three novels, four plays, eight philosophical essays, two books of poems, six short stories, and four versions of his autobiography. Jean Toomer died in obscurity in a Pennsylvania nursing home in 1967.

TROTTER, MONROE (1872-1934)   This editor and militant civil rights leader was born in Boston. He was educated there and at Harvard, from which he graduated *magna cum laude* in 1895. His family was fairly well off and he did not have to worry immediately about earning a living. In 1899 Trotter married and for a short while worked as a clerk for various firms, including a short stint as a statistical clerk for a genealogist. Then he went into the real estate business for himself as an insurance agent and mortgage negotiator. His business did well and he soon found himself owning several parcels of property. In 1901 Trotter organized the Boston Literary and Historical Association, a group that later developed into a sounding board for militant opinion on race issues. In that same year with partner George Forbes he established a black newspaper called the *Guardian.* The first issue of the newpaper appeared in November 1901. It became a national instrument for the blacks in their struggle for civil rights. Trotter as editor demanded full rights for black Americans and rejected all compromises. He opposed the accommodationist views of Booker T. Washington and became his bitter enemy. Trotter was involved in civil rights activities on behalf of the blacks until his death in 1934.

TURNER, DARWIN (1931-   )   This poet, literary critic, editor, and essayist was born in Cincinnati, Ohio. He was educated in the Cincinnati public schools and at the universities of Cincinnati and Chicago. During his academic career Darwin Turner has taught at Clark College, Morgan State College, Florida A and M, the University of Wisconsin, and the University of Michigan. His critical essays have been published in the *CLA Journal, Massachusettes Review, Negro Digest, Black World,* the *English Journal,* and the *Southern Humanities Review.* He has received an American Council of Societies Grant (1965) and the Duke University Humanities Fellowship.

TWEED RING, THE   During the period 1869-1871, New York City taxpayers were systematically swindled out of millions of dollars by a notorious group of crooked politicians and grafters. These men were led by William Marcy "Boss" Tweed of Tammany Hall and were known as the Tweed Ring. Contractors padded their bills and the difference went into the pockets of Tweed and his cohorts. Tweed bribed judges, newspapermen, and legislators in his operations. He tried to appear as benefactor of the public by giving handouts to the poor. Eventually Tweed was prosecuted, convicted, and died in jail in 1877. Hank Anderson, Tweed's black valet, was given the tasks of delivering the black vote to the Democrats, controlling the criminal elements in the black neighborhoods, and collecting payoffs to the ring. He was made the black leader of the area bounded by Minetta Lane and Baxter and Thompson streets. Anderson was the man the Democrats had to see if they wanted the black vote.

UMBRA   Established in 1963 in New York, this literary journal is still published on an irregular basis; the latest issue was published in 1974. The founding editors of *Umbra* were Thomas C. Dent, editor; David Henderson, associate editor; and Calvin C. Hernton. The first issue contained twenty-nine poems and one short play. In 1960 an anthology of the works of young black poets was published under the title *Umbra* and in 1970 another collection was published under the name *Umbra Blackworks.*

UNDERGROUND RAILROAD   A clandestine, changing network that fugitive slaves used to escape to freedom, the Underground Railroad was also known as the UGR. The antislavery organizers used railroad terms to refer to their operations. Guides were called "conductors," groups of slaves were known as "trains," hiding places were referred to as "stations," and the operators of such hiding places were designated "station masters." Food, clothing, and a means of transport were provided for the fugitive until the destination, usually Canada or a free state, was reached. The escape routes generally ran from Kentucky and Virginia across Ohio or from Maryland across Pennsylvania to New York, the New England states, and Canada. The UGR participants included free black writers such as William Wells Brown, Frederick Douglass, David Ruggles, and Martin Delaney, as well as Quakers and various other abolitionists. This system is thought to have been established about 1839 or 1840. Virginia Hamilton's book, *The House of Dies Drear*, is about one of the old houses used in the Underground Railroad.

UNIVERSAL NEGRO IMPROVEMENT ASSOCIATION   The UNIA was organized in Jamaica, West Indies, in 1914 by Marcus A. Garvey; but the success of the organization there was quite limited. In 1916 Garvey left Jamaica for New York and established headquarters in Harlem. Although the UNIA began slowly, by 1919 it had thirty complete branches, four hundred and twenty branches chartered, and approximately four hundred more in the process of being organized. The UNIA membership at one time was estimated at over two million. Its program was both national and international; it condemned colonialism in Africa and the exploitation of the African people. Lynching, job discrimination, race riots, poor schools, the lack of justice in the courts, and other violence and injustice inflicted upon the blacks in the United States were denounced. The blacks were urged to think of themselves in positive ways, to become aware of their African heritage, and to be proud of it. One of the basic tenets of the UNIA program was a "return to Africa" in spirit if not in fact. Efforts were made to transport to Africa those Afro-Americans who wanted to return. These efforts were largely failures. In 1925 Garvey was found guilty of using the mails to defraud and sentenced to five years in prison; he was released and deported from the United States in 1927. After Garvey's deportation, the UNIA began to decline and lose popular support. The organization ceased to exist nationally, although single branches still linger on in various cities in the United States today.

VAN DYKE, HENRY (1928-   )   This novelist, short story writer, and teacher was born in Allegan, Michigan. He was educated in the public schools of Kalamazoo and Lansing, Michigan, and at the University of Michigan. He has worked as an editor for the University of Michigan Research Institute in Ann Arbor (1956-1958), as an editor of Basis Books, and has been writer in residence at Kent State University, Kent, Ohio (1976). Mr. Van Dyke has received the Avery Hopwood Award from the University of Michigan, a Guggenheim Fellowship (1971), and an American Academy of Arts and Letters Award (1974).

VERA MANNING   This is a character in Jessie Fauset's novel, *There Is Confusion.*

VOODOO   The concept that voodoo and conjuring are part of the history and experience of the blacks in America and an important and valuable aid in sustaining them in their efforts to combat oppression appears in the work of contemporary black writers. Ishmael Reed employs the ideal of the black experience as a rich mixture of heritage in his latest novel, *The Last Days of Louisiana Red.* Charles Johnson employs the tenets of voodoo in the novel *Faith and the Good Thing* and it is evident in the short play *The Purple Flower,* by Marita Bonner.

VROMAN, MARY ELIZABETH (1923-1967)   This poet, teacher, essayist, and short story and screenwriter was born in Buffalo, New York, but grew up in the West Indies. She was educated in the West Indies and at Alabama State College. After completing her college work, Ms. Vroman taught at Camden Academy in Camden, Alabama. In 1951 she wrote the screenplay, *Bright Road,* which was based on her short story "See How They Run." Her essays and other writings have appeared in *Ladies Home Journal* and the *NEA Journal.* She received the Christopher Award for inspirational magazine writing.

WALDRON, ERIC (1898-1966)   This journalist and short story writer was born in Georgetown, British Guiana. When he was eight, his family moved to Barbados and later to Panama. He was educated in Barbados and the Canal Zone. He worked as a clerk in the Health Department of Cristobal and as a newspaper reporter. He left Panama for New York in 1918. He spent three years studying at City College of New York then continued his career as a journalist, first with the *Brooklyn and Long Island Informer* and later with Marcus Garvey's newspaper the *Negro World.* From 1925 to 1927 Waldron worked for the magazine *Opportunity,* the house organ of the Urban

League. Eric Waldron's articles and short stories began appearing in leading magazines as early as 1922. The *Messenger, Current History,* and *Smart Set* published his work. In 1926 *Tropic Death,* a collection of rather grim stories that depict black life in the Canal Zone, Guiana, and Barbados was published. Waldron's characters are in constant encounter with disaster in many forms, death, starvation, sickness, and white oppression. Writing in an intense and vivid style, he catches the dialects, heat, dust, sun, and lushness of the tropics. Although most of his stories have a West Indian setting, he wrote several stories about black life in New York. He is considered a part of the Harlem Renaissance. He died in London in 1966 while working on a book about the Panama Canal.

WALKER, ALICE (1944-   )   This poet, novelist, short story writer, essayist, and teacher was born in Eaton, Alabama. She was educated in local schools and at Spelman and Sarah Lawrence colleges. After completing her education, Ms. Walker became an instructor at Jackson State College. She has also taught and lectured at the University of Massachusetts, Wellesley College, Radcliffe College, and Case Western Reserve University. She is an editor for *Ms. Magazine.* Her writings have appeared in *American Scholar, Ms. Magazine, Black World, Freedomways, Harper,* and the *Harvard Advocate.* Alice Walker has received the Merril Fellowship for Writing (1966-1967), a fellowship from the McDowell Colony (1967), a National Endowment for the Arts Grant (1969), and the Lillian Smith and Rosenthall awards (1973).

WALKER, QUORK   Following the American Revolution, slavery was outlawed in several northern states. In Massachusetts the slave system was declared illegal as the result of several court cases involving a former slave named Quork Walker. On May 1, 1781, Quork Walker brought a suit in court against Nathaniel Jennison, claiming Jennison had assaulted him, imprisoned him, and claimed him as his slave. Walker insisted that he had been freed by his former owners. The jury decided the case in favor of Walker and awarded him fifty pounds damages. On May 28, 1781, Jennison brought a suit against John and Seth Caldwell, whose brother had owned Walker. He claimed that the Caldwells had lured Walker away from his service. Jennison was awarded twenty-five pounds. The Caldwells appealed the case to the Massachusetts Supreme Court. They were awarded court costs and found not guilty as charged. In April 1783 the question of Quork Walker's freedom again came before the Massachusetts high court in the case of *The Commonwealth* v. *Jennison*. The Massachusetts Supreme Court under Chief Justice Cushing ruled "that the ideal of slavery is inconsistent with our own conduct and constitution; and there can be no such thing as perpetual servitude of a rational creature, unless his liberty is forfeited by some criminal act or given up by personal consent or contract." This ruling in effect abolished slavery in the state of Massachusetts.

WARD, DOUGLASS TURNER (1930-)   This playwright, drama critic, actor, and director was born on a plantation in Burnside, Louisiana. His parents moved to New Orleans and he was educated in local schools and at Wilberforce University and the University of Michigan. After leaving the University of Michigan, he moved to New York, where he began to work with civil rights and radical groups. He began his career as a playwright with a political skit for a civil rights group. He became so interested in the theater that he enrolled in the Paul Mann Actors' Workshop. Mr. Ward's training in the Mann workshop led to role in Eugene O'Neill's play, *The Iceman Cometh*. Soon he was appearing in *Raisin in the Sun, One Flew over the Cuckoo's Nest,* and *Cariolanus*. He began his professional career as a playwright in 1965 with two one-act plays, *Happy Ending* and *Day of Absence,* which were presented by Robert Hooks, Inc., at the St. Marks Play House. These two plays won both the Vernon Rice Drama Desk Award and the Obie Award. In 1967 Ward, Robert Hooks, and Gerald Krone wrote a proposal for a black theatrical center, presented it to the Ford Foundation, and received a grant of $434,000 to establish the Negro Ensemble Company, with which he works closely.

WARING, LAURA WHEELER (1887-1948)   This painter and illustrator was born in Hartford, Connecticut. She studied art at the Pennsylvania Academy of Fine Arts and at the Grande Chaumere in Paris. After completing her training, Ms. Waring became an art teacher at Cheyney, now Pennsylvania State Teachers College; eventually she became the head of the arts department there. Many of her paintings are portraits of prominent black personalities, such as James Weldon Johnson, W. E. B. DuBois, and novelist Jessie Fauset. Her work has been exhibited at the Harmon Foundation, the Pennsylvania Academy of Fine Arts, the Art Institute of Chicago, and the Smithsonian Institute. Her paintings are in the collection of the National Archives, the Smithsonian Institution, and the National

Portrait Galley. She received the Harmon Gold Award and the Creason Traveling Scholarship. She died in Philadelphia in 1948.

WHEATLEY, PHILLIS (1753-1784)   This poet was born in Africa and was brought to America as a slave. In 1761 in Boston she was sold to John Wheatley, a wealthy tailor, to serve as a body servant for his wife. She was taught to read and write by the Wheatley family. A precocious child, she learned English and Latin easily. Phillis Wheatley began to write poetry when she was about thirteen years old. In 1773 a volume of her poems was published in London. When she was twenty-one years old, in 1774, she was emancipated. Phillis married John Peters, an intelligent black man who owned a grocery store and possessed a broad knowledge of the law as well as the ability to write well. He often pleaded before the court in the cause of the blacks. The marriage was not successful. At one time Peters was jailed for debt and Phillis had to work in a boardinghouse to care for herself and her three children. Phillis Wheatley died December 5, 1784, at the age of thirty-one.

WHITE, WALTER FRANCES (1893-1955)   This civil rights leader, novelist, and essayist was born in Atlanta, Georgia. He was educated in local schools and at Atlanta University and at the City College of New York. When he completed his studies, he went to work for the Atlanta Life Insurance Company and was active in the Atlanta branch of the NAACP. As a result of the Atlanta race riots of 1906, Walter White was an ardent opponent of racial injustice. In 1918 he was asked to become assistant secretary of the NAACP under James Weldon Johnson. In this capacity he investigated lynching and became deeply involved in the organization's work. In 1931, when James Weldon Johnson resigned from his post as executive secretary, Walter White was elected to fill his position. In spite of his work for the NAACP, he was able to find time to write. His essays appeared in *Survey Graphic* and *Negro Digest* and *Our World*. He was awarded the Spingarn Medal and a Guggenheim Fellowship.

WHITMAN, ALBERY A. (1851-1901)   This clergyman and poet was born a slave on a farm in Hart County near the town of Mumfordville, Kentucky. He remained a slave until 1863. Both his mother and his father died when he was twelve and he was left to fend for himself. He worked as a farm laborer near Mumfordville, then moved on to Louisville, where he held various jobs for a time before moving to Cincinnati, Ohio. He was employed by the A. J. Beedle Company in Troy, Ohio, and went to school at night. After leaving Troy, Whitman became a schoolteacher in Ohio and Kentucky. About 1870 he entered Wilberforce University, where he studied under Daniel A. Payne. By 1877 he had become both an A.M.E. minister and a financial agent for Wilberforce University.

WIDEMAN, JOHN (1941-   )   This short story writer, novelist, poet, critic, and teacher was born in Washington, D.C. He was educated in local schools and at the University of Pennsylvania. He was a Rhodes Scholar at New College, Oxford, and completed work at the University of Iowa as well. Mr. Wideman has taught at Howard University and the University of Pennsylvania since 1967. His writing has appeared in the *American Scholar* and *Black World*. He has received the Thouron Fellowship for Creative Writing and the Creative Writing Prize from the University of Pennsylvania.

DR. WILLIAM MILLER   This is a character in Charles Chesnutt's novel, *The Marrow of Tradition*.

WILLIAMS, JOHN A. (1925-   )   This novelist and essayist was born in Jackson, Mississippi, but grew up in Syracuse, New York, and attended the University of Syracuse. During World War II he served in the United States Navy. Mr. Williams has worked as a publishing director, a public relations director, a foreign correspondent for *Newsweek Magazine*, a television script writer and narrator, and a lecturer in Afro-American literature. He has written numerous articles that have appeared in *Holiday* and *Black World*.

WIND FROM NOWHERE, THE   This is a novel by Oscar Micheaux, published in 1941.

WONNIE   This is a character in Curtis Lucas's novel, *Third Ward Newark*.

WOODRUFF, HALE (1900-   )   This painter was born in Cairo, Illinois. He was educated in the local schools of Nashville, Tennessee, and at Hevon Art Institute in Indianapolis, Indiana. He studied further in 1927 under Henry A. Tanner in Paris and attended the Academie Moderne. When he returned to the United States in 1931, Woodruff accepted a post as instructor of art at Atlanta University. In 1938 he was commissioned to paint murals depicting the *Amistad* Revolt for the Slavery Library at Talledega College. Beginning in 1941, he began yearly art shows for black artists at Atlanta University. In 1945 Hale Woodruff became professor of art education at New York University. He held this post until 1968. His work has been exhibited numerous times in the Boston Museum of Fine Arts, Xavier University, the New York World's Fair, the Whitney Museum, Howard University, and the Los Angeles Art Museum. His paintings can be found in the Library of Congress, Newark Art Museum, and New York State University. Mr. Woodruff has received a Rosenwald Fellowship (1943-1945) and the Great Teacher Award of New York University.

WRIGHT, CHARLES STEVENSON (1932-   )   This short story writer, novelist and essayist was born in New Franklin, Missouri, and attended the public schools through the second year of high school there. In Sedalia, Missouri, Wright began writing for the black newspaper, the *Kansas City Call,* as a teenager. Although he left high school in his junior year, he studied writing from time to time at the Lawney Handy writing colony in Marshall, Illinois, where novelist James Jones was one of his associates. Charles Wright's essays have appeared in the *Village Voice,* for which he wrote a column called "Wrights World." His latest book, *Absolutely Nothing to Get Alarmed About,* consists in part of revised essays from his column in the *Village Voice.*

WRIGHT, RICHARD (1908-1960)   This novelist, short story writer, poet, and essayist was born on a plantation near Natchez, Mississippi. The education he acquired beyond the ninth grade was by his own efforts. As a young boy he held various jobs in several cities. In 1929 he became a post office worker in Chicago. He also worked at the South Side Boys Club, as acting manager of the Federal Writer's Project, and as an editor for *New Masses* magazine. In 1937 Wright moved to New York and continued with the Federal Writer's Project. Several of his books and articles were published during this period. In 1940 *Native Son* was published and he became widely known. In 1946 he left the United States and moved to France, where he remained and continued to write.

WRIGHT, SARAH E. (19   -   )   This novelist, poet, and critic was born in Wetipquin, Maryland. She was educated in local schools and at Howard University, the University of Pennsylvania, Cheney State Teachers College, and the New School for Social Rsearch. Ms.

Wright has worked as an arts and crafts teacher and in publishing. For several years she was involved with the Harlem Writer's Guild. Her essays have appeared in *Freedomways* and in anthologies. In 1969 her novel, *This Child's Gonna Live*, was chosen as one of the most outstanding books of the year by the *New York Times Book Review*. That same year she also received the Readability Award from the Baltimore Sun. In 1976 she received recognition from the Afro-American Writer's Conference in Washington, D.C.

X, MALCOLM (MALCOLM LITTLE) (1925-1965) This black nationalist leader was born in Omaha, Nebraska. When Malcolm X was small, his father moved the family to Lansing, Michigan. His father died when he was six years old and Mrs. Little was left with the task of raising eight children. Malcolm X's education ended in the eighth grade. As a young man he became involved in criminal activities and was arrested and sent to prison. While in prison, he read and studied a great deal and educated himself. While serving out his prison sentence, he became interested in the Muslim teachings of Elijah Muhammed. When his term of imprisonment was ended, he joined the Black Muslim Movement and rose rapidly to the position of minister of Muslim Temple Number Seven in New York. He became widely known as a spokesman for the Muslims as well as for the blacks of the United States in general. He spoke on television and radio, at universities and colleges. After a disagreement with Elijah Muhammed, he was forced out of the Muslim Movement. After a journey to Mecca he became an Orthodox Muslim and adopted the name El Hajj Malik El-Shabazz. He was in the process of establishing a new group, the Organization of Afro-American Unity, when he was assassinated.

YERBY, FRANK (1916-   ) This poet, teacher, novelist, and short story writer was born in Augusta, Georgia. He was educated in private schools and at Paine College, Fisk University, and the University of Chicago. ·He taught at Florida A&M College and Southern University. In 1942 he moved to Detroit and worked for the Ford Motor Company. His early writing appeared in *Harpers, Phylon, Tomorrow*, and *Common Ground*. In 1946 Mr. Yerby's first romantic novel was published and immediately became a best-seller. His public output has made him a wealthy man and he moved to Europe in 1952. One of his storys, "Health Card," won a special O'Henry Award for 1944.

Young, Al

YOUNG, AL (ALBERT JAMES YOUNG) (1939-   )   This poet, novelist, short story writer, and editor was born in Ocean Springs, Mississippi, but grew up in Detroit and was educated there. He attended the University of Michigan and the University of California at Berkeley. Young has had a varied career and has held many different jobs. He has been a musician, a railroad clerk, a disk jockey, an actor, a writing instructor, and a linguistic consultant. He has taught and lectured at Stanford University and the University of California. His work has appeared in *Changes,* the *Massachusetts Review,* and the *Journal of Black Poetry.* Al Young's poetry has appeared in many anthologies and he has read it at the Cooper Union Forum, the Academy of American Poets in Manhattan, and the YM/YMHA Poetry series in New York. Mr. Young has traveled all over the United States and to Canada, France, Portugal, Spain, and the Azores.

PART III

Author Bibliography

Margret Walker Alexander (1915-   )

Novel
Jubilee. Boston: Houghton Mifflin, 1966; Bantam, 1977.

Poetry
For My People. New Haven, Conn.: Yale University Press, 1942; (1968 reprint ed).

Prophets for a New Day. Detroit: Broadside Press, 1970.

Criticism
How I Wrote Jubilee. Black Paper Series. Third World Press, 1972.

"The Humanistic Tradition of Afro-American Literature." *American Liberties,* October 1970.

Other Writing
Book
A Poetic Equation: Conversations Between Nikki Giovanni and Margret Walker. Washington, D.C.: Howard University Press, 1974.

Articles
Education Age, May 1967; *Negro Digest,* 1951; *Freedomways,* Summer 1976.

Criticism and Biography on Margret Alexander
Current Biography, 1943.

Giddings Paula. "'A Shoulder Hunched Against a Sharp Concern': Some themes in the Poetry of Margret Walker." *Black World,* December 1971.

William Attaway (1911-   )

Novels
Blood on the Forge. New York: Doubleday, 1941; New York: Macmillan, 1970.

319

Let Me Breathe Thunder. New York: Doubleday, 1939; Chatham, N.J.: Chatham Bookseller, 1969.

Short Story

Challenge, June 1936.

Criticism and Biography on William Attaway

Bone, Robert. *The Negro Novel in America.* New Haven, Conn.; Yale University Press, 1966.

Current Biography, 1941.

Ellison, Ralph. "Transition." *The Negro Quarterly,* Spring 1942.

Felgar, Robert. "William Attaway's Unaccommodated Protagonists." *Studies in Black Literature,* Spring 1973.

JAMES BALDWIN (1924-   )

Novels

Another Country. New York: Dial, 1962.

Giovanni's Room. New York: Dial, 1956.

Go Tell It on the Mountain. New York: Knopf, 1953.

If Beal Street Could Talk. New York: Dial, 1974.

Tell Me How Long the Train's Been Gone. New York: Dial, 1968.

Short Stories

Going To Meet the Man. New York: Dial, 1965.

Plays

Amen Corner. New York: Dial, 1968

Blues for Mr. Charlie. New York: Dial, 1964.

One Day When I Was Lost. New York: Dial, 1973 (screenplay).

Essays

The Fire Next Time. New York: Dial, 1963.

No Name in the Street. New York: Dial, 1972.

Nobody Knows My Name. New York: Dial, 1961.

Notes of a Native Son. New York: Dial, 1957.

Criticism and Biography on James Baldwin

Contemporary Authors, 3.

Current Biography, 1964.

Mayfield, Julian. "And then Came Baldwin." *Black World,* Winter 1963.

Reilly, John. "Sonny's Blues: James Baldwin's Image of the Black Community." *Negro American Literature Forum,* No. 4, 1970.

Scott, Robert. "Rhetoric, Black Power, and James Baldwin's *Another*

Country. "Journal of Black Studies," September 1970.
Bibliographies
Fisher, Russel G. "James Baldwin: A Bibliography, 1947-1962," *Bulletin of Bibliography,* January-April 1965.
Standley, Fred L. "James Baldwin: A Checklist, 1963-1967."*Bulletin of Bibliography,* May-August 1968.

TONI CADE BAMBARA (1939-   )

Short Stories
Gorilla My Love and Other Stories. New York: Random House, 1972.
The Sea Birds Are Still Alive. New York: Random House, 1977.
Criticism and Biography on Toni Cade Bambara
Contemporary Authors, 29/32.
New York Times, December 3, 1972.

IMAMU BARAKA (LEROI JONES) (1934-   )

Novel
The System of Dante's Hell. New York: Grove Press, 1965.
Poetry
Black Magic: Poetry 1961-1967. Indianapolis: Bobbs-Merrill, 1969.
The Dead Lecturer. New York: Grove Press, 1964.
It's Nation Time. Chicago: Third World Press, 1970.
Preface to a Twenty Volume Suicide Note. New York: Corinth, 1961.
Short Stories
Tales. New York: Grove Press, 1967.
Plays
Baptism and the Toilet. New York: Grove Press, 1967.
The Death of Malcolm X. In Ed Bullins, ed. *New Plays From the Black Theater.* New York: Bantam, 1969
Dutchman and the Slave. New York: Morrow, 1964.
Four Black Revolutionary Plays. Indianapolis: Bobbs-Merrill, 1969. (Contents: *Experimental Death Unit 1, A Black Mass, Great Goodness of Life: A Coon Show, Madheart*)
J-E-L-L-O. Chicago: Third World Press, 1970.
Slave Ship. Negro Digest, April 1967.
Criticism
"The Black Aesthetic." Negro Digest, September 1969.
"Black (Art) Drama is the Same as Black Life." Ebony, February 1971.

"Black Revolutionary Poets Should Also Be Playwrights." *Black World*, April 1972.

"What The Arts Need Now. " *Negro Digest*, April 1967.

Other Writings

Black Music. New York: Morrow, 1967.

Blues People: Negro Music in White America. New York: Morrow, 1963.

Home: Social Essays. New York: Morrow, 1972.

Kawaida Studies: The New Nationalism. Chicago: Third World Press, 1972.

Raise, Race, Rays, Raze: Essays Since 1965. New York: Random House, 1971.

Criticism and Biography on Imamu Baraka

Benson, Kimberley. *Baraka: The Man and the Masks*. New Haven, Conn.: Yale University Press, 1976.

Bermel, Albert, "Dutchman, Or the Black Stranger in America." *Arts In Society*, Fall 1972.

Coleman, Larry G. "Comic-Strip Heroes: LeRoi Jones and the Myth of American Innocence." *Journal of Popular Culture*, Fall 1969.

Current Biography, 1940.

Gottlieb, Saul. "They Think You're an Airplane and You're Really a Bird." *Evergreen Review*, December 1967.

Hudson, Theodore R. *From LeRoi Jones to Amiri Baraka: The Literary Work*. Durham, N.C.: Duke University Press, 1973.

Jackson, Kathryn. "LeRoi Jones and the New Black Writers of the Sixties."*Freedomways*, Summer 1969.

Jeffers, Lance. "Bullins, Baraka and Elder: The Dawn of Grandeur in Black Drama." *CLA Journal*, September 1972.

Lederer, Richard. "The Language of LeRoi Jones's 'The Slave.'"*Studies in Black Literature*, Spring 1973.

Llorens, David. "Amiri (LeRoi Jones) Baraka." *Ebony*, August 1969.

Major, Clarence. "The Poetry of LeRoi Jones." *Negro Digest*, March 1965.

Miller, Jeanne-Marie. "The Plays of LeRoi Jones." *CLA Journal*, March 1971.

O'Brien, John. "Racial Nightmares and the Search for Self: An Explication LeRoi Jones's 'A chase: Aligheri's Dream.'" *Negro American Literature Forum*, Fall 1973.

Bibliography

Rush, T. G., C. F. Myers, and E. S. Arata. *Black American Writers*. Metuchen, Scarecrow, 1975.

ALDEN BLAND

Novels
Behold A Cry. New York: Scribner, 1947.
Criticism on Alden Bland
Fleming, Robert E. "Overshadowed by Richard Wright: Three Black Chicago Novelists." *Negro American Literature Forum*, Fall, 1973.

ROBERT BOLES (1943-   )

Novels
Curling. Boston: Houghton Mifflin, 1968.
The People One Knows. Boston: Houghton Mifflin, 1964.
Criticism on Robert Boles
Greenya, John. "A Colorless Sort of Gray." *Saturday Review*, February 1968

MARITA BONNER(1905-   )

Plays
The Pot Maker. Opportunity, February 1927.
The Purple Flower. In James V. Hatch and Ted Shine, eds. *Black Theater U.S.A.* New York: Free Press, 1974.
Short Stories
Crisis, June and December 1939; March 1940; February 1941.

ARNA BONTEMPS (1902-1973)

Novels
Black Thunder. New York: Macmillan, 1936; Boston: Beacon, 1968.
Drums at Dusk. New York: Macmillan, 1939.
God Sends Sunday. New York: Harcourt, 1931.
Poetry
Personals. London: Paul Breman, 1964. U.S. Distribution by Broadside Press.
Short Stories
The Old South: A Summer Tragedy and Other Stories of the Thirties. New York: Dodd, 1973.
"The Black Renaissance of the Twenties." *Black World*, November 1970.
"Famous WPA Authors." *Negro Digest*, June 1950.

Gwendolyn Brooks

"Harlem: The 'Beautiful' Years: A Memoir." *Negro Digest*, January 1965.
Books Edited by Arna Bontemps
With Langston Hughes. *American Negro Poetry*. New York: Hill and Wang, 1974.
—————. *The Book of Negro Folk Lore*. New York: Dodd, 1958. *Great Slave Narratives*. Boston: Beacon Press, 1969. *The Harlem Renaissance Remembered: Essays*. New York: Dodd, 1972.

Other Writings
Free At Last: The Life of Frederick Douglass. New York: Dodd, 1971. (Juv.)
Mister Kelso's Lion. Philadelphia: Lippincott, 1970. (Juv.)
100 Years of Negro Freedom. New York: Dodd, 1961.
Young Booker: The Story of Booker T. Washington's Early Days. New York: Dodd, 1972. (Juv.)
Criticism and Biography on Arna Bontemps
Baker, Houston A., Jr. "Arna Bontemps: A Memoir." *Black World*, September 1973.
Current Biography, 1946.
Davis, Arthur P. *From the Dark Tower*. Washington, D.C.: Howard University Press, 1974.
Bibliography
Rush, T. G., C. F. Myers, and E. S. Arata. *Black American Writers*, Metuchen, N.J.: Scarecrow, 1975.

GWENDOLYN BROOKS (1917-   )
Novel
Maud Martha. New York: Harper, 1953.
Poetry
Aloness. Detroit: Broadside Press, 1971.
Annie Allen. New York: Harper, 1949.
The Bean Eaters. New York: Harper, 1960.
Beckonings. Detroit: Broadside Press, 1975.
Bronzeville Boys and Girls. New York: Harper, 1956.
Family Pictures. Detroit: Broadside Press, 1971.
In the Mecca. New York: Harper, 1968.
Riot. Detroit: Broadside Press, 1970.
Selected Poems. New York: Harper, 1963.
A Street in Bronzeville. New York: Harper, 1945.

The Tiger Who Wore White Gloves or What You Really are. Chicago: Third World Press, 1974.

Short Stories

Hill, Herbert, ed. *Soon One Morning.* New York: Knopf, 1968.

Hughes, Langston, ed. *The Best Short Stories by Negro Writers.* Boston: Little Brown, 1967.

Sanchez, Sonia, ed. *We Be Word Sorcerers.* New York: Bamtam, 1973.

Criticism and Biography on Gwendolyn Brooks

Baker Houston A., Jr. "The Achievement of Gwendolyn Brooks." *CLA Journal,* September 1972.

Bambara, Toni Cade. "Report From Part One." *New York Times Book Review,* January 7, 1973.

Brooks, Gwendolyn, and Ida Lewis. "Conversation." *Essence,* April 1970.

_____. *Report From Part One.* Detroit: Broadside, 1972.

Cutler, B. "Long Reach, Strong Speech." *Poetry,* March 1964.

Davis, Arthur P. "The Black and Tan Motif in the Poetry of Gwendolyn Brooks." *CLA Journal.* December 1962.

_____. *From The Dark Tower.* Washington, D.C.: Howard University Press, 1974.

_____. "Gwendolyn Brooks: A Poet of the Unheroic." *CLA Journal,* December 1963.

Fuller, Hoyt. "Notes on a Poet." *Negro Digest,* August 1962.

Furman, Marva Riley. "Gwendolyn Brooks: The 'Unconditioned' Poet." *CLA Journal,* September 1973.

Garland, Phyliss. "Gwendolyn Brooks: Poet Laureate." *Ebony,* July 1968.

Hansell, William H. "Aestheticism Versus Political Militancy in Gwendolyn Brooks's 'The Chicago Picasso' and 'The Wall.'" *CLA Journal,* September 1973.

Hoff, Jon "Gwendolyn Brooks: A Bibliography." *CLA Journal,* September 1973.

Kent, George E. "The Poetry of Gwendolyn Brooks, Part I." *Black World,* September 1971.

_____. "The Poetry of Gwendolyn Brooks, Part II." *Black World,* October 1971.

Lee, Don L. "The Achievement of Gwendolyn Brooks." *Black Scholar,* Summer 1972.

McCluskey, John. "In The Mecca." *Studies in Black Literature,* Autumn 1973.

Rivers, Conrad Kent. "Poetry of Gwendolyn Brooks." *Negro Digest.* June 1964.

FRANK LONDON BROWN (1927-1962)

Novels

The Myth Makers. Chicago: Path Press, 1969.
Trumball Park. Chicago: Regnery, 1959.

Criticism

"Chicago's Great Lady Poet" *Negro Digest,* December 1961.

Criticism and Biography on Frank London Brown

Fleming, Robert E. "Overshadowed by Richard Wright: Three Black Chicago Novelists" *Negro American Literature Forum,* Fall 1973

Stuckey, Sterling. "Frank London Brown." In A. Chapman ed. *Black Voices.* New York: New American Library, 1968.

Short Stories

Clarke, John Henrick, ed. *American Negro Short Stories.* New York: Hill and Wang:, 1968.

Hill, Herbert ed. *Soon One Morning.* New York: Knopf, 1968

Hughes, Langston ed. *The Best Short Stories by Negro Writers.* Boston: Little Brown, 1967.

LLOYD LOUIS BROWN (1913-   )

Novel

Iron City. New York: Masses and Mainstream, 1951.

Short Stories

Masses and Mainstream, April 1948; December 1953.

Criticism

"Which Way for the Negro Writer?" *Masses and Mainstream,* March 1951; April 1951.

Essay

Freedomways, Spring 1964.

STERLING BROWN (1901-   )

Poetry

The Last Ride of Wild Bill and Other Narrative Poems. Detroit Broadside Press, 1974.

Southern Road. New York: Harcourt, 1932.

Criticism

"The American Race Problem as Reflected in American Literature." *Journal of Negro Education,* July 1939.

"Arna Bontemps: Co-Worker, Comrade." *Black World,* September 1973.

"The Blues." *Phylon*, Winter 1952.

"A Century of Negro Portraiture in American Literature." *Massachusetts Review*, Winter 1966.

"Negro Character as Seen by White Authors." *Journal of Negro Education*, January 1933.

"Negro Folk Expression: Spirituals, Seculars, Ballads, and Songs." *Phylon*, First Quarter 1953.

Negro Poetry and Drama and the Negro in American Fiction. New York: Atheneum, 1969.

Other Writings

With Arthur P. Davis and Ulysses Lee. *The Negro Caravan*. New York: Dryden, 1941; New York: Arno, 1969.

Criticism and Biography on Sterling Brown

Henderson, Stephen. "A Strong Man Called Sterling Brown."*Black World*, September 1970.

_____. *"Sterling Brown." Ebony*, July, 1976

Wagner, Jean. *Black Poets Of the United States*. Chicago: University of Illinois Press, 1973.

WILLIAM WELLS BROWN (1815-1884)

Novel

Clotel: or the President's Daughter. London: Partridge, Oakey, 1853; New York: Arno, 1969; New York: Colliers, 1970.

Play

Escape, or A Leap to Freedom: A Drama in Five Acts. In James V. Hatch and Ted Shine, eds. *Black Theater U.S.A.*, New York: Free Press, 1974.

Other Writings

The Black Man: His Antecedents, His Genius, and His Achievements. New York: Hamilton, 1863; New York: Arno, 1969 (reprint ed.).

Narrative of William W. Brown: A Fugitive Slave. New York: Johnson Reprint, 1970.

Criticism and Biography on William Wells Brown

Bone, Robert. *The Negro Novel in America*. New Haven, Conn.: Yale University Press, 1966.

Davis, Arthur P. Introduction to *Clotel: or The President's Daughter*. New York: Collier, 1970.

Farrison,W. Edward *William Wells Brown, Author and Reformer*. Chicago: University of Chicago Press, 1969.

Mary Burrill

Pawley, Thomas D. "The First Black Playwrights." *Black World,*
    April 1972.
Bibliography
Rush, T. G., C. F. Myers, and E. S. Arata. *Black American Writers.*
    Metuchen, N.J.: Scarecrow, 1975.

MARY BURRILL (-   )

Play
They That Sit in Darkness. In James V. Hatch and Ted Shine, eds.
Black Theater U.S.A. New York: Free Press, 1974.

CHARLES WADDELL CHESTNUTT (1858-1932)

Novels
The Colonel's Dream. New York: Doubleday, 1905. Reprints available.
The House Behind the Cedars. Boston: Houghton Mifflin, 1900.
    Reprints available.
The Marrow of Tradition. Boston: Houghton Mifflin, 1901. Reprints
    available.
Short Stories
The Conjure Woman. Boston: Houghton Mifflin, 1899. Reprints
    available.
Render, Sylvia L., ed. *The Short Fiction of Charles W. Chestnutt.*
    Washington, D.C.: Howard University Press, 1974.
*The Wife of His Youth and Other Stories of the Color Line.*Boston:
    Houghton Mifflin, 1889. Reprints available.
Criticism and Biography on Charles Chestnutt
Adams, Russell, *Great Negroes Past and Present: Chicago: Afro-*
    Am, 1969.
Andrews, William L. "Chestnutt's Patesville: The Presence and
    Influence of the Past in *The House Behind the Cedars.*" *CLA*
    Journal, March 1972.
Baldwin, R. E. "Art of the Conjure Woman." *American Literature,*
    November 1973.
Chesnutt, Helen M. *Charles Waddell Chesnutt: Pioneer of the Color*
    Line. Chapel Hill University of North Carolina Press, 1952.
Hovit, Theodore R. "Chesnutt's 'The Goophered Grapevine' as So-
    cial Criticism." *Negro American Literature Forum,* Fall 1973.

Reilly, J. M. "Dilemma in Chesnutt's *The Marrow of Tradition*." *Phylon*, Spring 1971.

Smith, R. A. "Note on the Folktales of Charles W. Chesnutt." *CLA Journal*, March 1962.

Turner, Darwin T. *"Introduction" to Charles Chesnutt's The House Behind the Cedars*. Toronto: Collier-Macmillan, 1969.

Walcott, Ronald. "Chesnutt's 'The Sheriff's Children' as Parable." *Negro American Literature Forum*, Fall 1973.

Wideman, John. "Charles Chesnutt: *The Marrow of Tradition*." *American Scholar*, Winter 1972-1973.

Bibliography

Rush, T. G., C. F. Myers, and E. S. Arata. *Black American Writers*. Metuchen, N.J.: Scarecrow, 1975.

COUNTEE CULLEN (1903-1946)

Novel

One Way to Heaven. New York: Harper, 1932.

Poetry

Ballad of a Brown Girl. New York: Harper, 1927.

The Black Christ. New York: Harper, 1929.

Color. New York: Harper, 1925; New York: Arno, 1970.

Copper Sun. New York: Harper, 1927

The Medea and Other Poems. New York: Harper, 1935.

On These I Stand. New York: Harper, 1947.

Books for Children and Young Adults

My Lives and How I Lost Them. Chicago: Follett, 1942.

The Lost Zoo. Chicago: Follett, 1969.

Criticism and Biography on Countee Cullen

Bontemps, Arna, ed. *The Harlem Renaissance Remembered*. New York: Dodd, 1972

Collier, Eugenia. "I Do Not Marvel Countee Cullen." *Crisis*, September 1967.

Daniel, Walter C. "Countee Cullen as Literary Critic." *CLA Journal*, March 1971.

Davis, Arthur P. *From the Dark Tower*. Washington, D.C.: Howard University Press, 1974.

Ferguson, Blanche. *Countee Cullen and the Harlem Renaissance*. New York: Dodd, 1966.

Bibliography

Rush, T. G., C. F. Myers, and E. S. Arata. *Black American Writers*. Metuchen, N.J.: Scarecrow, 1975.

GEORGE B. DAVIS

Novel

Coming Home. New York: Random House, 1971.

Short Stories

King, Woodie, ed. *Black Short Story Anthology.* New York: Columbia University Press, 1972.

Criticism and Biography on George B. Davis

Kent, George E. "Struggle for the Image: Selected Books by or About Blacks During 1971." *Phylon,* June 1972.

MARTIN DELANY (1812-1885)

Novel

Blake or the Huts of America: A Tale of the Mississippi Valley, the Southern United States and Cuba. Boston: Beacon Press, 1970.

Criticism and Biography on Martin R. Delany

Adams, Russell. *Great Negroes Past and Present.* Chicago: Afro-Am, 1969.

Brawley, Benjamin. *Early Negro American Writers.* Chapel Hill: University of North Carolina Press, 1935.

Fleming, Robert E. "Delany's Blake." *Negro History Bulletin,* February 1973.

Gayle, Addison, Jr. "Politics of Revolution: Afro-American Literature." *Black World,* November, 1971; October 1972.

Malveaux, Julianne. "Revolutionary Themes in Martin Delany's *Blake.*" *Black Scholar,* July, August 1973.

Sterling, Dorothy. *The Marking of an Afro-American: Martin Robison Delany.* New York: Doubleday, 1971.

Ullman, Victor. *Martin Delany: The Beginning of Black Nationalism* Boston: Beacon Press, 1971.

Bibliography

Rush, T. G. Rush, C. F. Myers, and E. S. Arata. *Black American Writers.* Metuchen, N.J.: Scarecrow, 1975.

WILLIAM DEMBY (1922-   )

Novels

Beetlecreek. New York: Rinehart, 1967; Chatham, N.J.: Chatham Booksellers, 1972 (reprint).

The Catacombs. New York: Pantheon, 1965.

Criticism and Biography on William Demby

Bayliss, John F. "*Beetlecreek*: Existential or Human Document." *Negro Digest*, November 1969.

Bone, Robert. "William Demby's Dance of life." *Tri-Quarterly*, no. 9, 1969.

_____. *The Negro Novel in America*. New Haven, Conn.: Yale University Press, 1966.

Hoffman, Nancy Y. "The Annunciation of William Demby." *Studies in Black Literature*, Spring 1972.

_____. "Technique in Demby's *The Catacombs*." *Studies in Black Literature*, Summer 1971.

O'Brien, John. "Interview with William Demby." *Studies in Black Literature*, Autumn 1972.

_____. *Interviews with Black Writers*. New York: Liveright, 1973.

Owen Dodson (1914-   )

Novel

Boy at the Window. New York: Farrar, 1951; Chatham, N.J.: Chatham Bookseller, 1972.

Poetry

The Confession Stone: A Song Cycle by Mary about Jesus. London: Breman, 1970. U.S. Distribution by Broadside Press.

Powerful Long Ladder: New York: Farrar, 1946; 1970 (reprint ed.)

Plays

Bayou Legend. In Darwin Turner, ed. *Black Drama in America*. New York: Fawcett, 1971.

Divine Comedy. In James V. Hatch and Ted Shine, eds. *Black Theater U.S.A.* New York: Free Press, 1974.

Criticism

"Countee Cullen (1903-1946)." *Phylon*, First Quarter 1946.

"Playwrights in Dark Glasses." *Negro Digest*, April 1966.

Criticism and Biography on Owen Dodson

O'Brien, John. *Interviews with Black Writers*. New York: Liveright, 1973.

Rush, T. G., C. F. Myers, and E. S. Arata. *Black American Writers*. Metuchen, N.J.: Scarecrow, 1975.

W. E. B. Du Bois (1868-1963)

Novels

The Black Flame: A Trilogy. New York: Mainstream, 1957-1961.

Dark Princess. New York: Harcourt, 1928. Reprints available.

The Quest of the Silver Fleece: A Novel. Chicago: McClurg, 1911;
New York: Arno, 1970.

Poetry

Selected Poems. New York: Panther House, 1971.

Essays

Darkwater: Voices from within the Veil. New York: Harcourt, 1921;
New York: AMS Press, 1969.

The Souls of the Black Folk: Essays and Sketches. Chicago: Mc-
Clurg, 1903; New York: Dodd, 1970.

Autobiography

The Autobiography of W. E. B. DuBois. New York: International,
1968.

*Dusk of Dawn: An Essay Toward an Autobiography of a Race
Concept.* New York: Harcourt, 1940.

Criticism and Biography on W. E. B. DuBois

Broderick, Francis L. *W. E. B. Dubois: Negro Leader in a Time of
Crisis.*Stanford, Cal.: Stanford University Press, 1959.

Clarke, John H., ed. *Black Titan: W. E. B. DuBois.* Boston: Beacon
Press, 1970.

Graham, Shirley. *His Day is Marching On: A Memoir.* Philadelphia:
Lippincott, 1971.

Lester, Julius, ed. *Seventh Son: The Thought and Writings of W. E. B.
DuBois.* New York: Random House, 1971.

Savory, Jerold J. "The Rending of the Veil in W. E. B. DuBois's *The
Souls of Black Folk.*" *CLA Journal,* March 1972.

Bibliographies

Aptheker, Herbert. *An Annotated Bibliography of the Writings of
W. E. B. DuBois.* Milwood, N.Y.: Kraus-Thompson, 1973.

Kaiser, Ernest."A Selected bibliography of the Published Writings
of W. E. B. DuBois." *Freedomways,* Winter 1965.

Paul Laurence Dunbar (1872-1906)

Novels

The Fanatics. New York: Dodd, 1901. Reprints available.

The Heart of Happy Hollow. New York: Dodd, 1904. Reprints
available.

The Love of Landry. New York: Dodd, 1900. Reprints available.

The Sport of the Gods. New York: Dodd, 1902; New York: Macmillan, 1972.

The Uncalled. New York: Dodd, 1898; New York: AMS Press, 1969.

Poetry

The Complete Poems of Paul Laurence Dunbar. New York: Dodd, 1951.

Short Stories

The Best Short Stories of Paul Laurence Dunbar. New York: Dodd, 1938.

Folks from Dixie. New York: Dodd, 1898.

In Old Plantation Days. New York: Dodd, 1903.

Martin, Jay, and Gossie Hudson, eds. *The Paul Laurence Dunbar.*

The Strength of Gideon and Other Stories. New York: Dodd, 1900. New York: Dodd, 1975.

Criticism and Biography on Paul Laurence Dunbar.

Baker, Houston A., Jr. "Paul Laurence Dunbar: An Evaluation." *Black World,* February 1973.

Gayle, Addison, Jr. *Oak and Ivy: A Biography of Paul Laurence Dunbar.* New York: Doubleday, 1971.

Hudson, Gossie Harold. "Paul Laurence Dunbar: Dialect et la Negritude." *Phylon,* September 1973.

Larsen, Charles R. "The Novels of Paul Laurence Dunbar."*Phylon,* Fall 1968.

Martin, Jay. "'Jump Back Honey': Paul Laurence Dunbar and the Rediscovery of American Political Traditions." *The Bulletin of the Midwest MLA,* Spring 1974.

_____. ed. *A Singer in the Dawn: Reinterpretations of Paul Laurence Dunbar.* New York: Dodd, 1975.

Redding, Saunders. *To Make a Poet Black.* Chapel Hill: University of North Carolina Press, 1939.

Turner, Darwin T. "Paul Laurence Dunbar: The Rejected Symbol." *Journal of Negro History,* January 1967.

Wagner, Jean. *Black Poets of the United States.* Chicago: University of Illinois Press, 1973.

Bibliographies

Blanck, Jacob. *Bibliography of American Literature,* vol. II, New Haven, Conn.: Yale University Press, 1957.

Rush, T. G., C. F. Myers, and E. S. Arata. *Black American Writers.* Metuchen, N.J.: Scarecrow, 1975.

RANDOLPH EDMONDS (1900-   )

Plays

Bad Man. In James V. Hatch and Ted Shine, eds. *Black Theater U.S.A.* New York: Free Press, 1974.

The Land of Cotton and Other Plays. Washington, D.C.: Associated Publishers, 1942 (contents: *Gangsters Over Harlem, The High Court of Historia, Silas Brown, Yellow Death*).

Shades and Shadows. Boston: Meador, 1930 (contents: *The Call of Jubah, Everymans Land, Hewers of the Wood, The Phantom Treasure, Shades and Shadows, The Tribal Chief.*

Six Plays for a Negro Theater. Boston: Baker, 1934 (contents: *Bad Man, Bleeding Hearts, The Breeders, Nat Turner, The New Window, Old Man Pete*).

Criticism and Biography on Randolph Edmonds

Brawley, Benjamin. *The Negro Genius.* New York: Dodd Mead, 1940. *Who's Who in Colored America.* New York Murry: 1940.

JUNIUS EDWARDS (1929-   )

Novel

If We Must Die. New York: Doubleday, 1963.

Short Stories

Hughes Langston, ed. *The Best Short Stories by Negro Writers.* Boston: Little, Brown, 1967.

RALPH WALDO ELLISON (1914-   )

Novel

The Invisible Man. New York: Random House, 1952.

Essays

Shadow and Act. New York: Random House, 1964.

Criticism and Biography on Ralph Ellison

Baumbach, Jonathan, "Nightmare of a Native Son: Ellison's *Invisible Man.*" in Donald Gibson, ed. *Five Black Writers.*

Bone, Robert. "Ralph Ellison and the Uses of Imagination." *Tri-Quarterly*, no. 6, 1963.

Brown, Lloyd W. "Ralph Ellison's Exhorters: The Role of Rhetoric in *Invisible Man.*" *CLA Journal*, March 1970.

Clarke, John Henrick. "The Visible Dimensions of *Invisible Man.*" *Black World*, December 1970.

Ford, Nick Aaron. "The Ambivalence of Ralph Ellison." *Black World,* December 1970.

Gibson, Donald B. *Five Black Writers.* New York: New York University Press, 1970.

Kaiser, Ernest. "A Critical Look at Ellison's Fiction and at Social and Literary Criticism By and About the Author." *Black World,* December 1970.

Klotman, Phyllis R. "The Running Man as Metaphor in Ellison's *Invisible Man." CLA Journal,* March 1970.

Lane, James B. "Underground to Manhood: Ralph Ellison's *Invisible Man." Negro American Literature Forum,* Summer 1973.

Neal, Larry. "Ellison's Zoot Suit." *Black World,* December 1970.

O'Brien, John. *Interviews with Black Writers.* New York: Liveright, 1973.

Sanders, A.D. "Odysseus in Black: An Analysis of the Structure of *Invisible Man." CLA Journal,* March 1970.

Turner, Darwin T. "Afro-American Authors: A Full House." *College English,* January 1972.

_____. "Sight in *Invisible Man."CLA Journal,* March 1970.

Volger, T. A. "*Invisible Man:* Somebody's Protest Novel." *The Iowa Review,* Spring, 1970.

Walcott, Ronald. "Ellison, Gordone, and Tolson: Some Notes on the Blues, Style and Space." *Black World,* December 1972.

Bibliography
Rush, T. G., C. F. Myers, and E. S. ARata. *Black American Writers: Past and Present.* Metuchen, N.J.: Scarecrow, 1975.

RONALD FAIR (1932-   )

Novels
Hog Butcher. New York: Harcourt, 1966; New York: Bantam, 1973.
Many Thousand Gone: An American Fable. New York: Harcourt, 1965; Chatham, N.J.: Chatham Bookseller, 1973.
We Can't Breathe. New York: Harper, 1971
World of Nothing. New York: Harper, 1972.

Short Stories
Essence, July 1971.
Hughes, Langston, ed., *The Best Short Stories by Negro Writers:* Boston: Little Brown, 1967. Baraka, Imamu, (LeRoi Jones) and Larry Neal, eds. *Black Fire.* New York: Morrow, 1968.

Criticism and Biography on Ronald Fair

Fleming, Robert E. "The Novels of Ronald Fair". *CLA Journal,* June 1972.

Klotman, Phyllis A. "The Passive Resistant in *A Different Drummer, Day of Absence,* and *Many Thousand Gone.*" *Studies in Black Literature,* Autumn 1972.

Jessie Remond Fauset (1886-1961)

Novels

The Chinaberry Tree. New York: Frederick A. Stokes, 1931; New York: AMS Press, 1969 (reprint).

Comedy American Style. New York: Frederick A. Stokes, 1933; New York: AMS Press, 1969 (reprint).

Plum Bun. New York: Frederick A. Stokes, 1929.

There Is Confusion. New York: Boni and Liveright, 1924.

Poetry

Adoff, Arnold, ed. *Poetry of Black America.* New York: Harper, 1972.

Hughes, Langston, and Arna Bontemps, eds. *Poetry of the Negro: 1746-1970.*

Criticism and Biography on Jessie Fauset

Adams, Russell. *Great Negroes Past and Present.* Chicago: Afro-Am, 1969.

Bone, Robert. *The Negro Novel in America.* New Haven, Conn.: Yale University Press, 1966.

Bontemps, Arna. *The Harlem Renaissance Remembered.* New York: Dodd, 1972.

Dannet, Sylvia. *Profiles of Negro Womanhood.* Yonkers, N.Y.:

Huggins, Nathan I. *Harlem Renaissance.* New York: Oxford, 1971.

_____. *Voices From the Harlem Renaissance.* New York: Oxford, 1976.

Lomax, Michael A. "Fantasies of Affirmation: The 1920's Novel of Negro Life." *CLA Journal,* December 1972.

Rudolph Fisher (1897-1934)

Novels

The Conjure Man Dies: A Mystery of Dark Harlem. New York: Covici-Freide, 1932.

The Walls Of Jericho. New York: Knopf, 1928.

Short Stories

Clarke, John Henrik, ed. *American Negro Short Stories.* New York: Hill and Wang, 1966.

Criticism and Biography on Rudolph Fisher

Bone, Robert. *The Negro Novel in America.* New Haven, Conn.: Yale University Press, 1966.

Huggins, Nathan I. *Harlem Renaissance.* New York: Oxford, 1971.

Lomax, Michael L. "Fantasies of Affirmation: The 1920's Novel Of Negro Life." *CLA Journal,* December 1972.

Wilamena, Robinson. *Historical Negro Biographies.* New York: Publishers Co., 1969.

"Rudolph Fisher." *Negro History Bulletin,* December 1938.

Turpin, Waters Edward. "Four Short Fiction Writers of the Harlem Renaissance: Their Legacy of Achievement." *CLA Journal,* September 1967.

ERNEST J. GAINES (1933-   )

Novels

The Autobiography of Miss Jane Pittman. New York: Dial, 1971.

Catherine Carmier. New York: Atheneum, 1954; Chatham, N.J.: Chatham Bookseller, 1972.

*Of Love and Dust.*New York: Dial, 1967.

Short Stories

Bloodline. New York: Dial, 1968.

Criticism and Biography on Ernest J. Gaines.

Beauford, Fred. "Conversation with Ernest Gaines." *Black Creation,* Fall 1972.

Bryant, Jerry. "From Death to Life: The Fiction of Ernest J. Gaines," *The Iowa Review,* Winter 1972.

Contemporary Authors, 11/12.

O,Brien, John. *Interviews with Black Writers.* New York: Liveright, 1973.

Schraufnagel, Noel. *From Apology to Protest: The Black American Novel.* Deland, Fla.: Everett Edwards, 1973.

Stoelting, Winifred. "Human Dignity and Pride in the Novels of Ernest J. Gaines." *CLA Journal,* March 1971.

LORENZ GRAHAM (1902-   )

Books for Children and Young Adults
David He No Fear. New York: Crowell, 1971.
Every Man Heart Lay Down. New York: Crowell, 1970.
God Wash the World and Start Again. New York: Crowell, 1971.
Hongry Catch the Foolish Boy. New York: Crowell, 1971.
I, Momolu. New York: Crowell, 1966.
North Town. New York: Crowell, 1965.
Return to South Town. New York: Crowell 1972
South Town. Chicago: Follett, 1958.
Whose Town? New York: Crowell, 1969.
Criticism and Biography on Lorenz Graham
"An Author Speaks." Elementary English, no. 50, February 1973.
Contemporary Authors, 9/10.
Small, Robert C., Jr. "South Town: A Junior Novel of Prejudice."
    Negro American Literature Forum, Winter 1970.

SAM GREENLEE (1930-   )

Novels
Bagdad Blues. New York: Emerson Hall, 1973.
The Spook Who Sat by the Door. New York: Bantam, 1970.
Poetry
Blues for an African Princess. Chicago: Third World Press, 1971.
Short Stories
Black World, August, 1973. Negro Digest, December, 1965; February,
    1966; September, 1966; January, 1967; October, 1970.
Criticism and Biography on Sam Greenlee
Burrell, W. "Rappin with Sam Greenlee." Black World, July 1971.
Rush, T. G., C. F. Myers, and E. S. Arata. Black American Writers.
    Metuchen, N.J.: Schockley, Ann A., and Sue Chandler. Living
    Black American Authors. New York: Bowker, 1973.

SUTTON GRIGGS (1872-1930)

Novels
The Hindered Hand: Or the Reign of the Repressionist. Nashville,
    Tenn.: Orion, 1902: New York: AMS Press, 1970.
Imperium In Imperio. Cincinnati: Editor Press, 1899; New York:
    Arno, 1969.

Overshadowed. Nashville, Tenn.: Orion, 1901; New York: AMS Press, 1970.

Pointing the Way. Nashville, Tenn.: Orion, 1908; New York: AMS Press, 1970.

Unfettered: A Novel. Nashville, Tenn.: Orion, 1902; New York: AMS Press, 1970.

Wisdom's Call. Nashville, Tenn.: Orion, 1911; Miami, Fla.: Mnemosyne, 1969.

Criticism and Biography on Sutton Griggs

Bone, Robert A. *The Negro Novel in America*, New Haven, Conn.: Yale University Press, 1966.

Rush, T. G., C. F. Myers, and E. S. Arata. *Black American Writers.* Metuchen, N.J.: Scarecrow, 1975.

Tatham, Campbell. "Reflections: Sutton Griggs' *Imperium In Imperio.*" *Studies in Black Literature,* Winter 1974.

ANGELINA WELD GRIMKE (1880-1958)

Play

Rachel. Washington, D.C.: McGrath, 1969.

Poetry

Adoff, Arnold, ed. *The Poetry of Black America.* New York: Harper, 1973.

Hughes, Langston, and Arna Bontemps, eds. *The Poetry of the Negro.* New York: Doubleday, 1970.

WILLIAM HARRISON GUNN (BILL) (1934-   )

Novel

All the Rest Have Died. New York: Dial, 1964.

Play

Johnnas. Drama Review, Summer 1968.

ROSA GUY (1925-   )

Novels

Bird at My Window. Philadelphia: Lippincott, 1966.

The Friends. New York: Holt, 1973.

Ruby. New York: Viking, 1976.

VIRGINIA HAMILTON (1936-   )

Books for Children and Young Adults

House of Dies Drear. New York: Macmillan, 1970.
Long Ago Tales of Jahdu. New York: Macmillan, 1969.
M.C. Higgins the Great. New York: Macmillan, 1974.
Paul Robeson, New York: Harper, 1974.
Planet of Junior Brown. New York: Macmillan, 1969.
W. E. B. DuBois: A Biography. New York: Crowell, 1972.
Zeely. New York: Macmillan, 1971.

Criticism and Biography on Virginia Hamilton

Commire. A. *Something About the Author,* vol. 4. Detroit: Gale, 1974.

JUPITER HAMMON (1720-1806)

Poetry

Ramson, Stanley A., ed. *America's First Negro Poet: The Complete Works Of Jupiter Hammon of Long Island.* Port Washington, N.Y.: Kennikat, 1969.

Criticism and Biography on Jupiter Hammon

Adams, Russell L. *Great Negroes Past and Present.* Chicago: Afro-Am, 1969.

Barksdale, Richard, and Keneth Kinnamon. *Black Writers of America.* New York: MacMillan, 1972.

Loggins, Vernon. *The Negro Author in America.* New York: Columbia University Press, 1959.

Malone, Dumas, ed. *Dictionary of American Biography.* New York: Scribner, 1958.

Williams, Kenny. *They Also Spoke.* Nashville, Tenn.: Townsend, 1970.

DELORIS HARRISON

Novel

Journey All Alone. New York: Dial, 1971.

Robert Hayden (1913-   )

Poetry

Angle of Ascent: New and Selected Poems. New York: Liveright, 1975.

A Ballad for Remembrance. London: Breman, 1962. U.S. Distribution by Broadside Press.

Figure in Time. Nashville, Tenn.: Hemphill Press, 1955.

Heart-Shape in the Dust. Detroit: Falcon, 1940.

The Night Blooming Cereus. Detroit: Broadside, 1972.

Selected Poems, 2nd ed. New York: October House, 1966.

Words in the Mourning Time. New York: October House, 1970.

Criticism and Biography on Robert Hayden

Davis, Charles T. "Robert Hayden's Use of History." In Donald B. Gibson, ed. *Modern Black Poets.* Englewood Cliffs, N.J.: Prentice-Hall, 1973.

Fetrow, Fred M. "Robert Hayden's 'Frederick Douglass': Form and Meaning in a Modern Sonnet." *CLA Journal,* September 1973.

O'Brien, John. *Interviews with Black Writers.* New York: Liveright, 1973.

O'Sullivan, Maurice J., Jr. "The Mask of Allusion in Robert Hayden's 'The Diver.'" *CLA Journal,* September 1973.

Pool, Rosey E. "Robert Hayden: Poet Laureate." *Negro Digest,* June 1966.

Whitlow, Roger. *Black American Literature.* Chicago, Nelson Hall, 1973.

Nathan Heard (1936-   )

Novels

Howard Street. New York: Dial, 1972.

To Reach A Dream. New York: Dial, 1972.

George Wylie Henderson (1904-   )

Novels

Jule. New York: Creative Age, 1946.

Ollie Miss. New York: Stokes, 1935.

Criticism and Biography on George W. Henderson

Bone, Robert. *The Negro Novel in America.* New Haven, Conn.: Yale University Press, 1966.

Calvin Hernton

Turner, Darwin T. "The Negro Novelists and the South." *Southern Humanities Review*, vol. 1, 1967.

Calvin Hernton (1932-   )

Novel
Scarecrow New York: Doubleday, 1974.
Essays
Sex and Racism in America. New York: Grove Press, 1965.
White Papers for White Americans. New York: Doubleday, 1967.
Poetry
The Coming of Chronos to the House of Nightsong: An Epical Narrative of the South. New York: Interim, 1964.

Chester Himes (1909-   )

Novels
All Shot Up. New York: Berkeley, 1960.
The Big Gold Dream. New York: Berkeley, 1966.
Blind Man with a Pistol. New York: Morrow, 1969.
Cast the First Stone. New York: New American Library, 1972.
Come Back Charleston Blue. New York: Berkeley, 1972.
The Crazy Kill. New York: Berkley, 1959.
If He Hollers Let Him Go. New York: Doubleday, Doran, 1945.
Lonely Crusade. New York: Knopf, 1947.
Pink Toes. New York: Dell, 1965.
The Primitive. New York: New American Library, 1955.
The Real Cool Killers. New York: Avon, 1959.
Run Man Run. New York: Dell, 1969.
The Third Generation. Cleveland, Ohio: World, 1954.
Criticism and Biography on Chester Himes
Baldwin, James. "History as Nightmare." *The New Leader*, October 25, 1947.
Contemporary Authors, 25/28.
Fabre, Michel. "A Case of Rape." *Black World*, March 1972.
Margolies, Edward. "Experiences of the Black Expatriate Writer: Chester Himes." *CLA Journal*, June 1972.
_____."The Thrillers of Chester Himes." *Studies in Black Literature*, Summer 1970.
Reed, Ishmael. "Chester Himes: Writer." *Black World*, March 1972.

Williams, John A. "My Man Himes: An Interview with Chester Himes." In John A. Williams and Charles F. Harris, eds. *Amistad 1.*

Autobiography

The Quality of Hurt: The Autobiography of Chester Himes. New York: Doubleday, 1972.

Bibliography

Fabre, Michel. "A Selected Bibliography of Chester Himes's Work." *Black World,* March 1972.

Rush, T. G., C. F. Myers, and E. S. Arata. *Black American Writers.* Metuchen, N.J.: Scarecrow, 1975.

LANGSTON HUGHES (1902-   )

Novels

Not Without Laughter. New York: Knopf, 1930; New York: Macmillan, 1969.

Simple Speaks His Mind. New York: Simon and Schuster, 1950.

Simple Stakes a Claim. New York: Rinehart, 1957.

Simple Takes a Wife. New York: Simon and Schuster, 1953.

Simple's Uncle Sam. New York: Hill and Wang, 1965.

Tambourines to Glory. New York: John Day, 1958.

Poetry

Ask Your Mama: 12 Moods for Jazz. New York: Knopf, 1961.

Don't You Turn Back. New York: Knopf, 1969.

The Dream Keeper and Other Poems. New York: Knopf, 1932.

Fields of Wonder. New York: Knopf, 1947.

Fine Clothes to the Jew. New York: Knopf, 1927.

Montage of a Dream Deferred. New York: Holt, 1951.

One Way Ticket. New York: Knopf, 1949.

The Panther and the Lash: Poems of Our Times. New York: Knopf, 1967.

Selected Poems of Langston Hughes. New York: Knopf, 1959.

Shakespeare in Harlem. New York: Knopf, 1942.

The Weary Blues. New York, 1924

Plays

Five Plays by Langston Hughes. Bloomington: Indiana University Press, 1963.

Short Stories

Laughing to Keep from Crying. New York: Holt, 1952.

Something in Common and Other Stories. New York: Hill and Wang, 1963.

The Ways of White Folks. New York: Knopf, 1934.

Kristin Hunter

Autobiography
The Big Sea: An Autobiography. New York: Knopf, 1940.
I Wonder as I Wander: An Autobiographical Journey. New York:
    Rinehart, 1956.
Essays
Berry, Faith, ed. *Good Morning Revolution: The Uncollected Protest
    Writings of Langston Hughes.* Westport, Conn: Lawrence Hill,
    1973.
Criticism and Biography on Langston Hughes
Current Biography, 1940.
Davis, Arthur P. *From The Dark Tower,* Washington, D.C.: Howard
    University Press, 1974.
Emanuel, James. *Langston Hughes.* New York: Twayne, 1967.
Meltzer, Milton. *Langston Hughes: A Biography.* New York: Apollo,
    1972.
Wagner, Jean. *Black Poets of the United States.* Chicago: University
    of Illinois Press, 1973.
Bibliographies
Dickinson, Donald C. *A Bio-Bibliography of Langston Hughes,
    1902-1967.* Hamden, Conn.: Archon Books, 1967.
O'Daniel, Therman, ed. *Langston Hughes: Black Genius, A Critical
    Evaluation.* New York: Morrow, 1971.

KRISTIN HUNTER (1931-   )

Books for Children and young Adults
Boss Cat. New York: Scribner, 1971.
Guests in the Promised Land. New York: Scribner, 1973.
The Soul Brothers and Sister Lou. New York: Scribner, 1968.
Novels
God Bless the Child. New York: Scribner, 1970.
The Landlord. New York: Scribner, 1966.
The Survivors. New York: Scribner, 1975.
Criticism and Biography on Kristin Hunter
Contemporary Authors, 13/14.
Rush, T.G., C.F. Meyers and E.S. Arata *Black American Writers.*
    Metuchen, New Jersey, Scarecrow, 1975.
Whitlow, Roger. *Black American Literature.* Chicago: Nelson Hall,
    1973.
Short Stories
Hughes, Langston, ed. *The Best Short Stories by Negro Writers.*
    Boston: Little Brown, 1976.

Turner, Darwin T, ed. *Black American Literature.* Columbus, Ohio: Charles E. Merrill, 1970.

Black World, June 1972; *Essence,* April, 1971; *Negro Digest,* June, 1968.

ZORA NEAL HURSTON (1903-1960)

Novels
Jonah's Gourd Vine. Philadelphia: Lippincott, 1934.
Moses Man of the Mountain. Philadelphia: Lippincott, 1939.
Seraph on the Suwanee. New York: Scribner, 1948.
Their Eyes Were Watching God. Philadelphia: Lippincott, 1937.

Short Stories
Barksdale, Richard, and Keneth Kinnamon, eds. *Black Writers of America.* New York: MacMillan, 1972.
Fire, December, 1926: *Opportunity,* December, 1924, May. 1925, January, 1926, August, 1926.

Plays
Fast and Furious. Best Plays of 1931-1932. New York: Dodd, 1932.

Books
Mules and Men. Philadelphia: Lippincott, 1935.
Tell My Horse. Philadelphia: Lippincott, 1938.

Essays
American Legion Magazine, November 1950: *American Mercury,* no. 57, 1943; *Negro Digest,* June 1943.
Journal of American Folklore: January-March 1930; October-December 1931; *Negro Digest,* May 1944; June 1944; April 1947; *Saturday Evening Post,* September 1942, December 1951; *Journal of Negro History,* October 1927.

Autobiography
Dust Tracks on the Road. Philadelphia: Lippincott, 1942; New York: Arno, 1970 (reprint).

Criticism and Biography on Zora Neal Hurston
Adams, Rusell. *Great Negroes Past and Present.* Chicago Afro-Am, 1969.
Barksdale, Richard, and Keneth Kinnamon. *Black Writers of America* (see Short Stories).
Blake, Emma L. "Zora Neal Hurston: Author and Folklorist." *Negro History Bulletin,* April 1966.
Davis, Arthur P. *From the Dark Tower.* Washington, D.C.: Howard University Press, 1974.

Giles, James. "The Significance of Time in Zora Neal Hurston's *Their Eyes Are Watching God.*" *Negro American Literature Forum,* April 1972.

Neal, Larry. "Eatonville's Zora Neal Hurston: A Profile." *Black Review,* no. 2 New York: Morrow, 1971.

Pratt, T. "Hurston, Zora Neal: A Memoir." *Negro Digest,* February 1962.

Taylor, Clyde. "Black Folk Spirit and the Shape of Black Literature." *Black World,* August 1972.

Turner, Darwin T. *In A Minor Chord: Three Afro-American Writers and Their Search for Identity.* Chicago: Southern Illinois University Press, 1971.

Walker, Alice "In Search of Zora Neal Hurston." *Ms,* March 1975.

Washington, Mary Helen. "Zora Neal Hurston: The Black Woman's Search for Identity." *Black World,* August 1972.

JESSE JACKSON (1908-   )

Books for Children and Young Adults

Anchor Man. New York: Harper, 1947.

Call Me Charley. New York: Harper, 1945.

Charley Starts from Scratch. New York: Harper, 1958.

The Fourteenth Cadillac. New York: Doubleday, 1972.

Make a Joyful Noise Unto the Lord. New York: Crowell, 1974.

Tessie. New York: Harper, 1968.

Criticism and Biography on Jesse Jackson

Commire, A. *Something About the Author,* vol. 2. Detroit: Gale, 1971

Rush, T. G., C. F. Myers, and E. S. Arata. *Black American Writers,* Metuchen, Scarecrow, 1975.

ROSCOE CONKLING JAMISON (1888-1918)

Poetry

Negro Soldiers and Other Poems. St. Joseph, Mo.: W.F. Neil, 1918.

Criticism and Biography on Roscoe Conkling Jamison

Brawley, Benjamin. *The Negro Genius.* New York: Dodd, Mead, 1940.

Kerlin, Robert. *Negro Poets and Their Poems.* Washington, D.C.: Associated, 1935.

Charles Johnson

Novel

Faith and the Good Thing. New York: Viking, 1974.

Fenton Johnson (1888-1958)

Poetry

A Little Dreaming. Chicago: Peterson, 1913; New York: McGrath, 1969 (reprint ed.)

Songs of the Soil. New York: By the Author, 1916; New York: McGrath, 1969 (reprint ed.)

Criticism and Biography on Fenton Johnson

Brawley, Benjamin. *The Negro Genius.* New York: Dodd, Mead, 1940.

Brown, Sterling. *Negro Poetry and Drama.* New York: Atheneum, 1969.

Kerlin, Robert. *Negro Poets and Their Poems,* Washington, D.C.: Associated, 1935.

Redding, Saunders. *To Make a Poet Black.* Chapel Hill: University of North Carolina Press, 1939.

Wagner, Jean. *Black Poets of the United States.* Chicago: University of Illinois Press, 1973.

James Weldon Johnson (1871-   )

Novel

The Autobiography of an Ex-Colored Man. New York: Knopf, 1927.

Poetry

Fifty Years and Other Poems. New York: Cornhill, 1917.

God's Trombones: Seven Negro Sermons in Verse. New York: Viking, 1927.

St. Peter Relates an Incident: Selected Poems. New York: Viking, 1935.

Other Writings

Along This Way. New York: Viking, 1933. (Autobiography)

Black Mountain. New York: Knopf, 1930.

The Book of American Negro Poetry. New York: Viking, 1940.

The Book of American Negro Spirituals. New York: Viking, 1940.

Negro Americans, What Now? New York: Viking, 1934.

Gayl Jones

Criticism and Biography on James W. Johnson
Baker, Houston A. "Forgotten Prototype." *Virginia Quarterly*, Summer 1973.
Collier, Eugenia. "Endless Journey of an Ex-Colored Man." *Phylon*, Winter 1971.
Davis, Arthur P. *From the Dark Tower*. Washington, D.C.: Howard University Press, 1974.
DuBois, W. E. B. "James Weldon Johnson." *Journal of Negro History*, April, July 1967.
Levy, Eugene. *James Weldon Johnson: Black Leader Black Voice*. Chicago: University of Chicago Press, 1973.

GAYL JONES (1949-   )

Novels
Corregidora. New York: Random House, 1975.
Eva's Man. New York: Random House, 1976.
Poetry
Jordon, June, ed. *Soulscript*. New York Doubleday, 1970.
Criticism and Biography on Gayl Jones
Rush, T. G., C. F. Meyers, and E. S. Arata. *Black American Writers*. Metuchen, Scarecrow, 1975.

JUNE MEYER JORDON (1936-   )

Poetry
New Days: Poems of Exile and Return. New York: Emerson Hall, 1973.
Some Changes. New York: Dutton, 1971.
Books for Children and Young Adults
Dry Victories. New York: Holt, 1972.
Fannie Lou Hamer. New York: Crowell, 1973.
His Own Where. New York: Crowell, 1973.
New Room: New Life. New York: Crowell, 1974.
Who Look At Me. New York: Crowell, 1969.
Criticism and Biography on June Jordon
Rush, T. G., C. F. Myers, and E. S. Arata. *Black American Writers*. Metuchen, Scarecrow, 1975.

WILLIAM MELVIN KELLEY (1937-   )

Novels

dem. New York: Doubleday, 1967.

A Different Drummer. New York: Doubleday, 1962.

A Drop of Patience. New York: Doubleday, 1965.

Dunsford Travels Everywhere. New York: Doubleday, 1969.

Short Stories

Book of Short Stories. New York: Doubleday, 1974.

Dancers on the Shore. New York: Doubleday, 1964.

Criticism

"The Task of the Negro Writer as Artist". *Negro Digest,* April 1965.

Articles

Negro Digest, January 1967; May 1968; November 1969; *Partisan Review* 1968; *New York Times Magazine,* May 20, 1960; *Mademoiselle,* 1960.

Criticism and Biography on William Melvin Kelley

Jarab, Joseph. "The Drop of Patience of the American Negro: W. M. Kelley's *A Different Drummer* (1962), *A Drop of Patience* (1965)." *Philologica Pragensia,* no. 12, 1969.

Kelley, William Melvin. "Ivy League Negro." *Esquire,* August 1963.

Klotman, Phyllis R. "Examination of the Black Confidence Man in Two Black Novels: *The Man Who Cried I Am* and *dem.*" *American Literature,* January 1973.

_____. "The Passive Resistant in *A Different Drummer, Day of Absence* and *Many Thousand Gone.*" *Studies in Black Literature,* Autumn 1972.

Nadeau, Robert L. "Black Jesus: A Study of Kelley's *A Different Drummer.*" *Studies in Black Literature,* Summer 1971.

Randall, Dudley F. "On the Conference Beat." *Negro Digest,* no. 16, 1967.

Schatt, Stanley. "You Must Go Home Again: Today's Expatriate Afro-American Writers." *Negro American Literature Forum,* Fall 1973.

ADRIENNE KENNEDY (1931-   )

Plays

Cities in Bezique: Two One Act Plays. (A Beast Story and *The Owl Answers)* New York: Samuel French, 1970.

Funnyhouse of a Negro. In Stanley Richards, ed. *Best Short Plays of 1970.* Philadelphia: Chilton, 1970.

A Lesson in Dead Language. In Edward Parone, ed. *Collision Course.* New York: Random House, 1968.

John O. Killens

A Rat's Mass. In William Couch, ed. *New Black Playwrights.* New
York: Avon, 1970.

Criticism and Biography on Adrienne Kennedy

Abramson, Doris E. *Negro Playwrights in the American Theater.*
Contemporary Dramatists New York: St. Martin. 1976.

Harrison, Paul Carter. *The Drama of Nommo.* New York: Grove,
1972.

Mitchell, Loften. *Black Drama.* New York: Hawthorne, 1967.

JOHN O. KILLENS (1914-   )

Novels

And We Heard the Thunder. New York: Knopf, 1963.

Cotillion: Or One Good Bull Is Half the Herd. New York: Trident,
1971.

'Sippi. New York: Trident, 1967.

Youngblood. New York: Dial, 1954.

Short Stories

Hughes, Langston, ed. *The Best Short Stories by Negro Writers.*
Boston: Little Brown, 1967

Criticism

"Another Time When Black Was Beautiful." *Black World,* December
1970.

Essays

Black Man's Burden. New York: Pocket Books, 1969.

Criticism and Biography on John Killens

Rush, T. G., C. F. Myers, and E. S. Arata. *Black American Writers:*
Past and Present. Metuchen, N.J.: Scarecrow, 1975.

NELLA LARSEN (1893-1963)

Novels

Passing, New York: Arno, 1970; New York: Macmillan, 1971.

Quicksand, New York: Macmillan, 1971.

Criticism and Biography on Nella Larsen

Bone, Robert. *The Negro Novel in America.* New Haven, Conn.: Yale
University Press, 1966.

Brown, Sterling. *The Negro in American Fiction.* Washington, D.C.:
Associates in Negro Folk Education, 1937.

Davis, Arthur P. *From the Dark Tower.* Washington, D.C.: Howard
University Press, 1974.

Huggins, Nathan. *Harlem Renaissance.* New York: Oxford, 1971.

Sato, Hiroko. "Under the Harlem Shadow: A Study of Jessie Fauset
and Nella Larsen." In Arna Bontemps. *The Harlem Renaissance
Remembered*. New York: Dodd, 1972.
Thornton, Hortense E. "Sexism as Quagmire: Nella Larsen's *Quicksand*." *CLA Journal*, March 1973.

GEORGE W. LEE (1894-1976)

Novel
River George. New York: Macauley, 1937.
Short Stories
Beal Street Sundown. New York: Field, 1942.
Other Writings
Beal Street Where the Blues Began. New York: R.O. Ballou, 1934.
Criticism and Biography on George W. Lee
Gloster, Hugh M. *Negro Voices in American Fiction*. Chapel Hill:
University of North Carolina Press, 1948.
Who's Who In in Colored America, 5th ed. 1938-1939. New York:
Murry, 1939.

JULIUS LESTER (1939-   )

Books for Children and Young Adults
Black Folktales. New York: R.W. Baron, 1969.
The Knee-high Man and Other Tales. New York: Dial, 1972.
Long Journey Home: Stories from Black History. New York: Dial,
1972.
To Be a Slave. New York: Dial, 1968.
Two Love Stories. New York: Dial, 1972.
Who I Am. New York: Dial, 1974.
Other Writings
Look Out Whitey—Black Power's Gon' Get Your Mamma. New
York: Dial, 1968.
Revolutionary Notes. New York: R.W. Baron, 1969.
Search for a New Land. New York: Dial, 1969.
Seventh Son: The Thoughts and Writings of W. E. B. DuBois, 2 vols.
New York: Random House, 1971.
Criticism and Biography on Julius Lester
Contemporary Authors, 17/18.
"Interview." *Arts in Society*, no. 5, 1968.
Meras, Phyllis, "Interview with Julius Lester." *Nation*, June 22, 1970.

Myrtle Smith Livingston

Autobiography
All is Well. New York: Morrow, 1976.

MYRTLE SMITH LIVINGSTON (1901-   )

Play
For Unborn Children. In James V. Hatch, and Ted Shine, eds. *Black Theater U.S.A.* New York: Free Press, 1974.

JOHN McCLUSKEY (1944-   )

Novels
Look What They Done to My Song. New York: Random House, 1974.
Short Stories
Foley, Martha ed. *Best American Short Stories.* Boston: Hougton Mifflin, 1976.
Black World, January 1973.
Coombs, Orde, ed. *What We Must See: Young Black Story Tellers.* New York: Dodd-Mead, 1971.
Criticism
"The City as a Force: Three Novels by Cyprian Ekwensi." *Journal of Black Studies.* December 1976.
"In the Mecca." *Studies in Black Literature,* Fall 1973.
Invisible Men: Protagonists of *Invisible Man* and *The Beautiful One are not Yet Born."* Juju, Spring 1976.
Book Reviews
Black World, September 1971.
Cleveland Magazine, August 1976.
Cleveland Plain Dealer, April 1975; April 10, 1977.
Essay
"On Black Language." *Black World,* Spring 1974.

CLAUDE McKAY (1890-1948)

Novels
Banana Bottom. New York: Harper, 1933.
Banjo: A Story without a Plot. New York: Harper, 1929; New York: Harcourt, 1970.
Home to Harlem. New York: Harper, 1928.
Poetry
Harlem Shadows: The Poems of Claude McKay. New York: Harcourt, 1922.

Selected Poems. New York: Bookman, 1953.

Spring In New Hampshire. London: Richards, 1920.

Essays and Other Writings

Harlem: Negro Metropolis. New York: Dutton, 1940.

American Mercury, August 1939; *Catholic Digest,* July 1945; *Crisis,*
    July 1921; April 1921; December 1923; *Ebony,* March 1946; *Negro
    History Bulletin,* April 1968; *Opportunity,* March 1937; Novem-
    ber 1939.

Autobiography

A Long Way From Home. New York: Lee Furman, 1937; New York:
    Harcourt, 1970.

Criticism and Biography on Claude McKay

Adams, Russell L. *Great Negroes Past and Present,* Chicago: Afro-
    Am, 1969.

Barksdale, Richard, and Keneth Kinnamon. *Black Writers of Amer-
    ica.* New York: MacMillan, 1972.

Bontemps, Arna, ed. *The Harlem Renaissance Remembered.* New
    York: Dodd, 1972.

Cartey, Wilfred. "Four Shadows of Harlem." *Negro Digest,* August
    1969.

Collier, Eugenia. "Heritage from Harlem." *Black World,* November
    1970.

Conroy, Sister Mary. "The Vagabond Motif in the Writings of
    Claude McKay." *Negro American Literature Forum,* no. 5, 1971.

Cooper, Wayne. "Claude McKay and the New Negro of the 1920's."
    Phylon, Fall 1964.

Jackson, Blyden. "The Essential McKay."*Phylon,* no. 14, 1953.

Kaye, Jacqueline. "Claude McKay's Banjo." *Presence Africaine,* no.
    73, 1970.

Kent, George E. "The Soulful Way of Claude McKay." *Black World,*
    November 1970.

Lang, Phyllis Martin. "Claude: Evidence of a Magic Pilgrimage."
    CLA Journal, June 1973.

Stoff, Michael B. "Claude McKay and the Cult of Primitivism." In
    Anna Bontemps *The Harlem Renaissance Remembered.* (see
    above).

Taylor, Clyde. "Black Folk Spirit and the Shape of Black Literature."
    Black World, August 1972.

Wagner, Jean. *The Black Poets of the United States.* Chicago: Uni-
    versity of Illinois Press, 1973.

CLARENCE MAJOR (1936-   )

Novels

All-Night Visitors. New York: Olympia, 1969.

No. New York: Emerson Hall, 1973.

Reflex and Bone Structure. New York: Fiction Collective, 1975.

Poetry

Cotton Club. Detroit: Broadside, 1972.

Human Juices. Omaha: Coericion, 1965.

Love Poems of a Blackman. Omaha: Coericion, 1964.

Private Line. London: Breman, 1971; U.S. Distribution by Broadside Press.

Swallow the Lake. Middletown, Conn.: Wesleyan University Press, 1970.

Symptoms and Madness. New York: Corinth, 1971.

The Syncopated Cakewalk. New York: Barlenmir House, 1974.

Short Stories

Black Creations. Summer 1972: *Essence,* December, 1973.

Criticism

"Black Criteria." *Journal of Black Poetry,* Spring 1967.

"Close to the Ground: A Note on Walt Whitman." *American Dialog,* 1969.

The Dark and Feeling. New York: Third Press, 1974.

"The Explosion of Black Poetry." *Essence,* 1972.

"Frank London Brown: A New American Voice." *Proof 1,* Summer 1960.

"The Poetry of LeRoi Jones: A Critique." *Negro Digest,* March 1965.

Other Writings

Dictionary of Afro-American Slang. New York: International, 1970.

Criticism and Biography on Clarence Major

Contemporary Authors, 23-24.

Jaffe, Daniel. "A Shared Language in the Poet's Tongue." *Saturday Review,* April 3, 1971.

O'Brien, John. *Interviews with Black Writers.* New York: Liveright, 1973.

Rush, T.G., C. F. Myers, and E. S. Arata. *Black American Writers.* Metuchen, Scarecrow, 1975.

Welburn, Ron. "All Night Travelers." *Nickel Review,* September 1969.

PAULE MARSHALL (1929-   )

Novels
Brown Girl, Brownstones. New York: Random House, 1959.
The Chosen Place, The Timeless People. New York: Harcourt, 1969.
Short Stories
Soul Clap Hands and Sing. New York: Atheneum, 1961.
Criticism
"The Negro Woman in American Literature." *Freedomways*, Winter 1966.
Criticism and Biography on Paule Marshall
Barksdale, Richard, and Keneth Kinnamon. *The Black Writers of America.* New York: MacMillan, 1972.
Braithwaite, Edward. "Rehabilitation." *Critical Quarterly*, Summer 1971.
_____. "West Indian History and Society in the Art of Paule Marshall's Novel." *Journal of Black Studies*, December 1970.
Kapai, Leela. "Dominant Themes and Technique in Paule Marshall's Fiction." *CLA Journal*, September 1972.
Stoelting, Winifred L. "Time Past and Time Present: The Search for Viable Links in *The Chosen Place, The Timeless People* by Paule Marshall." *CLA Journal*, September 1972.
Whitlow, Roger. *Black American Literature.* Chicago: Nelson Hall, 1973.

JOHN F. MATHEUS (1887-   )

Plays
Cruiter. In James V. Hatch and Ted Shine, eds. *Black Theater U.S.A.* New York: Free Press, 1974.
Criticism and Biography on John F. Matheus
Brawley, Benjamin. *The Negro Genius.* New York: Dodd, Mead, 1940.
Rush, T. G., C. F. Myers, and E. S. Arata. *Black American Writers.* Metuchen. N.J.: Scarecrow, 1975.

SHARON BELL MATHIS (1937-   )

Books for Children and Young Adults
Brooklyn Story. New York: Hill and Wang, 1970.
Listen to the Fig Tree. New York: Viking, 1974.

Julian Mayfield

Sidewalk Story. New York: Viking, 1971; New York: Avon, 1973.
Teacup Full of Roses. New York: Viking, 1972.
Criticism and Biography on Sharon Bell Mathis
Rush, T. G., C. F. Myers, and E. S. Arata. *Black American Writers,* vol. 2. Metuchen, N.J.: Scarecrow, 1975.
Black World, August 1973.

Julian Mayfield (1928-   )

Novels
The Hit. New York: Vanguard, 1957.
The Grand Parade. New York: Vanguard, 1961.
Criticism
"And Then Came Baldwin." *Freedomways,* Spring 1963.
"Crisis or Crusade: An Article-Review of Harold Cruse's *Crisis of the Negro Intellectual." Negro Digest:* June 1968.
"Into the Mainstream and Oblivion." *African Forum,* June 1960; also in James Emanuel and T. Gross, eds. *Dark Symphony.* New York: Free Press, 1968.
"The Negro Writer and the Stickup." *Boston University Journal,* Winter 1969.
"Tale of Two Novelists." *Negro Digest,* June 1965.
Criticism and Biography on Julian Mayfield
Contemporary Authors, 13/14.
Cruse, Harold. *The Negro Intellectual.* New York: Morrow, 1962.
O'Brien, John. *Interviews With Black Writers.* New York: Liveright 1973.
Rush, T. C., C. F. Meyers, and E. S. Arata. *Black American Writers.* Metuchin, N. J.: Scarecrow, 1975.

Louise Meriwether (19   -   )

Books for Children and Young Adults
Don't Ride the Bus on Monday: The Rosa Parks Story. Englewood Cliffs, New Jersey: Prentice-Hall, 1970.
The Freedom Ship of Robert Smalls. Englewood Cliffs, New Jersey: Prentice-Hall, 1971.
Heart Man: Dr. Daniel Hale Williams. Englewood Cliffs, New Jersey: Prentice-Hall, 1972.
Criticism
"Amen Corner." *Negro Digest January* 1965.

"James Baldwin: Fiery Voice of the Negro Revolt." *Negro Digest* August 1963.

Short Stories

Clarke, John Henrick, ed. *Harlem.* New York: New American Library, 1970.

King, Woodie, Jr. ed. *Black Short Story Anthology.* New York: Columbia Watkins, Mel, ed. *Black Review No. 2.* New York: Morrow, 1971.

Antioch Review, Fall 1967; *Essence,* June 1971.

Criticism and Biography on Louise Meriwether

"Daddy Was a Number Runner." *Ebony,* July 1970.

TONI MORRISON (1931-   )

Novels

The Bluest Eye. New York: Holt, 1970.

Sula. New York: Knopf, 1974.

Song of Solomon. New York: Harper 1977.

Essay

"Behind the Making of the Black Book." *Black World,* February 1974.

Criticism and Biography on Toni Morrison

Frankel, Haskel. *New York Times Book Review,* November 1, 1970.

Loftin, Elouise. *Black Creation,* Fall 1971.

Wilder. C. M. *CLA Journal,* December 1971.

CARL OFFORD (1910-   )

Novels

The Naked Fear. New York: Ace, 1954.

The White Face. New York: McBride, 1943.

Criticism and Biography on Carl Offord

Scraufnagle, Noel. *From Apology to Protest: The Black American Novelist.* Deland: Florida: Everett Edwards, 1973.

ROI OTTLEY (1906-1960)

Novel

White Marble Lady. New York: Farrar, 1965.

Other Writings

Black Odyssey. New York: Scribner, 1948.

Ann L. Petry

The Lonely Warrior: The Life and Times of Robert S. Abbott. Chicago: Regnery, 1955.

New World a'Coming: Inside Black America. Boston: Houghton Mifflin, 1943.

No Green Pastures. New York: Scribner, 1952.

Criticism and Biography on Roi Ottley

Current Biography, 1944.

ANN L. PETRY (1911-   )

Novels

Country Place. Boston: Houghton Mifflin, 1947; Chatham, N.J.: Chatham Booksellers, 1971.

The Narrows. Boston: Houghton Mifflin, 1953.

The Street. Boston: Houghton Mifflin, 1946.

Short Stories

Miss Muriel and Other Stories. Boston: Houghton Mifflin, 1971.

Books for Children and Young Adults

The Drugstore Cat. New York: T. Crowell, 1949.

Harriet Tubman: Conductor on the Underground Railway. New York: Crowell, 1955.

Legends of the Saints. New York: Crowell, 1970.

Tituba of Salem Village. New York: Crowell, 1964.

Criticism

"The Novel as Social Criticism." *The Writer's Book.* New York: Harper, 1950.

Criticism and Biography on Ann L. Petry

Adams, George R. "Riot as Ritual: Ann Petry's 'In Darkness and Confusion.'" *Negro American Literature Forum,* Summer 1972.

Barksdale, Richard, and Keneth Kinnamon. *The Black Writers of America* New York: Macmillan, 1972

Bone, Robert. *The Negro Novel in America.* New Haven, Conn.: Yale University Press, 1966.

Contemporary Authors, 7/8.

Davis, Arthur P. *From the Dark Tower.* Washington, D.C.: Howard University Press, 1974.

DeMontreville, Doris, and Donna Hill. *The Third Book of Junior Authors.* New York: Wilson, 1972.

Dempsey, David. "Uncle Tom's Ghost and the Literary Abolitionist." *Antioch Review,* no. 6, 1946.

"Has Anybody Seen Mrs. Dora Dean?" *New Yorker*, October 25, 1958.

O'Brien, John. *Interviews with Black Writers*. New York: Liveright, 1973.

DUDLEY F. RANDALL (1914-   )

Poetry

After the Killing. Chicago: Third World Press, 1973.

Cities Burning. Detroit: Broadside, 1968.

Love You, 2nd ed. London: Breman, 1971.

More to Remember: Poems of Four Decades. Chicago: Third World Press, 1971.

Criticism and Biography on Dudley F. Randall

Contemporary Authors, 25/28

Nicholas, A. X. "A Conversation with Dudley Randall." *Black World*, December 1971.

Redding, Saunders. "The Black Arts Movement in Negro Poetry." *American Scholar*, Spring 1973.

Rush, T. G., C. F. Myers, and E. S. Arata. *Black American Writers*. Metuchen, N.J.: Scarecrow, 1975.

JAY SAUNDERS REDDING (1906-   )

Novel

Stranger and Alone. New York: Harcourt, 1950.

Criticism

"The Alien Land of Richard Wright." In Herbert Hill, ed. *Soon One Morning*. New York: Knopf, 1968.

"American Negro Literature." *American Scholar*, no.18, 1949.

"The Black Arts Movement in Negro Poetry." *American Scholar*, Spring 1973.

"The Fall and Rise of Negro Literature." *American Scholar*, Spring 1949.

"The Negro Writer: The Road to Where." Boston University Journal, Winter 1969.

To Make A Poet Black. Chapel Hill: University of North Carolina Press, 1939.

Other Writings

With Arthur P. Davis. *Cavalcade: Negro American Writing from 1760 to the Present*. Boston: Houghton Mifflin, 1971.

The Lonesome Road: A Biographical History of Black America. New York: Doubleday, 1958.

They Came in Chains: Americans From Africa, rev. ed. Philadelphia: Lippincott, 1973.

Criticism and Biography on Saunders Redding

Arts in Society, Summer-Fall 1968.

Contemporary Authors, 4.

Current Biography, 1969.

Twentieth Century Authors. New York: Wilson, 1942.

ISHMAEL REED (1938-   )

Novels

Flight to Canada. New York: Random House, 1976.

The Free-Lance Pallbearers. New York: Doubleday, 1967.

The Last Days of Louisiana Red. New York: Random House, 1974.

Mumbo Jumbo. New York: Doubleday, 1972.

Yellow Back Radio Broke Down. New York: Doubleday, 1969.

Poetry

catechism of a neoamerican hoodoo church. London: Breman, 1970. U.S. Distribution by Broadside Press.

Chattanooga. New York: Random House, 1973.

Conjure: Selected Poems, 1963-1970. Amherst: University of Massachusetts Press, 1972.

Criticism

"Black Artist: 'Calling a Spade a Spade.'" Arts, May 1967.

"Can a Metronome Know the Thunder or Summon a God?" In Ishmael Reed, ed. 19 Necromancers from Now. New York: Doubleday, 1970.

Criticism and Biography on Ishmael Reed

Ambler, Madge. "Ishmael Reed Whose Radio Broke Down." Negro American Literature Forum, Winter 1972.

Beauford, Fred. "Conversation with Ishmael Reed." Black World, no. 4, 1973.

Bush, Roland. "Werewolf of the West." Black World, January 1973.

Contemporary Authors, 23/24.

Ford, Nick Aaron. "A Note on Ishmael Reed." Studies in the Novel, Summer 1971.

"An Interview with Ishmael Reed." Journal of Black Poetry, Summer-Fall 1969.

Newsweek, June 2, 1975.

O'Brien, John. *Interviews with Black Writers*. New York: Liveright, 1973.

Whitlow, Roger. *Black American Literature*. Chicago: Nelson Hall, 1973.

WILLIS RICHARDSON (1889-   )

Plays

Antonio Maceo. In Willis Richardson and May Miller, eds. *Negro History in Thirteen Plays*. Washington, D.C.: Associated Publishers, 1953.

Attucks: the Martyr. In Willis Richardson and May Miller, eds. *Negro History in Thirteen Plays*. Washington, D.C.: Associated Publishers, 1953.

The Broken Banjo. In Richard Barksdale and Keneth Kinnamon, eds. *Black Writers of America*. New York: Macmillan, 1972.

The Chip Woman's Fortune. In Darwin T. Turner, ed. *Black Drama In America: An Anthology*. New York: Fawcett, 1971.

Compromise: A Folk Play. In Alain Locke, ed. *The New Negro*. New York: Johnson Reprint, 1968.

The Danse Calinda. In Alain Locke and Montgomery Gregory, eds. *Plays Of Negro Life: A Sourcebook of Native American Drama*. New York: Harper, 1927. Reprint available from Negro Universities Press.

Flight of the Natives. In James V. Hatch and Ted Shine, eds. *Black Theater U.S.A.* New York: Free Press, 1974.

Idle Head. In James V. Hatch and Ted Shine, eds. *Black Theater U.S.A.* New York: Free Press, 1974. Richardson, Willis, comp. *Plays and Pagents from the Life of the Negro*. Washington, D.C.: Associated Publishers, 1930.

The Rider of the Dream. In Alain Locke and Montgomery Gregory, eds. *Plays of Negro Life*. New York: Harper, 1927.

Criticism and Biography on Willis Richardson

Brawley, Benjamin, *The Negro Genius*. New York: Dodd, Mead, 1940.

Who's Who in Colored America. New York: 1940.

GEORGE SAMUEL SCHUYLER (1895-   )

Novels

Black No More: Being an Account of the Strange and Wonderful

Gil Scott-Heron

Workings of Science in the Land of the Free A.D. 1933-1940. New York: Macauley, 1931; New York: Macmillan, 1970.

Slaves Today:A Story of Liberia. New York: Brewer, 1931; New York: AMS Press, 1969.

Criticism

"The Negro Art Hokum." *The Nation,* no.122, 1926.

"The Van Vechten Revolution." *Phylon,*no. 11, 1950.

"What's Wrong With Negro Authors." *Negro Digest,*May 1950.

Criticism and Biography on George S. Schuyler

Bone, Robert. *The Negro Novel in America.* New Haven, Conn.: Yale University Press, 1966.

Davis, Arthur P. *From The Dark Tower.* Washington, D.C.:Howard University Press, 1974.

Whitlow, Roger. *Black American Literature.* Chicago: Nelson Hall, 1973.

Winslow,H.F. "George S. Schuyler: Fainting Traveler." *Midwest Journal,* Summer 1953.

Bibliography

Rush, T. G., C. F. Myers, and E. S. Arata. *Black American Writers.* Metuchen, N.J.: Scarecrow, 1975.

GIL SCOTT-HERON (1949-   )

Novels

The Nigger Factory. New York: Dial, 1972.

The Vulture. Derby,Conn.: Belmont Tower, 1971.

Poetry

Small Talk on 125th and Lennox: A Collection of Black Poems. New York: New World, 1970.

Criticism and Biography on Gil Scott-Heron

Rush, T. G., C. F. Meyers, and E. S. Arata. *Black American Writers.* Metuchen, N.J.: 1975.

WILLIAM GARDNER SMITH (1927-1974)

Novels

Anger at Innocence. New York: Farrar, 1950.

The Last of the Conquerors. New York: Farrar, 1948.

South Street. New York: Farrar, 1954.

The Stone Face. New York: Farrar, 1963.

Essays

Return to Black America. Englewood Cliffs, N.J.: Prentice-Hall, 1970.

Criticism and Biography on William Gardner Smith

Bone, Robert. *The Negro Novel in America.* New Haven, Conn.: Yale University Press, 1966.

Bryant, Jerry H. "Individuality and Fraternity: The Novels of William Gardner Smith." *Studies in Black Literature,* Summer 1972.

Schatt, Stanley. "You Must Go Home Again: Today's Afro-American Expatriate Writers." *Negro American Literature Forum,* Fall 1973.

EULALIE SPENCE (1894-   )

Plays

Fool's Errand. New York: Samuel French, 1927.

Foreign Mail. New York: Samuel French, 1927.

Undertow. In James V. Hatch and Ted Shine, eds. *Black Theater U.S.A.* New York: Free Press, 1974.

Criticism and Biography on Eualie Spence

Hatch, James V., and Ted Shine, eds. *Black Theater U.S.A.* New York: Free Press, 1974.

WALLACE THURMAN (1902-1934)

Novels

The Blacker the Berry. New York: Arno Press, 1969.

Infants of the Spring. New York: Macaulay, 1929.

Play

*Harlem: A Melodrama of Negro Life in Harlem.*1929. In the James Weldon Johnson Collection at Yale University.

Short Stories

Barksdale, Richard, ed. *Black Writers of America.* New York: MacMillan, 1972.

Criticism

The Messenger, April to September 1926.

"Negro Artists and the Negro." *New Republic,* no. 52, 1927.

"Negro Poets and Their Poetry." *Bookman,* no. 67, 1928.

"Nephews of Uncle Remus." *Independent* no. 119, 1927.

Criticism and Biography on Wallace Thurman

Bone, Robert. *The Negro Novel in America.* New Haven: Yale University Press, 1966.

Brawley, Benjamin. *The Negro Genius.* New York: Dodd, 1940.

Henderson, Mae G. "Portrait of Wallace Thurman." In Arna Bontemps. *The Harlem Renaissance Remembered.* New York: Dodd, 1972.

West, Dorothy. "Elephant's Dance." *Black World,* November 1970.

JEAN TOOMER (1894-1967)

Poetry
Cane. New York: Boni and Liveright, 1923; New York: Harper, 1968.
Play
Balo. In James V. Hatch and Ted Shine, eds. *Black Theater U.S.A.* New York: Free Press 1974.
Criticism and Biography on Jean Toomer
Ackley, Donald G. "Theme and Vision in Jean Toomer's *Cane.*" *Studies in Black Literature,* Spring 1970.

Bell, Bernard. "A Key to the Poems in Cane." *CLA Journal,* March 1971.

Chase, Patricia. "The Women in *Cane.*" *CLA Journal* March 1971.

Duncan, Bowie. "Jean Toomer's *Cane:* A Modern Black Oracle." *CLA Journal,* March 1972.

Goede, William J. "Jean Toomer's Ralph Kabnis: Portrait of the Negro Artist as a Young Man." *CLA Journal,* Spring 1969.

Krasny, Michael J. "Design in Jean Toomer's *Balo.*" *Negro American Literature Forum,* Fall 1973.

Turner, Darwin T. "And Another Passing." *American Negro Literature Forum,* Fall 1967.

_____. "The Failure of a Playwright." *CLA Journal,* June 1967.

_____. *In A Minor Chord: Three Afro- American Writers and their Search for Identity.* Urbana: University of Southern Illinois Press. 1971

Wagner, Jean. *Black Poets of the United States.* Chicago: University of Illinois Press, 1973.

MELVIN VAN PEEBLES (1932-   )

Novels
Un american en enfer. Paris: Editions Denoel, 1965.

A Bear for the F.B.I. New York: Trident, 1968.
La Fete Harlem. Paris: J. Martineau, 1967.
Le Permission. Paris: J. Martineau, 1967.
The True American. New York: Morrow, 1976.
Plays
Ain't Supposed to Die a Natural Death. New York: Bantam, 1973.
Don't Play Us Cheap. New York: Bantam, 1973.
Short Stories
Le Chinois du XIVe. Paris: le Gadenet, 1966.
Criticism and Biography on Melvin Van Peebles
Coleman, Horace W. "Melvin Van Peebles." *Journal of Popular Culture,* Fall 1972.
Gussow, M. "Baadassssssss Success of Melvin Van Peebles."*New York Times Magazine,* August 20, 1972.
"Power to the Peebles." *Time,* August 16, 1971.
Scobie, W.I. "Supernigger Strikes." *London Magazine,* April-May 1972.
"Sweet Song of Success." *Newsweek,* June 21, 1971.
Wolf, William. "B**da*****s Peebles." *Milwaukee Journal Magazine,* September 17, 1972.

MARY ELIZABETH VROMAN (1923-1967)

Novels
Esther. New York: Bantam, 1963.
Harlem Summer. New York: Putnam, 1967.
Short Stories
Hughes, Langston, ed. *Best Short Stories by Negro Writers.* Boston: Little, Brown 1967.
Freedomways, Spring 1962; Spring 1963; *Ladies Home Journal,* June 1951.
Screenplay
Bright Road. Based on the short story "See How They Run." *Ladies Home Journal,* June 1951.
Other Writings
Book
Shaped to Its Purpose: Delta Sigma Theta, The First Fifty Years. New York: Random House, 1965.
Articles
Ladies Home Journal, September 1951; February 1957; *National Education Association Journal,* October 1951.

Alice Walker

Criticism and Biography on Mary Elizabeth Vroman
Bachner, Saul. "Black Literature: The Junior Novel in the Classroom,
    Harlem Summer." *American Negro Literature Forum,* Spring
    1973.
"Writing School Marm: Alabama Teacher Finds Literary Success
    with First Short Story." *Ebony,* July 1952.

ALICE WALKER (1944-   )

Novels
Meridian. New York: Harcourt, 1976.
The Third Life of Grange Copeland. New York: Harcourt, 1970.
Short Stories
In Love and Trouble: Stories of Black Women. New York: Harcourt,
    1973.
Poetry
Once:Poems. New York: Harcourt, 1968.
Revolutionary Petunias and Other Poems. New York: Harcourt,
    1973.
Criticism
"Beyond the Peacock: The Reconstruction of Flannery O'Connor."
    Ms, December 1975.
"The Black Writer and the Southern Experience." *New South,* Fall
    1970.
"In Search of Zora Neal Hurston." *Ms,* March 1975.
"The Unglamorous but Worthwhile Duties of the Black Revolution-
    ary Artist, or of The Black Writer Who Simply Works and
    Writes." *Black Collegian,* June 1971.
Articles
"Anais Nin." *Ms,* April 1977.
"In Search of our Mother's Gardens." *Ms,* May 1974.
"Lulls: A Native Daughter Returns to the Black South." *Ms,* January
    1977.

THEODORE WARD (1902-   )

Plays
Big White Fog: A Negro Tragedy. In James V. Hatch and Ted Shine,
    eds. *Black Theater U.S.A.* New York: Free Press, 1974.
Our Lan'. In Darwin T. Turner, ed. *Black Drama in America.* New
    York: Fawcett, 1971.

Criticism and Biography on Theodore Ward
Abramson, Doris. *Negro Playwrights in the American Theater.* Columbia University Press, 1969. Hughes, Langston, and Milton Meltzer. *Black Magic.* Englewood Cliffs, N.J.: Prentice-Hall, 1968.
Mitchell, Loften. *Black Drama.* New York: Hawthorne, 1967.

DOROTHY WEST (1910-   )

Novel
The Living is Easy. Boston: Houghton Mifflin, 1948.
Short Stories
Hughes, Langston, ed. *The Best Short Stories by Negro Writers.* Boston: Little, Brown, 1967.
Criticism
"Elephant's Dance: A Memoir of Wallace Thurman." *Black World,* November 1970.
Criticism and Biography on Dorothy West
Bardolph, Richard. *The Negro Vanguard.* New York: Rivehart, 1959.
Bone, Robert. *The Negro Novel in America.* New Haven, Conn.: Yale University Press, 1966.

JOHN E. WIDEMAN (1941-   )

Novels
A Glance Away. New York: Harcourt, 1967.
Hurry Home. New York: Harcourt, 1970.
The Lynchers. New York: Harcourt, 1973.
Criticism and Biography on John E. Wideman
O'Brien, John. *Interviews with Black Writers.* New York: Livewright, 1973.
Schraufnagel, Noel. *From Apolopy to Protest: The Black American Novel.* Deland: Florida: Everett Edwards, 1973.

JOHN A. WILLIAMS (1925-   )

Novels
The Angry Ones. New York: Ace, 1960.
Captain Blackman. New York: Doubleday, 1972.
The Junior Bachelor Society. New York: Doubleday, 1976.
The Man Who Cried I Am. Boston: Little, Brown, 1967.

Mothershill and the Foxes. New York: Doubleday, 1975.
Night Song. New York: Farrar, 1961.
Sissie. New York: Farrar, 1963.
Sons of Darkness and Sons of Light. Boston: Little, Brown, 1970.
Essays
Flashbacks: A Twenty Year Diary of Article Writing. New York: Doubleday. 1970.
Criticism and Biography on John A. Williams
Leonard, John. "Author at Bay." *New York Times Book Review,* October 29, 1967.
O'Brien, John. "Art of John A. Williams. *American Scholar,* Summer 1973.
_____. *Interviews with Black Writers.* New York: Livewright, 1973.
Bibliography
Rush, T. G., C. F. Myers, and E. S. Arata. *Black American Writers.* Metuchen, N.J.: Scarecrow, 1975.

CHARLES STEVENSON WRIGHT (1932-   )

Novels
The Messenger. New York: Farrar, 1963.
The Wig: A Mirror Image. New York: Farrar, 1966.
Essays
Absolutely Nothing to Get Alarmed About. New York: Farrar, 1973.
Criticism and Biography on Charles S. Wright
Foster, F.S. "Charles Wright: Black, Black Humorist." *CLA Journal,* September 1973.
O'Brien, John, ed. *Interviews with Black Writers.* New York: Livewright, 1973.

RICHARD WRIGHT (1908-1960)

Novels
Lawd Today. New York: Walker, 1963.
The Long Dream. New York: Doubleday, 1958; Chatham, N.J.; Chatham Bookseller, 1969.
Native Son. New York: Harper, 1969.
The Outsider. New York: Harper, 1953.
Savage Holiday. New York: Avon, 1954.

Short Stories
Bright and Morning Star. New York: International, 1938.
Eight Men. Cleveland Ohio: World, 1961.
Uncle Tom's Children. New York: Harper, 1938, 1965, 1969.
Autobiography
American Hunger. New York: Harper, 1977.
Black Boy. New York: Harper, 1945, 1965.
Criticism
White Man Listen. New York: Doubleday, 1957.
Other Writings
Black Power. New York: Harper, 1954.
Pagan Spain. New York: Harper, 1957.
12 Million Black Voices: A Folk History of the Negro in the United States. New York: Viking, 1941.
Criticism and Biography on Richard Wright
Baker, Houston A, ed. *Twentieth Century Interpretations of Native Son.* Englewood Cliffs, N.J.: Prentice-Hall, 1973.
Ellison, Ralph. "Richard Wright's Blues." *Antioch Review,* no. 5, 1945.
Fabre, Michel. *The Unfinished Quest of Richard Wright.* New York: Morrow, 1973.
Ford, Nick A. "The Ordeal of Richard Wright." *College English,* no. 15, 1953.
Jackson, Blyden. "Black Boy from America's Black Belt and Urban Ghettos." *CLA Journal,* June 1969.
Lawson, L.A. "Cross Damon, Kierkegaardian Man of Dread." *CLA Journal,* March 1971.
Webb, Constance. *Richard Wright: A Biography.* New York: Putnam, 1968.
Williams, John A. *Most Native Of Sons: A Biography of Richard Wright.* New York: Doubleday, 1970.
Bibliographies
Fabre, Michel, and William Margolies. "Richard Wright: A Bibliography." *Bulletin of Bibliography,* January 1965.
Kinnamon, Keneth. *The Emergence of Richard Wright: A Study in Literature and Society.* Urbana: University of Illinois Press, 1972.
Rush, T. G., C. F. Myers, and E. S. Arata. *Black American Writers.* Metuchen, N.J.: Scarecrow, 1975.

SARAH E. WRIGHT

Novel

This Child's Gonna Live. New York: Delacorte, 1969.

Poetry

Give Me a Child. Philadelphia: Kraft, 1955.

Criticism

"The Negro Woman in American Literature." *Freedomways*, Winter 1966.

AL YOUNG (1939-   )

Novels

Sitting Pretty. New York: Holt, 1976.

Snakes. New York: Holt, 1970.

Who Is Angelina? New York: Holt, 1975.

Poetry

Dancing: Poems. New York: Corinth, 1969.

Geography of the Near Past. New York: Holt, 1976.

The Song Turning Back Into Itself. New York: Holt, 1971.

Criticism and Biography on Al Young

Contemporary Authors, 29-32.

O'Brien, John. *Interviews with Black Writers.* New York: Livewright, 1973.

Rush, T. G., C. F. Myers, and E. S. Arata. *Black American Writers.* Metuchen, N.J.: Scarecrow, 1975.

PART IV

General Bibliography

Africa

African Encyclopedia. New York: Oxford,1974.

AWOONOR KOFI. *The Breast of the Earth: A survey of the History, Culture, and Literature of Africa South of the Sahara*. New York: Anchor Press, 1975.

BARNETT, DON and RAY HARVEY. *The Revolution in Angola*. New York: Bobbs-Merrill, 1972.

BEBEY, FRANCIS. *African Music: A People's Art*. New York: L. Hill, 1975.

BENNETT, NORMAN ROBERT. *Africa and Europe from Roman Times to the Present*. New York: Africana, 1975.

BEYER, BARRY K. *Africa South of the Sahara: A Resource and Curriculum Guide*. New York: Crowell, 1969.

BLANDIER, GEORGES, and Jaques Maquet. *Dictionary of Black African Civilization*. New York: Leon Amiel, 1974.

BRAVMAN, RENE. *West African Sculpture*. Seattle: University of Washington Press, 1970.

BROOKS, LESTER. *Great Civilizations of Ancient Africa*. New York: Four Winds Press, 1971.

BURNS, SIR ALAN. *History of Nigeria*. London: Allen Unwin, 1969.

The Cambridge History of Africa. New York: Cambridge University Press, 1976.

CHINWEIZER. *The West and the Rest of Us*. New York: Random House, 1975.

CHURCH, R. J. HARRISON. *West Africa*. New York: John Wiley, 1969.

DATHORNE, A. R. *The Black Mind: A History of African Literature*. Minneapolis: University of Minnesota Press, 1974.

DAVIDSON BASIL. *Lost Cities of Africa*. Boston: Little, Brown, 1959. Rev. ed., 1970.

DIHOFF, GRETCHEN. *Katsina: Profile of a Nigerian City*. New York: Praeger, 1970.

DuBois, W. E. B. *The World and Africa*. New York: International, 1965.

ELISOFON, ELIOT, and WILLIAM FAGG. *The Sculpture of Africa*. New York: Praeger, 1958.

FAGE J. D. *Africa Discovers Her Past*. New York: Oxford, 1969. *A History of West Africa*. London: Cambridge University Press, 1969.

GLAZIER, K. M. *Africa South of the Sahara: A Select Annotated Bibliography*. Los Angeles: Hoover Institute, 1969.

GRAHAM-WHITE, ANTHONY. *The Drama of Africa*. New York: French, 1974.

HALLETT, ROBIN. *Africa Since 1875*. Ann Arbor: University of Michigan Press, 1970.

JACKSON JOHN G. *Introduction to African Civilizations*. New York: University Books, 1970.

JONES, ELDRED D., ed. *African Literature Today*. New York: Holmes and Meier, 1975.

JULY, ROBERT W. *Precolonial Africa: An Economic and Social History*. New York: Scribner, 1975.

KLIMA, VLADIMIR. *Black Africa: Literature and Language*. Boston: Reidel, 1975.

LEGUM, COLIN. *Africa Contemporary Record, Annual Survey and Documentation 1974-75*. New York: Africana.

McEWAN, P., JR., ed. *Africa From Early Times to 1800*. London: Oxford 1968.

_____. ed., *Nineteenth-Century Africa*. London: Oxford, 1968.

_____. ed., *Twentieth Century Africa*. London: Oxford, 1968.

MEAUZE, PIERRE. *African Art: Sculpture*. New York: World, 1968.

MIDDLETON, JOHN. *Black Africa*. London: Macmillan, 1970.

MURPHY, E. JEFFERSON. *Understanding Africa*. New York: Crowell, 1969.

OLIVER, ROLAND. *The Dawn of African History*. New York: Oxford, 1965.

OLIVER, ROLAND, and J. D. FAGE. *A Short History of Africa*. Baltimore: Penguin, 1962.

PANOFSKY, HANS. *A Bibliography of Africana*. Westport, Conn.: Greenwood, 1975

ROTBERG, ROBERT I. *A Political History of Tropical Africa*. New York: Harcourt, 1965.

SHINNIE, MARGRET. *Ancient African Kingdoms.* New York: St. Martin's Press, 1965.

SOYINKA, WOLE, ed. *Poems of Black Africa.* New York: Hill and Wang, 1975.

WACHSMAN, KLANS, ed. *Essays on Music and History in Africa.* Evanston: Northwestern University Press, 1971.

WARREN, FRED. *The Music of Africa.* Englewood Cliffs, N.J.: Prentice-Hall, 1970.

WAUTHIER, CLAUDE. *The Literature and Thought of Modern Africa.* New York: Praeger, 1967.

WEBSTER, J. B., and A. A. Boahen. *History of West Africa.* New York: Praeger, 1970.

WILLETT, FRANK. *I Fe in the History of West African Sculpture.* New York: McGraw-Hill, 1967.

_____. *African Art.* New York: McGraw-Hill, 1971.

WILSON, HENRY S. *Origins of Western African Nationalism.* New York: St. Martin's Press, 1969.

Anthologies

ADOFF, ARNOLD, ed. *The Poetry of Black America.* New York: Harper, 1973.

BAKER, HOUSTON A., JR., ed. *Black Literature In America.* New York: McGraw-Hill, 1971.

BARKSDALE, RICHARD, and KENNETH Kinnamon, eds. *Black Writers of America.* New York: Macmillan, 1972.

BONTEMPS, Arna, ed. *American Negro Poetry,* rev. ed. New York: Hill and Wang, 1974.

BRAWLEY, BENJAMIN, ed. *Early Negro Writers.* Chapel Hill: University of North Carolina Press, 1935.

BREMAN, PAUL, ed. *You Better Believe It.* Baltimore: Penguin 1973.

_____. *Sixes and Sevens.* London: Breman, 1962.

BROOKS, GWENDOLYN. *A Broadside Treasury.* Detroit: Broadside, 1971.

_____. *Jump Bad: A New Chicago Anthology.* Detroit: Broadside, 1971.

BROWN, STERLING A, and ARTHUR P. DAVIS. *The Negro Caravan.* New York: Dryden, 1941; Arno, 1969, reprint.

CALVERTON, VICTOR F., ed. *Anthology of American Negro Literature.* New York: Modern Library, 1929.

CHAMETZKY, JULES, and SIDNEY KAPLAN, eds. *Black and White in American Culture.* Amherst: University of Massachusetts Press, 1969.

CHAPMAN, ABRAHAM, ed. *Black Voices.* New York: New American Library, 1968.

_____, ed. *New Black Voices,* New York: New American Library, 1972.

CLARKE, JOHN HENRICK, ed. *Harlem: Voices from the Soul of Black America.* New York: New American Library.

COOMBS, ORDE, ed. *We Speak As Liberators: Young Black Poets.* New York: Dodd, 1970.

CULLEN, COUNTEE, ed. *Caroling Dusk: An Anthology of Verse by Negro Poets.* New York: Harper, 1927; 1974, reprint.

CUNARD, NANCY, ed. *Negro: An Anthology.* London: 1934; New York: Frederick Ungar, 1970, reprint.

CUNEY, WARING, LANGSTON HUGHES, and BRUCE MCWRIGHT. *Lincoln University Poets.* New York: Fine Editions, 1954.

DAVIS, ARTHUR P., and SAUNDERS REDDING, eds. *Cavalcade: Negro American Writing from 1760 to the Present.* Boston: Houghton Mifflin, 1971.

DEE, RUBY. *Glowchild and Other Poems.* New York: Third Press, 1972.

EMANUEL, JAMES A., and THEODORE GROSS, eds. *Dark Symphony.* New York: Free Press, 1968.

GIOVANNI, NIKKI, ed. *Night Comes Softly.* New York: Nik-Tom Publications, 1970.

HAYDEN, ROBERT, ed. *Kaleidoscope: Poems by American Negro Poets.* New York Harcourt, 1967.

HAYDEN, ROBERT, DANIEL BURROWS, and FREDERICK LAPIDIES, eds. *Afro-American Literature: An Introduction.* New York: Harcourt, 1971.

HENDERSON, STEPHEN *Understanding the New Black Poetry.* New York: Morrow, 1973.

HILL, HERBERT, ed. *Soon One Morning: New Writing by American Negroes 1940-1962.* New York: Knopf, 1968.

HUGGINS, NATHAN I., ed. *Voices from the Harlem Renaissance.* New York: Oxford, 1976.

HUGHES, LANGSTON, ed. *La Poesie Negro Americaine.* Paris: Editions Seghers, 1966.

_____, ed. *New Negro Poets U.S.A.* Bloomington: Indiana University Press, 1964.

HUGHES, LANGSTON, and Arna Bontemps. *The Poetry of the Negro 1746-1970,* rev. ed. New York: Doubleday, 1970.

JOHNSON, CHARLES S., ed. *Ebony and Topaz: A Collection.* New York: National Urban League, 1927.

JOHNSON, JAMES WELDON, ed. *The Book of American Negro Poetry,* rev. ed. New York: Harcourt, 1931.

JONES, LEROI, and LARRY NEAL, eds. *Black Fire: An Anthology of Afro-American Writing.* New York: Morrow, 1968.

JORDON, JUNE, ed. *Soulscript: Afro-American Poetry.* New York: Doubleday, 1970.

KERLIN, ROBERT T., ed. *Negro Poets and Their Poems,* 2nd ed. Washington, D.C.: Associated, 1935.

KING, WOODIE, ed. *Black Spirits.* New York: Random House, 1972.

_____, ed, *The Forerunners: Black Poets in America.* Washington, D.C.: Howard University Press, 1975.

KNIGHT, ETHERIDGE, ed. *Black Voices from Prison.* New York: Pathfinder, 1970.

LOCKE, ALAIN, ed. *The New Negro: An Interpretation.* New York: Boni, 1925; New York: Arno, 1968, reprint.

LONG RICHARD A., and EUGENIA COLLIER. *Afro-American Writing: An Anthology of Prose and Poetry,* 2 vols. New York: New York University Press, 1972.

MAJOR, CLARENCE, ed. *The New Black Poetry.* New York: International, 1969.

MILLER, ADAM DAVID, ed. *Dices and Black Bones: Black Voices of the Seventies.* Boston: Houghton Mifflin, 1970.

MURPHY, BEATRICE, ed. *Ebony Rhythm.* New York: Exposition, 1948.

_____, ed, *Today's Negro Vioces: An Anthology by Young Negro Poets,* New York: Messner, 1970.

PATTERSON LINDSY, ed. *An Introduction to Black Literature in America from 1746 to the Present.* New York: Publishers Co., 1968.

_____, ed, *A Rock Against the Wind: Black Love Poems.* New York: Dodd, 1973.

PERKINS, EUGENE, ed. *Black Expressions: An Anthology of New Black Poets.* Chicago: Conda, 1967.

POOL, ROSEY E., ed. *Beyond the Blues: New Poems by American Negroes.* Kent, England: Lympne, 1962.

PORTER, DOROTHY, ed. *Early Negro Writing 1760-1837.* Boston: Beacon Press, 1971.

RANDALL, DUDLEY, and MARGRET BURROUGHS, eds. *For Malcolm.* Detroit: Broadside Press, 1969.

_____, eds, *The Black Poets.* New York: Bantam, 1971.

REDMOND, EUGENE, ed. *Sides of the River: A Mini Anthology of Black Writing.* Oberlin, Ohio: Author, 1969.

ROBINSON, WILLIAM H. *Early Black American Poets.* Dubuque: Wm. C. Brown and Co., 1969.

SANCHEZ, SONIA, ed. *Three Hundred and Sixty Degrees of Blackness Comin' At You.* New York: 5x Publishing Co. 1971.

STADLER, QUANDRA PRETTYMAN. *Out of Our Lives: A Selection of Contemporary Black Fiction.* Washington, D.C.: Howard University Press, 1976.

TURNER DARWIN, ed. *Black American Literature: Poetry.* Columbus Ohio: Merrill, 1970.

WILENZ TED, and TOM WEATHERLEY, eds. *Natural Process: An Anthology of New Black Poetry.* New York: Hill and Wang, 1970.

Autobiography

ALI, MUHAMMAD. *The Greatest: My Own Story.* New York: Ballentine, 1976.

ARMSTRONG HENRY. *Gloves, Glory and God.* Westwood, N.J.: Fleming Revell, 1956.

ARMSTRONG, LOUIS. *Sachmo: My Life in New Orleans.* Englewood Cliffs, N.J.: Prentice-Hall, 1954.

ASHE, ARTHUR, JR. *Advantage Ashe.* New York: Coward-McCann, 1976.

BAILEY, PEARL. *The Raw Pearl.* New York: Harcourt, 1968.

BARTON, REBECCA C. *Witnesses for Freedom: Negro Americans in Autobiography.* New York: Harper, 1948.

BECHET, SIDNEY. *Treat it Gentle.* New York: Hill and Wang, 1960.

BECKWOURTH, JAMES P. *The Life and Adventures of James P. Beckwourth.* Ed. by Bernard DeVoto. New York: Knopf, 1931.

Black Frontiersman: Jim Beckwourth's Story. New York: Baron, 1970.

BIBB, HENRY. *Narrative of the Life and Adventures of Henry Bibb, an American Slave.* Westport, Ct: Negro Universities Press, reprint.

BLASSINGAME, JOHN W. *Slave Testimony: Two Centuries of Letters Speeches, Interviews and Autobiographies.* Baton Rouge: Louisiana State University Press, 1977.

BRIGNANO, RUSSELL C. *Black Americans in Autobiography.* Durham: N.C.; Duke University Press, 1974.

BROOKS, GWENDOLYN ELIZABETH. *Report from Part One.* Detroit: Broadside Press, 1972.

BROONZY, WILLIAM LEE CONLEY. *Big Bill's Blues*. London: Cassell, 1955.

BROWN, CLAUDE. *Manchild in the Promised Land*. New York: Macmillan, 1965.

BROWN, HUBERT GEEROID (RAP). *Die Nigger Die*. New York: Dial, 1969.

BROWN, JIMMY. *Off My Chest*. New York: Doubleday, 1964.

BUTTERFIELD, STEPHEN. *Black Autobiography*. Amherst: University of Massachusetts Press, 1974.

CLAYTON, HORACE. *Long Old Road*. New York: Trident, 1965.

CHISHOLM, SHIRLEY. *Unbought and Ublossed*. Boston: Houghton Mifflin, 1970.

DOUGLASS, FREDERICK. *The Life and Times of Frederick Douglass*. Hartford, Conn.: Park Publishing Co. 1881; Collin Books, 1962, reprint.

DuBOIS, W. E. B. *The Autobiography of W. E. B. DuBois*. New York: International, 1968.

DUNHAM, KATHERINE. *A Touch of Innocence* New York: Harcourt, 1959.

FLIPPER, HENRY OSSIAN. *The Colored Cadet At West Point*. New York: Homer Lee and Co., 1978; Arno Press, 1969, reprint.

GIBBS, MIFFLIN WISTER. *Shadow and Light*. New York: Arno, 1968.

GIBSON, ALTHEA. *I Always Wanted to Be Somebody*. New York: Harper 1958.

GIOVANNI, Nikki. *Gemini*, Indianapolis: Bobbs-Merrill, 1971.

HARRIS, THEODORE D. *Negro Frontiersman: The Western Memoirs of Henry O. Flipper*. El Paso: Texas Western College Press, 1963.

HERNDON, ANGELO. *Let Me Live*. New York: Random House, 1937.

HUGHES, LANGSTON. *The Big Sea*. New York: Knopf. 1940.

_____. *I Wonder as I Wander*. New York: Rinehart, 1956.

HURSTON, ZORA NEAL *Dust Tracks on a Road*. Philadelphia: Lippincott, 1942; 1971, reprint.

JOHNSON, JAMES WELDON. *Along This Way: The Autobiography of James Weldon Johnson*. New York: Vikings, 1933

LESTER, JULIUS. *All is Well*. New York: Morrow, 1976.

LOVE, NAT. *The Life and Adventures of Nat Love*. New York: Arno Press, 1968.

MALVIN, JOHN. *North into Freedom: The Autobiography of John Malvin Free Negro 1795-1880*. Cleveland: The Press of Western Reserve University, 1968.

MAYS, BENJAMIN E. *Born to Rebel*. New York: Scribner, 1972.

MAYS, WILLIE. *Born to Play Ball*. New York: Putnam, 1955.

MULZAC, HUGH N. *A Star to Steer By*. New York: International, 1963.

NEWTON, HUEY P. *Revolutionary Suicide* New York: Harcourt, 1973.

NICOLS, CHARLES HAROLD. *Many Thousand Gone: The Slaves' Account of Their Bondage and Freedom*. Bloomington: Indiana University Press, 1963.

NORTHRUPT, SOLOMON. *Twelve Years a Slave*. Baton Rouge: Louisiana State University Press, 1968.

OWENS, JESSE. *Blackthink: My Life as a Black and White Man*. New York: Morrow, 1970.

PAIGE, LEROY. *Maybe I'll Pitch Forever*. New York: Doubleday, 1962.

PENNINGTON, JAMES W. C. *The Fugitive Blacksmith* 3rd ed. Reprint of 1850 ed. Westport, Ct.: Negro Universities Press, 1963.

ROBESON, PAUL. *Here I Stand*. New York: Othello Associates, 1958.

SAYERS, GAYLE. *I am Third*. New York: Viking, 1970.

SCHUYLER, GEORGE S. *Black and Conservative*. New Rochelle, N.Y.: Arlington House, 1966.

SEAL, BOBBY G. *Seize the Time*. New York: Random House, 1970.

SHORT, ROBERT WALTRYS (BOBBY). *Black and White Baby*. New York: Dodd, Mead. 1971.

SMITH, SIDONIA. *Where I'm Bound: Patterns of Slavery and Freedom in Black American Autobiography*. Westport, Conn.: Greenwood Press, 1976.

TARRY, ELLEN. *The Third Door: The Autobiography of an American Negro Woman*. New York: McKay, 1955.

TERRELL, MARY CHURCH. *A Colored Woman in a White World*. Washington, D.C.: Ransdell, 1940.

THOMPSON, ERA BELL. *American Daughter*. Chicago: University of Chicago Press, 1946.

_____. *Africa: Land of My Fathers*. New York: Doubleday, 1954.

VINCENT, THEODORE G., ed. *Voices of a Black Nation: Political Journalism in the Harlem Renaissance*. San Francisco: Ramparts, 1973.

WASHINGTON, BOOKER T. *Up From Slavery*. New York: Doubleday, 1963.

WATERS, ETHEL. *His Eye is on the Sparrow*. New York: Doubleday, 1951.

_____. *To Me Its Wonderful*. New York: Harper, 1972.

WELLS, IDA B. *Crusade for Justice*. Chicago: University of Chicago Press. 1970.

WHITE, WALTER. *A Man Called White*. New York: Viking, 1948.

X, MALCOLM, with ALEX HALEY. *The Autobiography of Malcolm X*. New York: Grove Press, 1965.

Bibliography

Afro-American, The. New York: Bellwether Publishing Co., 1976.

ARATA, FISHER S., and NICHOLAS J. ROTOLI. *Black American Playwrights, 1800 to the present: A Bibliography.* Metuchen, N.J.: Scarecrow, 1976.

BASKIN, WADE, and Richard Runes. *Dictionary of Black Culture.* New York: Philosophical Library, 1973.

BERGMAN, PETER M. *The Chronological History of the Negro in America.* New York: Harper, 1969.

BROOKS, ALEXANDER D. *Civil Rights and Civil Liberties in the United States: An Annotated Bibliography.* New York: Civil Liberties Educational Foundation, 1962.

CHAPMAN, ABRAHAM. *The Negro in American Literature: A Bibliography of Literature by and about Negro Americans.* Chicago: The National Council of Teachers of English, 1966.

DAVIS, JOHN P. *The American Negro Reference Book.* Englewood Cliffs, N.J.: Prentice-Hall, 1966.

DEODENE, FRANK and WILLIAM P. FRENCH. *Black American Fiction Since 1952.* Chatham, N.J.: Chatham Bookseller, 1970.

DICKINSON, DONALD C. *A Bio-Bibliography of Langston Hughes, 1902-1967.* Hamden, Conn.: Archon Books, 1972.

DODDS, BARBARA. *Negro Literature For High School Students.* Chicago: The National Council of Teachers of English, 1968.

DUMOND, DWIGHT LOWELL. *A Bibliography of Anti-Slavery in America.* Ann Arbor: University of Michigan Press, 1961.

Ebony Handbook, The. Chicago: Johnson Publishing Co., 1976.

FINNEY, FAMES E. *The Long Road to Now: A Bibliography of Material Relating to the American Blackman.* Farmingdale, N.Y.: C.W. Clark Co., 1969.

FISHER, RUSSELL G. "James Baldwin: A Bibliography, 1974-1962." In *Bulletin of Bibliography,* vol 24, January-April 1965, pp. 127-130.

INDIANA UNIVERSITY LIBRARIES. *Focus: Black America Bibliography Series.* Bloomington: Indiana University Libraries, 1969.

International Library of Negro Life and History. New York: Publishers Co., 1967.

IRWIN, LEONARD B. *Black Studies: A Bibliography.* Brooklawn, N.J.: McKinely, 1973.

JACKSON, MILES, JR. *A Bibliography of Negro History and Culture for Young Readers.* Pittsburgh: University of Pittsburgh Press, 1968.

JAHNEINZ, JOHN *A Bibliography of Neo-African Literature: From Africa, America and the Caribbean.* New York: Praeger, 1965.

JENKINS, BETTY LANIER, and SUSAN PHILLIS. *Black Separatism: A Bibliography.* Westport, Conn: Greenwood Press, 1976.

KAISER, ERNEST. "The History of Negro History." *Negro Digest,* February 1968, pp. 10-15.

LEFFAL, DELORES C., comp. *The Black Church: An Annotated Bibliography.* Washington, D.C.: Minority Research Center, 1973.

MC PHERSON, JAMES M. et. al. *Blacks in America; Bibliographical Essays.* New York: Doubleday, 1971.

MATTHEWS, GERALDINE O. *Black American Writers, 1773-1949: A Bibliography and Union List.* Boston: G.K. Hall, 1975.

MEYER, JON K. *Bibliography of the Urban Crisis.* Washington, D.C.: Government Printing Office, 1969.

MILLER, ELIZABETH W. *The Negro In America: A Bibliography.* Cambridge, Mass.: Harvard University Press, 1966.

The Negro Handbook. Chicago: Johnson Publishing Co., 1966.

NEW JERSEY LIBRARY ASSOCIATION. *New Jersey and The Negro: A Bibliography, 1715-1966.* Trenton, N.J.: MacCrellish and Quigley Co., 1967.

NEW YORK PUBLIC LIBRARY. *The Negro in the United States: A List of Significant Books,* 9th rev. ed. New York: New York Public Library, 1965.

—————. *The Negro in the United States: A List of Significant Books: A Supplement to the 9th rev. ed.* New York: New York Public Library, 1968.

PLOSKI, HARRY A., and ERNEST KAISER. *The Negro Almanac,* 2nd ed. New York: Bellwether, 1971.

PORTER, DOROTHY B. "Early American Negro Writings: A Bibliographical Study." In *Bibliographical Society of America.* Papers, vol 39. 1945, pp. 192-268.

—————. *The Negro in the United States: A Working Bibliography.* Ann Arbor: Mich. University Microfilms, 1969.

—————. *North American Negro Poets: A Bibliographical Checklist of Their Writings (1760-1944)* New York: Burt Franklin, 1963, reprint.

Reference Library of Black America. New York: Bellwether, 1971.

ROLLINS T.G., C.F. MYERS, and ESTHER S. ARATA. *Black American Writers, Past and Present: A Biographical and Bibliographical Dictionary.* Metuchen, N.J.; Scarecrow, 1975.

ROLLINS, CHARLEMAE H. *We Build Together: A Readers Guide to Negro Life and Literature for Elementary and High School Use.* Chicago: National Council of Teachers of English, 1967.

Ross, Frank A., and Louise V. Kennedy. *A Bibliography of Negro Migration*. New York: Columbia University Press, 1934.

Rush T. G., C. F. Myers, and Esther S. Arata. *Black American Writers, Past and Present: A Biographical and Bibliographical Dictionary*. Metuchen, N.J.; Scarecrow, 1975.

Salk, Erwin A. *A Layman's Guide to Negro History*. rev. ed. New York: McGraw-Hill, 1967.

Sanders, Charles L., comps. *Directory: National Black Organizations*. New York: Afro-Am, 1972.

Schatz Walter, comp. *Directory of Afro-American Resources*. New York: R.R. Bowker, 1970.

Smythe, Mabel. *The Black American Reference Book*. Englewood Cliffs, N.J.: Prentice-Hall, 1976.

Spangler, Earl. *Bibliography of Negro History: Selected and Annotated Entries*. Minneapolis: Ross and Haines, 1963.

Thompson, Edgar T. *Race and Region: A Descriptive Bibliography Compiled with Special Reference to the Relations between Whites and Negroes in the United States*. Chapel Hill: University of North Carolina Press, 1949.

Turner, Darwin T., comp. *Afro-American Writers*. Northbrook, Ill.: AHM, 1970.

Weinberg Meyer. *School Integration: A Bibliography*. Chicago: Integrated Education Association, 1967.

Welsch, Erwin K. *The Negro in the United States: A Research Guide*. Bloomington: Indiana University Press, 1965.

West, Earl H. *A Bibliography of Doctoral Research on the Negro 1933-1966*. Ann Arbor, Mich.: University Microfilms, 1969.

Westmoreland, Guy T., Jr *An Annotated Guide to Basic Reference Books on the Black American Experience*. Wilmington, Del.: Scholarly Resources, Inc., 1974.

Whiteman, Maxwell. *A Century of Fiction by American Negroes 1853-1952. A Descriptive Bibliography*. Philadelphia: Albert Saifer, 1968, reprint.

Work, Monroe N. *A Bibliography of the Negro In Africa and America*. New York: Octagon Books, 1965, reprint.

Biography

ANDERSON, JERVIS, *A. Philip Randolph: A Biographical Portrait.* New York: Harcourt, 1973.

ANDERSON, JOHN WEIR. *Eisenhower, Brownell and the Congress: The Tangled Origin of the Civil Rights Bill of 1956-57.* Tuscaloosa: University of Alabama Press.

BEARDEN, ROMARE. *Six Black Masters of American Art.* New York: Doubleday, 1972.

BEASLEY, DELIAH. *The Negro Trail Blazers of California.* San Francisco: Rand E. Research Associates, 1969, reprint.

BEDINI, SILVIO A. *The Life of Benjamin Banneker.* New York: Scribners, 1972.

BERNARD, JACQUELINE *Journey Toward Freedom; The Story of Sojourner Truth.* New York: Norton, 1963.

BONTEMPS, ARNA. *Young Booker.* New York: Dodd, 1972.

BRODERICK, FRANCIS L. *W. E. B. DuBois: Negro Leader in a Time of Crisis.* New York: Crowell, 1959.

CASH, EARL. *John A. Williams: The Evolution of a Black Writer,* New York: Third Press, 1974.

COLE, MARIA. *Nat King Cole.* New York: Morrow, 1971.

CRONON, E. DAVID. *Black Moses: The Story of Marcus Garvey and the Universal Negro Improvement Association.* Madison: University of Wisconsin Press, 1969.

CUTLER, JOHN H., ed. *Brooke: Biography of a Senator.* Indianapolis: Bobbs-Merrill, 1972.

DUBOIS, SHIRLEY GRAHAM. *His Day is Marching On.* New York: Lippincott, 1971.

ELLIOTT, LAURENCE. *George Washington Carver.* Englewood Cliffs, N.J.: Prentice-Hall, 1967.

EMBREE, EDWIN. *Thirteen Against the Odds.* New York: Viking, 1945.

FABRE, MICHEL. *The Unfinished Quest of Richard Wright.* New York: Morrow, 1973.

FARRISON, WILLIAM E. *William Wells Brown.* Chicago: University of Chicago Press, 1969.

FAX, ELTON. *Garvey: The Story of a Pioneer Nationalist.* New York: Dodd, Mead, 1972.

FELTON, HAROLD. *William Rose: Negro Trail Blazer.* New York: Dodd, 1965.

——. *Jim Beckwourth: Negro Mountain Man.* New York: Dodd, 1966.

FONER, PHILLIP S. *Frederick Douglass A Biography.* New York: Citadel Press, 1964.

FOX, STEPHEN R. *Guardian of Boston: William Monroe Trotter.* New York: Atheneum, 1971.

GAMOND, PETER. *Scott Joplin and the Ragtime Era.* New York: St. Martin's Press, 1975.

GAYLE, ADDISON, JR. *Oak and Ivy: A Biography of Paul Laurence Dunbar.* New York: Doubleday, 1971.

GILLIAM, DOROTHY BUTLER. *Paul Robeson: All American.* Washington, D.C.: New Republic Book Co., 1976.

GILMORE, AL-TONY. *Bad Nigger: The Impact of Jack Johnson.* Port Washington, N.Y.: Kennikat Press, 1975.

GOLDMAN, PETER. *The Death and Life of Malcolm X.* New York: Harper, 1973.

HABER, LAWS. *Black Pioneers of Science and Invention.* New York: Harcourt, 1972.

HAMILTON, VIRGINIA. *W. E. B. DuBois.* New York: Crowell, 1972.; _____. *Paul Robeson.* New York: Harper, 1974.

HARLAN, LOUIS. *Booker T. Washington: The Making of a Black Leader.* New York: Oxford, 1972.

HARRIS, SHELDON H. *Paul Cuffee and the African Return.* New York: Simon and Schuster, 1972.

HASKINS, JAMES . *A Piece of the Power: Four Black Mayors.* New York: Dial Press 1972.

_____. *Profiles in Black Power.* New York: Doubleday, 1972.

_____. *Pinckney Benton Stewart Pinchback.* New York: Macmillan, 1973.

HELM, MACKINLEY. *Angel Mo and Her Son Roland Hayes.* Boston: Little, Brown, 1942.

HUDSON, THEODORE R. *From LeRoi Jones to Amiri Baraka.* Durham, N.C.: Duke University Press, 1973.

JONES, HETTIE *Big Star Fallin' Mama: Five Women in Black Music.* New York: Viking, 1974.

LEVY, EUGENE. *James Weldon Johnson.* Chicago: University of Chicago Press, 1973.

LEWIS, DAVID. *Martin Luther King.* New York: Praeger, 1970.

MANN, PEGGY. *Ralph Bunche, UN Peace Maker.* New York: Coward, 1975.

MARSHALL, HERBERT, and MILDRED STOCK. *Ira Aldridge: The Negro Tragedian.* New York: Macmillan, 1959.

MATHEWS, MARCIA M. *Richard Allen.* Baltimore: Helicon Press, 1963. _____. *Henry Ossawa Tranner.* Chicago: University of Chicago Press, 1969.

MELTZER, MILTON. *Langston Hughes.* New York: Crowell, 1968.

OTTLEY, ROI. *The Lonely Warrior: The Life and Time of Robert Abbott*. Chicago: Henry Regnery, 1955.

PARKHILL, FORBES. *Mister Barney Ford*. Denver: Sage Books, 1963.

PEPE PHIL. *Come Out Smokin: Joe Frazier the Champ Nobody Knew*. New York: Coward, 1972.

PONTON, M. M. *Life and Times of Henry M. Turner*. New York: Negro Universities Press, 1970.

RUDWICK, ELLIOT. *W. E. B. DuBois: Propagandist of the Negro Protest*. New York: Atheneum, 1968.

TALMADGE, MARIAN, and IRIS GILMORE. *Barney Ford: Black Baron*. New York: Dodd, 1973.

THORNBROUGH, EMMA LOU. *T. Thomas Fortune*. Chicago: University of Chicago Press. 1972.

ULLMAN VICTOR. *Martin R. Delaney*. Boston: Beacon Press, 1971.

WEBB, CONSTANCE. *Richard Wright*. New York: Putnam, 1968. *Who's Who in Colored America, 1927-1950.*

WILLIAMS, JOHN A. *The Most Native of Sons. A Biography of Richard Wright*. New York: Doubleday, 1970.

Black Art

ALBRIGHT, THOMAS. "The Blackmans Art Gallery." *Art Gallery*, April 1970.

ANDREWS, BENNY. "On Understanding Black Art." *New York Times*, June 21, 1970. "And the Migrants Kept Coming." *Fortune*, November 1941.

"Artist in an Age of Revolution: A Symposium." *Arts and Society*, Summer and Fall 1968.

BEARDEN, ROMARE. "The Negro Artist and Modern Art." *Opportunity*, December 1934.

_____. and Harry Henderson. *Six Black Masters of American Art*. New York: Doubleday, 1972.

_____. "Black Artists in America: A Symposium,." *Metropolitan Museum Bulletin*, January 1969.

_____. "Black Lamps: White Mirrors." *Time*. October 3, 1969.

BLODGETT, GEOFFREY. "John Mercer Langston and the Case of Edmonia Lewis, Oberlin, 1862." *Journal of Negro History*, July 1968.

BOSTON MUSEUM OF FINE ARTS. *Afro-American Artists, New York and Boston.* Boston: Museum of Fine Arts, 1970.

BOWLING, FRANK. "Black Art." *Arts Magazine,* December 1969; January 1969.

CAMPBELL, LAURENCE. "The Flowering of Thomas Sills." *Art News,* March 1972.

CHASE, JUDITH WRAGG. *Afro-American Art and Craft.* New York: Van Nostrand, 1971.

DAVIS, DOUGLAS. "What is Black Art?" *Newsweek,* June 1, 1970.

DOVER, CEDRICK. *American Negro Art.* New York: New York Graphic, 1960.

DRISKELL, DAVID C. *Two Centuries of Black Art.* New York: Knopf, 1976.

ELLISON, RALPH. "Romare Bearden: Paintings and Projections." *Crisis,* March 1970.

FAX, ELTON. *17 Black Artists.* New York: Dodd, Mead, 1971.

_____. *Black Artists of the New Generation.* New York: Dodd, 1977.

FINE, ELSA HONIG. *The Afro-American Artist.* New York: Holt, Rinehart, Winston, 1973.

GENOVESE, EUGENE. "Harlem on His Back." *Artform,* February 1969.

GHENT, HENRI. "Forum: Black Creativity in Quest of An Audience." *Art in America,* May, June 1970.

GLUECK, GRACE. "A Brueghel from Harlem." *New York Times,* February 22, 1970.

HUNTER, WILBUR H., JR. "Joshua Johnson: 18th Century Negro Artist." *American Collector,* February 1948.

KILLENS, JOHN O. "The Artist in the Black University." *The Black Scholar,* November 1969.

KRAMER, HILTON. "Black Experience and Modernist Art." *New York Times,* February 19, 1970.

LE GRACE, BENSON G. "Sam Gilliam: Certain Attitudes." *Artform,* September 1970.

LEWIS, SAMELLA S., and RUTH WADDY. *Black Artists on Art,* 2 vols. Los Angeles: Contemporary Crafts, 1969, 1971.

LOCKE, ALAIN. "American Negro As Artist." *American Magazine of Art,* September 1931.

_____. *The Negro in Art.* New York: Hacker Art Books, 1968, reprint.

MC CAUSLAND, ELIZABETH. "Jacob Lawrence." *Magazine of Art,* November 1945.

MCILVAINE, DONALD. "Art and Soul." *Art Gallery,* April 1970.

MATTHEWS, MARCIA M. *Henry Ossawa Tanner.* Chicago: University of Chicago Press, 1969.

MELLOW, JAMES. "Black Community, the White Art World." *New York Times,* June 9, 1969.

NEAL, LARRY. "Any Day Now: Black Art and Black Liberation." *Ebony,* August 1970.

NORA, FRANCOISE. "From Another Country." *Art News,* March 1972.

PATTERSON, LINDSAY *The Negro in Music and Art.* New York: Publishers Co., 1968.

PERREAULT, J. "Henry Ossawa Tanner." *Art News,* December 1967.

PINCUS-WITTEN, ROBERT. "Black Artists of the 30's." *Artform,* February 1969.

PORTER, JAMES. "Afro-American Art at Flood Tide." *Arts and Society,* Summer-Fall 1968.

—————. *Modern Negro Art.* New York: Dryden Press, 1943.

RODMAN, SELDON. *Horace Pippin: A Negro Painter in America.* New York: Quadrangle, 1947.

ROSE, BARBARA. "Black Art in America." *Art in America,* September-October 1970.

SIEGEL, JEANNE. "Robert Thompson and the Old Masters." *Harvard Art Review,* Winter 1967.

SPRIGGS, EDWARD S. "The Studio Museum in Harlem." *Art Gallery,* April 1970.

—————. "Symposium Black Art: What is It? *Art Gallery,* April 1970.

—————. "What is Black Art?" *Time,* July 1, 1970.

WOODRUFF, HALE. "My Meeting With Henry O. Tanner." *Crisis,* January 1970. ·

Black Church

BRAGG GEORGE F. *History of the Afro-American Group of the Episcopal Church.* New York: Johns Reprint, 1968.

CLEAGE, ALBERT. *Black Christian Nationalism.* New York: Morrow, 1972.

CONE, JAMES H. *Black Theology and Black Power.* New York: Seabury Press, 1969.

—————. *Black Theology of Liberation.* Philadelphia: Lippincott, 1970.

DESAI, RAM, ed. *The Lord Ain't White No More.* Chicago: Swallow Press, 1970.

GEORGE, Carol V. R. *Segregated Sabbaths: Richard Allen and the Rise of Independent Black Churches 1760-1840.* New York: Oxford, 1973.

GILLARD, JOHN T. *The Catholic Church and the American Negro.* New York: Johnson Reprint, 1968.

HOLLAND, DEWITTE. *Preaching in America.* Nashville: Abingdon, 1969.

HOUGH, J. C. *Black Power and White Protestants: A Christian Response to the New Negro Pluralism.* New York: Oxford, 1968.

JOHNSON, CLIFTON, ed. *God Struck Me Dead.* Philadelphia: Pilgrim Press, 1969.

LECKY, R. S., and H. E. WRIGHT, eds. *Black Manifesto: Religion, Racism and Reparation.* New York: Sheed, 1969.

MITCHELL, HENRY H. *Black Preaching.* Philadelphia: Lippincott, 1970.

MURRY, ANDREW E. *Presbyterians and the Negro.* Philadelphia: Presbyterian Historical Society. 1966.

NELSON, H. M. *Black Church in America,* New York; Basic Books, 1971.

PAYNE, DANIEL A. *Recollections of Seventy Years.* New York: Arno Press, 1968.

RICHARDSON, HARRY V. *Dark Salvation: The Story of Methodism as It Developed among Blacks in America.* New York: Anchor Press, Doubleday, 1976.

WASHINGTON, JOSEPH R. *Black and White Power Subreption.* Boston, Beacon Press, 1969.

Civil Rights

APTHEKER, HERBERT. *Soul of the Republic.* New York: Marzani, 1964.

BARNET, RICHARD, and JOSEPH GARAI. *Where the States Stand on Civil Rights.* New York: Sterling, 1962.

BERGER, MARROE. *Equality by Statute: Legal Controls over Group Discrimination.* New York: Columbia University Press, 1952.

BERMAN, DANIEL M. *A Bill Becomes Law: The Civil Rights Act of 1960.* New York: Macmillan. 1962.

BERRY, M. *Black Resistence- White Law.* New York: Appleton-Century, 1971.

BICKEL, ALEXANDER M. *Politics and the Warren Court.* New York: Harper, 1965.

BITTKEN, BORIS I. *The Case for Black Reparations*. New York: Random House, 1973.

BLAUSTEIN, ALBERT P. *Civil Rights and the Black American: A Documentary History*. New York: Washington Square Press, 1970.

BRACEY, JOHN H., JR. et al. *Conflict and Competition: Studies in the Black Protest Movement*. Belmont, Cal.: Wadsworth, 1971.

BROOKS, THOMAS R. *The Walls Came Tumbling Down. A History of the Civil Rights Movement 1940-1970*. Englewood Cliffs, N.J.: Prentice-Hall, 1970.

BUREAU OF NATIONAL AFFAIRS. *The Civil Rights Act of 1964: Operations Manual*. Washington, D.C.: Government Printing Office, 1964.

BURKE, JOAN M. *Civil Rights: A Current Guide to the People Organizations and Events*, 2nd ed. New York: R. R. Bowker, 1974.

CABLE, GEORGE W. *The Negro Question: A Selection of Writings on Civil Rights in the South*. New York: Doubleday, 1958.

COUNTRYMAN, VERNON, ed. *Discrimination and the Law*. Chicago: University of Chicago Press, 1965.

COX, ARCHIBALD et al. *Civil Rights, the Constitution and the Courts*. Cambridge, Mass.: Harvard University Press, 1967.

DULLES, FOSTER R. *Civil Rights Commission 1957-1965*. Ann Arbor: University of Michigan Press, 1968.

ETZKOWITZ, HENRY, and GERALD SCHAFLANDER. *Ghetto Crisis: Riots and Reconciliation*. Boston: Little, Brown, 1969.

FAGER, CHARLES E. *Selma 1965*. New York: Scribner, 1974.

FRANKLIN, JOHN H., and ISADORE STARR. *The Negro in Twentieth Century America: A Reader on the Struggle for Civil Rights*. New York: Vantage, 1967.

FRIEDMAN, LEON, ed. *Southern Justice*. New York: Pantheon, 1965.

GARFINKLE, HERBERT. *When Negroes March*. Boston: Atheneum, 1969.

GOLDMAN, PETER. *Civil Rights: The Challenge of the Fourteenth Amendment*, rev. ed. New York: Coward, 1970.

GOVERNMENT PRINTING OFFICE. *To Secure These Rights*. Washington, D.C.: Government Printing Office, 1947.

GRANT, JO ANNE. *Black Protest*. Greenwich, Conn.: Fawcett, 1968.

GREENBERG, JACK. *Race Relations and American Law*. New York: Columbia University Press, 1959.

HANDLIN, OSCAR. *Fire Bell in the Night: The Crisis in Civil Rights*. Boston: Little, Brown, 1964.

HARRIS, ROBERT J. *The Quest for Equality: The Constitution, Con-*

gress and the Supreme Court. Baton Rouge: Louisiana State University Press, 1960.

Hartman, PAUL. Civil Rights and Minorities, 5th ed. New York: Anti-Defamation League, 1962.

HARVEY, JAMES C. Civil Rights During the Johnson Administration. Jackson: University Press of Mississippi, 1973.

HERBERS, JOHN. The Lost Priority. New York: Funk and Wagnalls, 1970.

HUGHES, LANGSTON. Fight for Freedom: The Story of the N.A.A.C.P. New York: Norton, 1962.

JORDON, JUNE. Dry Victories. New York: Holt, Rinehart, Winston, 1972.

KEESINGS. Race Relations in the U.S.A. 1954-1968. New York: Scribner, 1970.

KELLOG, CHARLES F. N.A.A.C.P.: A History of the National Association for the Advancement of Colored People 1909-1920. Baltimore: Johns Hopkins University Press, 1967.

KING, MARTIN LUTHER. Stride Toward Freedom. New York: Harper, 1958.

LEVITAN SAR, A. et al. Still A Dream: The Changing Status of Blacks Since 1960. Cambridge, Mass.: Harvard University Press, 1975.

McGRAW, JAMES R., ed. Up from Nigger. New York: Stein and Day, 1976.

MAJOR, REGINALD. A Panther Is a Black Cat. New York: Morrow, 1971.

MARSHALL, BURKE. Federalism and Civil Rights, New York: Columbia University Press, 1964.

MEIRER, AUGUST. Negro Protest Thought in the 20th Century. Indianapolis: Bobbs-Merrill, 1965.

_____. Black Protest in the Sixties. Chicago: Quandrangle, 1970.

_____. C.O.R.E.: A Study in the Civil Rights Movement 1942-1968. New York: Oxford, 1973.

MILLER, LOREN. The Petitioners: The Story of the Supreme Court of the United States and the Negro. New York: Pantheon, 1966.

NEWMAN, EDWIN. Civil Liberty and Civil Rights. New York: Oceana, 1970.

PARRIS, GUICHARD. Blacks in the City: A History of the National Urban League. Boston: Little, Brown, 1971.

PETTIGREW, THOMAS, ed. Racial Discrimination in the United States. New York: Harper, 1975.

PIOUS, RICHARD M. *Civil Rights and Liberties in the 1970's.* New York: Harper, 1973.

RUSTIN, BAYARD. *Down the Line.* Chicago: Quadrangle, 1971.

_____. *Stratagies for Freedom: The Changing Pattern of Black Protest.* New York: Columbia University Press, 1976.

SOBLE, LESTER A., ed. *Civil Rights 1960-1966.* New York: Facts on File, 1967.

SUTHERLAND, A. E. *Civil Rights and the South: A Symposium.* New York: Da Capo, 1971.

Drama

ABRAMSON, DORIS. *Negro Playwrights in the American Theater, 1925-1959.* New York: Columbia University Press, 1969.

ARCHER, LEONARD C. *Black Images in American Theater.* Nashville: Pageant Press, 1973.

BARAKA IMAMU AMIRI (LEROI JONES). *Black Revolutionary Plays.* Indianapolis: Bobbs-Merrill, 1969.

_____. *Black Quartet.* New York: New American Library, 1970.

BOND, FREDERICK W. *The Negro and Drama.* Washington, D.C.: Associated Publishers, 1940.

BRASMER, WILLIAM et al. *Black Drama: An Anthology.* Columbus, Ohio: Merrill, 1970.

BROWN, STERLING *Negro Poetry and Drama,* New York: Atheneum, 1969.

BULLINS, ED. *Black Theater Magazine.* New York: New Lafayette, 1968-1972.

_____. *Five Plays by Ed Bullins.* Indianapolis: Bobbs-Merrill, 1969.

_____. *New Plays From the Black Theater.* New York: Bantam, 1969.

_____. *The Theme is Blackness.* New York: Morrow, 1973.

CHILDRESS, ALICE. *Black Scenes.* New York: Doubleday, 1971.

COUCH, WILLIAM, JR. *New Black Playwrights.* Baton Rouge: Louisiana State University Press, 1968.

DAVIS, OSSIE. "Flight From Broadway." *Negro Digest,* April 1966.

DENT, THOMAS et al., eds. *The Free Southern Theater.* Indianapolis: Bobbs-Merrill, 1969.

DODSON, OWEN. "Playwrights in Dark Glasses." *Negro Digest,* April 1968.

EDMONDS, RANDOLPH. *The Land of Cotton and Other Plays.* Washington, D.C.: Associated Publishers, 1943.

_____. *Shades and Shadows.* Boston: Meador, 1930.

_____. *Six Plays for a Negro Theater.* Boston: Walter H. Baker, 1934.

FLETCHER, TOM. *100 Years of the Negro in Show Business.* New York: Buidge Co., 1954.

FULLER, HOYT W. "Black Theater in America." *Negro Digest,* April 1968.

HARRISON, PAUL CARTER. *The Drama of Nommo.* New York: Grove Press, 1972.

HATCH, JAMES V., ed. *Black Theater U.S.A.* New York: Free Press, 1974.

_____. *Black Image on the American Stage, A Bibliography of Plays and Musicals 1770-1970.* New York: Drama Book Specialists, 1970.

HUGHES, LANGSTON, and MILTON MELTZER. *Black Magic.* Englewood Cliffs, N.J.: Prentice-Hall, 1968.

KING, WOODIE, and RON MILNER. *Black Drama Anthology.* New York: New American Library, 1971.

LEONARD, CLAIRE, "Dark Drama." *Negro Digest,* August 1944.

LOCKE, ALAIN ed. *Plays of Negro Life.* New York: Harper, 1927.

LONG, RICHARD A. "Crisis of Consciousness." *Negro Digest,* May 1968.

MILNER, RON. "Black Magic: Black Art." *Negro Digest,* April 1967.

MITCHELL, LOFTEN. *Black Drama: The Story of the American Negro in the Theater.* New York: Hawthorne, 1967.

_____. *Voices of the Black Theater.* Clifton, N.J. James T. White Co., 1976.

MOLETTE, CARLTON W. II. "The First Afro-American Theater." *Negro Digest,* September 1970.

NEAL, LARRY. "The Black Arts Movement." *Drama Review,* Summer 1968.

OLIVER, CLINTON, and STEPHANIE SILLS. *Contemporary Black Drama.* New York: Scribner, 1971.

PATTERSON, LINDSAY. *Anthology of the American Negro in the Theater.* New York: Publishers Co., 1967.

_____. *Black Theater.* New York: Dodd, 1971.

REARDON, WILLIAM, and THOMAS PAWLEY. *The Black Teacher and the Dramatic Arts.* Westport, Conn.: Negro Universities Press, 1970.

RICHARDSON, WILLIS. *The Kings Dilemma and Other Plays for Children.* New York: Exposition 1956.

_____. and May Miller. *Negro History in Thirteen Plays.* Washington, D.C.: Associated Publishers, 1935.

_____. *Plays and Pageants from the Life of the Negro.* Washington, D.C.: Associated Publishers, 1936.

SMALLEY, WEBSTER. *Five Plays by Langston Hughes.* Bloomington: Indiana University Press, 1968.

TOLL, ROBERT C. *Blacking Up: The Minstrel Show in the Nineteenth Century.* New York: Oxford, 1974.

TURNER, DARWIN T. "The Negro Dramatist's Image of the Universe."*CLA Journal,* December 1961.

_____. "Negro Playwrights and the Urban Negro." *CLA Journal,* September 1968.

_____. "Past and Present in Negro Drama." *American Negro Literature Forum,* Summer 1968.

_____. *Black Drama in America: An Anthology.* New York: Fawcett, 1971.

TURNER, SHERRY. "An Overview of the New Black Arts." *Freedomways,* no. 9, 1969.

WARD, THEODORE. "The South Side Center of the Performing Arts, Inc." *Black Theater,* no. 2, 1969.

X, MARVIN. "An Interview with Le Roi Jones." *Black Theater,* no. 2 1968.

Economics and Labor

ALLEN, ROBERT. *Black Awakening in Capitalist America.* New York: Doubleday, 1969.

AMERICAN ASSEMBLY. *Black Economic Development: Report of the 35th American Assembly Arden House.* New York: Harriman, 1969.

BAILEY, R. W. *Black Business Enterprise: Historical and Contemporary Perspectives.* New York: Basic Books, 1971.

BLOOM, GORDON F. *Black Capitalism and Black Supermarkets.* Cambridge, MIT Press, 1969.

BLUMROSEN, ALFRED W. *Black Employment and the Law.* New Brunswick, N.J.: Rutgers University Press, 1971.

BRACEY, JOHN H., Jr., et al. *Black Workers and Organized Labor.* Belmont, Cal. Wadsworth, 1971.

BRAMWELL, JONATHAN. *Courage in Crisis: The Black Professional Today.* Indianapolis: Bobbs-Merrill, 1973.

CROSS, THEODORE L. *Black Capitalism* New York: Atheneum, 1969.

DuBois, W. E. B. *The Negro in Business.* New York: Arno Press 1968, reprint.

FOLEY, EUGENE P. *The Achieving Ghetto.* Washington, D.C.: National Press, 1968.

FONER, PHILLIP. *Organized Labor and the Black Worker.* New York: Praeger, 1974.

FORTUNE, THOMAS. *Black and White: Land, Labor and Politics in the South.* Chicago: Johnson Publishing Co., 1970, reprint.

GELBER, STEVEN M. *Black Men and Businessmen.* Port Washington, N.Y.: Kennikat, 1974.

GIBSON, PARKER D. *The $30 Billion Dollar Negro.* New York: Macmillan, 1969.

GINZBERG, ELI. *The Negro Potential.* New York: Columbia University Press, 1956.

_____. *Business Leadership and the Negro Crisis.* New York: McGraw-Hill, 1968.

HADDAD, WILLIAM, and DOUGLAS PUGH. *Black Economic Development.* Englewood Cliffs, N.J.: Prentice-Hall, 1969.

HARRIS, ABRAM, L. *The Negro as Capitalist: A Study of Banking and Business among American Negroes.* Philadelphia: American Academy of Political and Social Science, 1936.

HARRISON, BENNETT. *Education and Training in the Black Ghetto.* Baltimore: Johns Hopkins University Press, 1973.

HAYNES, GEORGE E. *The Negro at Work in New York City.* New York: AMS Press, 1968, reprint.

HENRI, FLORETTE. *Black Migration: Movement North 1900-1920.* New York: Doubleday, 1976.

HUND, J. *Black Entrepreneurship.* Belmont, Cal.: Wadsworth, 1970.

JACOBSON, JULIUS, ed. *The Negro and the American Labor Movement.* New York: Doubleday, 1968.

JONES, E. H. *Black Businessman in America: His Beginning, His Problems, His Future.* New York: Grossett, 1971.

KAIN, JOHN F. *Race and Poverty: The Economics of Discrimination.* Englewood Cliffs, N.J.: Prentice-Hall, 1969.

KENTUCKY COMMISSION ON HUMAN RIGHTS. *Black Business in Louisville.* Louisville, Ky.: Kentucky Commission on Human Rights, 1968.

MARSHALL, F. RAY. *The Negro Worker.* New York: Random House,

MARSHALL, F. RAY and VERNON BRIGGS. *The Negro and Apprenticeship.* Baltimore: Johns Hopkins University Press, 1967.

NORGEN, PAUL H., and SAMUEL HILL. *Toward Fair Employment.* New York: Columbia University Press, 1964.

OAK, VISHNU. *The Negro's Adventure in Business.* Yellow Springs, Ohio: Antioch Press, 1949.

PURCELL, T. VINCENT, and G. F. CAVANAUGH. *Blacks in the Industrial World: Issues for the Manager.* New York: Free Press, 1973.

RITTENOUER, R. LYNN. *Black Employment in the South: The Case of the Federal Government.* Austin: Bureau of Business Research, University of Texas, 1976.

ROSS, ARTHUR, and HERBERT HILL. *Employment, Race and Poverty.* New York: Harcourt, 1969.

RUCHAMES, LOUIS. *Race, Jobs and Politics.* New York: Negro Universities Press, 1972, reprint.

RUTLEDGE, AARON L., and GERTRUDE GASS. *19 Negro Men: Personality and Manpower Retraining.* San Francisco: Jossey Bass, 1967.

SHAW, CAROLYN BELL. *Economics of the Ghetto.* New York: Pegasus, 1970.

SOHIN, DENNIS P. *Working Poor: Minority Workers in Low-Wage, Low Skill Jobs.* Port Washington, N.Y.: Kennikat, 1974.

SPERO, STERLING D., and ABRAM L. HARRIS. *The Black Worker: The Negro and the Labor Movement.* New York: Atheneum, 1968.

SULLIVAN, LEON H. *Build Brother Build.* Philadelphia: Macrae-Smith, 1969.

SWIFT, WILLIAM F. *The Negro in the Offshore Maritime Industry.* Philadelphia: University of Pennsylvania Press, 1974.

TWENTIETH CENTURY FUND. *Task Force on Employment Problem of Black Youth: The Job Crisis and Black Crisis and Black Youth.* New York: Twentieth Century Fund, 1971.

ULMER, AL. *Cooperatives and Poor People in the South.* Atlanta: Southern Regional Council, 1969.

WEAVER, ROBERT C. *Negro Labor: A National Problem.* Port Washington, N.Y.: Kennikat, 1969.

Education

ANDREWS, CHARLES. *The History of the African Free Schools.* New York: Negro Universities Press, 1969.

ASHMORE, HARRY S. *The Negro and the Schools.* Chapel Hill: University of North Carolina Press, 1954.

BALDWIN, CAROL. *The Buses Roll.* New York: Norton, 1974.

BALLARD, ALLEN B. *The Education of Black Folk.* New York: Harper, 1973.

BAUGHMAN, E. EARL. *Negro and White Children.* New York: Academic Press, 1968.

BERMAN, DANIEL. *It is So Ordered: The Supreme Court Rules on School Segregation.* New York: Norton, 1966.

BOND, HORACE MANN. *The Education of the Negro in the American Social Order.* New York: Octagon Books, 1966, reprint.

BOWERS, MELVIN K. *Between Two Worlds.* New York: McGraw, 1976.

BOYD, WILLIAM M. *Desegregating America's Colleges.* New York: Praeger, 1974.

BULLOCK, HENRY ALLEN. *A History of Negro Education in the South: from 1619 to the Present.* Cambridge, Mass.: Harvard University Press, 1967; New York: Praeger, 1970.

CLARK, KENNETH BANCROFT. *A Possible Reality.* New York: Emerson-Hill, 1972.

CLIFT, VIRGIL, ed. *Negro Education in America: Sixteenth Yearbook of the John Dewey Society.* New York: Harper, 1962.

COLEMAN, JAMES S. *Equality of Educational Opportunity.* Washington, D.C.: Department of Health, Education and Welfare, 1966.

CONANT, JAMES BRYANT. *Slums and Suburbs: A Commentary on Schools in Metropolitan Areas.* New York: McGraw, 1961.

CORSON, WILLIAM R. *Promise on Peril: The Black College Student in America.* New York: W.W. Norton. 1970.

CROSS, GEORGE LYNN. *Blacks in White Colleges: Oklahoma's Landmark Cases.* Norman: University of Oklahoma Press, 1975.

DUBOISE, W. E. B. *The Education of Black People.* Amherst: University of Massachusetts Press, 1973.

EDWARDS, HARRY. *Black Student.* New York: Free Press, 1970.

EPPS, EDGAR G. *Black Students in White Schools.* Worthington, Ohio: Jones, 1972.

FULLER, EDMUND. *Prudence Crandall.* Middletown, Conn. Wesleyan University Press, 1971.

GITTELL, MARILYN. *Educating an Urban Population.* Beverly Hills, Cal.: Sage Publications, 1967.

GREENBERG, POLLY. *The Devil Has Slippery Shoes.* New York: MacMillan, 1969.

GROSSMAN, B. *Black Means,* New York: Hill and Wang, 1970.

HOLDEN, ANNA. *The Bus Stops Here.* New York: Agathon Press, 1974.

KOZOL, JONATHAN. *Death at an Early Age.* Boston: Houghton Mifflin, 1967.

LEVEY, GERALD. *Ghetto School.* New York: Pegasus, 1970.

LEVIN, HENRY M. *Community Control of Schools.* Washington, D.C.: Brookings Institution, 1970.

LOGAN, RAYFORD W. *Howard University 1867-1967.* New York: University Press, 1968.

McEVOR, JAMES, and ABRAHAM MILLER. *Black Power and Student Rebellion: Conflict on the American Campus,* Belmont, Cal.: Wadsworth, 1969.

MEREDITH, JAMES. *Three Years in Mississippi.* Bloomington: Indiana University Press, 1966.

MOORE, WILLIAM. *Black Educators in White Colleges.* San Francisco: Jossey Bass, 1974.

RACHE, RICHARD J. *Catholic Colleges and the Negro Student.* Washington, D.C.: Catholic University of America Press, 1948.

RECORD, WILSON. *Little Rock U.S.A.* San Francisco: Chandler, 1960.

RILES, WILSON C. *The Urban Education Task Forces, New York: Praeger, 1970.*

RODGERS, FREDERICK A. *The Black High School and its Community.* Lexington Mass.: Lexington Books, 1975.

RUBINSTEIN, ANNETTE T. *Schools against Children.* New York: Monthly Review Press, 1970.

SAARATT, REED. *The Ordeal of Desegregation: The First Decade.* New York: Harper, 1966.

ST. JOHN, NANCY. *School Desegreation: Outcomes for Children.* New York: Wiley, 1975.

Scott, IRVING E. *The Education of Black People in Florida.* Philadelphia: Dorrance, 1974.

SMITH, ROBERT. *They Closed their Schools: Prince Edward County, Virginia 1951-1964.* Chapel Hill: University of North Carolina Press, 1965.

SOWELL, THOMAS. *Black Education: Myths and Tragedies.* New York: McKay, 1972.

THOMPSON, DANIEL CALBERT. *Private Black Colleges at the Cross roads.* Westport, Conn.: Greenwood, 1973.

TRILLIN, CALVIN. *An Education in Georgia: The Integration of Charlayne Hunter and Hamilton Holmes.* New York: Viking 1964.

U.S. COMMISSION ON CIVIL RIGHTS. *Racial Isolation in the Public Schools,* Washington, D.C.: Government Printing Office, 1967.

WEST, EARL H., ed. *The Black American and Education.* Columbus, 054Ohio: Merrill, 1972.

WOODSON, CARTER G. *The Education of the Negro Prior to 1861.* Washington, D.C.: Associated Publishers, 1915; Arno Press, 1968, reprint.

WRIGHT, NATHAN, JR. *What Black Educators are Saying.* New York: Hawthorn Books, 1970.

Folklore and Language

ABRAHAMS, ROGER D. *Deep Down in the Jungle: Negro Narrative Folklore from the Streets of Philadelphia.* Hatboro, Pa.: Folklore Associates, 1964.

_____. *Positively Black.* Englewood Cliffs, N.J.: Prentice-Hall, 1970.

ANDREWS, MALACHI, and PAUL OWENS. *Black Language,* Berkeley: University of California Press, 1973.

BONTEMPS, ARNA, and LANGSTON HUGHES. *The Book of Negro Folklore.* New York: Dodd, 1958.

BRASCH, IDA W., and WALTER M. Brasch, comps. *A Comprehensive Annotated Bibliography of American Black English.* Baton Rouge, State University of Louisiana Press, 1974.

BREWER, JOHN MASON "American Negro Folklore." *Phylon,* no. 6, 1945. *"Dog Ghost" and other Texas Negro Folk Tales.* Austin: University of Texas Press.

_____. *Worser Days and Better Times: The Folklore of the North Carolina Negro.* Chicago: Quadrangle, 1965

_____. *American Negro Folklore.* Chicago: Quadrangle, 1968.

BROOKES, STELLA BREWER. *Joel Chandler Harris: Folklorist.* Athens: University of Georgia Press, 1950.

BYRD, JAMES W. *J. Mason Brewer: Negro Folklorist.* Austin: Steck-Vaughn, 1967.

CARMER, CARL. *Stars Fell on Alabama.* New York: Hill and Wang, 1934.

CLAERBAUT, DAVID. *Black Jargon in White America.* Grand Rapids, Mich.: Eerdmans, 1972.

CORBETT, EDWARD P. J. "Students' Right to Their Own Language." *College Composition and Communication, Fall 1974.*

DAVIS, OSSIE. "The English Language is My Enemy." *American Teacher,* April 1967.

DE STEFANO, JOHANNA S. *Language, Society and Education: A Profile of Black English.* Worthington, Ohio: Charles A. Jones Co., 1973.

DILLARD, JOEY LEE. *Black English: Its History and Usage in the United States.* New York: Random House, 1972.

DOBIE, FRANK J. *Follow De Drinkin Gou'd.* Austin: Texas Folklore Society, 1928.

_____. *Tone the Bell Easy.* Dallas: Southern Methodist University Press, 1932.

DORSON, RICHARD M. *Negro Folktales in Michigan.* Cambridge, Mass.: Harvard University Press, 1956

_____. *American Negro Folktales.* Bloomington: Indiana University Press, 1958.

DUNDES, ALAN, ed. *Mother Wit from the Laughing Barrel: Readings in the Interpretation of Afro-American Folklore.* Englewood Cliffs, N. J.: Prentice-Hall, 1973.

FABIO, SARAH WEBSTER. "What Is Black?" *College Composition and Communication,* December 1968.

FARRISON, W. EDWARD. "Dialectology Versus Negro Dialect." *CLA Journal,* September 1969.

FLEMING, ROBERT E. "Playing the Dozenas' in the Black Novel." *Studies in Black Literature,* Autumn 1972.

HARRIS, JOEL C. *Uncle Remus, His Songs and Sayings.* New York: Appleton, 1880

_____. *Tar-Baby and Other Rhymes of Uncle Remus.* New York: Appleton, 1904

_____. *Uncle Remus and Brer Rabbit.* New York: Stokes, 1906.

HASKINS, JAMES, and HUGH F. BUTTS. *The Psychology of Black Language.* New York: Barnes and Noble, 1973.

HAYWOOD, CHARLES. *A Bibliography of North American Folklore and Folksong.* New York: Dover, 1951.

HUGHES, LANGSTON, ed. *The Book of Negro Humor.* New York: Dodd, 1966.

HURSTON, ZORA N. *Mules and Men.* Philadelphia: Lippincott, 1935.

_____. *Tell My Horse.* Philadelphia: Lippincott, 1938.

JACKSON, BRUCE. *The Negro and His Folklore in Nineteenth Century Periodicals.* Austin: University of Texas Press, 1967.

_____, ed. *Get Your Ass in the Water and Swim Like Me: Narrative Poetry from the Black Oral Tradition.* Cambridge, Mass.: Harvard University Press, 1974.

JOHNSON, GUY B. *John Henry: Tracking Down a Negro Legend.* Chapel Hill: University of North Carolina Press, 1929.

JORDON, JUNE. "Black English: The Politics of Translation." *Library Journal,* May 1973.

_____."*White English: The Politics of Language.*" *Black World,* August 1973.

KOCHMAN, THOMAS. *Rappin and Stylin Out: Communication in Urban Black America.* Chicago: University of Illinois Press, 1972.

MAJOR, CLARENCE, ed. *A Dictionary of Afro-American Slang.* New York: International, 1969.

SMITH, ARTHUR L. *Language, Communication and Rhetoric in Black America,* New York: Harper, 1972.

SMITHERMAN, GENEVA. "God Don't Never Change: Black English from a Black Perspective." *College English,* March 1973.

_____. *Black Language and Culture: Sounds of Soul.* New York 1975.

_____. "*White English in Black Face: Who Do I Be?*" *Black Scholar,* May-June 1973.

SPAULDING, HENRY D. *Encyclopedia of Black Folklore and Humor.* Middle Village, N.Y.: Jonathan David, 1972.

STERLING, PHILIP. *Laughing on the Outside.* New York: Grosset, 1966.

SULLIVAN, PHILIP E. "Buh Rabbit: Going Through the Changes." *Studies in Black Literature,* Summer 1973.

TURNER, LORENZO D. *Africanisms in the Gullah Dialect.* Chicago: University of Chicago Press, 1949.

WOLFRAM, WALT, and NONA H. CLARKE, eds. *Black-White Speech Relationships.* Washington, D.C.: Center for Applied Linguistics, 1971.

History

APTHEKER, HERBERT. *American Negro Slave Revolts.* New York: International, 1963.

BARBEAU, ARTHUR, and FLORETTE HENRI. *Unknown Soldiers: Black American Troops in World War I.* Philadelphia: Temple University Press, 1975.

BENNETT, LERONE. *Confrontation Black & White.* Chicago: Johnson Publishing Co., 1965

_____. *Before the Mayflower: A History of Black America,* 4th rev. ed. Chicago: Johnson Publishing Co., 1969.

_____. *The Challenge of Blackness*. Chicago: Johnson Publishing Co., 1972.

BERLIN, IRA. *Slaves Without Masters: The Free Negro in the Antebellum South*. New York: Pantheon, 1974.

BERRY, F.M. *Black Resistance and White Law: A History of Constitutional Racism in America*. New York: Appleton, 1970.

BRACEY, JOHN H. et al. *Black Nationalism in America*. Indianapolis: Bobbs-Merrill, 1970.

BROWN, LETITIA WOODS. *Free Negroes in the District of Columbia 1790-1846*. New York: Oxford, 1972.

CARROLL, J. *Black Military Experience in the American West*. New York: Liveright, 1971.

CLEAVER, ELDRIGE. *Soul on Ice*. New York: McGraw-Hill, 1968.

COOMBS, NORMAN. *The Black Experience in America*. New York: Twayne, 1972.

CORNISH, DUDLEY T. *The Sable Arm: Negro Troops in the Union Army, 1861-1865*. New York: Norton, 1965.

DRIMMER, MELVIN, ed. *Black History*. New York: Doubleday, 1968.

DuBOIS, W. E. B. *Black Reconstruction in America, 1860-1880*. New York: Meridian, 1964.

_____. *The Negro*. New York: Oxford, 1970.

DUMOND, DWIGHT LOWELL. *Anti-Slavery: The Crusade for Freedom in America*. Ann Arbor: University of Michigan Press, 1961.

DUNHAM, PHILIP, and EVERETT JONES. *The Negro Cowboys*. New York: Dodd, 1965.

FISHEL, LESLIE H., and BENJAMIN QUARLES. *The Black American*, 3rd ed. Glenview, Ill.: Scott-Foresman, 1976.

FONER, PHILIP S. *History of Black Americans*. Westport, Conn.: Greenwood Press, 1975.

FOWLER, A. L. *Black Infantry in the West 1869-1891*. New York: Negro Universities Press, 1971.

FRANKLIN, JOHN HOPE. *Reconstruction After the Civil War*. Chicago: University of Chicago Press, 1961.

_____. *The Emancipation Proclamation*. New York: Doubleday, 1963.

_____. *An Illustrated History of Black Americans*. New York: Time-Life, 1970.

_____. *From Slavery to Freedom*, 4th rev. ed. New York: Knopf, 1970.

GATEWOOD, WILLARD B., JR. *"Smoked Yankees" and the Struggle for Empire: Letters from Negro Soldiers 1898-1902*. Chicago: University of Illinois Press, 1971.

GOLDSTEIN, RHODA L., ed. *Black Life and Culture in the United States.* New York: Crowell, 1971.

GREEN, CONSTANCE M. *The Secret City: A History of Race Relations in the Nation's Capital.* Princeton, N.J.: Princeton University Press, 1967.

GREENE, LORENZO J. *The Negro in Colonial New England, 1620- 1776.* New York: Columbia University Press, 1942.

GRIFFITH, CYRIL E. *The African Dream: Martin Delany and the Emergence of Pan-African Thought.* University Park, Penn.: State University Press, 1975.

GROH, GEORGE M. *The Black Migration.* New York: McKay 1972.

HEARD, NORMAN, JR. *Black Frontiersmen: Adventure of Negroes among the American Indians 1528-1918.* New York: John Day, 1969.

HENRI, FLORETTE. *Bitter Victory: A History of Black Soldiers in World War I.* New York: Doubleday, 1970.

IRVINE, KEITH. *The Rise of the Colored Races.* New York: W.W. Norton 1970.

JAMES, C. L. R. *A History of Pan African Revolt.* Washington, D.C.: Drum and Spear Press, 1969.

JOHNSON, E. *A History of Negro Soldiers in the Spanish-American War.* New York: Johnson Reprint, 1970.

JORDON, WINTHOP D. *White over Black.* Chapel Hill: University of North Carolina Press, 1968.

KATZ, W. L. *Black West.* New York: Doubleday, 1971.

KLEIN, A. E. *The Hidden Contributors: Black Scientists and Inventors in America.* New York: Doubleday, 1971.

LACY, DAN. *The White Use of Blacks in America.* New York: Atheneum, 1971.

LANE, ANN J. *The Brownsville Affair.* Port Washington, N.Y.: Kennikat, 1971.

LECKIE, WILLIAM H. *Buffalo Soldiers: A Narrative of the Negro Cavalry in the West.* Norman: University of Oklahoma Press, 1967.

LITWACK, LEON. *North of Slavery: The Negro in the Free States.* Chicago: University of Chicago Press, 1961.

LOGAN, FRENISE A. *The Negro in North Carolina, 1876-1894.* Chapel Hill: University of North Carolina Press, 1964.

McPHERSON, JAMES M. *The Negro's Civil War.* New York: Pantheon, 1964.

MEIER, AUGUST. *Negro Thought in America 1880-1915: Racial Ideologies in the Age of Booker T. Washington.* Ann Arbor: University of Michigan Press, 1963.

MELVILLE, SAMUEL. *Letters from Attica.* New York: Morrow, 1972.

MOTLEY, MARY P. *The Invisible Soldier: The Experience of Black Soldiers in World War II.* Detroit: Wayne State University Press, 1976.

PAINTER, NELL IRVIN. *Exodusters: Black Migration to Kansas after Reconstruction.* New York: Knopf, 1977.

PEASE, WILLIAM H., and J. H. PEASE. *Black Utopia: Commual Experiments in America.* Madison: State Historical Society of Wisconsin, 1963.

PURDON, ERIC. *Black Company: The Story of Subchaser 1264.* New York: McKay, 1972.

QUARLES, BENJAMIN. *The Negro in the Civil War.* Boston: Little, Brown, 1953.

——————. *The Negro in the American Revolution.* Chapel Hill: University of North Carolina Press, 1961.

——————. *Black Abolitionists.* New York: Oxford, 1969.

——————. *The Negro in the Making of America.* New York: Macmillan, 1969.

REDDING, SAUNDERS. *They Came in Chains: Americans from Africa.* Philadelphia: Lippincott, 1973.

STAMPP, KENNETH MILTON. *The Era of Reconstruction 1865-1877.* New York: Knopf, 1965.

STILLMAN, RICHARD J. II. *Integration of the Negro in the U.S. Armed Forces.* New York: Praeger, 1968.

THORPE, EARL E. *Negro Historians in the United States.* Baton Rouge, La.: Fraternal Press, 1958.

——————. *Black Historians: A Critique.* New York: William Morrow, 1971.

TUTTLE, WILLIAM, JR. *Race Riot: Chicago in the Red Summer of 1919.* New York: Atheneum, 1970.

WALVIN, JAMES. *The Black Presence.* New York: Schocken, 1972.

WEISBROD, ROBERT G. *Ebony Kinship: Africa, Africans, and the Afro-Americans.* Westport, Conn.: Greenwood, 1973.

WESLEY, CHARLES. *Neglected History: Essays in Negro-American History.* Washington, D.C.: Association for the Study of Negro Life and History, 1969.

WESLEY, CHARLES H. *In Freedom's Footsteps.* New York: Publishers Co., 1968.

WILLIAMS, LEE E., and LEE E. WILLIAMS II. *Anatomy of Four Race Riots.* Jackson: University and College Press of Mississippi, 1972.

WINKS, ROBIN. *The Blacks in Canada.* New Haven, Conn.: Yale University Press, 1971.

WOLSELEY, ROLAND. The Black Press U.S.A. Ames: Iowa State University Press, 1971.

WOLTERS, RAYMOND. Negroes and the Great Depression: The Problem of Economic Recovery. Westport, Conn.: Greenwood, 1970.

WRIGHT, J. M. Free Negro in Maryland 1634-1860. New York: Octogon, 1971.

Literary Criticism and History

ALLEN, SAMUEL. "Negritude and its Relevance to the American Negro Writer." The American Negro Writer and His Roots. New York: American Society of African Culture, 1960.

AMANN, CLARENCE A. "Three Negro Classics: An Estimate." Negro Literature Forum, no. 4, 1970.

ANDERSON, JERVIS. "Black Writing: The Other Side." Dissent, no. 15, 1968.

BAKER, HOUSTON A. Singers at Daybreak: Studies in Black American Literature. Washington, D.C.: Howard University Press, 1974.

_____. Long Black Song: Essays in Black American Literature and Culture. Charlottesville: University of Virginia Press, 1973.

BARKSDALE, RICHARD, and KENETH KINNAMON. Black Writers of America. New York: Macmillan, 1972.

BIGSBY, C. W. E., ed. The Black American Writer, 2 vols. Deland, Florida: Everett Edwards, 1969.

BONTEMPS, ARNA, ed. The Harlem Renaissance Remembered. New York: Dodd, 1972.

_____. "The New Black Renaissance." Negro Digest, November 1961.

BRAITHWAITE, WILLIAM S. "Alain Locke's Relationship to the Negro in American Literature." Phylon, no. 18, 1957.

BRAWLEY, BENJAMIN. "The Negro in American Literature." The Bookman, October 1922.

_____. "The Negro Literary Renaissance." Southern Workman, April 1927.

_____. The Negro in Literature and Art. New York: Duffield, 1930.

BREMEN, PAUL, and ROSEY POOL, eds. Ik Zag Hoe Zwart ik Was. Den Haag: Daamen, 1958.

BRONZ, STEPHEN H. *Roots of Negro Consciousness: The 1920's Three Harlem Renaissance Authors.* New York: Libra, 1964.

BROOKS, GWENDOLYN. "Poets Who Are Negro." *Phylon*, no.11, 1950.

BROWN, LLOYD L. "Which Way for the Negro Writer?" *Masses and Mainstream*, March 1951.

Brown, Lloyd W. "Black Entitles: Names as Symbols in Afro-American Literature." *Studies in Black Literature*, Spring 1970.

BROWN, STERLING A. "The American Race Problem as Reflected in American Literature." *The Journal of Negro Education*, no.8, 1939.

_____. "A Century of Negro Portraiture in American Literature." *The Massachusetts Review*, Winter 1966.

BUTCHER, MARGARET. *The Negro in American Culture.* New York: Mentor, 1971.

CALVERTON VICTOR. "The Negro and American Culture." *Saturday Review of Literature*, September 21, 1940.

CAYTON, HORACE R. "Ideological Forces in the Work of Negro Writers." (Herbert Hill,) ed. *In Anger and Beyond.* New York: Knopf, 1968.

CHAPMAN, ABRAHAM. "The Harlem Renaissance in Literary History." *CLA Journal*, no.9, 1967.

CLARKE, JOHN HENRIK. "The Neglected Dimensions of the Harlem Renaissance." *Black World*, November 1970.

_____. "Transition in the American Negro Short Story." *Phylon*, Winter 1960.

_____, ed., *William Styron's Nat Turner: Ten Black Writers Respond.* Boston: Beacon Press, 1968.

COOK, MERCER, and STEPHEN HENDERSON. *The Militant Black Writer in Africa and the United States.* Madison: University of Wisconsin Press, 1969.

CRUSE, HAROLD. *The Crisis of the Negro Intellectual.* New York: Morrow, 1967.

CULLEN, COUNTEE. "The Dark Tower." *Opportunity*, Monthly Column, 1926-1928.

DAVIS, ARTHUR P. *From the Dark Tower.* Washington, D.C.: Howard University Press, 1974.

_____. "Growing up in the New Negro Renaissance: 1920-1935." *Negro American Literature*, Forum no.2, 1968.

DEODENE, FRANK, and WILLIAM P. FRENCH. *Black American Fiction Since 1952: A Premliminary Checklist.* Chatham, N.J.: Chatham Bookseller, 1970.

DOVER, CEDRIC. "Notes on Coloured Writing." *Phylon*, no.8, 1947.

ELLISON, RALPH. *Shadow and Act.* New York: New American Library, 1964.

EMANUEL, JAMES A. "America Before 1950: Black Writers' Views." *Negro Digest,* August 1969.

_____. "The Invisible Men of American Literature." *Books Abroad,* no.37, 1963.

EVANS, MARI. "Contemporary Black Literature." *Black World,* June 1970.

_____. "In With You." *Negro Digest,* May 1968.

FABIO, SARAH WEBSTER. "A Black Paper." *Negro Digest,* July 1969.

FORD, NICK AARON. "Black Literature and the Problem of Evaluation," *College English,* no.32, 1971.

_____. "A Blueprint for Negro Authors." *Phylon,* no.9, 1950.

"Confessions of a Black Critic." *Black World,* June 1971.

FULLER, HOYT W. "Black Images and White Critics." *Negro Digest,* November 1969.

_____. "The Negro Writer in the United States." *Ebony,* November 1964.

GAYLE, ADDISON, JR. "Black Literature and the White Aesthetic." *Negro Digest,* July 1969.

_____, ed. *The Black Aesthetic,* New York: Doubleday, 1971.

_____. *The Way of the New World: The Black Novel in America.* New York: Doubleday, 1975.

JEFFERS, LANCE. "Afro-American Literature: The Conscience of Man." *Black Scholar,* January 1971.

LOGGINS, VERNON. *The Negro Author: His Development in America to 1900.* Port Washington, N.Y.: Kennikat, 1964.

MARTIN, JAY, ed. *A Singer in the Dawn.* New York: Dodd, 1975.

_____ and Gossie Hudson. *The Paul Laurence Dunbar Reader.* New York: Dodd, 1975.

PERRY, MAGARET. *Silence to the Drums: A Survey of the Literature of the Harlem Renaissance.* Westport, Conn.: Greenwood, 1976.

RAMPERSAND, ARNOLD. *The Art and Imagination of W. E. B. DuBois.* Cambridge, Mass.: Harvard University Press, 1976.

REDDING, SAUNDERS. "American Negro Literature." *The American Scholar,* no.18, 1949.

SCOTT, NATHAN A., JR. "Judgement Marked by a Cellar: The American Negro Writer and the Dialectic of Despair." *The Denver Quarterly,* Summer 1967.

SINGH, AMRITJIT. *The Novels of the Harlem Renaissance: Twelve Black Writers 1923-1933.* University Park: Pennsylvania State University Press, 1976.

Music

ARMSTRONG, LOUIS. *Satchmo: My Life in New Orleans.* Englewood Cliffs, N.J.: Prentice-Hall, 1956.

BALLIET, WHITNEY. *New York Notes: A Journal of Jazz, 1972-1975.* Boston: Houghton Mifflin, 1976.

BAXTER D. S. *Ma Rainey and the Classic Blues Singers.* New York: Stein and Day, 1970.

BERENDT, JOACHIN ERNEST. *Blues.* Munchen: Mymphenburger Verlagshandlung, 1960.

_____. *The New Jazz Book: A History and Guide.* New York: Hill and Wang, 1962.

BRUNN, HARRY O. *The Story of the Original Dixieland Jazz Band.* Baton Rouge: Louisiana State University Press, 1960.

CARAWAN, GUY, comp. *We Shall Overcome! Songs of the Southern Freedom Movement.* New York: Oak Publications, 1963.

CHARTERS, SAMUEL. *The Country Blues.* New York: Rinehart, 1959.

_____. *Jazz: New Orleans 1885-1963.* New York: Oak Publications, 1963.

_____. *The Poetry of the Blues.* New York: Oak Publications, 1963.

COURTLANDER, HAROLD. *Negro Folk Music U.S.A.* New York: Columbia University Press, 1963.

DELERMA, DOMINIQUE-RENE. *Black Music in Our Culture.* Kent, Ohio: Kent State University Press, 1970.

_____. *Readings on Afro-American Music.* Kent, Ohio: Kent State University Press, 1973.

FEATHER, LEONARD. *The Encyclopedia of Jazz in the Sixties.* New York: Horizon, 1966.

FERNETT, GENE. *Swing Out.* Midland, Mich.: Pendell, 1970.

FISHER, MILES MARK. *Negro Slave Songs in the United States.* New York: Atadel, 1953.

HAAS, ROBERT B., ed. *William Grant Still and the Fusion of Cultures in American Music.* Los Angeles: Black Sparrow Press, 1972.

HANDY, WILLIAM C., ed. *A Treasury of the Blues.* New York: Boni, 1949.

HARE, MAUD CUNEY. *Negro Musicians and Their Music.* Washington, D.C.: Associated Press, 1936.

HAYES, ROLAND. *My Songs: Aframerican Religious Folk Songs.* Boston: Little, Brown, 1948.

HEILBUT, TONY. *The Gospel Sound: Good News and Bad Times,* New York: Simon and Schuster, 1972.

JEWELL, DEREK. *Duke: A Portrait of Duke Ellington.* New York: Norton, 1977.

JOHNSON, JAMES WELDON. *The Book of American Negro Spirituals.* New York: Viking, 1926.

_____. *The Books of American Negro Spirituals.* New York: Viking, 1940.

JONES, LEROI. *Black Music.* New York: Morrow, 1967.

_____. *Blues People.* New York: Morrow, 1963.

KATZ, BERNARD, ed. *The Social Implications of Early Negro Music in the U.S.* New York: Arno, 1969.

KEEPNEWS, ORRIN. *A Pictorial History of Jazz.* New York: Crown, 1966.

KEIL, CHARLES. *Urban Blues.* Chicago: University of Chicago Press, 1966.

LEONARD, NEIL. *Jazz and the White Americans.* Chicago: University of Chicago Press, 1962.

LEVINE, LAWRENCE W. *Black Culture and Black Consciousness.* New York: Oxford, 1977.

LILJE, HANNS. *Das Buch Der Spirituals und Gospel Songs.* Hamburg: Furche-Verlag, 1961.

LOCKE, ALAINE. *The Negro and His Music.* Port Washington, N.Y.: Kennikat, 1936.

LOVELL, JOHN. *Black Song: The Forge and the Flame.* New York: Macmillan, 1972.

NATHAN, HANS. *Dan Emmet and the Rise of Early Negro Minstrelsy.* Norman: University of Oklahoma Press, 1962.

NEFF, ROBERT, and ANTHONY CONNOR. *Blues.* Boston: David Godine, 1975.

OLIVER, PAUL. *Aspects of the Blues Tradition.* New York. Oak Publications, 1970.

_____. *Savannah Syncopators.* New York: Stein and Day, 1970.

_____. *Conversation with the Blues.* New York: Horizon, 1965.

PANASSIE, HUGUES. *The Real Jazz.* New York: Barnes, 1960.

PLEASANTS, HENRY. *Serious Music and All That Jazz.* New York: Simon and Schuster, 1969.

RAMSEY, FREDRIC. *Been Here and Gone.* New Brunswick, N.J.: Rutgers University Press, 1960.

ROACH, HILDRED. *Black American Music: Past and Present.* Boston: Crescendo Publishing Co., 1973.

ROBERTS, JOHN. *Black Music of Two Worlds.* New York: Praeger, 1972.

RUSSELL, ANTHONY. *Blacks, Whites and Blues.* New York: Stein and Day. 1970.

SACKHEIM, ERIC., comp. *The Blues. Line* New York. Grossman, 1969.

SCHAFER, WILLIAM J. *The Art of Ragtime: Form and Meaning of An Original Black American Art.* Baton Rouge: Louisiana University Press, 1973.

SOUTHERN, EILEEN. *The Music of Black Americans: A History.* New York: Norton, 1972.

_____. *Readings in Black American Music.* New York: Norton, 1971.

SPELLMAN, A. B. *Black Music.* New York: Schocken, 1970.

STERNS, MARSHALL. *The Story of Jazz.* New York: Oxford, 1957.

ULANOV, BARRY. *A Handbook of Jazz.* New York: Viking, 1957.

WILLIAMS, MARTIN T. *The Art of Jazz.* New York: Oxford, 1970.

WORK, JOHN W. *I John Saw the Holy Number.* New York: Galaxy Music Corp., 1962.

Poetry

BAILEY, LEONARD. *Broadside Authors: A Biographical Directory.* Detroit: Broadside, 1971.

BAKER, HOUSTON, JR. *A Many Colored Coat of Dreams: The Poetry of Countee Cullen.* Detroit: Broadside, 1975.

BARKSDALE, RICHARD K. "Trends in Contemporary Poetry." *Phylon,* no. 19, 1958.

_____. "Urban Crisis and the Black Poetic Avant Garde." *American Negro Literature Forum,* no. 3, 1969.

_____. "Humanistic Protest in Recent Black Poetry."In *Modern Black Poets.* Donald Gibson, ed., Englewood Cliffs, N.J.: Prentice Hall, 1973.

BONE, ROBERT. "American Negro Poets: A French View." *Tri-Quarterly,* no. 4., 1965.

BROOKS, GWENDOLYN. "Poets Who Are Negro." *Phylon,* no. 9, 1950.

BROWN, STERLING A. "The Blues." *Phylon,* no. 8, 1952.

_____. "Negro Folk Expression, Spirituals, Seculars, Ballads and Songs." *Phylon,* no. 16, 1953.

CARTEY, WILFRED. "Four Shadows of Harlem." *Negro Digest,* August, 1969.

CHAPMAN, ABRAHAM. "Black Poetry Today." *Arts in Society,* no. 5, 1968.

COLLIER, EUGENIA W. "Heritage from Harlem." *Black World,* November 1970.

_____. "I Do Not Marvel, Countee Cullen." *CLA Journal,* no. 9, 1967.

DAVIS, ARTHUR P. "The New Poetry of Black Hate." *CLA Journal* no. 13, 1970.

DAYKIN, WALTER. "Race Consciousness in Negro Poetry." *Sociology and Social Research,* no. 20, 1036.

ECHERUO, M. J. C. "American Negro Poetry." *Phylon,* no. 24, 1963.

ELLISON, MARTHA. "Velvet Voices Feed On Bitter Fruit: A Study of American Negro Poetry." *Poet and Critic,* Winter 1967.

EMERUWA, LEATRICE. "Black Art and Artists in Cleveland, Ohio." *Black World,* January 1973.

FURAY, MICHAEL. "Africa in Negro American Poetry to 1929." *African Literature Today,* no. 2, 1969.

GARRETT, DE LOIS. "Dream Motif in Contemporary Negro Poetry." *English Journal,* no. 59, 1970.

GARRETT, NAOMI M. "Racial Motifs in Contemporary American and French Negro Poetry." *West Virginia University Philological Papers,* no. 14, 1963.

GOOD, CHARLES HAMLIN. "The First American Negro Literary Movement." *Opportunity,* no. 10, 1932.

HORNE, FRANK S. "Black Verse." *Opportunity,* no. 2, 1924.

JACKSON, BLYDEN. *The Waiting Years: Essays in American Negro Literature.* Baton Rouge: Louisiana State University Press, 1976.

_____. *Black Poetry in America: Two Essays in Historical Interpretation.* Baton Rouge: Louisiana State University Press, 1974.

KILGORE, JAMES C. "Toward the Dark Tower." *Black World,* June 1970.

LEE, DON L. "Black Poetry: Which Direction?" *Negro Digest,* September-October 1968.

_____. *Dynamite Voices: Black Poets of the 1960's.* Detroit: Broadside, 1971.

MURPURGO, J. E. "American Negro Poetry." *Fortnightly,* July 1947.

POOL, ROSEY. "The Discovery of American Negro Poetry." *Freedomways,* no. 3, 1963.

RAMSARAN, J. A. "The 'Twice Born' Artist Silent Revolution." *Black World,* May 1971.

REDDING, J. SAUNDERS. *To Make a Poet Black.* Chapel Hill: University of North Carolina Press, 1939; McGrath, 1968, reprint.

REDMOND, EUGENE B. "The Black American Epic: Its Roots, Its Writers." *Black Scholar,* January 1971.

_____. *Drumvoices: The Mission of Afro-American Poetry: A Critical History.* New York: Doubleday, 1976.

RODGERS, CAROLYN M. "Black Poetry—Where It's At." *Negro Digest,* September 1969.

THURMAN, WALLACE. "Negro Poets and Their Poetry." *Bookman,* no. 58, 1928.

"The Umbra Poets." *Mainstream,* July 1963.

WAGNER, JEAN. *Les Poetes Negres des Etats-Unis: Le Sentiment Racial et Religieux dans la Poesie P.L. Dunbar a Langston Hughes.* Paris: Istra, 1963.

──────. *Black Poets of the United States: From Paul Laurence Dunbar to Langston Hughes.* Chicago: University of Illinois Press, 1973.

WALKER, MAGARET. "New Poets." *Phylon,* no. 11, 1950.

Politics

ARKINS, CHARLES, ed. *The Negro Votes.* San Francisco: Chandler, 1962.

BAILEY, HARRY A., JR., ed. *Negro Politics in America.* Columbus, Ohio: Charles E. Merrill, 1967.

BILLINGTON, MONROE. *The Political South in the Twentieth Century.* New York: Scribner, 1974.

BOND, JULIAN. *A Time to Speak, A Time to Act: The Movement in Politics.* New York: Simon and Schuster, 1972.

BRYANT, LAWRENCE C., ed. *Negro Legislators in South Carolina 1865-1894.* Orangeburg: South Carolina State College Press, 1966.

BULLOCK, CHARLES S., and HARRELL R. RODGERS, JR., eds. *Black Political Attitudes.* Chicago: Markham, 1972.

BUNI, ANDREW. *The Negro in Virginia Politics 1902-1965.* Charlottesville: University Press of Virginia, 1967.

CALLCOTT, MAGARET. *The Negro in Maryland Politics 1870-1912.* Baltimore: Johns Hopkins University Press, 1969.

CHRISTOPHER, MAURINE. *America's Black Congressmen,* rev. ed. New York: Crowell, 1976.

DAVIS, LENWOOD G. *Blacks in Politics: An Exploratory Bibliography.* Monticello, Ill.: Council of Planning Librarians, 1975.

DUBOIS, W. E. B. *Black Reconstruction in America.* New York: World, 1964.

DYMALLY, M. M. *The Black Politician: His Search for Power.* Belmont, Cal.: Wadsworth, 1971.

EDMONDS, HELEN G. *The Negro and Fusion Politics in North Carolina 1894-1901.* Chapel Hill: University of North Carolina Press, 1951.

GILLIAN, REGINALD E. *Black Political Development: An Advocacy Analysis.* Port Washington, N.Y.: Kennikat, 1975.

GOSNELL, HAROLD F. *Negro Politicians: The Rise of Negro Politics in Chicago.* Chicago: University of Chicago Press, 1966, reprint.

GREENBERG, EDWARD S. et al. *Black Politics.* New York: Holt, 1971.

HASKINS, JAMES. *A Piece of the Power: Four Black Mayors.* New York: Dial, 1972.

HENDERSON, LENNEAL J. *Black Political Life in the United States* New York: Chandler, 1972.

HOLDEN, MATTHEW, JR. *The Politics of the Black "Nation."* New York: Chandler, 1973.

KEY, V. O. *Southern Politics in State and Nation.* New York: Knopf, 1949.

LADD, EVERETT C., JR. *Negro Political Leadership in the South.* Ithaca, N.Y.: Cornell University Press, 1966.

LEVINE, ROBERT A. *Black Power, White Style.* Washington, D.C.: United States Office of Economic Opportunity, 1968.

LEWINSON, PAUL. *Race, Class, and Party.* New York: Grossett and Dunlap, 1965.

LUVISINSON EDWIN R. *Black Politics in New York City.* New York: Twayne, 1974.

McFARLEN, ANNJENNETS S., comp. *Black Congressional Reconstruction Orators and Their Orations.* Metuchen, N.J.: Scarecrow, 1976.

McQUILKIN, FRANK. *Think Black: An Introduction to Black Political Power.* New York: Bruce, 1970.

MATTHEWS, DONALD R., and JAMES W. Protho. *Negroes and New Southern Politics.* New York: Harcourt, 1966.

MOON, HENRY LEE. *Balance of Power: The Negro Vote.* New York: Doubleday, 1948.

OGDEN, FREDERICK D. *The Poll Tax in the South.* Tuscaloosa: University of Alabama Press, 1958.

PAINSETT, ALEX. *Black Power Gary Style.* Chicago: Johnson Publishing Co, 1970.

PATTERSON, ERNEST. *Black City Politics.* New York: Dodd, 1974.

SILVERMAN, SANDRA. *The Black Revolt and Democratic Politics.* Boston: Heath, 1970.

413

STOKES, CARL B. *Promises of Power*. New York: Simon and Scuster, 1973.

STONE, CHARLES SUMNER. *Black Political Power*. New York: Dell, 1970.

TURNER, ROBERT P. *Up to The Front of the Line: Blacks in the American Political System*. Port Washington, N.Y.: Kennikat, 1975.

VINCENT, T. *Black Power and the Garvey Movement*. New York: Simon and Schuster, 1970.

WAGSTAFF, THOMAS. *Black Power*. Beverly Hills, Cal.: Glencoe Press, 1969.

WALTON, HAYNES, JR. *The Negro in Third Party Politics*. Philadelphia: Dorrance, 1969.

_____. *Black Politics*. Philadelphia: Lippincott, 1972.

_____. *Black Republicans: The Politics of the Black and Tans*. Metuchen, N.J.: Scarecrow, 1975.

WARREN, ROLAND L. *Politics and the Ghettos*. New York: Athenton, 1969.

WILSON, JAMES Q. *Negro Politics: The Search for Leadership*. Glencoe, Ill.: Free Press, 1960.

WRIGHT, NATHAN, JR. *What Black Politicians Are Saying*. New York: Hawthorn, 1972.

YOUNG, RICHARD P. *Roots of Rebellion: The Evolution of Black Politics and Protest Since World War II*. New York: Harper, 1970.

Slavery

ASIEGBU, JOHNSON U. J. *Slavery and the Politics of Liberation 1787-1861*. New York: Africana, 1969.

BALLAGH, JAMES C. *A History of Slavery in Virginia*. Baltimore: Johns Hopkins University Press, 1902.

BLASSINGAME, JOHN W. *The Slave Community: Plantation Life in the Antebellum South*. New York: Oxford, 1972.

BOURNE, H. F. *Slave Traffic in Portuguese Africa*. Chicago: Afro-Am, 1970.

BOXER, C. R. *The Dutch Seaborne Empire*. New York: Knopf, 1965.

_____. *Portuguese Seaborne Empire 1600-1800*. New York: Knopf, 1970.

CURTIN, PHILLIP I. *Africa Remembered: Narratives by West Africans from the Era of the Slave Trade.* Madison: University of Wisconsin Press, 1968.

DANIEL, PETE. *The Shadow of Slavery: Peonage in the South 1901-1969.* Chicago: University of Illinois Press, 1972.

DONNAN, ELIZABETH. *Doucments Illustrative of the History of the Slave Trade to America.* New York: Octagon Books, 1965.

DOW, G. F. *Slave Ships and Slaving.* New York: Dover, 1970.

DUBOIS, W. E. B. *The Suppression of the African Slave Trade to the United States 1638-1870.* New York: Russell and Russell, 1965, reprint.

DUFF, JOHN B. *The Nat Turner Rebellion: The Historical Event and the Modern Controversy.* New York: Harper, 1971.

FAGEL, ROBERT W., and STANLEY L. ENGERMAN. *Time on the Cross: The Economics of American Negro Slavery.* Boston: Little, Brown, 1974.

FILLER, LOUIS. *Slavery in the United States of America.* New York: Van Nostrand, 1972.

FISHER, A. G., and H. J. FISHER. *Slavery and Muslim Society in Africa.* New York: Doubleday, 1971.

GENOVESE, EUGENE et al. *Race and Slavery in the Western Hemisphere.* Princeton, N.J.: Princeton University Press, 1974.

_____. *Roll Jordan Roll.* New York: Pantheon, 1974.

GUTMAN HERBERT G. *Slavery and the Numbers Game: A Critique of Time on the Cross.* Chicago: University of Illinois Press, 1975.

HOETINK, H. *Slavery and Race Relations in the Americas.* New York: Harper and Row. 1973.

JOHNSTON, JAMES HUGO. *Race Relations in Virginia and Miscegenation in the South.* Amherst: University of Massachusetts Press, 1970.

KILLON, RONALD, comp. *Slavery time When I was chillun Down on Marster's Plantation: Interviews with Georgia Slaves.* Savanah, Ga.: Beehive Press, 1973.

KLEIN, HERBERT S. *Slavery in the Americas: A Comparative Study of Virginia and Cuba.* Chicago: University of Chicago Press, 1967.

LYND, STAUGHTON. *Class Conflict: Slavery and the United States Consitiution:* Indianapolis: Bobbs-Merrill, 1971.

MACLEOD, DUNCAN J. *Slavery, Race and the American Revolution.* New York: Cambridge University Press, 1974.

MCMANUS, EDGAR J. *A History of Negro Slavery in New York:* Syracuse, N.Y.: Syracuse University Press, 1966.

_____. *Black Bondage in the North.* Syracuse, N.Y.: Syracuse University Press, 1973.

MARSH, HENRY. *Slavery and Race: A Story of Slavery and Its Legacy for Today.* New York: St Martin's Press, 1974.

MELLON, MATTHEW T. *Early American Views on Negro Slavery.* New York: Bergman, 1969.

MILLER, ELINOR, comp. *Plantation Town and Country.* Urbana: University of Illinois Press, 1974.

MOORE, GEORGE H. *Notes on the History of Slavery in Massachusetts.* New York: Negro Universities Press, 1968.

MULLIN, GERALD W. *Flight and Rebellion: Slave Resistance in Eighteenth Century Virginia.* New York: Oxford, 1972.

OLMSTEAD, FREDERICK L. *A Journey in the Back Country.* New York: Shocken, 1970, reprint.

PARRY, J. H. *The Spanish Seaborne Empire.* New York: Knopf, 1966.

PATTERSON, ORLANDO. *The Sociology of Slavery.* London: MacGibbon and Kee, 1967.

POPE HENNESY, JOHN. *The Sins of the Fathers.* New York: Knopf, 1968.

PRICE, RICHARD. *Maroon Societies: Rebel Slave Communities in the Americas.* New York: Anchor Press, 1974.

RICHARDSON, PATRICK. *Empire and Slavery.* New York: Harper and Row, 1971.

ROSE, WILLIE LEE, ed. *A Documentary History of Slavery in North America.* New York: Oxford, 1976.

SCHERER, LESTER. *Slavery and the Churches in Early America 1619-1819.* Grand Rapids, Mich.: Eerdmans, 1975.

SMITH, ELBERT B. *The Death of Slavery: The United States 1837-1865.* Chicago: University of Chicago Press, 1967.

Stammp, Kenneth. *The Peculiar Institution: Slavery in the Antebellum South.* New York: Knopf, 1956.

STAROBIN, ROBERT S., ed. *Denmark Vesey: The Slave Conspiracy of 1822.* Englewood Cliffs, N.J.: Prentice Hall. 1970.

_____. *Industrial Slavery in the Old South.* New York: Oxford, 1970.

_____. *Blacks in Bondage: Letters of American Slaves.* New York: New Viewpoints Press, 1974.

WARD, W. E. F. *The Royal Navy and the Slavers.* New York: Shocken, 1970.

WHITE, JOHN, M. A. *Slavery in the American South.* Magnolia Mass.: Peter Smith, 1973.

WHITE, JOHN, and RALPH WILLETT. *Slavery in the American South.* New York: Harper, 1971.

WOOLMAN, JOHN. *Some Considerations on the Keeping of Negroes.* New York: Grossman, 1976.

_____. *The First Emancipation: The Abolition of Slavery in the North.* Chicago: University of Chicago Press, 1967.

Sociology and Psychology

BANKS, JAMES A. *Black Self-Concept.* New York: McGraw-Hill, 1972.

BAUGHMAN, E. *Black Americans.* New York: Academic Press, 1971.

BILLINGS, CHARLES E. *Racism and Prejudice.* Rochelle Park, N.J.: Hayden, 1976.

BILLINGSLEY, ANDREW. *Black Families and the Struggle for Survival.* New York: Friend Press, 1974.

BLACKWELL, JAMES, and MORRIS JANOWITZ. *Black Sociologists: Historical and Contemporary Perspectives.* Chicago: University of Chicago Press, 1974.

BOGART, LEO, ed. *Social Research and the Desegregation of the U.S. Army.* Chicago: Markham Publishing Co. 1969.

CLARK, KENNETH B. *Dark Ghetto. Dilemmas of Social Power.* New York: Harper, 1965.

COLES, ROBERT. *Children of Crisis: A Study of Courage and Fear.* Boston: Little, Brown, 1967.

CONYERS, JAMES E., and WILLIAM J. FARMER. *Black Youth in a Southern Metropolis.* Atlanta: Southern Regional Council, 1968.

COTTLE, THOMAS. *Black Children, White Dreams.* New York: Delta, 1975.

DAVIS, ALLISON, and JOHN DOLLARD. *Children of Bondage.* Washington, D.C.: American Council on Education, 1940.

DRAKE, St. CLAIR, and HORACE CAYTON. *Black Metropolis.* New York: Harper, 1964.

DuBOIS, W. E. B. *The Philadelphia Negro.* New York: Schocken, 1967, reprint.

ERCEG, DONALD. *The Image Is You.* Boston: Houghton Mifflin, 1960.

FRAZIER, FRANKLIN E. *The Negro in the United States,* rev. ed. New York: Macmillan, 1957.

_____. *The Negro Family in the United States.* New York: Macmillan, 1957.

_____. *Black Bourgeoisie.* Glencoe, Ill.: Free Press, 1957.

_____. *The Negro Family in the United States.* Chicago: University of Chicago Press, 1966.

GRIER, WILLIAM H., and PRICE M. Cobbs. *Black Rage.* New York: Basic Books, 1968.

GUTMAN, HERBERT. *The Black Family in Slavery and Freedom 1720-1925.* New York: Pantheon, 1976.

HANNERZ, ULF. *Soulside.* New York: Columbia University Press, 1969.

HARRIS, MARVIN. *Patterns of Race in America.* New York: Norton, 1974.

HAUSER, S. T. *Black and White Identity Formation.* New York: John Wiley, 1971.

HILL, ROBERT B. *The Strengths of Black Families.* New York: Emerson Hall, 1971.

HIPPLER, ARTHUR. *Hunters Point: A Black Ghetto in America.* New York: Basic Books, 1971.

HOUGH, J. *A Year in the Ghetto.* Boston: Little, Brown, 1970.

JOHNSON, CHARLES S. *Patterns of Negro Segregation.* New York: Harper, 1943.

JOHNSON, JAMES WELDON. *Black Manhattan.* New York: Knopf, 1930; Arno Press, 1969, reprint.

JORDON, WINTHROP D. *The White Man's Burden.* New York: Oxford, 1974.

KINLOCH, GRAHAM. *The Dynamics of Race Relations: A Sociological Analysis.* New York: McGraw-Hill, 1974.

KORDINER, ABRAM, and LIONEL OVESEY. *The Mark of Oppression.* New York: World Publishing, 1962.

KORNIVEIBLE, THEODORE. *No Crystal Stair: Black Life and the Messenger.* Westport, Conn.: Greenwood, 1975.

KRAMER, JUDITH R. *The American Minority Community.* New York: Crowell, 1970.

KVARACEUS, C. WILLIAM. *Negro Self-Concept.* New York: McGraw-Hill, 1965.

LYMAN, STANFORD M. *The Black American in Sociological Thought: A Failure in Perspective.* New York: Capricorn, 1972.

MYRDAL, GUNNAR. *American Dilemma: The Negro Problem and Modern Democracy.* New York: Harper, 1944.

NEARING, SCOTT. *Black America.* New York: Johnson Reprint Corp., 1970.

PARSONS, TALCOTT, and KENNETH CLARK. *The Negro American.* Boston: Houghton Mifflin, 1966

PETTIGREW, THOMAS F. *A Profile of the Negro American.* Princeton, N.J.: Van Nostrand, 1964.

PINKEY, ALPHONSO. *Black Americans.* Englewood Cliffs, N.J.: Prentice-Hall, 1969.

_____. *Red, Black and Green.* New York: Cambridge University Press, 1976.

PORTER, JUDITH D. R. *Black Child, White Child.* Cambridge, Mass.: Harvard University Press, 1971.

RAINWATER, LEE. *Behind Ghetto Walls: Black Families in a Federal Slum.* Chicago: Aldine Publishing Co., 1970.

RICH, ANDREA L. *Interracial Communication.* New York: Harper, 1974.

ROSS, C. J., and R. H. WHEELER. *Black Belonging.* Westport, Conn.: Greenwood, 1971.

SHERRAND, THOMAS R., ed. *Social Welfare and Urban Problems.* New York: Columbia University Press, 1968.

SPEAR A., ed. *Black Chicago 1890-1920.* Chicago: University of Chicago Press, 1967.

THOMPSON, DANIEL C. *Sociology of the Black Experience.* Westport, Conn.: Greenwood, 1974.

WILLIAMS, JOHN E. *Race, Color, and the Young Child.* Chapel Hill: University of North Carolina Press, 1976.

WILLIE, CHARLES V., ed. *Black/ Brown/ White Relations: Race Relations in the 1970's.* New Brunswick, N.J.: Transaction Books, 1976.

Magazines and Journals

Amistad 1 and 2

Anglo-African, The

Black Academy Review

Black American Literature Forum (formerly *Negro American Literature Forum*)

Black Books Bulletin

Black Orpheus: A Journal of African and Afro-American Literature

Black Position, The

Black Review 1 and 2

Black Scholar, The

Black Theater

Black World (formerly Negro Digest)
Challenge and New Challenge
C.L.A. Journal
Colored American, The
Crisis, The
Ebony
Encore
Essence
Fire
Freedomways
Harlem Quarterly
Hoodoo
Journal of Black Poetry, The
Journal of Black Studies, The
Journal of Negro Education, The
Journal of Negro History, The
Juju
Liberator
Messenger, The
Negro American Literature Forum (now Black American Literature
        Forum)
Negro History Bulletin
Negro Quarterly, The
Obsidian: Black Literature in Review
Opportunity: A Journal of Negro Life
Phylon
Presence Africaine
Soul Book
Studies in Black Literature
Voice of the Negro, The
Yardbird

CHRONOLOGICAL INDEX

Events in United States History and Literature

1619   The first blacks arrived in the English colony of Virginia; the House of Burgesses established.

1620   The Pilgrims landed in New England.

1630   The city of Boston founded.

1635   The Boston Latin School established.

1636   Harvard College established.

1638   *The Desire*, the first American slave ship, sailed from Salem, Massachusetts.

1640   *The Bay Psalm Book* published; the Virginia colony made slavery legal.

1641   Shepherd's *Sincere Convert* published.

1647   Nathaniel Ward's *The Simple Cobbler of Aggawam* published.

1650   Anne Bradstreet's *Tenth Muse* published.

1656   The Quakers appeared in Massachusetts.

1664   The English captured New Netherlands and renamed the colony New York.

1670   Charleston, South Carolina, founded.

1672   The Royal African Company organized.

1682   William Penn came to Pennsylvania.

1688   The Germantown Quaker Protest written.

1692   The Salem witchcraft trials occurred.

1700   Samual Sewall's *The Selling of Joseph* published.

1701   Yale College founded; the Society for the Gospel in Foreign Parts founded.

1702	Cotton Mather's *Magnalia Christi: History of the Puritan Movements* published.
1704	The first American newspaper, *The Boston Newsletter*, appeared.
1732	George Washington born in Virginia (died 1799).
1732-1757	Benjamin Franklin's *Poor Richard's Almanac* published; Peter Zenger, newspaper publisher, went to trial and won a case for freedom of the press.
1740-1745	*The Great Awakening*, a religious revival.
1741	Jonathan Edwards's *Sinners in the Hands of an Angry God* published.
1743	Thomas Jefferson born in Virginia (died 1826).
1749	The University of Pennsylvania founded.
1750	Anthony Benezet arrived in Philadelphia.
1754-1763	The French and Indian War.
1765	The Stamp Act passed.
1769	Samuel Adams's *Appeal to the World* published.
1771	Benjamin Franklin's *Autobiography* published.
1774	The First Continental Congress met in Philadelphia.
1775-1783	The American Revolutionary War.
1775	The Battle of Bunker Hill fought.
1776	General Washington recommended the acceptance of free blacks in the Continental armies; the American colonies declared themselves free from England; Thomas Jefferson wrote the Declaration of Independence; Thomas Paine's *The Crisis* and *Common Sense* published; the Phi Beta Kappa Society founded.
1779	Francis Hopkinson's *The Battle of the Kegs* published.
1781	British General Cornwallis surrendered at Yorktown, Virginia.
1791	William Bartram's *Travels Through North and South Carolina* published.
1792-1806	H. Henry Brackenridge's *Modern Chivalry* published.
1793	Fugitive Slave Law enacted by Congress.
1794	William Cullen Bryant born in Cummington, Massachusetts (died 1878); Timothy Dwight's *Greenfield* published.
1797	John Adams's presidency (1797-1801).

1849   The Great Gold Rush to California began.

1850   U.S. population 23,191,876; Nathaniel Hawthorne's *The Scarlet Letter* published; the Compromise of 1850 arranged.

1851   Herman Melville's *Moby Dick,* and Nathaniel Hawthorne's *The House of Seven Gables* published.

1852   Harriet Beecher Stowe's *Uncle Tom's Cabin* published.

1854   The Kansas-Nebraska Bill passed by the U.S. Congress; Henry David Thoreau's *Walden* published.

1855   Walt Whitman's *Leaves of Grass* published.

1856   The Kansas-Nebraska border war began.

1857   The Dred Scott Decision delivered by the U.S. Supreme Court; the magazine *The Atlantic Monthly* first published.

1860   U.S. population 31,443,790; Abraham Lincoln elected president; Nathaniel Hawthorne's *The Marble Faun* published.

1861-
1865   The U.S. Civil War.

1862   The Battle of Antietam.

1863   President Lincoln issued the Emancipation Proclamation; the Battle of Gettysburg.

1865   President Lincoln assassinated; the Freedmens' Bureau established; the Ku Klux Klan organized in Tennessee; the Thirteenth Amendment to the Constitution passed; Walt Whitman's *Drum Taps* published.

1866   A civil rights bill passed by the U.S. Congress; John Greenleaf Whitter's *Snow-Bound* published.

1870   U.S. population 38,818,449; Ralph Waldo Emerson's *Society and Solitude* published; novelist Frank Norris born in Chicago, Illinois (died 1902).

1871   The Tweed Ring destroyed in New York; the Great Chicago Fire occurred; writer Stephen Crane born Newark, New Jersey (died 1900).

1876   Barbed wire invented; the Battle of Little Big Horn; The Hayes-Tilden election disputed; Mark Twain's *Tom Sawyer* and Henry James's *Roderick Hudson* published; Jack London born in San Francisco, California (died 1916).

1877   Rutherford B. Hayes presidency (1877-1881); Sarah Orne Jewett's *Deephaven* and Henry James's *The American* published.

1878   The "Solid South" political structure formed; Henry James's *Daisy Miller* and *The European* published.

1880   U.S. population 50,155,783.

1900   U.S. population 75,994,575; the Boxer Rebellion in China; Theodore Dreiser's *Sister Carrie* published; Thomas Wolfe born in Asheville, North Carolina (died 1938).

1901   Theodore Roosevelt's presidency (1901-1909); Frank Norris's *The Octopus* published; Glenway Wescott born in Wisconsin.

1902   William James's *Varieties of Religious Experience*, Owen Wister's *The Virginian*, and Henry James's *The Wings of the Dove* published; John Steinbeck born in California (died 1968).

1903   Orville and Wilbur Wright flew an airplane for the first time at Kitty Hawk, North Carolina; Frank Norris's *The Pit* and Jack London's *The Call of the Wild* published; novelist Kay Boyle born in Minnesota.

1904   The American Academy of Arts and Letters founded; Henry James's *The Golden Bowl* and Jack London's *The Sea Wolf* published; novelist James T. Farrell born in Chicago, Illinois.

1906   A great earthquake and fire occurred in San Francisco, California; William Sidney Porter's (O'Henry) *The Four Million* and Upton Sinclair's *The Jungle* published; playwright Clifford Odets born in Philadelphia, Pennsylvania (died 1963).

1907   Henry Adam's autobiography, *The Education of Henry Adams,* published.

1909   William Howard Taft's presidency (1909-1913); novelist Eudora Welty born in Mississippi.

1910   U.S. population 91,972,266.

1912   *Poetry: a Magazine of Verse* founded in Chicago.

1913   Woodrow Wilson's presidency (1913-1921); Willa Cather's *O Pioneers* and Robert Frost's *A Boy's Will* published; poet Karl Shapiro born in Baltimore, Maryland.

1915   The Ku Klux Klan revived; Edgar Lee Master's *The Spoon River Anthology* and William McFee's *Casuals of the Sea* published.

1917   U.S. entered World War I; *The Cambridge History of American Literature* and Joseph Hegeshimer's *Three Black Penneys* published; John F. Kennedy born Brookline Massachusetts (died 1963).

1918   The battles of Belleau Wood, Chateau-Thierry, the Argonne Forest, and the second Battle of the Marne fought;

Carl Sandburg's *Cornhuskers* and Booth Tarkington's *The Magnificent Ambersons* published.

1919   The Treaty of Versailles (U.S. did not sign); John Reed's *Ten Day's That Shook the World*, Sherwood Anderson's *Winesburg, Ohio* and Henry L. Mencken's *The American Language* published.

1920   U.S. population 105,710,620; Carl Sandburg's *Smoke and Steel*, F. Scott Fitzgerald's *This Side of Paradise*, and Eugene O'Neill's *Emperor Jones* published.

1921   Warren G. Harding's presidency (1921-1923); the first trial of Nicola Sacco and Bartolomeo Vanzetti held; John Dos Passos's *Three Soldiers*, Ben Hecht's *Erik Dorn*, and Edwin A. Robinson's *Collected Poems* published.

1922   Thomas Stearns Eliot's *The Waste Land* and Edward Estlin Cummings's *The Enormous Room* published.

1923   Calvin Coolidge's presidency (1923-1929); the Teapot Dome scandal; Edna V. Millay's *The Harp Weaver and Other Poems* and D. H. Lawrence's *Studies in Classic American Literature* published.

1925   The J. T. Scopes Trial held in Tennessee; Robinson Jeffers's *The Roan Stallion* and Sinclair Lewis's *Arrowsmith* published.

1926   Carl Van Vechten's *Nigger Heaven* published.

1927   Charles A. Lindbergh flew from New York to Paris alone; Nicola Sacco and Bartolomeo Vanzetti executed in Massachusetts; the U.S. Marines invaded Nicaragua; Edvart Rolvaag's *Giants in the Earth* and Vernon Parrington's *Main Currents in American Thought*, vols. 1 and 2, published.

1928   The first Mickey Mouse cartoon produced.

1929   Herbert Hoover's presidency (1929-1932); the crash of the stock market on October 24 and 29 began the Great Depression; Ernest Hemingway's *Farewell to Arms* and Thomas Wolfe's *Look Homeward Angel* published.

1930   U.S. population 122,775,046; Hart Crane's *The Bridge* and William Faulkner's *As I Lay Dying* published.

1933   Franklin D. Roosevelt's presidency (1933-1945); the Civilian Conservation Corp established; the Twentieth and Twenty-first Amendments to the Constitution ratified; Hervey Allen's *Anthony Adverse* and Eugene O'Neill's *Ah! Wilderness* published.

1935   The Works Progress Administration and the National Youth Administration established; the Federal Writer's Project begun; Clifford Odets's *Waiting for Lefty* produced.

1936   Franklin D. Roosevelt reelected president; the Federal Theater Project established (1936-1939); Margaret Mitchell's *Gone with the Wind* and Irwin Shaw's *Bury the Dead* published.

1937   John Steinbeck's *The Red Pony* published.

1938   Howard Hughes flew around the world in ninety-one hours; Robert Sherwood's *Abe Lincoln in Illinois* and Thornton Wilder's *Our Town* published.

1940   U.S. population 131,669,275; *The Dictionary of American History*, Carson McCullers's *The Heart Is a Lonely Hunter*, Thomas Wolfe's *You Can't Go Home Again*, and Willa Cathers' *Sapphia and the Slave Girl* published; Franklin D. Roosevelt became president for the third time.

1941   The Japanese Naval Air Force attacked Pearl Harbor and the United States entered World War II; Edmund Wilson's *The Wound and the Bow*, F. Scott Fitzgerald's *The Last Tycoon*, and Edna St. Vincent Millay's *Collected Sonnets* published.

1942   U.S. military forces in the Philippine Islands surrendered; Bataan and Corregidor captured; U.S. war planes under the command of General James Dolittle bombed Tokyo, Japan; the naval battles of Midway, Coral Sea, and the Solomon Islands and the battle for Guadalcanal Island fought; U.S. forces landed in North Africa; Douglass Southall Freeman's *Lee's Lieutenant's*, William Faulkner's *Go Down Moses*, and E. B. White's *One Man's Meat* published.

1943   Allied military forces led by General Dwight D. Eisenhower forced the German army to abandon North Africa; Sicily and Italy invaded; the Japanese offensive in the Pacific halted; Thomas Stearns Eliot's *Four Quartets*, Betty Smith's *A Tree Grows in Brooklyn*, and John Dos Passos's *Number One* published.

1944   General Douglas MacArthur led U.S. and Philippine military forces in a return to the Philippine Islands; Western Europe invaded by Allied forces on D Day, June 6; John Hershey's *A Bell for Adano*, Charles Jackson's *The Lost Week End*, and Karl Shapiro's *V-Letter* published; Franklin D. Roosevelt elected president for a fourth term and died shortly after inauguration; Harry S. Truman's presidency (1944-1953).

1945   Germany surrendered to the Allies; V-E Day; the battles of Iwo Jima and Okinawa fought; atomic bombs dropped on the Japanese cities of Hiroshima and Nagasaki; Japan surrendered; V-J Day; the United Nations chartered; Arthur Schlesinger's *The Age of Jackson,* Glenway Wescott's *An Apartment in Athens,* and Tennessee Williams's *The Glass Menagerie* published.

1946   The United Nations met for the first time; Carson McCullers's *Member of the Wedding* and Robert Lowell's *Lord Weary's Castle* published.

1947   The Marshall Plan, developed by General George C. Marshall to help in European reconstruction, begun; the Taft-Hartley Labor Relations Act passed by the U.S. Congress; Bernard DeVoto's *Across the Wide Missouri* and Allen Nevin's *The Ordeal of the Union* published.

1948   Harry S. Truman elected to a full term as president of the United States; the Berlin Airlift began; William Faulkner's *Intruder in the Dust* and Truman Capote's *Other Voices Other Rooms* published

1950   U.S. population 150,597,361; North Korea invaded South Korea; Thomas Stearns Eliot's *The Cocktail Party* and Ernest Hemingway's *Across the River and into the Trees* published.

1952   Dwight D. Eisenhower's presidency (1953-1960); Ernest Hemingway's *The Old Man and the Sea* and Bernard DeVoto's *The Course of Empire* published.

1953   A truce arranged in the Korean War; Saul Bellow's *The Adventures of Augie March* and Thomas Stearns Eliot's *The Confidential Clerk* published; death of Eugene O'Neill.

1954   The U.S. Supreme Court declared racial segregation in the public schools unconstitutional in *Brown v. The Board of Education of Topeka Kansas;* the U.S. became involved in the Vietnam conflict; Eudora Welty's *The Ponder Heart* and William Faulkner's *A Fable* published.

1955   The Salk polio vaccine developed; Arthur Miller's *The View from the Bridge* published.

1956   Dwight Eisenhower reelected president; *The Letters of Thomas Wolfe,* Nelson Algren's *A Walk on the Wild Side,* and Edwin O'Connor's *The Last Hurrah* published.

1957   President Eisenhower ordered U.S. troops and Arkansas National Guardsmen into Little Rock, Arkansas, in the school desegregation crisis; James Agee's *A Death in the Family*, Jack Keroac's *On the Road*, and Richard Wilbur's *Poems* published.

1958   Governor Orval Faubus of Arkansas closed the public schools and reopened them as private schools; the National Aeronautic and Space Administration established; Alaska admitted to the Union as the forty-ninth state; Archibald MacLeish's *J.B.*, James Jones's *Some Came Running*, and Robert Penn Warren's *Promises* published; death of James Branch Cabell.

1959   Hawaii admitted to the Union as the fiftieth state; Phillip Roth's *Good Bye Columbus* and William Snodgrass's *The Heart's Needle* published.

1960   U.S. population 170,323,175; John F. Kennedy's presidency (1960-1963); the U2 spy plane incident; John Updike's *Rabbit Run* and William Faulkner's *The Mansion* published.

1961   John Glenn orbited the earth in a space craft; John Steinbeck's *The Winter of Our Discontent*, Irving Stone's *The Agony and the Ecstacy*, and Marc Shorer's *Sinclair Lewis* published.

1962   The drug Thalidomide caused children to be born deformed; Edward Albee's *Who's Afraid of Virginia Woolf*, Edmund Wilson's *Patriotic Gore*, and Philip Roth's *Letting Go* published.

1963   President John Fitzgerald Kennedy assassinated in Texas; intense and widespread civil rights demonstrations by blacks and their white allies; Robert Frost's *In the Clearing* and John Updike's *The Centaur* published; death of playwright Clifford Odets; death of poet Theodore Rothke; death of poet William Carlos Williams.

1964   Lyndon Baines Johnson elected president; civil rights bill passed by Congress; Gore Vidal's *Julian* and Saul Bellow's *Herzog* published.

1965   U.S. troops sent to the Dominican Republic to settle a revolt; military support for South Vietnam increased; Norman Mailer's *The American Dream*, Shirley Ann Grau's *The Keepers of the House*, Arthur Schlesinger's *The Thousand Days*, and John Berryman's *Seventy-Seven Dream Songs* published.

implicated President Nixon in the Watergate Affair; Vice-President Spiro Agnew resigned from office; Congressman Gerald R. Ford became vice-president of the United States;Kurt Vonnegut's *Breakfast of Champions*; Thomas Pynchon's *Gravity's Rainbow*, and Malcolm Cowley's *A Second Flowering* published.

1974   Richard Nixon resigned as president of the United States; Gerald R. Ford became the thirty-ninth president; President Ford granted Richard Nixon a pardon for any criminal offenses he may have committed while in office; James A. Michener's *Centennial*; Joseph Heller's *Something Happened*, and Robert Lowell's *The Dolphin* published.

1975   The Vietnam War ended; two assassination attempts made on the life of President Ford, both of them in California; Judith Rossner's *Looking for Mr. Goodbar*, E. L. Doctorow's *Ragtime*, and Gary Snyder's *Turtle Island* published.

1976   James Earl (Jimmy) Carter, ex-governor of Georgia elected president; NASA's Viking landers searched for life on the planet Mars; Chaim Potok's *In the Beginning*, Joseph Wambaugh's *The Choirboys*, and John Ashberry's *Self Portrait in a Convex Mirror* were published.

1977   Death of novelist Vladimir Nabokob.

1978   The Memiors of Richard Nixon were published.

Events in United States Afro-American History and Literature

1526   Black slaves brought to the Carolinas by the Spanish.

1619   Blacks appeared in Jamestown, Virginia.

1637   Black Slaves appeared in Boston and the New Netherlands.

1640   Slavery made legal in Virginia.

1645   Slavery made legal in New York.

1692   Tituba Indian, a black woman slave, was the central figure in the Salem witchcraft trials.

1720   Poet Jupiter Hammon born in New York (died 1800).

1753   Phillis Wheatley born in Africa (died 1784).

1754-
1763   The French and Indian war; black troops fought.

1798	James P. Beckwourth, explorer and mountain man, born in Virginia (died 1867).
1800	U.S. black population 1,002,037; Gabriel Prosser's slave rebellion in Henrico County, Virginia.
1809	Antislavery leader and writer James W. C. Pennington born a slave in Maryland (died 1870).
1810	U.S. black population 1,337,808; black abolitionist Charles Lennox Remond born in Salem, Massachusetts (died 1873).
1811	Daniel A. Payne, church leader and writer, born in Charleston, South Carolina (died 1893).
1812	War of 1812 (1812-1815); Martin R. Delaney, black abolitionist, editor, and novelist, born in Charlestown, Virginia (died 1885).
1813	James McCune Smith, black abolitionist and writer, born in New York City (died 1864).
1814	The blacks of Philadelphia built and manned fortifications to defend the city against British attacks; Henry Highland Garnet, black abolitionist and writer, born in New Market, Maryland (died 1884).
1816	William Wells Brown, novelist and playwright, born in Lexington, Kentucky (died 1884); William Cooper Nell, black abolitionist, editor, and historian, born in Boston, Massachusetts (died 1874).
1817	Frederick Douglass, black abolitionist leader, editor and writer, born in Talbot County, Maryland (died 1895).
1820	U.S. black population 1,771,656; Robert Duncanson, painter, born in Cincinnati, Ohio.
1821	William Still, historian of the Underground Railroad and writer, born in Maryland (died 1902); Harriet Tubman, black abolitionist, born in Maryland (died 1913); the African Players, a black theatrical troupe, performed in New York City.
1822	The Denmark Vesey Rebellion in Charleston, South Carolina.
1825	Frances Ellen Watkins Harper, poet and novelist, born in Baltimore, Maryland (died 1911).
1827	*Freedom's Journal*, the first black newspaper in the United States edited by Samuel Cornish and John B. Russwurm, founded in New York City.
1828	The Reading Room Society of Philadelphia founded.
1829	The New York African Clarkson Society, a literary club, founded in New York City; David Walker's antislavery

pamphlet, *Appeal in Four Articles Together With A Preamble To The Colored Citizens Of The United States*, better known as *The Appeal*, and George Moses Horton's poem, *The Hope of Liberty*, were published.

1830   U.S. black population 2,328,642; the New York Philomathean Society, a reading club, founded in New York City.

1831   The first Convention of People of Color held in Philadelphia; a violent revolt led by slave Nat Turner in Virginia; the Female Literary Society of Philadelphia and the Theban Literary Society of Pittsburgh founded.

1832   The Afric-American Female Society and the Boston Philomathean Society founded in Boston.

1833   The Library Company of Colored People in Philadelphia, the Phoenix Society, a reading and literary club in New York City, and a literary society in Providence, Rhode Island founded.

1834   The Minerva and the New York Garrison Literary Society in New York City and the Washington D.C., Convential Society, a literary group, established; David Ruggles's pamphlet, *The Extinguisher Extinguished*, published.

1835   The Thompson Literary and Debating Society founded.

1837   The Institute for Colored Youth set up in Pennsylvania; P. B. S. Pinchback, black Reconstruction leader, born Mississippi (died 1920); the *Weekly Advocate*, a newspaper edited by Samuel Cornish, founded in New York City.

1838   Frederick Douglass escaped from slavery; David Ruggles, black abolitionist, editor and writer, established the first black magazine in the United States, the *Mirror of Liberty*, in New York City; the *National Reformer*, a newspaper, founded; Charlotte Forten, a writer, born in Philadelphia (died 1914).

1840   U. S. black population 2,873,648; the pamphlet *The Colonization Scheme Considered and Its Rejection by the Colored People* published in Newark, New Jersey.

1841   William Lloyd Garrison and Frederick Douglass met at an antislavery meeting in Nantucket, Massachusetts; J. W. C. Pennington's *Textbook on the Origin and History of the Colored People* published; J. W. Loguen, a future bishop of the A.M.E. Church, moved to Syracuse, New York.

1845   Edmonia Lewis, a black sculptress, born in New York

State; Frederick Douglass's *Narrative on the Life of Frederick Douglass* and *Les Cenelles,* the first anthology of verse by black poets in the United States, published.

1847   The *North Star.* a newspaper founded by Frederick Douglass, began publication; an autobiography, *The Narrative of William Wells Brown,* published.

1848   William Wells Brown's *The Anti-Slavery Harp* published.

1849   Harriet Tubman, abolitionist and Underground Railroad official, escaped from slavery; George Washington Williams, historian, born in Bedford Springs, Pennsylvania, (died 1891); Archibald H. Grimke, writer and civil rights leader, born in Charleston, South Carolina (died 1930); the autobiographies *The Life of Josiah Henson, the Narrative of Henry "Box" Brown,* and, in London, J. W. C. Pennington's *The Fugitive Blacksmith* published.

1850   U.S. black population 3,638,808; an autobiography, *Narrative of Sojourner Truth a Northern Slave,* published.

1851   Poet, Albery A. Whitman born in Kentucky (died 1902); William Cooper Nell's *The Services of Colored Americans in the Wars of 1776 and 1812* published.

1852   William Wells Brown's *Three Years in Europe* published in London and Martin Delaney's *The Condition, Elevation, Emigration, and Destiny of the Colored People of the United States* appeared.

1853   William Wells Brown's *Clotel or the President's Daughter,* the first novel by a black American writer, published in London; Solomon Northrupt's *Twelve Years A Slave* published.

1854   The case of escaped slave Anthony Burns's return to Virginia taken to court in Boston, Massachusetts; Lincoln University founded in Pennsylvania, Frances Ellen Watkin's *Poems on Miscellaneous Subjects* published; songwriter James Bland born in Flushing, New York (died 1911).

1855   Frederick Douglass's autobiography, *My Bondage My Freedom,* and, in London, Samuel Ringold Ward's *Autobiography of a Fugitive Negro* published.

1856   Wilberforce founded by the Methodist Episcopal Church in Ohio; Timothy Thomas Fortune, poet, editor, and author, born in Florida (died 1928); Booker T. Washington. black leader and writer, born in Hales Ford, Virginia (died 1915).

1857   Frank Webb's *The Garies and Their Friends* published.

poser and musician, born in Jacksonville, Florida (died 1954); the Colfax Massacre in Louisiana.

1874　William Wells Brown's collection of biographies, *The Rising Son*, published.

1875　Mary McLeod Bethune, educator and writer, born in South Carolina (died 1955); Carter G. Woodson, historian, born in Virginia (died 1950).

1876　Bert Williams, vaudeville star, born in the West Indies (died 1924)

1877　Meta Vaux Warrick Fuller, sculptress, born in Philadelphia (died 1967); Sculptress May Howard Jackson born in Philadelphia (died 1930); Albery Whitman's *Not A Man and Yet A Man* published.

1878　Henry Ossian Flipper's autobiography, *The Colored Cadet at West Point*, published.

1879　The *Washington Bee*, a newspaper, founded in Washington, D.C.

1880　U.S. black population 6,580,793; William Wells Brown's *My Southern Home* published; Booker T. Washington opened Tuskeegee.

1882　Benjamin Brawley, literary critic, historian, and poet, born in Columbia, South Carolina (died 1939); the third edition of Frederick Douglass's *The Life and Times of Frederick Douglass* published.

1883　George Washington Williams's *History of the Negro Race in America* published.

1884　William Scott, painter, born in Indiana (died 1964); Albery Whitman's *The Rape of Florida* published.

1885　Huddie Ledbetter, folksinger, born in Louisiana (died 1949); Joseph "King" Oliver, musician and band leader, born in Louisiana (died 1938); George Washington Williams's *The Negro in the American Rebellion* published.

1886　Alain Locke, literary critic, born in Philadelphia (died 1954).

1887　Marcus Garvey, black nationalist leader born in Jamaica, West Indies (died 1940); John F. Matheus, poet, short story writer, critic, born in Keyser, West Virginia; Charles Chesnutt's *The Goopherd Grapevine* published.

1888　Fenton Johnson, poet, born in Chicago, Illinois, Sargent Johnson, sculptor, born in Boston, Massachusetts (died 1967); Horace Pippin, painter, born in West Chester, Pennsylvania (died 1946); Daniel A Payne's *Recollections of Seventy Years* published (he was a Bishop of the A.M.E. Church and a poet).

1889   Willis Richardson, playwright, born in Wilmington, North Carolina.

1890   U.S. black population 7,448,676; Claude McKay, poet and novelist born in Jamaica, West Indies (died 1948).

1891   Charles H. Wesley, historian, born in Louisville, Kentucky; Archibald Motley, painter, born in New Orleans, Louisiana; Archibald Grimke's *The Life of Charles Sumner* published.

1892   The *Baltimore Afro-American,* a newspaper, founded by John Murphy; blues singer William "Big Bill" Broonzy born in Scott, Mississippi (died 1957).

1893   Paul Laurence Dunbar's *Oak and Ivy* published.

1894   E. Franklin Frazier, sociologist, born in Baltimore, Maryland (died 1962); Bessie Smith, blues singer, born in Clarksdale, Mississippi (died 1937); George W. Lee, novelist born in Indianola, Mississippi (died 1976).

1895   Florence Mills, singer, born in Washington D.C. (died 1927); death of Frederick Douglass; William Grant Still, composer, born in Woodville, Mississippi; Paul Laurence Dunbar's *Majors and Minors* published

1896   Malvin Gray Johnson, painter, born in Greensboro, South Carolina (died 1934); Josua Henry Jones's *Hearts of Gold,* Paul Laurence Dunbar's *Lyrics of a Lowly Life,* and W. E. B. DuBois's *The Suppression of the Slave Trade to the United States of America, 1638-1870* published.

1897   The American Negro Academy founded in Washington, D.C., by Alexander Crummel and others; James Edwin Campbell's *Echos from the Cabin and Elsewhere* and Daniel Webster's *Weh Doun Souf* published.

1898   A black musical, *Clorindy,* book by Paul Laurence Dunbar and music by Will Marion Cook, opened in New York City: Paul Robeson, singer and actor, born in Princeton, New Jersey (died 1976); Joseph S. Cotter, Sr.'s *Links of Friendship* and Paul Laurence Dunbar's *Folks from Dixie* and *The Uncalled* published.

1899   Edward K. "Duke" Ellington born in Washington, D.C. (died 1974); Aaron Douglass born in Topeka, Kansas; Charles Chestnutt's *The Wife of His Youth, The Conjure*

Woman, and *Frederick Douglass*, Paul Laurence Dunbar's *Lyrics of the Hearthside,* and *W. E. B. DuBois's The Philadelphia Negro* published.

1900   U.S. black population 8,833,994; James Wledon Johnson composed the black national anthem, "Lift Every Voice and Sing"; Augusta Savage, sculptress, born in Green Cover Springs, Florida (died 1962); Hale Woodruff, painter, born in Cairo, Illinois; Charles Chesnutt's *The House behind the Cedars,* Paul Laurence Dunbar's *The Love of the Laundry,* and Booker T. Washington's *Up from Slavery* published.

1901   The *Boston Guardian,* a newspaper, founded by Monroe Trotter; Albery Whitman's *The Octoroon,* Paul Laurence Dunbar's *The Fanatics* and *The Sport of Gods,* and Charles Chesnutt's *The Marrow of Tradition* published.

1902   Arna Bontemps, novelist and poet, born in Alexandria, Louisiana (died 1973).

1903   Countee Cullen, poet and novelist, born in New York City (died 1946); Zora Neal Hurston, novelist, born in Eatonville, Florida (died 1960); Ralph J. Bunche born in Detroit, Michigan (died 1971); W. E. B. DuBois's *The Souls of Black Folk,* Paul Laurence Dunbar's *Lyrics of Love and Laughter,* and *In Old Plantation Days,* and Joseph Scotter's *Cableb the Degenerate* published.

1904   A race riot in Springfield, Ohio; Paul Laurence Dunbar's *The Heart of Happy Hollow,* William Stanley Braithwaite's *Lyrics of Life and Love,* and James Madison Bell's *Poetic Works* published.

1905   W. E. B. DuBois organized the Niagara Movement in Niagara Falls, Canada; Frank Marshall Davis, poet, born in Arkansas City, Kansas; George Edmund Haynes's *The Negro At Work in New York City,* Charles Chesnutt's *The Colonel's Dream,* and Paul Laurence Dunbar's *Lyrics of Sunshine and Laughter* published.

1906   A race riot involving black U.S. Army troops in Brownsville, Texas; the Equal Rights Association, a civil rights organization, formed in Macon, Georgia; literary critic Jay Saunders Redding born in Wilmington, Delaware; J. Mord Allen's *Rhymes, Tales and Rhymed Tales* published.

1907   Robert Weaver, the first black presidential cabinet member, born in Washington, D.C.; William Stanley Braithwaite's *The House of Falling Leaves* published.

1908   A severe race riot in Springfield, Illinois.

1909   The National Association for the Advancement of Colored People (NAACP) founded; Kelly Miller's *Race Adjustment* and Booker T. Washington's *The Story of the Negro* published.

1910   U.S. black population 9,827,763; Cyrus Colter, short story writer and novelist born in Nobelsville, Indiana; Benjamin Brawley's *The Negro in Literature and Art in the United States* appeared; the *Crisis Magazine,* house organ of the NAACP, began publication.

1911   The National Urban League organized; the Phelps Stokes Fund for the education of Afro-American, African, North American Indian, and poor white students established; W. E. B. DuBois's *The Quest of the Silver Fleece* published.

1912   James Weldon Johnson's *The Autobiography of an Ex-Colored Man* published.

1913   Robert Hayden, poet and critic, born in Detroit, Michigan; William Stanley Braithwaite began to edit *The Anthology of Magazine Verse;* Paul Laurence Dunbar's *Complete Poems* and Oscar Micheaux's *The Conquest* published; death of Harriet Tubman.

1914   Dudley Randall born in Washington D.C.; Owen Dodson, poet and novelist born in Brooklyn, New York; Romare Bearden, painter, born Charlotte, North Carolina; Ralph Waldo Ellison, novelist and essayist, born in Oklahoma City.

1915   The Association For the Study of Negro Life and History (Washington, D.C.) and Karamu Theater (Cleveland, Ohio) founded; Scott Joplin, musician and composer, wrote *Tree-monisha,* a ragtime opera; John Hope Franklin, historian, born in Rentiesville, Oklahoma; Ray Durem, poet, born in Seattle, Washington; (died 1963); John W. Work's *Folk Songs of the American Negro,* and W. E. B. DuBois's *The Negro* published; death of Booker T. Washington.

1916   The *Journal of Negro History* founded; the Amenia Conference held in New York State; in Georgia were born novelists and short story writers John O. Killens in Macon and Frank Yerby in Augusta.

1916- The Great Migration of Blacks from the rural South to
1920   northern industrial cities; George Marion McClellan's *The Path of Dreams* published.

1917 A violent race riot in East St. Louis, Illinois; the *Negro World*, a newspaper, founded by Marcus Garvey; Samuel W. Allen (Paul Vesey), poet, born in Columbus, Ohio; Gwendolyn Brooks, poet and novelist, born in Topeka, Kansas; Ossie Davis, actor and playwright, born in Cogsdell, Georgia; Jacob Lawrence, painter, born in Atlantic City New Jersey; James Weldon Johnson's *Fifty Years and Other Poems* published.

1918 William Stanley Braithwaite received the Springarn Medal; Bruce M. McWright, poet, was born in Princeton, New Jersey; publisher John H. Johnson born in Arkansas City Arkansas; Kelly Miller's *The Appeal to Conscience* published.

1919 Savage race riots in Washington, D.C., and Chicago; because of the numerous lynchings and riots that took place, the summer of 1919 called the Red Summer; Charles White, artist, born in Chicago; Lance Jeffers, poet, born in Fremont, Nebraska; M. Carl Holman, poet, born in Minter City, Mississippi.

1029 U.S. black population 10,436,131; W. E. B DuBois's *Darkwater* published.

1921 Bibliographer Robert L. Southgate born in Cincinnati, Ohio; James Farmer, civil rights leader born in Marshall, Texas; James Emanuel, poet and critic, born in Alliance, Nebraska, James Weldon Johnson's *The Book of American Negro Poetry* and Benjamin Brawley's *A Social History of the Negro* published.

1922 The home of Frederick Douglass became a museum; the Harmon Foundation founded; Carter G. Woodson's *The Negro in Our History,* Claude McKay's *Harlem Shadows* and Leslie Pinckney Hill's *Wings of Oppression* published.

1923 The Abyssinian Baptist Church opened in a new building in Harlem, New York; *Opportunity,* the house magazine of the Urban League, began publication under the editorship of Charles Spurgeon Johnson; Naomi Long Madgett, poet, born in Norfolk, Virginia; Jean Toomer's *Cane* published.

1924 Roland Hayes, concert singer, awarded the Spingarn Medal; Charles S. (Chuck) Stone, novelist, born in St. Louis, Missouri; James Baldwin, novelist and essayist, born in Harlem, New York; John Biggers, a painter, born in Gastonia, North Carolina; Sidney Poiter, actor and director, born in Miami, Florida; Kelly Miller's *The Everlasting*

Stain, Jessie Fauset's *There Is Confusion*, and W. E. B. DuBois's *Gift of Black Folk* published.

1925   Marcus Garvey, black nationalist leader, imprisoned; James Weldon Johnson, poet, novelist, essayist, awarded the Spingarn Medal; John A. Williams, novelist, born in Jackson, Mississippi; Black leader Malcolm X (Malcolm Little) born in Omaha, Nebraska (died 1965); Lerman (Zack) Gilbert, poet, born in McMullen, Missouri; Countee Cullen's *Color*, Alain Locke's *The New Negro*, Walter White's *The Fire in the Flint*, and James Weldon Johnson's *The Book of Negro Spirituals*, published; Garland Anderson's *Appearances* opened on Broadway; Wallace Thurman's *Harlem* opened at the 42nd Street Apollo Theater.

1926   Carter Woodson, historian, awarded the Spingarn medal; Langston Hughes's "The Negro Artist and the Racial Mountain" appeared in *Nation Magazine;* the literary magazine *Fire* founded and ceased to exist after the first issue; Langston Hughes's *The Weary Blues* and Walter White's *Flight* published; death of classical scholar William S. Scarborough.

1927:   Marcus Garvey, black nationalist leader, deported to Jamaica, West Indies; during the Coffeeville, Kansas, race riot street fighting between blacks and whites went on for three days; critic Hoyt Fuller born in Atlanta, Georgia; Russel Atkins, poet, born in Cleveland, Ohio; opera singer Leontyne Prince born in Laurel, Mississippi; James Weldon Johnson's *God's Trombones*, Langston Hughes's *Fine Clothes to the Jew*, and Charles S. Johnson's *Ebony and Topaz*, published.

1928   Charles Chesnutt, novelist, awarded the Spingarn Medal; James C. Kilgore, poet, born in Ansley, Louisiana; Eugenia Collier, literary critic, born in Baltimore, Maryland; Tad Joans, poet, born in Cairo, Illinois; Julian Mayfield, novelist, born; Henry Van Dyke, novelist born in Alegan, Michigan; Rudolph Fisher's *The Walls of Jericho*, Claude McKay's *Home to Harlem*, W. E. B. DuBois's *Dark Princess*, Nella Larsen's *Quicksand*, and Jesse Fauset's *Plum Bun* published.

1929   Martin Luther King, civil rights leader and writer, born in Atlanta, Georgia (died 1968); Paule Marshall, novelist and short story writer, born in Brooklyn, New York; Countee Cullen's *Black Christ*, Claude McKay's *Banjo*, and Wallace Thurman's *The Blacker the Berry* published.

1930   U.S. black population 11,891,143; Sam Greenlee, novelist, born in Chicago; Lorraine Hansberry, playwright, born in Chicago (died 1965); Bobb Hamilton, poet, born in Cleveland, Ohio; Langston Hughes's *Not without Laughter*, Charles S. Johnson's *The Negro in American Civilization*, and James Weldon Johnson's *Black Manhattan* published.

1931   *The Journal of Negro Education* founded; Kristin Hunter, novelist, born in Philadelphia; Martin J. Hamer, short story writer, born in New York City; Darwin Turner, literary critic and poet, born in Cincinnati, Ohio; Jesse Fauset's *The Chinaberry Three*, Arna Bontemps's *God Sends Sunday*, and George S. Schulyer's *Slaves Today* published.

1932   The blacks deserted the Republican party and voted for the Democratic party candidate, Franklin D. Roosevelt, in the presidential elections; Melvin Van Peebles, novelist and film maker, born in Newport News, Virginia; Calvin Hernton, poet and novelist born in Chattnooga, Tennessee; Cifford Mason, playwright and critic, born in Brooklyn, New York; Sterling Brown's *Southern Road*, Claude McKay's *Gingertown*, Rudolph Fisher's *Conjure Man Dies* (first detective novel by a black writer in the United States) published.

1933   The first the Scottsboro trials began; Conrad Kent Rivers, poet, born in Atlantic City, New Jersey (died 1968); Etheridge Knight, poet, born in Corinth, Mississippi; James Weldon Johnson's *Along This Way*, Claude McKay's *Banana Bottom*, and Jesse Fauset's *Comedy American Style*, published.

1934   The literary magazine *Challenge* founded; W. E. B. DuBois resigned as editor of *Crisis;* Imamu Amiri Baraka (Everett LeRoi Jones), poet and short story writer, born in Newark, New Jersey; Sonia Sanchez, poet, born in Birmingham, Alabama; Edward S. Spriggs, poet and painter, born in Cleveland, Ohio; Audre Lorde, poet, born in New York City; Henry Dumas, poet, born in Sweet Home, Arkansas (died 1968); Langston Hughes's *The Ways of White Folks*, Zora Neal Hurston's *Jonas Gourd Vine*, Charles S. Johnson's *The Shadow of the Plantation* and James Weldon Johnson's *Negro Americans What Now?* published.

1935   A race riot in Harlem, New York; Lanston Hughes's *Mulatto* opened for a long run in New York City; William Grant Still's *Afro-American Symphony* performed by the New

York Philharmonic Orchestra; Johari Amini (Jewel Lattimore), poet, born in Philadelphia; Eldridge Cleaver, essayist, born in Wabbseka, Arkansas; A. B. Spellman, poet, born in Elizabeth City, North Carolina; Jay Wright, poet, born in Albuquerque, New Mexico; Ed Bullins, playwright, born in Philadelphia; Frank Marshall Davis's *Black Man's Verse* and George Wylie Henderson's *Ollie Miss* published.

1936   The National Negro Congress founded; Neil Harris, playwright, born in Valhala, New York; Clarence Major, poet, critic, and novelist, born in Atlanta, Georgia; Benjamin Brawley's *Paul Laurence Dunbar* and O'Wendell Shaw's *Greater Need Below* published.

1937   Joe Louis Barrow became heavyweight boxing champion of the world; Walter White, civil rights leader and writer, awarded the Spingarn Medal; Eugene Redmond, poet and critic, born in St. Louis; Jane Cortez, poet, born in Arizona; Sharon Bell Mathis, writer of children's stories, born in Atlantic City, New Jersey; Joe Goncalves, poet and critic, born in Boston; William Melvin Kelley, novelist and short story writer, born in New York City; Laurence P. Neal, poet and literary critic, born in Atlanta, Georgia; Waters E. Turpin's *These Low Grounds*, Zora Neal Hurston's *Their Eyes Were Watching God*, George W. Lee's *River George*, and Frank Marshall Davis's *I Am the American Negro* published; death of blues singer Bessie Smith.

1938   Henry Armstrong became both lightweight and welterweight boxing champion of the world; James A. Randall, poet, born in Detroit, Michigan; Ishmael Reed, poet and novelist, born in Chattanooga, Tennessee; poet Julia Fields was born in Uniontown, Alabama; Richard Wright's *Uncle Tom's Children*, Benjamin Brawley's *Negro Builders and Heroes*, and Sterling Brown's *The Negro in American Fiction* and *Negro Poetry and Drama* published.

1939   *Harlem on the Prairie*, the first all-black western produced by Jed Buell; Toni Cade Bambara, short story writer, born in New York City; Jaqueline Earley, poet, born in Buffalo, New York; Julius Lester, poet, critic, and editor, born in St. Louis; Al Young, poet and novelist, born; David Llorens, critic, born in Chicago; Walters E. Turpin's *O Canaan*, Franklin Frazier's *The Negro in the United States*, Jay Saunders Redding's *To Make a Poet Black*, and William Attaway's *Let Me Breathe Thunder* published.

1940   The literary magazine *Phylon* founded with W. E. B. Du-
        Bois as editor; Frenchy Jolene Hodges, poet, born in Dublin,
        Georgia; Geneva Smitherman, critic and editor, born in
        Brownsville, Tennessee; Richard Wright's *Native Son*,
        Langston Hughes's *The Big Sea*, Claude McKay's *Harlem
        Negro Metropolis*, and Robert Hayden's *Heart Shape in the
        Dust* published.

1941   John Wideman, novelist, born in Washington, D. C.; Alain
        Locke's *The Negro in Art*, Richard Wright's *Twelve Million
        Black Voices*, William Attaway's *Blood on the Force*, Ster-
        ling Brown's *The Negro Caravan*, and Jay Saunders Red-
        ding's *No Day of Triumph* published.

1942   Margaret Walker won the Yale University Younger Poets
        Award for *For My People*; David Henderson, poet, born in
        Harlem, New York; Stokley Carmichael, civil rights leader
        and writer, born in Trinidad; Don. L. Lee (Haki R.
        Maghabuti) poet, born in Little Rock, Arkansas.

1943   Violent race riots in Detroit, Harlem, and Mobile, Alabama;
        the Congress of Racial Equality (CORE) began its first sit-
        in demonstration at Stoner's Restaurant on the Chicago
        Loop; Nikki Giovanni, poet, born in Knoxville, Tennessee;
        Langston Hughes's *Freedom's Plow* and *Jim Crow's Last
        Stand*, and Roi Ottley's *New World A Comin* published.

1944   The U.S. Supreme Court declared the "white primary"
        unconstitutional; the United Negro College Fund estab-
        lished; Frank Yerby won the O'Henry Award for "Health
        Card"; Alice Walker, poet, critic, and novelist, born in
        Eaton, Georgia; Ron Wellburn, poet, editor, and short story
        writer, born in Bryn Mawr, Pennsylvania; John Mc-
        Cluskey, novelist and short story writer, born in Middle-
        town, Ohio; Barbara McBain (Mahone), poet, born in
        Chicago; Melvin Tolson's *Rendevous with America*, and
        Langston Hughes's *Lament for Dark Peoples* published.

1945   Sharyn Jeanne Skeeter, poet and critic, born in New York
        City; Chester Himes's *If He Hollers Let Him Go* and Gwen-
        dolyn Brooks's *A Street in Bronzeville* published.

1946   William H. Hastie, a black man, became governor of the
        Virgin Islands; Mae Jackson, poet, born in Earl Arkansas;
        Frank Yerby's *The Foxes of Harrow* and Owen Dodson's
        Powerful Long Ladder published; death of Countee Cullen.

1947   *Ebony* magazine founded in Chicago by John H. Johnson;

Jackie Robinson became the first black to play officially on a major league team, the Brooklyn Dodgers; CORE began its first Freedom Ride into the South; Theodore Ward's *Our Land* produced on Broadway; Stephany Fuller (Stephany), poet, born in Chicago.

1948   Lisbeth Grant, literary critic and short story writer, born in Chicago; William Thigpen, poet, born in Detroit, Michigan (died 1971); Frank Marshall Davis's *47th Street*, Robert Hayden and Myron O'Higgins's *The Lion and the Archer*, Jonathan H. Brooks's *The Ressurrection and Other Poems*, and William Gardener Smith's *The Last of the Conquerers* published.

1949   Congressman William L. Dawson became chairman of the House of Representatives Expenditure Committee; Gayl Jones, poet and novelist, born in Lexington, Kentucky; Willard Savoy's *Alien Land* published.

1950   U.S. black population 15,042,286; James Weldon Johnson Memorial Collection of Negro Arts and Letters established at Yale University from materials given by Carl Van Vechen; the University of Virginia Law School ordered to admit blacks; Dr. Ralph Johnson Bunche received the Nobel Peace Prize; poet Gwendolyn E. Brooks became the first black person to be awarded a Pulitzer Prize, for *Annie Allen;* William Demby's *Beetlecreek* and Jay Saunders Redding's *They Came in Chains* published.

1951   The University of North Carolina Law School ordered by the courts in the case of *McKissick v. Carmichael* to admit blacks as students; Jersey Joe Walcott became heavyweight boxing champion of the world; James Baldwin's *Go Tell It on the Mountain,* Owen Dodson's *Boy at the Window,* and Willard Motley's *We Fished All Night* published.

1952   Archie Moore became the light heavyweight champion of the world; Ralph Ellison's *The Invisible Man* and Jay Saunders Redding's *On Being a Negro American* published.

1953   Mark Kennedy's *The Pecking Order,* Ann Petry's *The Narrows,* and Gwendolyn Brooks's *Maude Martha* published; Louis Peterson's *Take A Giant Step* opened on Broadway and had a successful run.

1954   The United State Supreme Court declared, in the case of *Brown* v. *Board of Education of Topeka, Kansas,* public school segregation to be unconstitutional; Charles Diggs elected to the House of Representatives from Detroit; white citizens councils organized in many parts of the South; John O. Killens *Youngblood* published; Charles Seebree and Greer Johnson's Mrs. *Patterson* and William Branch's *In Splendid Error* produced in New York City.

1955   Fourteen-year-old Emmet Till from Chicago, visiting relatives, kidnapped and lynched in Money, Mississippi, because he whistled at a young white woman; a boycott of the public transportation system began in Montgomery, Alabama, with Martin Luther King as leader of the blacks; James Baldwin's *Notes of a Native Son* published; Alice Childress's *Trouble in Mind* produced off Broadway in New York City.

1956   Rioting occurred after black student Autherine Lucy was admitted to the University of Alabama; John Hope Franklin's *The Militant South*, James Baldwin's *Giovanni's Room*, and Gwendolyn Brooks's *Bronzville Boys and Girls* published.

1957   The Southern Christian Leadership Conference founded with Martin Luther King as leader; the Civil Rights Act of 1957 passed by the U.S. Congress; Jim Brown of the Cleveland Browns football team broke NFL ground gaining record; Julian Mayfield's *The Hit* published; Langston Hughes's *Simply Heavenly* produced on Broadway; Loften Mitchell's *Land Beyond the River* produced off Broadway in New York City.

1958   NAACP youth councils began a series of sit-ins at a lunch counter in Oklahoma City; Martin Luther King, Jr., stabbed in the chest by a demented black woman while autographing books in a Harlem department store; Jay Saunders Redding's *The Lonesome Road* and Willard Motley's *Let No Man Write My Epitaph* published.

1959   Lorraine Hansberry's *A Raisin in the Sun* opened on Broadway; Frank London Brown's *Trumbull Park* published.

1960   U.S. black population 18,871,831; four North Carolina A & T College students began the sit-in movement at a five-and-ten-cent store in Greensboro, North Carolina; Imamu Baraka (LeRoi Jones) edited *Yugen*, an important literary journal; President Eisenhower signed the Civil Rights Act of 1960; May Miller's *Into the Clearing*, Waring Cuney's *Puzzles*, published; death of Roi Ottley.

1961   Thirteen CORE members led by James Farmer began a freedom ride from Washington, D.C., through the South to test the integration of interstate transportation facilities; the Alvin Ailey Dance Troupe organized; Adam Clayton Powell, Jr., became chairman of the House of Representatives Education and Labor Committee; John Hope Franklin's *Reconstruction after the Civil War*, James Baldwin's *Nobody Knows My Name*, John A. Williams's *Night Song*, Imamu Baraka's (LeRoi Jones) *Preface to a Twenty Volume Suicide Note*, and Paule Marshall's *Soul Clap Hands and Sing* published; Ossie Davis's *Purlie Victorious* opened on Broadway.

1962   Escorted by U.S. marshals, James H. Meredith registered at the University of Mississippi; James Baldwin's *Another Country*, William Melvin Kelly's *A Different Drummer*, and Robert Hayden's *A Ballad of Remembrance* published; Errol John's *Moon on A Rainbow Shawl* produced off Broadway in New York City.

1963   Two-hundred fifty-thousand people, both black and white, took part in a march on Washington, D.C., as a civil rights demonstration; four little black girls killed in the bombing of a church in Birmingham, Alabama; John Hope Franklin's *The Emancipation Proclamation*, James Baldwin's *The Fire Next Time*, Imamu Baraka's *Blues People*, John A. Williams's *Sissie*, and John O. Killens's *And Then We Heard the Thunder* published; William Hairston's *Walk in Darkness* and Langston Hughes's *Tambourines to Glory* opened off Broadway in New York City.

1964   Sidney Poitier won an Academy Award as best actor for his role in the film *Lilies of the Field*; the bodies of three young civil rights workers, two white, one black, found in an earth dam near Philadelphia, Mississippi; riots in Harlem, Rochester, Jersey City, Paterson, Dixmoor (Illinois), and Philadelphia; Martin Luther King, Jr., awarded the Nobel Prize for Peace; William Melvin Kelly's *Dancers on the Shore*, Ralph Ellison's *Shadow and Act*, and Imamu Baraka's *The Dead Lecturer* published; Imamu Baraka's *The Dutchman*, James Baldwin's *Blues for Mr. Charlie*, and Lorraine Hansberry's *The Sign in Sidney Brustein's Window* produced; Adrienne Kennedy's *The Funny House of a Negro* opened at the Cricket Theater in New York City.

1965   Malcolm X (Malcolm Little) assassinated at the Audubon Ball Room while addressing his followers; the Voting Rights Act of 1965 passed by Congress; John O. Killens's *The Black Man's Burden, The Autobiography of Malcolm X,* John A. Williams's *This Is My Country Too,* Claude Brown's *Manchild in the Promised Land,* Imamu Baraka's *System of Dante's Hell,* William Melvin Kelly's *A Drop of Patience,* and William Demby's *The Catacombs* published; James Baldwin's *The Amen Corner* produced on Broadway; Imamu Baraka's *The Slave and the Toilet* produced off Broadway in New York City.

1966   Robert Weaver became secretary of Housing and Urban Development (HUD) and was the first black member of a president's cabinet; James Meredith shot from ambush as he began a march near Hernando, Mississippi; Edward Brooke of Massachusetts became the first black elected to the U.S. Senate since the Reconstruction Period and the first black ever elected from a northern state; Imamu Baraka's *Home* and James Baldwin's *Going to Meet the Man* published; Douglass Turner Ward's *Happy Ending* and *Day of Absence* produced off Broadway in New York City.

1967   Muhammad Ali convicted of breaking the draft laws and sentenced to five years in prison. Released on bond pending the appeal of his case. Earlier this same year he lost his status as heavyweight boxing champion when the World Boxing Association and the New York Athletic Commission withdrew their recognition; Carl B. Stokes and Richard Hatcher became mayor of Cleveland, Ohio, and Gary, Indiana, respectively; William Melvin Kelly's *Dem,* John A. Williams's *The Man Who Cried I Am,* John O. Killens's *Sippi,* Imamu Baraka's *Tales,* and Ishmael Reed's *The Free Lance Pall Bearers* published.

1968   Martin Luther King, Jr., assassinated by a sniper in Memphis, Tennessee; James Baldwin's *Tell Me How Long the Train's Been Gone,* Lerone Bennet's *What Manner of Man,* Eldridge Cleaver's *Soul on Ice,* Julius Lester's *Look Out Whitey Black Power's Gonna Get Your Mama,* Imamu Baraka and Larry Neal's *Black Fire,* Lucille Clifton's *The Good Times,* and Johari Amini's (Jewel C. Latimore) *Black Essence* published.

1969   The Urban Coalition report, *One Year Later,* published; Fred Hampton, Black Panther leader in Illinois, killed in a police raid in Chicago; the Black Academy of Arts and Letters organized and Clifton Wharton elected president of Michigan State University; Bernie Casey's *Look at the People*, James M. Cone's *Black Theology and Black Power*, Tom Dent et al. *Free Southern Theater*, Benjamin Quarles's *Black Abolitionists*, Sarah E. Wright's *This Child's Gonna Live*, and June Jordon's *Who Look at Me* published.

1970 The Mormon Church continued its policy of barring blacks from the priesthood; Daniel P. Moynihan, advisor to President Nixon, suggested in a report to the president on the race issue that this subject should undergo a period of "benign neglect"; Kenneth A. Gibson elected Mayor of Newark, New Jersey; rioting in Augusta, Georgia; Judge Harold J. Haley and two San Quentin convicts killed in a gun battle after an attempted escape in San Rafael, California; Angela Davis implicated in the affair; John Wideman's *Hurry Home*, John A. Williams's *The King God Didn't Save*, George Jackson's *Soledad Brother*, Mari Evens's *I Am a Black Woman*, Nikki Giovanni's *Black Feelings, Black Judgement, Black Talk*, Haki Mahabuti's (Don L. Lee) *We Walk the Way of the New World*, Audre Lorde's *Cables of Rage*, and Alice Walker's *The Third Life of Grange Copeland* published.

1971 The Dance Theater of Harlem, a classical ballet company, founded by dancer Arthur Mitchell; Samuel Lee Gravely, Jr. promoted to the rank of admiral and became the first in U.S. history; George Jackson, one of the "Soledad Brothers," killed in San Quentin; prison inmates at Attica Prison in New York rebelled against the prison authorities causing the death of thrity-two prisoners and ten prison guards; Angela Davis and others collection of essays, *If They Come in The Morning*. Alice Childress's *Black Scenes*, Addison Gayle's *Oak and Ivy*, Ernest Gaines's *The Autobiography of Miss Jane Pittman*, Frenchy Jolene Hodges's *Black Wisdom*, Norman Jordon's *Above Maya*, and *Destination Ashes*, and June Jordon's *Some Changes* published.

1972 Bobby Seal, former chairman of the black Panther party, ran for the office of mayor of Oakland, California; Angela Davis acquitted of murder and kidnapping charges that grew out of the San Rafael, California, escape attempt of 1970; Frank Wills, a black security guard, called the police to Washington, D.C.'s Watergate Complex; five men arrested for breaking into the Democratic National Committee offices; the secretary of the Army cleared the records of the soldiers involved in the Brownsville, Texas, race riot of 1906; fighting between black and white sailors aboard the aircraft carrier *Kitty Hawk*; Addison Gayle's *Claude McKay: The Black Poet at War* and Nikki Giovanni's *My House* published.

1973   The National Black Network, the first black owned and operated news network, began operation in New York City; Thomas Bradley, a black politician, elected mayor of Los Angeles; June Jordon's *Fannie Lou Hamer*, Stephen E. Henderson's *Understanding the New Black Poetry*, Alice Walker's *Revolutionary Petunias and other Poems*, and *In Love and Trouble*, Booker T. Washington's *Writings*, vol. 1, edited by Louis Harlan, and Leon Forrest's *There Is a Tree More Ancient Than Eden* published.

1974   Mrs. Martin Luther King, Sr. shot to death while attending church services; random killings of whites referred to as the Zebra killings in San Francisco, California; golfer Lee Elder played in the Masters' Golf Tournament; Nate Shaw's *All God's Dangers*, James Baldwin's *If Beal Street Could Talk*, Angela Davis's *Angela Davis*, Toni Morrison's *Sula*, John McCluskey's *Look What They Done to My Song*, Ishmael Reed's *The Last Days of Louisianna Red*, Charles Johnson's *Faith and the Good Thing*, and Calvin Hernton's *Scarecrow* published; death of writer Ted Poston.

1975   The congressional black caucus sought aid for jobless blacks; a race riot in Boston; CORE recruited black war veterans to serve as military advisors and medics in Angola; Gayle Jones's *Corregidora*, Gwendolyn Books's *Beckonings*, Nikki Giovanni's *The Women and the Men*, Sterling Plumpp's *Steps to Break the Circle*, Al Young's *Who is Angelina*, Addison Gayle's *The Way of the New World*, and Sterling Brown's *The Last Ride of Wild Bill* published.

1976   Congressman Andrew Young of Georgia appointed ambassador to the United Nations, the first black to hold that post; former chairman of SNCC, H. "Rap" Brown, freed from prison and all charges against him dropped; Clarence Norris, the last of the Scottsboro defendants, pardoned by Governor George C. Wallace of Alabama; Eldridge Cleaver, former defense minister of the Black Panther party, returned from exile in France to face charges in California; Robert Hayden appointed poetry consultant to the Library of Congress, the first black poet to hold this post; composer Scott Joplin posthumously received a special Pulitzer Award; Ishmael Reed's *Flight to Canada,* Gayle Jones's *Eva's Man,* Alex Haley's *Roots,* Alice Walker's *Meridan,* Eugene Redmond's *Drumvoices,* and Kimberly Benson's *Baraka* published; death of concert singer Roland Hayes.

1977   Alex Haley received a special Pulitzer Prize for *Roots* as well as a special National Book Award; Hughey Newton, founder and leader of the Black Panther party returned to the United States from exile in Cuba. Toni Morrison's *Song of Solomon;* Leon Forrests' *Bloodworth Orphans* published.

1978   James McPhereson received the Pulitzer Prize for *Elbow Room;* the Mormon church changed its policy concerning black priests. Ishmael Reed's *Shrove Tuesday* in old New Orleans published.

AUTHOR INDEX TO PART I